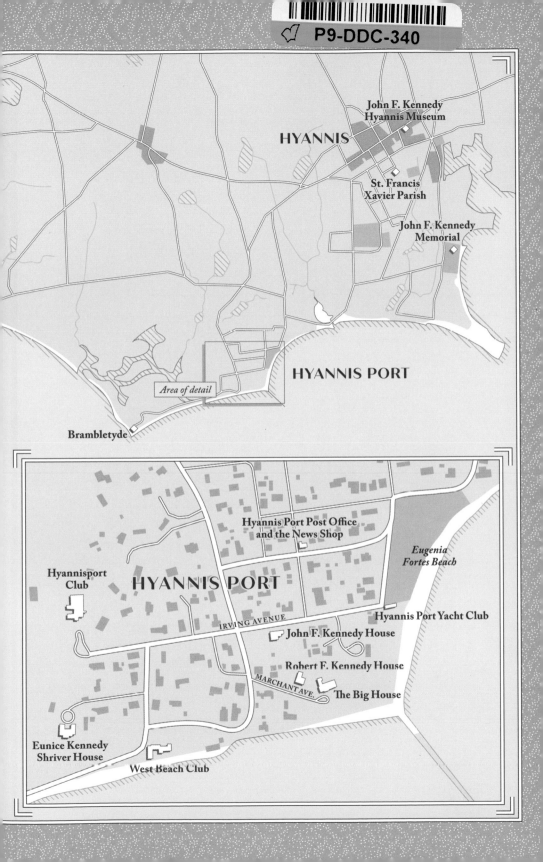

P9-DDC-340

John F. Kennedy
Hyannis Museum

HYANNIS

St. Francis
Xavier Parish

John F. Kennedy
Memorial

HYANNIS PORT

Area of detail

Brambletyde

Hyannis Port Post Office
and the News Shop

*Eugenia
Fortes Beach*

Hyannisport
Club

HYANNIS PORT

Hyannis Port Yacht Club

IRVING AVENUE

John F. Kennedy House

Robert F. Kennedy House

MARCHANT AVE.

The Big House

Eunice Kennedy
Shriver House

West Beach Club

More Praise for *White House by the Sea*

"Kate Storey invites us to witness the saga of Camelot as it unfolded at the family's famous summer compound.... Monumental political decisions were made here. Terrible news was delivered.... But we also witness small family moments of love and beauty. In Storey's hands, the Kennedys come alive in a whole new way—more intimate and real."

—Neal Thompson, author of *The First Kennedys: The Humble Roots of an American Dynasty*

"Profoundly empathetic, rich in detail, this is a Kennedy book that must be read and once read will not be forgotten."

—Laurence Leamer, author of *The Kennedy Women* and *The Kennedy Men*

"A special book ... Storey takes us inside the Kennedys' most private space.... In these pages you get the sense that the family felt most free to be themselves when they were by the sea."

—Kate Andersen Brower, author of *The Residence: Inside the Private World of the White House*

"Kate Storey has given us a treat. ... *White House by the Sea* offers illuminating 'if these walls could talk' stories, affirming how a house can stand like a witness tree."

—Kate Clifford Larson, author of *Rosemary: The Hidden Kennedy Daughter*

"Storey is a brilliant storyteller and a relentless researcher who has uncovered sources that no one has seen before. [This is] impossible to put down."

—Steven M. Gillon, author of *America's Reluctant Prince: The Life of John F. Kennedy Jr.*

WHITE HOUSE BY THE SEA

A Century of the Kennedys at Hyannis Port

Kate Storey

SCRIBNER

NEW YORK   LONDON   TORONTO   SYDNEY   NEW DELHI

Scribner
An Imprint of Simon & Schuster, Inc.
1230 Avenue of the Americas
New York, NY 10020

First Scribner hardcover edition June 2023

SCRIBNER and design are registered trademarks of The Gale Group, Inc., used
under license by Simon & Schuster, Inc., the publisher of this work.

For information about special discounts for bulk purchases,
please contact Simon & Schuster Special Sales at 1-866-506-1949 or
business@simonandschuster.com.

The Simon & Schuster Speakers Bureau can bring authors to your live event. For
more information or to book an event, contact the Simon & Schuster Speakers
Bureau at 1-866-248-3049 or visit our website at www.simonspeakers.com.

Interior design by Jaime Putorti

Manufactured in the United States of America

1 3 5 7 9 10 8 6 4 2

Library of Congress Cataloging-in-Publication Data has been applied for.

ISBN 978-1-9821-5918-4
ISBN 978-1-9821-5920-7 (ebook)

For Heath and Finn

CONTENTS

WHITE HOUSE
BY THE SEA

PROLOGUE

T ed Kennedy walks up the stairs. As he passes the old grandfather clock on the landing, he leans forward with each step, the floors creaking under the cream-colored runner. He reaches the top of the staircase and looks into his childhood bedroom. As the youngest of nine, he'd received the worst of most things, including the worst room. It's at the front of the house, facing away from Nantucket Sound, so it's stuffy and stale with no breeze. And it's loud with the mingled noises of two floors.

Today, Ted is seventy-one and his thick, wavy hair is a shock of white. He's gone from baby of the family to one of the grown-ups, both a grandfather and bearer of the family legacy. The house, though, looks a lot like it always did. Today, the hallway is quiet. His stepdaughter, Caroline, is in his sister Jean's old room. He walks down the hall past his sister Pat's old room. Then his sister Eunice's. Then his oldest sister Rosemary's. Rosemary had loved it here, before the surgery in the early 1940s changed her, before she could no longer come home. There are rooms on each side of the narrow hallway. The room facing south belonged to Ted's sister Kathleen—they called her Kick. Kick's room changed hands in the 1940s, too, after she died in the plane crash. The kids had always squabbled over the bedrooms. *No, I hate that bed. I can't sleep in that bed. Well, all right, if nobody wants that bed, I'll take it.* The one who never complained was Kick.

There's been so much loss here on the Cape. A couple of days ago,

Ted was out sailing when his gaze fell on the endless stretch of deep blue water where his nephew John F. Kennedy Jr.'s airplane disappeared into the sea. "You look out over that water and you see no-man's-land, and it just is too . . . ," he starts to say, "it's too powerful. And so that's difficult." This house, though, has been the shelter: the walls behind which the family grieved, laughed, exhaled. Being in the Big House, the heart of the Kennedy Compound, is like walking through a family photo album, suspended somewhere between the past and the present. You can almost hear Ted's father, Joe, calling him to come downstairs to go to their farm to ride horses. Above him, the floors creaking, his brothers in the attic playing toy soldiers. His older siblings banging on the door of the bathroom they shared, shouting, *Hurry up! Hurry up in there!* His mother downstairs in the living room playing "Sweet Adeline" on the piano, the signal that it was time for dinner.

On the other end of the hallway, separated by a door, was where the revolving cast of staff slept: governesses who were like family, cooks, nurses. But the family didn't spend much of their time upstairs—the rooms were cramped with small beds. The place to be was the first floor, which led out to the backyard and the ocean. While the second floor has been updated over the years, the first floor feels like stepping back in time.

There used to be two bedrooms on the first floor. Joe Jr., the firstborn son, the one who was supposed to go on to the greatest things, had the nicest one. Next to him in the smaller room was John, the second son who went by the name Jack. Their bedrooms were connected by a modest bathroom, which the boys shared. After Joe Jr. died in the war, his room was turned into a TV room during the big 1940s home renovation. But Jack's room hasn't changed for nearly a century: trim secretary desk in the corner, matching twin beds with carved wooden posts, floral, pleated bed skirts, and matching drapes, family pictures on the walls.

Ted still calls it The President's Room.

Outside Jack's room, there's the living room, where the Pope's sofa sits. Cardinal Pacelli visited the Kennedy family home in Bronxville, New York, in the 1930s and sat on that very sofa—he later became pope, so Ted's mother, Rose Kennedy, brought it to Hyannis Port and proudly slapped a plaque on it so visitors would know a future pope had sat there.

And there's the black baby grand piano in the west corner covered with silver frames: Jack walking along the beach, and Rose in pearls. Next to the piano, Ted's sister-in-law Jackie taught everyone in the family how to dance the Twist. Some things have changed—the living room walls were once a vivid kelly green and now they're a crisp, modern white. But the bookshelves are still lined with inscribed copies of *Finnegans Wake* by James Joyce and *The Collected Poems* of Robert Frost. There's Arthur Schlesingers's *A Thousand Days: John F. Kennedy in the White House* peppered with Rose Kennedy's marginalia, alongside creased copies of books by Mary Higgins Clark—this *is* a beach house, after all.

Through the living room there's the sunroom. Over the wooden fireplace mantel hangs the 1790s gilt leaf and painted mirror that Ted's parents brought back from Europe in 1932. In front of that mirror, the whole family had posed for their only group picture the day Jack was elected president. Tucked away in the corner of the first floor is the kitchen, which has barely changed since the 1940s—old cabinets painted white, nicks touched up over the years, and the big butcher block island where Ted used to swipe cookies set out to serve guests.

The hardwood floors on this level—oh, how Ted's father had loved them—they still have each scratch and scuff, marks of the people who've passed through this house. Take a deep breath on this main floor and you breathe in the comforting old smell of wood mixed with a tinge of beachy moisture that all these old beach houses have. It smells like the first day of summer after a long, cool spring, like anticipation of the ten weeks ahead. That first day of the season, the first step into the house, you don't really see the rooms at all. You don't notice the Early American antiques, the reclaimed pine floors from the 1700s, the family photos that could fill a history book. What you see is that view of Nantucket Sound. Each window frame looks like it holds a watercolor—blue skies fading into blue water, white dunes, green lawn. The best views, though, are from the two rooms in the corner on the second floor: Ted's parents' rooms, which are connected by a deck. Over those weathered planks Joe and Rose could walk to visit each other without their kids, guests, and staff knowing. Ted's father had the room at the very end of the hall with the picture windows. Now, there's an elevator—put in after Joe's stroke in 1961—that opens discreetly into that room and leads down to the first floor and the movie theater in the basement. It was in that upstairs bedroom where Joe Kennedy found out his second son had been gunned down in Dallas, where he learned his third son had been shot in California, where his youngest son told him that there'd been a terrible accident and that a young woman was dead. It was where Joe Kennedy took his last breath.

Today, Ted shares his father's old room with his wife, Vicki. From there, Ted can see the sailboats holding up the blue sky as they bob with the wake, a hypnotic back-and-forth. He watches as a family of ospreys build a nest outside his window, each day adding twigs from the neighborhood, sometimes flying over with trash they've found to weave into it. Ted is so invested in the story of these birds. "Come look at the osprey!" he calls out to his family. His stepchildren humor him by coming to look. The ospreys return to the same nest summer after summer, each year adding more sticks and trash to make it stronger.

Next to Ted's room is Mother's Room. Long after Rose Kennedy died, this is still Mother's Room. "This is where my mother lived for the last thirty, thirty-five years. And this is where she actually died . . . in this room," Ted says, his big voice catching in his throat. "So this is a very . . . you know . . . a sort of a special room in the house. And it's been difficult for many of my sisters . . . all of us. It has such memories, but it's also . . . there's new life and joy and . . ."

Ted has been thinking a lot lately about the past. He's been thinking about his parents, his siblings. He doesn't have many summers left here in the Big House.

CHAPTER ONE

The house was white, simple. It sat on about three acres at the end of a short dead-end street—no longer than a long driveway. It looked out onto endless Nantucket Sound. Immense and empty. Sitting on the stretch of sandy private beach at the edge of the property felt like being on a boat with no land in sight. There were no sounds of traffic, shops, or crowds. Just waves lapping on the shore. The house faced south to take advantage of the cool summer breeze and warm winter sun. To the left there was an old, craggy breakwater made of granite links slicing through the water—the spine of the half-moon harbor, protecting the land from waves, keeping the view peaceful, still, unchanged. The view from the wraparound porch of 50 Marchant Avenue was one of the best on Cape Cod.

The house was nice but by no means the nicest in town. The exterior was shingles painted a stark white, not the weathered natural gray favored by most of the Cape. There was no fence. No elaborate landscaping surrounding it. Nothing special about it at all, really. At least not from the outside. Other than that view. The house was built by a local, L. Frank Paine, who worked with his dad, Lucius K. Paine. Everyone in town knew the Paine men, who built sturdy homes—homes that would last. Frank Paine built the house at the end of Marchant Avenue in 1904 for a local named Beulah Malcolm. There'd been a different house on that lot before, but the whole thing was picked up and moved down the street, over to

Irving Avenue, where another wealthy family used it as a guest house. Most of these old Cape houses were built right on the sand without foundation, making them easy to shift around as families expanded. Hyannis Port, a quiet neighborhood tucked into the curve of Cape Cod, is the kind of place where people named their second homes, which stayed in the family for generations. When the new house on Marchant Avenue was built, it was called Malcolm Cottage—until 1928, when Joseph P. Kennedy bought it and doubled its size. For the next century it was, simply, the Big House.

Joseph P. Kennedy drove a Rolls-Royce. Well, he was driven in it. He was tall with perfectly erect posture, handsome with square shoulders, and ginger-haired in the sunlight—and he was quick with a smile that crinkled his eyes. By the time he bought Malcolm Cottage, his main residence was in New York, but he still clung to his insouciant Boston drawl. He was married to Rose Fitzgerald, the daughter of John F. Fitzgerald, the former mayor of Boston better known as "Honey Fitz." And, by the time Joe rolled into the Port, he'd made enough money in banking that he had his own chauffeur. There was already plenty of wealth in Hyannis Port when the Kennedys arrived—steel money flowed in from Pittsburgh early in the century. But people didn't flaunt their wealth. They called their homes "cottages"; they were quick to say with a sneer that this wasn't *Newport*. It wasn't chichi *Bar Harbor*. So, people noticed when Joe Kennedy arrived in the back of his loud, flashy car. They'd look back and say that was the first thing they remembered about the Kennedys. You couldn't help but notice Joe Kennedy, and he seemed to like being noticed.

Before the Rolls-Royce and the house with the view, Joe and Rose's story began at the beach. They were from political Boston families, and their fathers knew each other. Joe's father was born to Irish Catholic immigrants and had gone from owning bars in East Boston to a political career as a ward boss. The Kennedys and Fitzgeralds had enough money to summer somewhere other than the city, escaping the stifling and dusty streets of East Boston for breezy summer months on the coast of Maine with other powerful families. They rented cottages in Old Orchard, a beach community tucked between Kennebunkport and Cape Elizabeth. Rose and Joe were just kids when they were introduced at a picnic for Boston politicians when Rose was five and Joe seven. Years later, they fell in love at Old Orchard.

Rose's father rented the prize house in the community, an impressive place called Bleak House overlooking Saco Bay, a small gulf on the Atlantic. Honey Fitz was at the center of social activity those summers. He loved nothing more than entertaining a crowd with his stories. He got such a kick out of himself that he often collapsed into a fit of laughter before getting to his punch line. Tears streamed down his round face as he gasped for air, his audience giggling, too, even if he couldn't make it to the end of the tale. Slight with neatly middle-parted sandy hair, the mayor was driven around in his chauffeured car with his kids and their friends piled in the back with him. You could hear him coming from down the street, belting out "Sweet Adeline." Those summers at the beach were working vacations—Honey Fitz began by taking the three o'clock train, which was full of Boston Irish heading to Old Orchard. After a few weeks of making the trek, he knew everyone on that train's name, and everything about their families. Then, he took the four o'clock train for a few weeks. Same thing—he'd get to know each and every four o'clock passenger. Then it was the five o'clock train. By the end of the summer, he'd gotten to know dozens of people—potential voters in the next election.

Even with all that campaigning and socializing, Honey Fitz made time to swim in the ocean with his oldest daughter, a petite, dark-haired girl named Rose. While Rose and the rest of the kids played, her mother, Josie, the much more reserved half of the couple, sat on the porch with all the other mothers positioned just so, rocking back and forth, back and forth, watching their children play in the waves.

After they married in 1914, the Kennedys spent the first summers of their marriage trying to recapture those childhood memories. First, they explored the coast of Massachusetts looking for a place to spend July and August. By 1915, Rose's parents had moved on from Old Orchard to Hull, a town on a peninsula at the southern edge of Boston Harbor, where they rented a rambling Victorian home on Nantasket Beach. Rose and

Joe rented a smaller gray cottage nearby. It was there, at the cottage, where their first child, a blue-eyed, dimple-cheeked boy named for his father, was born. Joseph P. Kennedy Jr. was a delight to Honey Fitz, who'd paced the beach waiting for his first grandson's arrival. Two years later, Rose and Joe's second son was born. They named him John Fitzgerald Kennedy for his grandfather and called him Jack. Then, in 1918, came their first girl, Rosemary, named for her mother. Two more girls followed—Kick was born in 1920, and Eunice arrived in 1921.

The family of seven rented a two-story summer home in Cohasset, a more upscale resort town. Joe, Jack, and Rosemary waded into the calm water of the Massachusetts Bay, learning to maneuver the small but steady rowboats they rented from the beach vendors. They were so little, you couldn't see their heads. It looked from shore as if the boats were empty.

Their grandfather Honey Fitz splashed around with the children while their father, clad in full work attire despite the heat, watched from a distance. Joe Jr., by then already an adventurous and scrappy kid, saw the wind take the bigger boats with their crisp white sails farther and farther away from the safety of the shore. He was determined to learn himself.

The summer of 1922, Joe, who was ready to establish a home base for Rose and the kids, applied to be a member of the Cohasset Golf Club. There should have been no question that Joe would be admitted to the club. After all, by then he was making a name for himself in the Boston banking world. Cohasset, however, was the home of the Protestant elite and the Kennedys were Irish Catholic—rare at the exclusive golf club. There *were* a few, including Joe's close friend and assistant Eddie Moore. But the club's election committee delayed making a ruling on Joe's application. As June faded into July and then August, Joe never heard back. The board didn't even dignify the application with a rejection.

"It was petty and cruel," said Ralph Lowell, one of Joe's associates. "The women of Cohasset looked down on the daughter of Honey Fitz, and who was Joe Kennedy but the son of Pat, the barkeeper?"

Still, the family continued to rent in Cohasset while they explored the rest of the coastline, looking for a more permanent place where they'd be accepted. Cohasset was an easy drive to Joe's family summer home in Sagamore, in the pit of Cape Cod's arm, so Rose, Joe, and their young kids shuttled back and forth, making their way farther along the Cape.

In June 1923, the family made the drive south to the Cape's elbow to celebrate Rose's birthday. The men golfed at the stately Wianno Club right on the water in Osterville. Rose and the women spent their day shopping in Hyannis.

The next summer, the family rented a home down the road from Hyannis's Main Street. Tucked just south of Hyannis was the neighborhood of Hyannis Port. You had to know where you were going to find Hyannis Port. No main roads passed through. Kids ran from lawn to lawn barefoot, cutting through the neighbors' freshly cut grass to meet up at the narrow wooden pier right in the middle of the village, where sailboats launched off into Nantucket Sound. The waters were so shallow that splashing children stayed waist-deep and local sailors memorized where the biggest rocks were beneath the clear surface. The shoreline was almost always still thanks to the 1,100-foot-long breakwater that had been built in 1826 and reached out toward the private spit of land across the way called Great Island. In the summer, the water was just right—warmer than the north side of the Cape. On a sunny day, groups picnicked on the breakwater while kids dove off it.

To the left of the breakwater was the only public beach in the village, to the right was a stately mansion with carved columns, like a smaller version of the White House. That was the Taggarts' place, built in 1911 by Indianapolis mayor and chair of the Democratic Party Thomas Taggart. Next to that sat Malcolm Cottage.

When Joe rented the cottage the summers of 1924 and 1925, it was really for Rose and the children. He was at a critical point in his career, having decided a few months earlier to move from banking to the film business by bidding on the movie company Film Booking Offices of America, or FBO. He spent most of the summer of 1925 preparing for the proposal. In August, he ended his summer early to sail from New York City to London, where he'd make his official $1 million offer.

A letter for Rose arrived at the little Hyannis Port post office from Joe: "I know it's terrible to tell you in every letter how homesick I am but it is terrible. I can't seem to shake it off at all. I think of you and the children all the time and almost go silly."

As the blooms began to burn off in the late-summer heat, the air was humid and thick with mosquitos. Along the beach, groans of "Pesky skeeters!" were followed by slaps of the skin to squash the pests. In the weeks before it was time for Rose to return the family to Boston, eight-year-old Jack was confident enough to sail with two friends, neighbors Rhona and William Brown, out into Hyannis Harbor. One minute they were maneuvering the sail, using a gust to take them farther from shore. The next, they'd capsized.

Fortunately, neighbors George Davis and Walter Wright spotted the kids kicking and gasping to keep their heads above water and jumped into a tender to come to their aid. The next day, August 13, the local newspaper the *Hyannis Patriot* landed on lawns with an account of the rescue. The story's last line was "It was a close call."

The next summer, Jack signed up for swimming lessons.

In February 1926, Joe finalized the deal to buy FBO, officially becoming a movie man. That summer, he'd be traveling back and forth from the Cape to New York and California. But he rented Malcolm Cottage again for Rose, the kids, and his father, who was spending more time with the family after the death of Joe's mother. Joe Jr., however, wouldn't be joining his now seven siblings. The Kennedys had added another girl to the family, Patricia, and a third boy, Robert, whom they called Bobby. Joe Jr. was eleven, which Rose decided was old enough to be sent to summer camp in New Hampshire. Each child would have a summer away from the beach when they were old enough. They'd learn about nature and camping, and it would lighten the load back in Hyannis Port.

"This turned out to be one of my least successful ventures in child rearing," Rose would later reflect. "Most of the older ones went, as I recall, for short times but didn't really care for the experience at all and said loudly and clearly they would rather have been at home with the family in Hyannis Port."

*   *   *

After a few summers renting in Hyannis Port, Joe started to think about buying. He looked in Oyster Harbors, with its grand estates on sprawling plots of land, down the street in the ritzier village of Osterville. But it reminded him of Cohasset, where his family had been so unwelcome. He surveyed his neighbors, trying to figure out the best home he could buy in Hyannis Port—for the best deal. He was renting the family's primary residence in Riverdale, a New York City suburb, after selling their Boston home to be closer to his movie studio's Manhattan office. He hated the thought of paying off someone else's mortgage, and he was doing it on two homes. He asked his neighbor James Woodward, who'd just moved to the Port, what was for sale. Joe had his eye on the biggest house on the water: the Taggart house with its impressive columns framing the front. But the yard wasn't very big—not enough open space for the kids to run around or play sports. And Rose liked Malcolm Cottage, the house they'd been renting the last few summers, where she could sit on the porch and watch the children play on the lawn, like her mother had done when she was a kid.

"I can buy this place for $25,000," he told Woodward about Malcolm Cottage. "I was just interested to see if you could do better."

"I don't think I can do any better," Woodward answered, "and I don't think *you* can do any better."

In November 1928, the Kennedys purchased Malcolm Cottage. They went right to work on plans to expand, making it big enough for their still-growing family. They brought on L. Frank Paine, the man who'd built it in 1904, to create an addition that would double the size of the house to twenty-one rooms, including twelve bedrooms, a steam room, and a theater in the basement. While most of the homes in the Port sat quiet and empty in January 1929, 50 Marchant Avenue was full of work crews as new walls began going up. The day after Paine broke ground, the Kennedys set off for a long European vacation. By the time the family returned, the addition on the east side was nearly done—three new bedrooms upstairs and a couple more rooms downstairs, plus a dazzling new sunroom. But Joe decided a plain old motion picture machine in the home's bottom-floor movie theater just wouldn't do. He was a movie man now, his name appearing on the posters of the pictures FBO produced. He called a radio engineer from the Radio Corporation of America who visited the house and determined that the latest, state-of-the-art technology could be installed for $15,000. They just had to figure out how to make the RCA Photophone—which was meant for public theaters, not basements—work.

In June, neighbors arriving back at their summer homes noticed a van with a crew of workers and an enormous roll of special two-inch cables in the circular driveway at the end of Marchant Avenue. As the Kennedy kids wrapped up their semesters at boarding school, the finishing touches were put on the home theater, the first of its kind in New England. Facing the screen where the movies would be projected in the small, dark room were about two dozen fixed chairs with iron legs and, also, fold-down wooden seats. Cumulatively, the setup could comfortably seat forty, but if Marchant Avenue moviegoers really squeezed into the aisles, they could fit as many as fifty. There was a simple mural of shoppers in Paris on one of the walls. Once the Kennedys were all moved in, with their furniture and decorations collected from their trips to Europe, the family hosted movie night three or four times a week, inviting their staff and the kids' friends. Thanks to Joe's connections, they got movie reels before they were released to the public.

Hyannis Port has its own post office, so it's sometimes mistakenly referred to as a village, but it's just a small dead-end neighborhood in the village of Hyannis. Hyannis is one of the seven villages of Barnstable— the others are Centerville, Osterville, Cotuit, Marstons Mills, Barnstable, and West Barnstable. The Port, as locals call it, is just over nine square miles with the post office smack in the middle. The post office, which was smaller than most cottages in the village, was attached to a little store called the News Shop that sold newspapers for five cents, coffee, penny candy, and homemade ice cream. When the Kennedy kids turned five, they earned a weekly allowance of ten cents. Like most other Port kids, they went straight to the News Shop to spend their money on the colorful assortment of sweets lining the walls. In the 1920s, there was just one hotel in town, The Gables, which had a nice pool that local kids would sneak into. The other two Port hotels had burned down in freak back-to-back Labor Day accidents—one in 1905, the other in 1909. Sally Fowler's Shop, which sold knickknacks and whatnots, sat across from the News Shop. The public beach, smaller than most homes' private beaches, was just down the street from the post office. Next to the beach was the Hyannis Port Yacht Club, though when the Kennedys moved into town in the 1920s the yacht club hadn't been functioning for years.

In the summer months only two Port churches stood open. There was the little Union Chapel just down the street from the Kennedy house, and perched high on a hill overlooking the neighborhood was St. Andrews By-the-Sea, the Episcopal church. Up that hill, there was the Hyannisport Club, where Joe Kennedy was accepted upon the family's move to town. The golf course, which had always been a fine course, was in the midst of a massive renovation that would turn it into a great—and competitive—one. Around the corner from the golf club, the West Beach Club sat facing Nantucket Sound. A modest building with wood-paneled walls and wide, creaky floorboards, the private club served as a hangout for the local families who paid for a membership. The big event of the week was the Wednesday picnic—Wednesday because that's when most families gave their cooks the night off.

And that was about it for the Port. Houses, private clubs, a few churches, and a couple of shops. Hyannis was the Port's much more populated neighbor. The Hyannis Main Street lights shone so bright that on an overcast night, they reflected off the clouds lighting up Hyannis Port. There were big stores like Megathlin's drugstore, and the Idle Hour Theatre. The Hyannis downtown smelled of sweet berries, which Colonial Candle of Cape Cod on Main Street boiled down to make its souvenir candles. Around the corner from the candle factory sat St. Francis Xavier, the white-columned Catholic church that the Kennedys attended every Sunday morning. They piled into a couple of cars to get to church two miles away—but Rose always went alone.

The streets of Hyannis Port teemed with children. On nice afternoons, kids in the neighborhood ran down Marchant Avenue to get to the Big

House in time for kickoff—it was widely agreed that the Kennedy yard
was best suited for touch football, flat and long. There were the Keavy
boys who lived across from the post office, who were about the same
age as Jack and Bobby and just as competitive and athletic. And there
were the Bell boys up by the fire station on Scudder Avenue. The Bells
were Irish Catholic year-rounders with five kids about the same age as
the Kennedy children—their dad was an engineer and their mom did
ironing for the families in town. One afternoon, Bobby went to get his
best friend, Jack Bell, for a game of football. Jack told Bobby he couldn't
come to play—his father said he had to mow the lawn. Bobby left. Then
he came back a few minutes later in the back of his chauffeured car. The
driver hopped out with their family's big power mower to finish the job
more quickly than Bell ever could with his dinky sickle bar mower.

The girls didn't usually play football. Eunice cut across the lawns
along Marchant Avenue to get over to Irving Avenue, the street just before hers, to play dolls with Tish Mumford in the yard. Kick made fast
friends with the bubbly, dark-haired, bright-eyed neighbor girl directly
across the street, Nancy Tenney—in spite of her parents' attitude toward
the Kennedys. The Tenneys came from old Boston banking money, and
Nancy's father made clear his disdain for the new-money Irish Catholics
next door. Rockwell Tenney's credo was "Good fences make good neighbors," so a tall white one went up when they built their house next door
in 1929. But Kick and Nancy, or "Ken and Ten" as they referred to each
other, met up to swim in the ocean that connected their backyards beyond
the fence. After dinner, they met up again, playing until nine or until they
heard Rose yell out, *"Kathleeeeen!"* At night, they weren't allowed to use
the phone, so they connected a long string from Kick's window above the
Kennedy front porch to Nancy's bedroom window, using a basket to pass
notes back and forth until their eyelids got too heavy. Thursday nights
were Kick's favorite because she got to go over to the Tenney house for
dinner, and the girls stayed up late to eat cereal with cream on it in the
kitchen. Then they did jigsaw puzzles while everyone else went to sleep.

On Sunday mornings, Nancy stood at the end of her driveway to
catch a ride with the Kennedys to church—she was Episcopalian but
Eunice, who was also friends with Nancy, was always encouraging her

to become a Catholic. The children all filed into the pews with their perfectly combed hair, the boys in navy sweaters, the girls in navy dress coats
with matching shoes and purses. It was the one morning a week the kids
weren't salt-soaked from the ocean, dirty from the lawn. Rockwell Tenney waited at the end of his driveway for Nancy to come home. "Where
were you?" he asked, irritation showing. "With those mackerel snatchers
again?" He never hid his disdain for Catholicism.

When Joe Jr. was around, Rudy Vallee's or Fred Waring's voice echoed
from his record player over the noise of his siblings—there was another
girl by now, Jean. But Joe Jr. also had a life in the Port away from the Big
House—many of his friends from Brookline or from boarding school
had summer homes in Hyannis Port. For the rich, New England was
a small world. When he could, Joe Jr. took off with the other teenagers. There was Whitney Wright, a boarding school friend, whose family had long ties to the Port. Whitney's father, Walter, was one of the
first people the Kennedys had met a few years earlier, when he saved
Jack from drowning. The Wrights, who owned a Boston wool business,
bought their waterfront home from a Johns Hopkins professor. They
were snobs who didn't think much of the Kennedys—with their loud
children pouring out of the house. Still, despite what parents might say
about neighbors over the dinner table, kids of the same age banded together when they were in the Port. Joe Jr. walked over to Ocean Avenue,
passing by Keyes Beach, to get to the Wright house. Whitney and Joe Jr.
hung out with two other locals, Bert Ellis and Bobby Fogan, and the
four boys formed a club they called BoBeWiJo. They filled their days
with chatter about what school would be like in the fall or by preparing
for school sports by working out, playing football, and digging holes in
the sand behind Joe Jr.'s house. Their other project was redecking the
small, twelve-by-ten-foot boathouse on the Wright property. At the end
of the day, they sized up their progress then decided what to do before
it was time to go home and clean up for dinner. It was Joe Jr. who usually persuaded the group to come to his house—he was the ringleader.
His younger siblings watched the teenagers through the windows, not

daring to disturb him for fear of his wrath later. The boys hung out in the backyard or on the beach behind the house, their shadows long as the sun began to set, while Joe Jr. went inside to get them drinks. Usually, he offered water instead of ginger ale because, he said, soda was expensive and led to flatulence.

Like his parents, Joe Jr. fell in love for the first time at the beach. When he was thirteen, the oldest Kennedy child was already tall with square shoulders and a sardonic half smile that crinkled his eyes, just like his dad. The summer of '28, there was a girl a year his senior in town visiting family friends. Her name was Eleanor Leavens, and she was fourteen with dark hair, bright blue eyes, and a hearty laugh. Joe Jr. and Eleanor met right around the corner from his house on the pier that ran alongside the breakwater and served as the Port's social center. On a nice day, kids knew that, if they rode their bikes to the pier, they'd run into someone they could hang out with. On that clear summer day, Joe Jr. walked over to the pier to find a girl about his age he'd never noticed before. She stood next to a boy, her host's son, who it was assumed would act as her date. Joe Jr. could barely see her face because she was hunched over, staring into the sea, frantic, drawing in sharp breaths.

"What's going on?" Joe Jr. asked. Eleanor had dropped her ring in the water, she explained breathlessly.

"Go sailing with him," Joe Jr. told Eleanor, gesturing at the other boy, as he began to undress. "I'll dive for it."

Eleanor went off with her date but not before noticing Joe Jr.'s bare white bottom beneath the water as he scanned the shallow water for her ring. Joe Jr. never did find it, but Eleanor accepted his offer to go sailing with him the next time.

After four trips out on his Wianno Junior sailboat, Eleanor and her mother left town. It wasn't much of a courtship, but it meant something to Joe Jr. After Eleanor left, he sulked around the house, uninterested in anything—even sailing—and became even more short-tempered than usual with his siblings. That fall, he wrote to Eleanor, "I have been thinking about you ever since you went away. I was going to kiss you goodbye but you didn't give me any encouragement when I see you I will if you don't mind. Really I love you a lot."

* * *

Joe Jr. could be charming. He was smart. But he was also a bully. He was once described as the kind of kid who wouldn't "leave an unprotected shin unkicked." And nobody was on the receiving end of his violence more than Jack, who, at two years younger, was the sibling closest in age. In contrast to Joe Jr., Jack was slight and sickly. The rule was that when you were late for lunch, you missed your meal. But when Jack was late—and he was *always* late—he snuck into the kitchen to charm the cook into slipping him a pile of leftovers. "I knew what he was doing. And he knew that I knew," his mother, Rose, said. "But I let him get away with it, despite my theoretically inflexible rule, because he was so skinny I felt he needed the nourishment more than the discipline." So, physically, Joe Jr. and Jack were unevenly matched. When they raced around the block in opposite directions, colliding face-on, it was Jack who wound up with twenty-eight stitches. Joe Jr. was unscathed.

One day Eunice sat with her older sister Rosemary and younger brother Bobby on the staircase watching their older brothers roll around the living room. The trio's eyes were wide as they looked through the banister's uprights to see Joe Jr. land punch after punch, Jack trying to wiggle away, legs kicking in the air. The rest of the kids stayed out of it when they went after each other like this. Nobody wanted to catch a stray punch, first of all, but they also knew Jack usually managed to hold his own, figuring out a way to break free. There was always some reason for Joe Jr. to beat the crap out of his brother, but that day's fight had started nearly a week before when Jack mistakenly took his older brother's swimsuit. Jack hadn't taken the time to look at the name on the tag, which was Rose's method for keeping the kids' matching outfits in order. How else was she to keep an eye on all those kids out in the ocean if not for identical bathing caps and suits at the West Beach Club? When Joe Jr. looked in his drawer and realized his suit was missing, his blue eyes narrowed as he stormed into Jack's room to see the trunks sagging on Jack's thin frame. He erupted.

"Jack just made a mistake," Rose told her older son, putting herself between them. "It won't happen again. Just calm down."

Joe Jr. knew better than not to listen to his mother. The boys separated and traded suits. But four days later, the same mistake happened again, and this time Rose wasn't there to diffuse the situation. As soon as Joe Jr. saw Jack in the swimsuit, he took off after him. Jack jumped over the stairs, weaving through the furniture and out to the lawn. He made it to the breakwater, crawling up while glancing behind him, stepping gingerly from stone to slippery stone. He turned one more time to see his brother gaining on him.

They both stopped cold when they heard a voice yell, "Stop that!"

It was their father's friend Eddie Moore.

"You two get yourselves back here!" he bellowed. "Right now!"

Sheepishly, they made their way back to the house. It wasn't until Moore was gone that they had it out on the living room floor.

Sometimes, the boys played together nicely. They liked to climb up to the attic on rainy days, away from all the little kids, so they could spread their toy soldiers across the floor and let the figurines battle. But as Jack got older and more confident, he did things to intentionally get under Joe Jr.'s skin. Joe Jr. may have been big and brash like their father, but Jack took after their grandfather Honey Fitz with his cunning and cleverness. Jack knew Joe Jr.'s favorite part of the day was devouring cook Margaret's chocolate pie. The oldest Kennedy boy would sneak into the kitchen before dinner to request his slice and place it next to his plate, so he could anticipate and admire it for the entire meal. This evening, Jack knew it was time for his revenge on his older brother.

When Joe Jr.'s glance drifted from the sweet, sweating slice, Jack, with a sly smile, swiped the plate and, in one seamless movement, shoved the whole thing into his mouth as he took off in a sprint. Jack, covered in chocolate, ran straight to the breakwater. This time, Joe Jr. didn't follow. He just waited. Seething. Standing on the shore, he watched the still waters, protected by the large stones. Jack took a dive, his slim body piercing the surface, which silently rippled as he held his breath under the water. Joe Jr. waited until his brother's head emerged, gasping for air as he bobbed up and down. Then Joe Jr. went after him, the two wrestling while the rest of the family looked on from the lawn.

*   *   *

Rose mostly kept to herself. She and Joe rarely socialized with their neighbors, and she had no interest in entertaining. They only invited their very closest Boston or Bronxville friends to the Cape. Joe's good friend, Joseph Timilty—when he was appointed Boston police commissioner in 1936, they just called him the Commish—journeyed to the Cape once in a while. Joe wasn't one for dancing, so Timilty would take out Rose, who got dressed to the nines for a night of dancing at the Wianno Club. But mostly, their house was very much a family home—Rose wanted it to be a place where the children were comfortable, where they could be together in summers away from school. It was the longest stretch of the year where they were all in one place.

The kids had their friends and fought like all siblings do, but most of the time they preferred playing with each other. Neighbors noticed that the eight Kennedy kids cheered for each other louder than for anyone else, and they were always hugging and kissing. "No matter what anyone else had done, the Kennedy children always praised each other's accomplishments to the skies," said one observer. "While it was amusing and touching for a time, it got to be rather tiresome after a while."

Rose was particularly uninterested in getting to know the other women in the neighborhood. Her days were full with Mass and her children, and her husband when he was there. And for herself, when she had a spare moment to steal away. She didn't like being out on the water, but she had a little prefabricated hut built on the edge of the property, overlooking the sea, which was just for her. She loved her large family, but motherhood sometimes overwhelmed her. There was nowhere in that big house that was completely quiet, where she could breathe, be with her own thoughts. There was always someone knocking on the door, someone who needed something from her. "It's solitary confinement not splendor I need," she once said. "Any mother will know what I mean." She went out to her little hut to sit and think, or read, or pray.

Some of the women in the Port separately went over to welcome the family after they moved in, only to be met with a cold stare from Rose or a brush-off from someone working for her. Neighbor Madelaine Blackburn told writer Laurence Leamer about trying to get to know Rose.

One afternoon, Blackburn made her way down Marchant Avenue and knocked on the front door.

"I live right down the street," Blackburn said brightly to a maid who looked at her from the other side of the threshold, "and I'm here to say hello to Mrs. Kennedy."

After a few seconds of silence, the housekeeper asked, "Do you have an appointment to see Mrs. Kennedy?"

"Have a what?"

"An appointment."

"No," Blackburn said, "of course not."

"I'll get Mrs. Kennedy's secretary if you would like to make an appointment to meet with her."

As she turned on her heel back down the steps, Blackburn said under her breath, "The hell with that, I'm not going to bother these people."

Everyone was in Hyannis Port that first weekend of August 1929. The streets were full of kids riding their bikes, the beaches packed with sunbathers. The church in Hyannis was so crowded an extra tray was brought out to administer Communion. So, when a Sikorsky amphibious plane landed on the ocean behind the Kennedy house, it had an audience. Those with houses on the water fetched their binoculars and pressed their faces against their windows. A line formed along the beach's edge to see who on earth was making such a grand entrance. A petite woman barely five feet and a hundred pounds, her wide eyes lined with heavy makeup and displaying a perfectly black beauty mark on her chin, stepped carefully from the plane to a boat then onto the pier and over to Marchant Avenue. "Gloria Swanson," gawkers on the beach said to one another, as if the person next to them didn't know. Swanson was one of the biggest stars in the world. It was nearly impossible to go to the movie theater to see a silent film in which she wasn't the star. She epitomized Hollywood glamour and glitz, always pictured draped in pearls and silk gowns. There was no mistaking Gloria Swanson. The Port was a place for holey sweaters and bare feet, not celebrities or glamour. But here was Gloria Swanson and her friends—in the Port! Visiting the new family in town.

Swanson and Joe Kennedy had met when his studio tried to recruit her for its pictures. Joe soon took on a role managing her and overseeing her finances. She was already successful, but he thought she needed more prestigious roles to elevate her reputation and his film studio along with it. He told her over and over that he wanted to create important films. She would be his important star. Then, in January 1928, they had sex. Their affair became an open secret in Hollywood—and Swanson would later confirm the relationship in her autobiography, as would a biography of Joe written by David Nasaw. When Swanson came to Hyannis Port that hot August weekend, they'd been sleeping together for more than a year.

Like Joe, Swanson was married with children. When Joe was away from the Cape, he was often with Swanson at the villa he rented for her so they could be together when he was in California. He was infatuated, bringing her on family trips, and now—to his family's home. Rose's father, Honey Fitz, had had public affairs, including an explosive relationship that ended his political career and humiliated his wife, Josie. Rose never talked about Joe's unfaithfulness, but it was assumed the couple had some sort of unspoken agreement—that Joe not flaunt it, that he not embarrass her and the family. But here was Swanson in their family's most sacred place, their new neighbors watching and whispering.

Rose treated Swanson like any other work colleague of her husband's: cordially, politely. Joe showered Swanson with his attention and charm even in front of his wife, but Rose never let on if she was jealous. Swanson strode along the beach and visited with the Kennedy kids. She even signed her name on the wall next to the movie posters hung in the clubhouse above the garage where Kick and her friends Nancy Tenney and Mary Frances "Sancy" Falvey held meetings for their movie club.

"I was told if I wanted to be in the club, that I had to be in the Gloria Swanson club," said Nancy Tenney. "And I said, 'What other club is there?' And they said, 'Well, Constance Bennett,' and I said, 'but I want to be in the Constance Bennett club.' I couldn't because *they* were in the Constance Bennett club so *I* had to be in the Gloria Swanson club."

Swanson was expected to end her weekend trip with a Hyannis airport departure, and indeed, her group of friends arrived at the airport laughing and carrying on. Swanson wasn't with them, though. She'd changed her mind. She and Joe left quietly with another friend of hers by train.

Swanson would later write that her romantic relationship with Joe ended the following year. But for summers to come, neighbors whispered that when Rose left for one of her shopping trips to Europe, a chauffeur-driven Duesenberg would roll up the driveway in front of the Big House. Gloria's Duesenberg, they assumed.

When August turns into September, the sun sets earlier, the air cools, and the crowds begin to thin. In September 1929, Rose and Joe left for their trip to Europe, and the kids stayed back before returning to their various boarding schools. It was their grandparents' fortieth wedding anniversary.

To celebrate, Honey Fitz and Josie spent their day swimming at Craigville Beach, the sprawling public beach between Hyannis and Osterville. Then they had their grandchildren and some friends over to their rental in West Hyannisport—a part of town with homes more modest than where Rose and Joe lived. After dinner, everyone went back to the house on Marchant Avenue for a movie in the basement theater. Honey Fitz spent a lot of his time over on Marchant Avenue with his grandkids and their neighbor and his friend, Thomas Taggart, the former senator. Honey Fitz loved nothing more than regaling a captive audience, and that night he went on about the beauty and uniqueness of Cape Cod. Hyannis Port—and the Cape in general—was no hidden gem by this point. Rapid development early in the century was increasingly luring tourists to the small Cape communities. A Boston news columnist had recently railed about the "Floridization of Cape Cod." But with the perfect sailing conditions, calm shores, a scattering of freshwater ponds, and summers that were never too hot or too cold, there were more tourism dollars to be had, Honey Fitz believed.

"The right kind of publicity would bring the whole country here!" the diminutive former mayor proclaimed over dinner. It was often a crisp seventy degrees at Craigville Beach in the summer, which he believed was the absolute ideal temperature. What more could a person need?

The party ended. The Fitzgeralds went back to Boston. The Kennedy kids returned to their private schools. The house on Marchant Avenue sat quiet, dark, and empty. Most of the houses in the Port were second homes, with a scattering of year-rounders who stayed after the leaves changed.

Then came October 29, 1929. The stock market saw the worst crash it had ever seen. The plummet would spin into a depression, changing the country forever. Longtime residents of the Cape held their breath, waiting to see what it would mean for these little communities bloomed from wealth. Of course, there were bigger, much more important questions, but for the Port the question was: What would happen next summer?

CHAPTER TWO

On a summer Friday afternoon, Joe Kennedy's chauffeur drove through Whitman, Massachusetts, and slowed as the vehicle approached a big white sign with a soldier pointing to a white Cape Cod–style building. It was Joe's tradition to stop on the way to the Cape at the Toll House Inn, a restaurant owned by his friends Ruth and Kenneth Wakefield, which reputedly had the best desserts in Massachusetts. Joe started his meal with the French onion soup and ended with decadent Boston cream pie—the Wakefields made sure Joe was served a double-sized slice and sent him home with boxes full of cookies and cakes to bring to the kids. Before he left, Joe went to the kitchen to visit the staff before getting back in the car.

Joe Kennedy had been some combination of strategic and lucky before the catastrophic stock market crash. He'd moved his investments around and stepped away from Hollywood after a three-and-a-half-year run. With money sunk into his new homes in Bronxville and Hyannis Port and healthy trust funds established for the children, Joe had created a level of financial security for his family that contrasted with that of nearly everyone else in the country who faced devastation and ruin. While houses around the country were being foreclosed on, Joe prepared to buy a third home to be used as the family's winter residence: a mansion in Palm Beach, Florida, grander than the house on the Cape. And he hired the renowned Olmsteds—the family that designed Manhattan's Central Park—to overhaul the landscape for the Big House.

In Hyannis Port, life went on, too. The long-planned renovation of the Hyannisport Club, the golf club up the hill from the Kennedys, stalled briefly—memberships were down, fewer people were using the greens and the tennis courts. Club fees were reduced to encourage members not to quit. But the club quickly made up for the diminished fees with donations from other members, like Joe Kennedy. The club was doing well enough by late 1930 to buy up nearly forty more acres of Hyannis Port land west of the sixth hole. It was now an impressive 140 acres for golf: a manicured course framed by swampy wetlands set above the rest of the Port.

In Hyannis, the summer kicked off in early June with the largest gathering Main Street had ever seen for the annual Odd Fellows Parade. It was the start of the Great Depression, but summer homes were filled, and people still came to Hyannis from across the Cape to celebrate. A reporter for the local paper the *Hyannis Patriot* noted, "Hyannis never looked better."

The same could be said for Rose and Joe's relationship. Done with Hollywood, Joe was spending more time at home with his family than he had in years. Rose would later look back on this time as "a golden interval" in their lives. She and her husband began playing golf together at the beautiful renovated course up the hill. They thumbed through antiques catalogs, noting Early American antiques they wanted to bid on to decorate their home on the Cape. They went for long walks, hand in hand— just as in their relationship's early days. Sunday afternoons were theirs. They set off down the driveway, up Marchant, into town, talking about the children, their lives, everything. Sometimes the kids trailed behind, but eventually they gave up trying to catch up to their parents, who'd walk too fast and too far. After dinner, Rose and Joe sat on the far end of the porch wrapped in blankets while symphonies softly played on the record player. Out on the lawn in front of them, knives of light sliced through the yard, and giggles and shrieks echoed off the placid water. One of the kids' favorite games to play on nice summer nights was "Murder," which was their version of flashlight tag. When the kids were finally in their beds, Rose and Joe went for one last walk through the dark.

The acute focus that had made Joe a successful businessman was aimed squarely on his family now that he was home so often. He didn't know what he'd do next in his career, and he had enough money to take his time figuring it out. He sat on the balcony that connected his and Rose's rooms. He had a phone line set up out there, and a comfortable chair where he could recline and conduct business calls while sunning himself. His bellowing commands to whoever was on the other end of the line reverberated from the second-floor balcony out across the lawn, out to sea, where the kids could hear him as they played along the shoreline. There was no one else in town quite like Joe Kennedy.

"We would sit in our house and look at that big Kennedy house and know that somebody in that big house was going to be president of the United States," Nancy Tenney said. With a grandfather who'd served as mayor of Boston, and a father whose ambitions knew no limit, the Kennedy children saw nothing but a bright future. "We didn't know whether it was going to be Big Joe or Little Joe or Jack, but we knew it was going to be somebody in there."

Joe's intensity had always been dispensed in small doses—he'd come home for a weekend and suck up all the energy with his stories and his expectations for the children. But now, he was always there. And he seemed to be everywhere.

There was Joe standing in the hall to make sure the kids' fingernails were clean before they left the house in the morning. He stood in the yard wearing his dress shoes watching their swimming lessons. He was on the sidelines for their tennis matches on the court he'd had built in the backyard's east corner. When the older kids went sailing, Joe was right behind them in the water, puttering along in his motorboat. (He wasn't a sailor.) He'd always expected excellence from his children but now he was trailing a few feet behind shouting out their mistakes. "Coming in second was just no good," said Eunice, his fifth child.

There was Joe in his swim trunks out on the balcony attached to his room looking out on the harbor with his book in his lap, listening to his kids below on the wraparound porch whispering and gossiping about what they'd done on the weekends with their friends at boarding school. They never realized their father, up on his perch, could hear every conversation. "So," Joe said, clearing his throat over lunch the next day, "my spies in New York tell me they saw some of you kids at the nightclubs down there. Is that true?" They all looked at one another around the table, eyes wide. *How did he know?* It would be years before some of the girls happened to be up on their father's deck and realized he could hear everything that was being said down below. Jack, though, knew to be careful when his father was up there keeping watch. When he and his friend Jack Bell from up on Scudder Avenue took their dry, folded sails out to the boats, they carefully tucked a bag of beer under them so Joe, from his spot above, wouldn't see them sneaking it.

And there was Joe in his special chair in the movie theater basement. He was done with Hollywood, but he was still able to work his film studio connections to secure early copies of movies like *Dumbo* and *Snow White*. Sometimes the invited audience was just family and staff—family in the front, staff in the back—other nights the kids invited their friends from the neighborhood. Joe invited the pretty girls to come sit up front next to him. But they whispered to each other not to accept the invitation, because "Big Joe," as he was called, liked to pinch the girls who sat next to him.

"My friend Sancy was cute and blonde, and he'd say, *Sancy, how nice to see you, come sit with me,* and she'd roll her eyes," Nancy Tenney said. "He leans over this way so she has to lean this way. I never sat next to him—I was like one of the children."

Other times, Nancy noticed there were women down in the cellar for the movie night whom she hadn't seen around the house during the day—it was her guess that they'd come down from Boston. Rose, though, was rarely down there for movies. After the lights went out, the movie started rolling with someone on the Kennedy staff running the projector. Many of the films were from Joe's studio, so he stopped the film with a button next to his chair to interject little behind-the-scenes tidbits. And as soon as a couple on-screen started holding hands, Joe shouted, "Teddy! Teddy! Teddy, I think it's time for you to go to bed."

"Jean!" he shouted to the second-youngest when there was kissing. "Jean! You've got to go up to bed."

*   *   *

Just down the street from Marchant Avenue there was a tiny building that had once been home to the Hyannis Port Yacht Club. The building sat empty for years, just an abandoned hut at the end of the pier everyone in the Port walked down, often to catch a motorboat. From there they'd shuttle over to their sailboats anchored offshore. But in 1932, a few summer residents decided to raise money to fix up the club and get it going again.

With excitement for sailing rising in the neighborhood that summer, Joe decided it was time for his boys to have a real, competitive sailboat. A Wianno Senior. He went over to the neighboring town of Osterville to see what was available at the Crosby Yacht building, where the Crosbys, a longtime Cape family, built the impressive Wianno sailboats that filled Nantucket Sound. Anyone who wanted to compete in the many one-design races in the area needed to have a Wianno Senior—no other boats were allowed to compete so that each sailor was evenly matched. The Kennedy kids had been sailing on the smaller version—the sixteen-foot Wianno Junior. They had two Juniors—the first was named *Tenovus*, for the ten Kennedys. After their ninth child, Teddy, was born in 1932, they bought another and called it *Onemore*. But Joe Jr., Jack, and Eunice—the most competitive sailors in the family—were ready for the big leagues. Their friends, like Whitney Wright, already had the bigger boat to compete in the bigger races. The Kennedys needed a Senior.

In the Crosby Yacht yard that afternoon sat a boat labeled number 94: a sleek Senior that had been made on spec. Like the ninety-three Seniors made before it, the boat had a white oak frame, sturdy cypress planks, and a rich mahogany tiller. It was twenty-five feet long overall. Sturdy. It had a keel centerboard, suited for the shallow, sometimes choppy south side of the Cape. In the water, it was steady, slicing through waves gracefully without slapping the surface. Joe bought it on the spot for Jack's fifteenth birthday. Jack named it *Victura*, "about to conquer."

Jack shared the boat with Joe Jr., and they were out on the water behind the house whenever the wind was above five knots. After returning to shore, they carried their soaked sails up the stairs to the attic. Up in the attic, you could see where the old house ended—the boys walked across the house's original shingle roof to get to the beams where they'd nailed pins and hooks on the support beams overhead so they could hang their heavy sails. The next day, the sails were dry and ready to take back out again.

Most kids in the Port took their sailing lessons at the reopened Hyannis Port Yacht Club. The building was spruced up, but there was still almost nothing to it—no parking lot, no kitchen, no dining room, not even a toilet. It was merely a wooden building smaller than a freestanding garage at which to meet up for a lesson. In grandeur, it couldn't be further from the impressive Wianno Yacht Club the next town over. The Kennedy kids, however, didn't take their lessons through the Hyannis Port Yacht Club—they practiced on their own with Jimmie MacLean, a Coast Guard Academy graduate and merchant mariner whom Joe hired to give his kids a competitive edge.

"If there was a tough race of any kind, the [skipper] would be down by the docks scrubbing the bottoms of Joe Jr.'s and Jack's boats with oil. He didn't bother with Kick's or Eunice's boat. But Jack and Joe's boat, there was always some action on the underbelly to make it go smoother," Nancy said.

On race days, Jack and Joe Jr. showed up at the start line with their well-oiled sailboats, ready to collect their trophies. "All the kids in the neighborhood wanted to sail with the Kennedys in those days," said Sam Keavy, one of the Keavy boys from down the street, "because the opportunities for coming in first were much much better than coming in second or third."

The only one of the older children not allowed to go out on the water on her own was Rosemary. She was just a year younger than Jack—the oldest girl in the family. She was beautiful, with full cheeks and thick, dark curls. Of all the children, Rosemary looked most like her mother. It had been clear for a while that Rosemary was slower to develop than the rest of her siblings. It wasn't something the family talked about—with each other or anyone else. The kids were just told their sister was "a little slow." Childhood and adolescence were sometimes difficult for Rosemary as she tried to keep up with her siblings and was shuttled between schools and doctor's appointments. But she loved those summers in Hyannis Port. Rose made sure Rosemary was included in everything the other kids did. Jack was the one who brought Rosemary to the weekly twelve-and-over dances at the Wianno Yacht Club. Kids in the neighborhood spent all week looking forward to the dances, which drew a mix of teenagers from the wealthy summer families, the young people working for those families, and the year-rounders. It was a night to get out of your environment and meet other kids—maybe even start a summer romance. Joe Jr. loved the dances. He threw his whole body into dancing, projecting absolute enthusiasm, full gusto. He was the life of the party. And he loved to tease his sisters. If one got stuck with a would-be suitor for too long, they'd spy him out of the corner of their eye with that mischievous smirk of his, delighting in their misfortune. Eventually, he'd cut in, relieving them of their discomfort. Jack spent most of the dances with his sister Kick, who was much more outgoing than Jack and pulled him out of his shell by introducing him to other kids. And she was popular. A tradition at the dances was for the girls to throw a shoe into the center of the dance floor, at which point the boys would run and grab a shoe, the prize being the opportunity to dance with the shoe's owner. All the boys paid attention to which shoes Kick was wearing when she walked into the dance, and they'd fight over that shoe when she threw it.

Once in a while, Rose and the family's governess, Alice Cahill, followed the kids to the dance. They stood outside the building, peering through a window to see how Rosemary was doing. One of those nights, they spotted her standing all by herself. Joe Jr. was off dancing; Jack and Kick were somewhere else—probably chatting up some group. And Rosemary was alone. Rose was furious. When the kids got home, she told the boys it was their responsibility to dance with Rosemary, to make sure she was having a good time.

While the older kids could be too self-absorbed to include Rosemary, it was Eunice, three years her junior, who was the most patient with her. Eunice was the one to make sure Rosemary was included when the kids headed out to the yard with their tennis rackets and their mother called out after them, "Make sure to take Rosemary with you!" Eunice—the middle child, lanky with big, round eyes and wild, curly hair she never cared about taming—was also one of the most competitive Kennedy children. She was as aggressive on the water as it gets.

Rosemary wasn't a strong sailor, but Eunice still invited her to come crew for her that summer. She knew how much it meant to Rosemary. Their thick hair whipped their faces, the mast popping with each gust as they hugged the shore. The mark was in sight. Eunice's eyes focused on the mast and then straight ahead and back again. Her mouth set in a determined line. Rosemary gazed at her sister as the sun beat down and the water splashed against the hull. Her grasp on the jib loosened as she turned back to her sister with a sweet smile. She was content.

"Rosemary!" Eunice shouted. "Get the jib, Rosemary! Rosemary, *look*, the jib is flapping! Pull it in! For God's *sake*, Rosemary, pull in the blasted jib!" Years later, Eunice would think back on that day. "Despite my tone, she would never lose her somewhat distant but happy smile."

When they got home after the race, Joe asked how they did. Performance was, as always, top of mind. "We came in third, Dad," Eunice told her father. He responded, "For God's sake. Can't you do better than that?" Winning was just as important to Eunice. But she'd seen the look on her sister's face. And that meant something, too.

As his first semester of Harvard wrapped up, Joe Jr. invited a friend from school to come back with him to Hyannis Port. Thomas Bilodeau was a year older and lived in the Winthrop House dormitory with Joe Jr. Bilodeau figured there'd be sailing and athletics. He knew Joe Jr. was an avid sailor who came from a big family. But he wasn't prepared for the intensity of Hyannis Port. To an outsider, visiting the Big House was like entering a whole new world where touch football was a blood sport and Joe was king.

When the boys arrived from Boston, Joe Jr. introduced the rest of his siblings to his new friend. When the Kennedys spilled out onto the lawn and split into teams for touch football, Bilodeau noticed Jack waited for Joe Jr. to pick a team—then he stepped over to the opposite side. The rivalry that began with swiped slices of pie and chases down the breakwater continued after Joe Jr. left for school, but the difference in Jack's and

Joe Jr.'s size had narrowed. Still, Jack was much thinner, his threadbare T-shirts hanging on his bony shoulders as if they were a wire hanger. Bilodeau quickly realized these games weren't what he'd come to know as typical touch football: the kind where players replace tackles with two-hand tags. Joe Jr. and Jack took every opportunity to block each other with a full-body slam, to roughhouse each other to the ground between plays. "Touch football was not a matter of strategy with the Kennedy family. It was a matter of blood and thunder," Bilodeau said. "You tried to get on the side that had the most weight or else you'd get killed."

As Bilodeau sat with the family in the living room while they waited for dinner, he observed the clear family hierarchy. The kids, especially Joe Jr. and Jack, worshiped their father. If Joe Kennedy was in the room, everything centered around him: the attention, the energy, the conversation. Bilodeau found his new friend's father and his stories about life in Hollywood fascinating. And though they were surely stories they'd heard a million times, Joe Jr. and Jack hung on their dad's every word. "When the father was present," Bilodeau said, "he ran the show."

When Bobby went away to boarding school in Boston at Milton Academy, everyone knew who his father was—he was Bobby Kennedy, son of the Hollywood bigwig, and he was treated as the kid of a famous person. So, when he brought his friend from school Dave Hackett back home to Hyannis Port, Hackett was curious what the Kennedy house would be like. After a particularly depleting visit, he wrote up his "Rules for Visiting the Kennedys."

"Prepare yourself by reading *The Congressional Record*, *U.S. News & World Report*, *Time*, *Newsweek*, *Fortune*, *The Nation*, *How to Play Sneaky Tennis*, and *The Democratic Digest*," it started. "Anticipate that each Kennedy will ask you what you think of another Kennedy's (a) dress, (b) hairdo, (c) backhand, (d) latest public achievement. Be sure to answer 'Terrific.' This should get you through dinner. Now for the football field. It's touch, but it's murder." And it went on from there.

As Rose once said, "I suppose if you're not used to it, a weekend with us can be exhausting. *Pooping*, I believe, is the word."

When Jack brought home Ralph "Rip" Horton Jr., a friend from Choate, Horton was most struck by the patriarch—like Joe Jr.'s friend

Bilodeau had been. "Jack and Joe Jr. would ask questions and Mr. Kennedy would answer in great detail. But if I asked a question, he'd treat me like a piece of dirt," Horton said. "He'd ignore me. He was only really interested in his own family."

The lull in Joe's work ended in the summer of 1934. He was appointed by President Franklin D. Roosevelt—whom he'd campaigned for two years earlier—to oversee Wall Street corruption as the first head of the Securities and Exchange Commission, drawing on his own experiences in banking. His new role in D.C. took him away from home more often, and he split his time going back and forth to the house he rented in Maryland. The dizzying cycle of lessons, races, dances, and dinners went on as usual on Marchant Avenue for Rose and the kids.

The summer of 1934, Joe Jr. arrived home later than the rest of the family—he'd gone on a three-week trip to Russia before coming back to the Cape for the end of the summer. It was important to Joe that his sons travel extensively—he wanted them to be as worldly as they were well-educated. At dinner on Joe Jr.'s first night back, all attention was on the eldest son as he told the table about his trip. He talked about communism, explaining that he saw on his trip a system of sharing in which everyone got what they needed. He was impressed by it.

His father's blue eyes turned as dark as a night storm. The other children went quiet as everyone turned to the head of the table to see what their father's response would be. "I don't want to hear any more of it until you go out and sell your boat and get rid of your new car and get rid of your horse I just purchased for you," Joe said sternly. "After you do that, so you can be equal with everyone else, then you can come back to the dinner table and continue the conversation."

When Joe Jr. had written home that spring about his trip to Germany a letter full of shocking praise for Adolf Hitler and the Nazis—"Hitler is building a spirit in his men that could be envied in any country" and "he has passed the sterilization law which I think is a great thing"—his father hadn't offered a reply. Not even about his son's apparent reference to the "Law for the Prevention of Offspring with Hereditary Diseases," which mandated forced sterilization of people with physical and mental disabilities. Rose and Joe had wanted their sons to travel so they could form their own opinions. But now, as Joe Jr. went on about the benefits of communism over capitalism, his father exploded. Joe set down his knife and fork, pushed back his chair, and stomped out of the dining room.

The rest of the family sat silent. Rose turned to her oldest son. "You shouldn't get your father so upset."

The next day, everything went back to normal. There was no more talk of it.

Nancy Tenney and Pat sat on the sunporch listening to Pat's big radio. Pat had her mother's straight nose and dark eyebrows, and usually wore her thick hair pulled back halfway. She loved music and going into town for matinees. Above the girls a number of loud thuds could be heard. "That's Daddy," Pat told Nancy. "He's mad it's too loud but I don't care because I like it like that."

The stomping stopped for a few minutes. Then, the downstairs phone rang. Nancy went over to answer it. It was Joe calling from upstairs. Only then did Pat turn down the music.

"Pat spoke up," Nancy said. "None of the others ever spoke up to their parents."

The summer of 1937, it was Bobby's and Pat's turn to go away for summer camp. Bobby was eleven, just a hair over five feet, with hazel eyes, a face full of freckles, and a head full of licks that were impossible to keep down. He was the one most likely to be left out of things—he wasn't one of the big kids and he wasn't one of the little kids—so he spent most of his time with his friend Jack Bell. Bobby was a quiet boy with a red-hot temper, and when he did talk, his voice was louder than you'd expect out of a boy his size. "Bobby was a brat! He was the only one that was sort of with any discord," Nancy said. "If they were all going this way, he was going that way. The others all had wonderful dispositions. I didn't see meanness in anybody except Bobby. He was mean."

Pat had just turned thirteen, and she and Bobby begged not to be sent away—they didn't want to leave Hyannis Port and the rest of the family for the summer. But just like their siblings before them, they didn't have a choice. Eighteen-year-old Rosemary was away at camp that summer, too. She was old enough to be out on her own, but her parents decided additional supervision would be good for her, so they arranged for her to have an adult companion go with her. With the three kids gone and Joe Jr. and Jack both back and forth visiting, the house at the end of Marchant Avenue was quieter that summer.

Halfway through their camp session, Bobby and Pat got their wish to leave when they were both admitted to the hospital at the same time: Bobby with pneumonia, Pat with an acute case of appendicitis that required emergency surgery. While recovering in hospital rooms down the hall from each other, the kids formed a bond with one of six nurses attending to them, Luella Hennessey, who was only two years out of training. Their father rushed to the hospital from Washington, and Rose booked a flight back from Paris, where she'd been on a shopping trip. By the time they got there, the kids were starting to feel better. They told their parents of the plan they'd hatched for the rest of the summer: they wanted Hennessey to come back with them to the Cape—to be the nurse who'd oversee their recovery at the Big House.

Rose only had one screening question for the nurse.

"Do you smoke?" Rose asked. She wouldn't be able to stand the Big House stinking with smoke. "No ma'am," Hennessey answered, "I don't."

Hennessey was hired. The plan was for her to help with Pat's recovery through Labor Day. Then she'd return to her hospital job. Hennessey, Joe, Rose, Bobby, and Pat made the trip from Boston back home to Hyannis Port—Hennessey's first time there. As they pulled into the circular driveway at the dead end of Marchant Avenue, they were greeted by the rest of the kids lined up on the white porch waving. They looked straight out of a picture with their matching smiles in front of that big, beautiful house framed by the sea. "Hi, Miss Hennessey!" they shouted.

On the second floor, she was shown the staff quarters, which were to the left of the stairs. Hennessey unpacked in her new room, which was small but neat and comfortable. That night, she had a place setting at the dinner table with the rest of the family, and the kids excitedly explained sailing to her. "You'll come out with us tomorrow, won't you?" they asked.

The sailing invitation wasn't just to make the new nurse feel welcome—the older kids were often in need of people to help crew for them. Anyone who stepped foot in their house was a possible crew member for the next day's race. And they didn't go easy on Hennessey just because she was new—and a medical professional employed by the family. Just as she was beginning to settle in, she was roped into crewing for Jack, who was back from Harvard for a sailing race.

Out there in the sunshine, she felt so lucky to be on the Cape that summer. She'd go back to her regular life eventually, but now, she just wanted to enjoy being by the beach for a couple of months. She snapped back to attention when Jack asked if she'd mind jumping overboard. You see, they were behind, and he thought eliminating her weight might help his chances of a win.

"Teddy!" Honey Fitz shouted down to the lawn. "Teddy!"

Little Teddy tried to ignore his grandfather, instead picking up the football and drawing back his arm to toss it to his brother for another play. All the older kids—his siblings and the kids from the neighborhood—waited impatiently for Teddy to answer his grandfather's call. The game had to stop every hour or so for the same reason.

"Teddy!" Honey Fitz yelled. "Just come in!"

Honey Fitz liked to read each and every newspaper edition. There were several editions a day, and the close follower of current events relied on his grandson to bike over to the News Shop with a nickel as soon as each new edition arrived. Honey Fitz liked to read on the sunporch right above the playing field, his leathered face slathered in cocoa butter, which, he told anyone who'd listen, was healthy for the skin. Teddy was never terribly excited to see his grandfather.

It wasn't easy being the youngest of nine. The older kids adored their baby brother—Teddy was four years younger than Jean, the second-youngest Kennedy kid. He was seventeen years younger than Joe Jr., the oldest. Jack had written a letter to his mother when he found out there'd be a ninth Kennedy sibling, asking to be the baby's godfather. And when Joe Jr. got his own boat, he named it *Teddy*. The neighbors in the Port remember a spunky, round-faced, freckled little Teddy following his older siblings around like an afternoon shadow.

"Teddy was darling," Nancy Tenney said, "little cute, fat Teddy, and everybody adored him."

If Jack and Bobby were feeling charitable they'd include him, but more often than not, they stayed a few steps ahead, shouting over their shoulders, "Hit it, squirt!" They loved their baby brother—that didn't always mean they wanted him hanging around. It was Jean who was most often stuck with Teddy—the two youngest siblings banished to the little table off to the side of the dining room table at dinnertime. Jeannie, as they called the youngest girl, was shy, her head usually hung low as she sat on the lawn while the rest of the kids played. If Joe Jr. or Jack had a friend over, Bobby would begrudgingly be demoted to the kids' table, too.

It was Rose's idea to host her sister's children in the summers to give Teddy a playmate in his cousin Joey Gargan, a sandy-haired boy about his age. Rose's sister Agnes—whom she was close to and who served as her maid of honor when she married Joe—died in 1936, which was a traumatic blow to Rose. Agnes's children—Joey and his sisters Mary Jo and Ann—bounced around between relatives. But their summers would be in Hyannis Port with the Kennedys.

Teddy and Joey were as close as brothers those summers. But still, there was nothing like attention from Teddy's real big brothers—especially Joe Jr. It was Teddy's dream to go sailing with Joe Jr. He asked. He begged. He pleaded. Then, one day, it happened.

The *Victura* was repaired from the electrical damage the year before—lightning had split the mast and ripped a hole in the hull. And Joe Jr. was ready to take the mended Wianno Senior for a spin in one of the local races. When Teddy asked to join him, Joe Jr. said okay. Teddy could hardly believe it. He'd write about that momentous day years later when Jack put together a book of remembrances about Joe Jr. Five-year-old Teddy followed on Joe Jr.'s heels down to the pier in the final minutes before the race. Their sail raised just as the gun exploded to start the event. Teddy's first race. He was soaking it in when his brother shouted at him to pull in the jib. *Pull in the jib?* Teddy had no idea what he was talking about. Joe Jr.

said it again. This time louder. Teddy felt confused, panicked. He watched the other boats drift farther away. Joe Jr. jumped over Teddy to grab the sail. Teddy's eyes widened, a little scared about what was going to happen. Next thing Teddy knew, his brother had picked him up by the pants, and he was flying clear over the stern, landing with a splash in the frigid water. Teddy drew in a sharp breath as he broke through the surface, gasping, spinning around looking for the boat. He was scared to death. His brother had thrown him in! Then he heard another splash and felt a pull as Joe Jr. dragged him back over the side into the boat. They kept racing, silently, dripping, two pools of water beneath them on the cockpit floor. They came in second.

As they walked back to the house, Joe Jr. said to Teddy, "Keep quiet about what happened this afternoon."

The lead editorial in the local paper, the *Hyannis Patriot*, on Thursday, December 16, 1937, was headlined "Our New Ambassador."

> The news of the appointment of Joseph P. Kennedy of Boston as Ambassador to the Court of St. James is as gratifying to the people of Cape Cod as to all the other parts of the country which are hailing this selection as one of the achievements of the Roosevelt Administration. For many years the Kennedys have had a summer home in Hyannis Port and have proved good neighbors with a genuine interest in the Cape and who have given the sort of distinction to this section of New England that is helpful.

Joe Kennedy finally had the respect he'd so long thirsted for. And the Kennedys were going to London.

"Look at this, Rosie," Joe said to his wife in their new home at 14 Prince's Gate overlooking Hyde Park in London. He was holding a list of all the exclusive clubs to which he was automatically granted membership as the American ambassador. "I am now a member of at least six exclusive golf clubs. I wonder what the people in Cohasset would think if they saw me now. It sure shows that if you wait long enough, the wheel turns."

Joe and Rose had moved their entire family with them to Europe, where they were warmly welcomed. The Kennedys were constantly in the papers—the British were fascinated by the large, lively family and Rose's style. The kids were happy there, too—particularly Kick and Jack, who were quick to make a group of upper-crust friends. But the family still made the long trip to Hyannis Port for June and July of 1938. When they came back, they were met with new neighbors—the Taggart family had sold the large, columned house next door to the McKelvys from Pittsburgh. But most everything else was the same.

Jack and Joe Jr. had a big race coming up—the intercollegiate sailing championship, which was called the McMillan Cup. That year, it was being held a town over at the Wianno Yacht Club, and the brothers were representing Harvard. On race day, the weather was perfect, with a crisp southwest breeze. It was just like when they were kids—packing up their sails to head out together for a race on Nantucket Sound. Jack sailed Harvard's second division, while Joe Jr. sailed the first division. Their father had accepted a guest seat on the committee board—now that Joe was a dignitary, he had special access, attention, and respect. In back-to-back races, Joe Jr. came in fourth and Jack second, helping Harvard win that week.

Ten months later, the days slowly got longer, the fluffy hydrangeas bloomed indigo again, and Hyannis Harbor filled with sailboats. The Kennedys were still in Europe, so Honey Fitz and Josie opened their house for the season. Honey Fitz loved his daughter's house in Hyannis Port. He and Josie had rented houses all around the area, but he spent as much time as he could at Rose and Joe's home. When his grandkids were around, he danced a jig through the halls with his fingers pointing up, singing, "I love the ladies! I love the ladies! The fat ones, the slim ones, the tall ones, the short ones. I love them all!" But when there was nobody to entertain, he sat for hours on the wall that surrounded the deck, enjoying the sun and the sound of the breaking waves. He loved, too, to walk down to the beach, where he lay on the rocks, covering himself with seaweed because he thought the bromides were good for his skin. But when he and his wife arrived that summer of '39 to open the house, the terns had claimed the end of Marchant Avenue as their own. They were everywhere, the sand black with a blanket of birds. Honey Fitz and Josie tried to ignore them, passing the enormous flock and their nests to go down for a swim. The terns set off a chorus of *kik, kik, kik*, their wings flapping, swooping down at the couple, snapping their orange beaks.

"The birds are a nuisance! A public nuisance!" Honey Fitz said, exasperated. "One of these days those birds will be picking someone's eyes out!"

He called the board of selectmen for help. The full board of local government officials came to the property, but they found only a dozen or so birds. There wasn't much they could do, they explained patiently. The terns were protected by the Department of Conservation.

That week, Honey Fitz told a local reporter that he was on the verge of getting a trench helmet to wear for his daily swims. What he actually did, though, was wrap a white towel around his head, shaking it at the birds when they squawked at him.

Then, one quiet afternoon, the neighbors heard gunshots. *Pop, pop, pop, pop, pop, pop.* Followed by a series of splashes in the water. Honey Fitz, it turned out, had hired Norton Sherman, a local who'd worked on the family's boats a few seasons earlier, to shoot all those terns clear out of the sky. When Joe Kennedy heard about what his father-in-law had done, Honey Fitz was no longer invited to the Big House. It would be a few seasons before he was invited back.

CHAPTER THREE

The Kennedy kids pushed open the windows on the first floor facing their driveway and leaned out as far as they could. Their hands firmly on the white windowsills, they watched their friend George Mead turn down Dale Avenue, then onto Marchant. "Go home, George!" they yelled in unison. Through giggles they shouted, "Not enough food!"

George Mead was a Jack and Kick friend who lived across Lewis Bay on Great Island. While Hyannis Port is crowded with summer houses of the wealthy, Great Island is home to the secluded estates of the filthy rich. Mead, whose family was one of the oldest and most prominent in Dayton, Ohio, and owned the Mead Paper Company, was as competitive as the Kennedys but small—just five foot eight and 140 pounds—and spent so many meals over at the Kennedy house that the family teased him endlessly about it. The Kennedys loved to needle each other and their friends, and Jack and Kick, in particular, had a similar sense of humor. As they got older, the two were inseparable, their heads always together sharing an inside joke.

Mead laughed and made his way in. Rose was on the phone talking to Archbishop Spellman, while Pat, in a sweatshirt and worn-in dungarees, told a story she'd just read in the news about a plane crashing near where their family had lived in London, and Joe Jr. explained something happening in the Soviet Union. Bobby tried unsuccessfully to get everybody to play charades. Jack was downstairs surrounded by piles of *Why England*

Slept, the book he'd written from his Harvard senior thesis. It came out in July 1940, and it was everywhere, including proudly on display at the tiny News Shop down the street from the Big House. Jack's room was a mess of laundry and his research materials; letters from congressmen and notes from prime ministers lay crumpled beneath the twin beds. Jack talked about the publicity he had planned for the book. There were interviews, radio programs, and autographed copies to send out. As he laid out the next few months of work ahead of him, Honey Fitz burst into the room.

The former mayor and his wife, Josie, had rented a house on Lighthouse Lane, overlooking Keyes Beach and just a ten-minute walk from the Big House. By then, Joe had forgiven Honey Fitz for the terns, letting him continue his visits to Marchant Avenue. Teddy had brought his grandfather that day's papers, which Honey Fitz waved back and forth furiously. There was, he explained in fits and starts, a scathing article about his time as mayor. Jack listened patiently, then, with an innocent smile, began teasing him. "Well, grandfather," Jack said, "let's be honest about it. You're really lucky to be here."

Joe and his oldest daughter, Rosemary, were the last to return from England. Joe had argued that Rosemary should stay behind and live in Europe. He'd written to Rose a year earlier: "She is much happier when she sees the children just casually. For everyone's peace of mind, particularly hers, she shouldn't go on vacation or anything else with them . . . I'm not sure she isn't better staying over here indefinitely with all of us making our regular trips, as we will be doing, and seeing her then. I have given her a lot of time and thought and I'm convinced that's the answer. She must never be at home for her sake as well as everyone else's."

But either Rose didn't agree to the plan or Joe had a change of heart—Rosemary and her father came home in the heat of the Second World War. Joe had gone to London a respected diplomat; he'd left in disgrace after publicly contradicting President Roosevelt by saying the United States should stay out of the war.

The rest of the family had taken a boat back to the States, arriving in September 1939. Rosemary flew home with Joe's friend Eddie Moore and his wife in June 1940, and Joe finally left that October, bringing with him an 1888 baton from conductor Arturo Toscanini to decorate the Big House's living room mantel and, also, an air raid siren to call the children in from swimming.

The summer of 1941, everyone was back home. In the morning, as the clocks ticked over to six, the sun rising in the back of the house, Joe, in his flannel shirt and riding boots, knocked on nine-year-old Teddy's door. "You can come riding if you're downstairs in five minutes!" Teddy hopped out of bed, pulled on his clothes, and bounded down the stairs. Teddy was Joe's favorite riding partner. Often Joe rode alone—his long rides were meditation for him. The kids nicknamed his favorite horse Mount Sinai, where, in the Bible, Moses received the Ten Commandments. If Joe wanted to ride with someone, he brought along one of his boys. But Jack was allergic to the horses, Bobby didn't like to ride, and Joe Jr. liked to go solo. Teddy, who coveted rare time alone with his father, was his most enthusiastic riding partner.

The family had a farm in Osterville on some land Joe had bought. Osterville was the village over from Hyannis—the houses were bigger there and it had the more opulent golf and yacht clubs. But Osterville also had sprawling rural land away from the ocean. It was only a fifteen-minute drive out to the farm, but leaving the crowded streets of Hyannis Port for the tranquil open land shaded by a canopy of trees, father and son could sense a certain shift in the air. If it was low tide, Joe dropped Teddy off at the bridge that led to Osterville with a couple of buckets and shovels. While Joe went riding, Teddy walked along the shore looking for little holes in the sand where he could dig for steamers. But if the tide was high, Teddy got to ride with his father. Joe mounted his horse, while Teddy rode Blue Boy, a gentle, old stallion that his brothers had ridden for years. Joe had his horses brought over from Ireland. He liked to say it cost more to ship them over than the value of the horses themselves, but they all had good, sweet dispositions. Joe and Teddy ambled together along the wet cranberry fields, the horses' hooves sinking into the ground with each step, cranberry trucks rattling alongside them from time to time. If

Joe was in a good mood, he peppered his youngest with questions about school, sports, books. He listened intently and, in turn, talked about the rest of the family. The ride went quickly, and they were back at the farm before they knew it. If Joe wasn't in a good mood, he was so quiet you could hear the swishing of the horses' tails. The morning sun beat down on them as they looked ahead in silence. "His temperament was never hard to discern," Teddy later wrote.

The Kennedys would think back to that summer of 1941 for the rest of their lives. The ones who lived to see their hair turn gray would sit on their porches, talking about those months when the family was together, whole and happy. "The summer of 1941 was the last one that our family would ever have together," Rose would reminisce. Reflecting on that same summer, Teddy wrote six decades later, "I can look back and see all of them as they might well have been on a given weekend morning, each one distinct yet a part of the whole."

That summer was a peak for the Kennedys but, outside of Marchant Avenue, there was a heavy, expectant feeling on the Cape as the country braced for the war that Joe had left behind in Europe the previous fall. Joe Jr. and Jack had both entered the draft, and Joe Jr. was set to leave for the navy soon. Before he left, Joe Jr. took the *Victura* for one last race on July 10.

After the Kennedys closed the Big House at the end of that summer, Joe and Rose made the decision to sell their home in Bronxville, New York. The older kids were all out of the house, so Joe and Rose would split their time with Pat, Bobby, Jean, and Teddy between Hyannis Port and Palm Beach. The older kids would visit as often as they could. But it would be decades before their sister Rosemary returned home to Hyannis Port.

Joe was becoming more and more frustrated with Rosemary's condition. Her learning delays from childhood had never improved, and as a young adult, she sometimes displayed emotional outbursts and unpredictable and intense moods. She was unable to live on her own, and the doctors who'd been seeing her since she was a child weren't able to give Joe any satisfactory answers or solutions. When Joe heard about an experimental medical procedure that promised to subdue Rosemary's moods but required surgery on the brain, he signed her up—without talking to his wife or anyone else about it.

It was clear as soon as the lobotomy was completed that it was a horrific mistake—Rosemary was left permanently disabled. Joe made the next decision, too, to take his daughter away from the family to live in a private psychiatric hospital and eventually a Catholic institution in Wisconsin. The neighbors in Hyannis Port noticed that Rosemary suddenly stopped coming home to the Cape, but they didn't dare ask where she'd gone. The question of what happened to Rosemary was never discussed—within the family or with anyone else. Rosemary simply vanished.

In December 1941, America officially entered World War II. There was a heavy quiet across the neighborhood. Car headlights were painted half-black. Inside homes, windows facing Nantucket Sound were draped with thick, dark curtains: precautions to keep light from reflecting off American tankers and ships traveling along the coastline. On December 9, Cape Cod experienced its first air raid alarm, the dull, constant noise echoing through the afternoon, followed by workers in civilian defense taking to their stations.

When the Port families returned to their homes the next summer, fewer sons came with them. Applications for the June session at the Cape Cod Secretarial School skyrocketed as those who hadn't been drafted prepared for defense-related secretarial work. Jean, Pat, and Bobby, all home from boarding school, signed up for the courses there. And Jean went to the Red Cross on Mondays and Thursdays to make bandages for the soldiers. Jack and Joe Jr., who were away for training, came home for weekends as often as they could. It was hard for the younger kids to grasp the severity of the looming war and what it would mean for their community and their family. On July 10, Pat, then eighteen, wrote to her older brother Jack:

> Dear Jack,
>   Well how's every little thing with you good looking? . . .
>   The Cape is duller than ever and your sister more unpopular (if that's possible). There is a Senior race at the Port and Bobby is

racing at Hyannis. Whitney Wright is the only other Senior in the
Port . . . Nancy Tenney is home for a month and Kick arrives tomor-
row after her little trip to see Johnny before he goes in the Navy. Eu-
nice's 21st birthday is Friday (don't forget). Do you think you will be
down again? Well that's about all. Write soon.
　　Lots of love,
　　Pat

In August 1942, the kids' first friend died in the war. George Mead
was Jack and Kick's friend from over on Great Island, the one who never
passed up a dinner invitation and who was just as likely to roll up his
sleeves to clean dishes after the meal. Mead, who spent so many evenings
playing board games in the Big House living room, died while serving as
a Marine on a reconnaissance mission in the Solomon Islands. Kick, in
particular, was devastated.

With food rations in place, Joe converted the farm in Osterville where
he kept his Irish horses into a working farm that could supply his family with vegetables, meat, and dairy products. He had cows, pigs, lambs,
and vegetable gardens. "Your father is nuts about the farm. He is reading
farm reports assiduously and discussing the merits of having registered
cattle," Rose wrote the children that summer. "He is also busy preserving
everything from string beans to steers." Joe wrote to his son Jack about
the farm: "I hope to keep it going until two or three years after the war, at
least, and possibly as long as we stay at the Cape."

Joe Jr., who'd just been commissioned as a naval pilot, came home to
Hyannis Port to see his family in September 1943 before leaving for England. He shook hands, embraced his younger siblings in hugs, and said
his final words before saying goodbye. The family watched as he drove off,
turning right on Scudder Avenue, which would take him out of Hyannis
Port, unsure when they'd see him again.

With their older brothers fighting in the war, Bobby would pick up
Teddy and they'd drive up from their boarding schools to the closed Big
House. It was dark, quiet, frigid. The noise of radios and phonographs,
telephones and barking dogs, which normally vibrated through the walls
in the summer, was gone, replaced by the biting wind and the waves lap-

ping on the shore. After the early sunsets, they walked together along the dunes talking about how much their lives were changing. They were finally old enough—and had been through enough together—that the six-year age difference between them didn't matter as it had. When it got too cold to walk any farther, they came back. They slept in the musty, cobwebbed apartment above the garage, which was a little warmer than the main house, bundled together to share body heat.

Teddy would later recall, "Those chilly weekends at the Cape cast a quiet spell on both of us . . . that is hard to describe."

Rose sat in Joe's bedroom, a large room overlooking the yard and the Sound beyond it. She was waiting for the morning news to begin on the radio when she received a phone call just after eight. It was a reporter from the *Boston Globe*. Joe was over at the farm on his morning horse ride, Rose explained to the journalist before hanging up. She wondered what a reporter could possibly be calling Joe about.

While Joe steered his way back to the Big House, he listened to the news on the radio. The announcer said that navy lieutenant John F. Kennedy, who after an encounter with a Japanese destroyer had been missing for several days, had been found. And he was safe. Joe was so excited that he jerked at the steering wheel, driving the car off the road and into a grassy field somewhere between Osterville and Hyannis Port.

The kids, who didn't know their brother had been missing, found out that day when they rode their bikes over to the News Shop to get the evening papers and saw the *Boston Evening Globe*: "Kennedy's Son Hero of PT-Boat Saga" it read. When Jack's boat was hit by a Japanese destroyer just south of the Solomon Islands, Jack had ordered the rest of the crew off the boat before it went up in flames—and he was the one who helped the other survivors swim the three and a half miles to the closest island. From there Jack swam from island to island looking for food, fresh water, and help. Finally, three days after his boat had sunk, Jack and a member of his crew came across two men—islander scouts working with the Allies. Jack scratched an SOS into a coconut, which the scouts delivered, resulting in the rescue of his crew. It was a heroic saga worthy of one of his father's films.

The kids ran the three blocks home from the News Shop, shouting down the street that their brother was a hero. Joe admitted to his family that he'd been notified several days earlier that Jack had been missing. He didn't want to worry anyone—not the kids at home, not Joe Jr. who was away at war, not even Rose—with the news. By now Joe was plenty skilled at keeping secrets. Rose and the kids, who crowded around her, were just relieved that Jack was safe, and proud they had a war hero in the family.

Soon after Jack's rescue, Joe Jr. was back home on the Cape in time for his father's fifty-fifth birthday celebration. With one son home, and another son safe after a harrowing ordeal, the Big House was energetic, jubilant. Jack's rescue was the talk of the Port. Judge John Burns, a friend of Joe's, raised a glass, quieting the dining room for a toast. "To Ambassador Joe Kennedy," Burns began, "father of our hero, our own hero, Lieutenant John F. Kennedy of the United States Navy."

The guests held their glasses raised. And the judge sat down. His brief toast ended with no mention of Joe Jr., who sat across from him. Joe Jr. raised his glass with a tight smile stretched across his face.

That night, a guest heard Joe Jr. crying in his bedroom.

Joe Jr. and Jack had been competing since they could walk, chasing each other since they could run. But Joe Jr. was always the family's star, the one destined for great things.

The summer of 1944, everyone anxiously awaited that day's mail at the little post office in Hyannis Port. A letter from Kick arrived for her best friend, Nancy Tenney, from Europe. Kick's and Nancy's lives had changed a lot in the last years, since they were kids passing notes back and forth through their bedroom windows. Nancy had gotten married and had a baby named Tangley. Kick, who'd moved back to England, was the baby's godmother. Nancy opened the letter from Kick—she'd written that she couldn't wait to come back to the Cape to introduce Nancy to her new husband. She'd married William "Billy" Cavendish, the Marquess of Hartington, whom she'd met during her first trip to England in 1938. Everyone was beginning to think about what their lives would be like when the war ended.

Jack received a letter from Joe Jr. who wrote that he'd be home around the first of September, good for about a month's leave. Jack was heading home to mend his injuries, and Joe Jr. wanted his brother to set him up with a woman when they were both back. "Perhaps you, too, will be available at that time, and will be able to fix your old brother up with something good," Joe Jr. wrote. "I have already sent a notice home about my graying hair. I feel I must make a pretty quick move, so get something that really wants a tired old aviator."

That was also the summer when Pat, Jean, and Eunice were next door with Nancy when she got a telegram from the War Department with no stars—a letter marked with stars meant that the message would begin "I regret to inform you . . ." It meant that someone had died. But this envelope didn't have the stars, so Nancy, who was feeding her infant daughter, opened it in front of her friends. Her husband, aviation cadet Demarest Lloyd, had been shot down, and he was missing in action. "It was supposed to have stars on it but didn't have any," Nancy said. They'd barely been married two years.

"It was just one after the other all summer long. It was terrible. It was a mess, and so we were getting used to it, sort of," Nancy said. "Nobody knew what happened, you see, you don't read about it. You would just know that there was something terrible that happened. But it was never really discussed. It was a terrible summer."

Rose Kennedy sat alone on the porch of the Big House. It was a hot, humid August afternoon. She rocked back and forth in her favorite rocking chair that faced the Sound, just like the one her mother had occupied while watching to make sure her children were safe playing along the shore when Rose was a child. The family had just had a picnic lunch out there with her, but now Joe was upstairs taking a nap and the kids were playing quietly in the living room right inside. Bing Crosby's "I'll Be Seeing You" wafted from a turntable.

Rose didn't hear the dark car as its tires crunched down the driveway. She didn't hear them make their way to her front door. But she looked up from her Sunday paper when she heard a pounding knock. She pushed herself up from the rocking chair, walked through the house, and opened the door to see two men who looked like priests. They introduced themselves. They asked to speak to Mr. Kennedy. Rose didn't think much of it. She assumed they were there to ask her husband to get involved with some church charity event or another. She invited them in to sit with her family until Joe was up from his nap. No, they said. They needed to speak to her and her husband now. Their son was missing in action. He was presumed lost. The kids in the other room made out a few words. *Missing. Lost.*

Rose ran up the stairs, down the hall, into Joe's room. He looked at her confused, half-asleep, waiting for her to speak. But she froze, her thoughts garbled. After a few moments she explained that priests were there and she repeated what they told her. She followed her husband back down the stairs, and they sat with the priests in the small room just off the living room where Rose liked to make her flower arrangements. She listened as they explained what had happened—he'd been on a classified mission and his plane had gone down but there were few details. As she listened, though, she understood Joe Jr. was dead. That there was no hope. Neither Rose nor Joe cried. Joe stood and walked into the sunroom, his face twisted as he looked at his other children. He told them their brother wasn't coming home. It was quiet for a beat, then the children all burst into tears. Some groaned with pained wails. Joe told them they needed to be strong. That they should race that afternoon on their sailboats—that's what their brother would have wanted. Then Joe turned and stumbled up the stairs back to his room. Most of the kids listened to their father and left home to go get their boats. Jack stayed behind. Rose watched him walk alone on the beach. Past the breakwater where she'd watched him run away from his older brother so many times. Past the boats they'd sailed on their whole lives. The tide coming in and out under his feet. Rose called Joe's good friend, former police commissioner Joe Timilty, and asked him to drive down from Boston to take Bobby and Bobby's friend from school up to Boston for the night to stay with her father, Honey Fitz. At around four that afternoon, Bobby and his friend left. Then Rose went up to see her husband and they embraced for a long time, weeping silently. Until Joe finally said, "We've got to carry on. We must take care of the living. There is a lot of work to be done."

Joe stayed in his bedroom for days, the sound of classical music pouring out of the open windows, enveloping the grounds. Wilbert, the caretaker who'd been with the family so long people liked to joke he came with the house, listened to the somber music coming from above as he tended to the marigolds, the verbenas, the roses, made sure everything looked the way it always had. He'd watched the priests arrive. He saw them leave. He heard that Joe Jr. wasn't coming home. He listened to the music seep from Big Joe's bedroom for the rest of the summer. And watched as Rose held her head up, put on a brave face, and moved forward.

Kick returned home from Europe as soon as she heard about her brother. And Jack was still back home on the Cape, recovering from the operation on his back. He made his way through the first floor with the help of a cane. His first-floor bedroom helped him avoid using the stairs. More and more friends from his PT-109 navy mission were returning to the Boston area. Though Joe Jr. had died just weeks earlier, Jack invited his navy friends over to the Big House for a Labor Day weekend party. It would be good to see the familiar faces, and to get his mind off grieving—a way to lighten the heaviness lingering in the house since the priests left that fateful day.

Bobby came home from Harvard for the long weekend, too. It was good for the family to be together again. The house was once again filled with the sounds of young people coming in and out from sports in the backyard and lively conversations on the wraparound porch, which began to drown out the sound of Joe's records coming from his room upstairs. There was the annual Labor Day sailing race that weekend, which Eunice was competing in. By now, the yacht club was full of trophies engraved EMK—Eunice Mary Kennedy. She was just as good as her older brothers were. Maybe better. That weekend, she needed someone to help crew for her, so she tapped one of Jack's visitors. She unapologetically barked orders at her—guest or not, anyone on Eunice's boat was expected to help her cross that finish line first. And she did win that day.

When the group was back on dry land after the race, they wanted to unwind with some cocktails back at the house. The Kennedys, however, had a long-standing rule about drinking. Joe had never cared much for alcohol, and he didn't want his kids to be drinkers, either. When the kids were little, he didn't keep liquor in the house. He'd offered each of his children a deal: $1,000 for not smoking or drinking until they turned twenty-one. Everyone but Jack collected the earnings. But now that some of the kids were past that age, typically, on a given night, they'd be invited to imbibe the single cocktail Joe served his guests before dinner. He blended creamy daiquiris to be passed out in small glasses. That weekend, though, Jack and his navy friends ignored the rule, sneaking into the kitchen after the cook left for the night to steal the scotch from his parents' liquor cabinet. Eighteen-year-old Bobby saw them walking out with the brown bottles. He warned them not to do it, telling Jack and Kick what they already knew—that their father would be furious. Kick told their little brother to get lost.

After Rose and Joe and the rest of the kids went to bed, Kick, Jack, and his friends stayed out on the lawn, catching up. It sounded like it had before the kids started leaving home—laughing, singing, telling stories. For a little while that night, they were all happy. The war seemed far away. There wasn't another sound out on the end of the street, and their voices carried up into Joe's bedroom. And the more they drank, the louder they got. Finally, Joe leaned his head out his window and shouted at them down below: "Jack, don't you and your friends have any respect for your dead brother?"

The night went still.

Less than a week later, Kick's husband would be dead, too. Billy Cavendish died after being shot by a German sniper, on September 9, 1944. Kick wouldn't learn about his death until a few days later, on September 16, while on a shopping trip to New York with her family.

Back in Cape Cod, military units were dispatched as a violent hurricane generating eighty-mile-per-hour winds made its way up the East Coast. Jack was home by himself, still nursing his back. The rest of the kids were off at school, and Rose and Joe had packed up and gone to Palm Beach for the cold months. The Big House was so far out on the end of the street that, when storms came, it wasn't protected by much of anything. The wind roared through the empty house, the windowpanes shaking in their wooden sashes. The green wooden shutters rattled. The black waves broke farther and farther up the lawn, threatening the porch. Jack sat inside in the dark, waiting for the house to quiet down, for the storm to pass. Suddenly, he heard a door swing open. "Jack?" he heard a panicked, breathless voice. He went to see who it was and found his father's chauffeur, David Deignan, who lived year-round in the small apartment above the garage. Deignan had tied himself to one end of a rope, the other end attached to a tree in the yard. He'd carefully made his way from the garage to the Big House, terrified he'd be taken away with the wind or the waves.

"I've come here to check on you," Deignan said, paddling through the water that was now lapping onto the porch.

"For God's sakes, Dave!" Jack said. "Untie yourself and go to bed and go to sleep! Up here, we're going to be fine."

"Well," Deignan said, "I'm worried. I think we've got to evacuate."

There'd been an evacuation notice for anyone living in waterfront homes in the storm's path. Jack and Deignan had stayed, along with their neighbors next door, the McKelvys. Now, the water was seeping into the cellar. It seemed to be rising closer to the ceiling by the moment. The yard was gone—gulped up by feet of angry ocean water.

"You can't evacuate," Jack said. "We haven't got a boat. And we'll just—we'll keep moving up flights of stairs. It's a long way to go, up to the attic."

And so they stayed there together in the house, trying to ignore the violent gusts. With the water rising, it was hard to get much sleep.

Next door, the McKelvys were trapped, too. As Jack and Deignan tried to hold out until morning, the McKelvys were desperately trying to escape *their* house, which sat closer to the water than the Kennedys'. The bottom of the McKelvys' home was submerged. Two Coast Guard officers plunged through the surf to get to the family as they tried to get to higher ground in front of their house. After reaching them, one guardsman tied a rope around the waists of Mr. and Mrs. McKelvy as well as around their dog. The couple followed the officers to the shore, but when they got there, they realized their dog had been knocked loose from the rope. They spun around, desperately looking for any sign of the dog—and saw their pet swimming right behind, following them to safety on high ground.

When Jack and Deignan woke the next day, all they could see was sand, each house on the street its own island. Rose's peaceful little hut had been washed away. Jack had been right—they were safe up on the second floor. But it had been one of the worst hurricanes to ever hit the Cape. The Hyannisport Club, where the kids had gone to dances and where Joe and Rose went to play golf together, had the roof ripped straight off, sections of it carried a thousand feet by the violent wind. Sailboats that the family had raced against were tossed like toy boats onto the shore. The West Beach Club down the street was demolished, along with the small Union Chapel that had stood in the Port's center. In the off-season, workers hurried to rebuild before the summer population returned. The Big House fared much better than some of its neighbors, but the family would face further devastation before they came together to see it again.

The old, scratched-up floors were ripped up, room by room. Debris piled up on the Big House lawn. A truck arrived with the new floors Joe picked out. They were long, wide planks of eastern white pine varying in width. This wasn't just a beautiful pile of planks—it was one of the rarest types of flooring in the country. In fact, it had once been illegal to make flooring out of eastern white pine because it was sourced from New England trees able to grow more than two hundred feet tall. There was a penalty if planks wider than two feet were used for home building—but Joe had gotten around that rule by buying them from an old house that had been built in 1706. And he'd gotten a deal—the floors had been free except for the cost to remove them from the old house and transport them to the Cape. Joe loved the history of his rich, knotty pumpkin-colored floors and the original hand-molded nails, which he left in. The first floor, where the family spent its time, would be different, special, better than before.

* * *

Jack's friends from the navy continued to visit as he recovered at the Big House from surgery and figured out what was next for him now that he wouldn't be going back to the war. After Joe Jr. died there seemed to be a change in how Jack saw his future. Joe Jr. was always supposed to be the politician. Jack, now in his late twenties, would be a journalist or a writer—he already had a bestseller with *Why England Slept*. He was also less outgoing than his extroverted older brother, who just seemed a more natural fit for the spotlight. Hyannis Port neighbors would remember Joe Jr. proclaiming from a young age that he'd be the first Catholic president. And Joe lavished special attention on his first son. But soon after Joe Jr.'s death, Joe shifted that attention to his second son. Jack stepped into the role his father was creating for him.

Jack's navy buddy Jim Reed sat with Jack and his family around the dining room table at the Big House along with Joe's friend and journalist Arthur Krock, Honey Fitz, and some others. Joe was there, back at the head of the table, laughing with his family and his guests. The talk turned to politics and someone joked to Jim that one day he'd be president. Jack jumped into the conversation to say "After me!" Honey Fitz, never one to pass up a speech, a song, or a toast, raised a glass: "To the future president of the United States, my grandson, John Fitzgerald Kennedy."

In late 1945, Jack stayed in Massachusetts to prepare to run for office. His only tie to the state, at that point, was Hyannis Port. The family had left Boston long ago and his time at Harvard was behind him. But Joe and Rose had maintained the family's connection to Massachusetts with their house on the Cape. In June 1946, twenty-nine-year-old Jack won the Democratic primary for the Eleventh District of Massachusetts, far outpacing the other nine candidates. He followed the victory with a two-week vacation back home at the Big House racing the *Victura*. And in November, Jack won the general in a landslide.

He was now a congressman.

Jack moved to Washington, D.C., bringing his sister Eunice and the family cook, Margaret Ambrose, with him. Jack and Eunice lived in a town house in Georgetown, but they still took the nearly five-hundred-mile trip up north to the Cape as often as they could. Jack's pain from his injuries and the surgery wasn't going away, so when he was back home, he spent a lot of time in bed in his little room on the first floor, which was filled with his books—the ones he'd read and loved as a kid as well as new ones he brought back with him, nearly all nonfiction. Jack almost never read a novel. When the neighbors did see their newly minted congress-man neighbor out and about, they noticed he still had trouble walking, leaning on a cane to help him get around. Wherever Jack was, Joe was usually somewhere close behind, constantly checking in on his son, asking if he was okay.

Coming home was a break from work and the Washington social scene. But it was also a way to regroup, to be reminded of the family val-ues that had gotten the Kennedys this far—a way to go back in time to childhood when things were simple and Joe had the answers. Inside the walls of the Big House, things just seemed to make the most sense to the Kennedy kids. But as they became adults and started their own lives, they brought people from the outside into their sanctuary. Their little world, which revolved around Joe, didn't always seem so idyllic to those seeing it for the first time—in fact, it could seem peculiar.

Jack and Eunice brought Mary Pitcairn, a friend they'd made in D.C., back to the Big House for a few days to relax on the beach. Pitcairn had dated Jack off and on, and she'd met his father when Joe came down to Washington. When he was in town, Joe had a reputation for taking the women Jack was dating out to dinner. It struck Pitcairn and the other women as unusual. But she tried to write it off as the eccentricity of a man from another generation. When she was at the Big House, there was Joe again. She was polite, as she would be to any of her friends' parents. But after dinner with the family, she went up to the room she was staying in on the second floor to get ready for bed. She heard footsteps coming down the hall, getting louder the closer they got to her room. There was Joe in the doorframe.

"He came into my bedroom to kiss me goodnight!" Pitcairn later told writers Joan and Clay Blair Jr. "I was in my nightgown, ready for bed. Eunice was in her bedroom. We had an adjoining bath. The doors were open. He said, 'I've come to say goodnight,' and kissed me. Really kissed me. It was so silly. I remember thinking, 'how embarrassing for Eunice!' but beyond that, nothing."

* * *

Eugenia Fortes was the cook at the Falvey house, right behind the Kennedys on Irving Avenue. Before that, she worked as a server for the Tenneys across the street from the Kennedys. So, she knew the Kennedy kids well. She said hi to Kick and Eunice when the little girls ran across their yard to come play with Sancy, the Falvey daughter. When she lined the lobsters up on the porch while she brought the pot of salty water to a boil before family barbecues, she knew to look out for Teddy's dimpled little hands. He was always lingering, ready to swipe one to bring home. Fortes's nephew remembered about his aunt: "She had to beat his butt a couple of times."

As a girl, Fortes had sailed with her mother to the States in 1920 on a three-masted schooner from Cape Verde. It took them thirty-one days to cross. They went to New Bedford to look for Eugenia's father, who'd sailed over without them years earlier. He and many other Cape Verdeans had moved to the States looking for a better life for their families. The Fortes family stayed there for a couple of years before they were invited to a wedding in Harwich, a little town in the crook of the Cape, and Fortes liked it so much she worried the family sick until they moved to Cape Cod, where her father got a job in the cranberry bogs and building roads. The work was seasonal, and making it through the winter, when work dried up, took planning. Her mother made clothes for her siblings out of printed grain bags, and Fortes cooked to help her family, but her favorite part of the week was when she finished up her work and could go to the library. Then, there were only a couple dozen Cape Verdeans in the town, and the school she went to was segregated by race.

When she was old enough to move out on her own, Fortes moved to Hyannis. As a Black woman, there weren't many options for work. It was either clean houses or cook. So, she cooked, working for the rich white families in the Port. She bought her own two-bedroom cottage up on Pitchers Way, which she liked to jokingly call "the slums of Hyannis," and drove over to waterfront Hyannis Port for work. The closer you got to the water, the bigger the houses got and the more manicured the lawns. But the more time Fortes spent in those houses as an outsider, the more she learned about the families living in them.

"They're not happy," Fortes once said of the rich white families of the Cape. "I've lived with too many and I've worked for too many. I mean, the dinners at night I cook and serve, and you'd listen to them. Scared to death of losing that money. And they'll do anything to keep it, I don't care what."

One summer day in 1945, Fortes had the afternoon off. Her friend Marie was visiting from Ohio, and just after lunchtime they took the Falveys' pit bull Peter out for a walk on the beach. Fortes loved pit bulls. The two women walked along the small public beach next to the Hyannis Port pier that connected to the strip of private beachfront running behind the Tenneys', the McKelvys', and the Kennedys' homes. Fortes and Marie slid down into the gray sand, leaning against the pier to catch up. They talked and watched the waves break against the shore as Peter panted next to them.

"I'm sorry," Fortes remembered a police officer saying as he walked up to them, "colored sits on the other side [of the beach]." His short shadow cast over their feet.

"They do?" Fortes asked, confused, flustered, embarrassed. Her friend was so excited to see the Cape, which Fortes had been telling her about for years. This was her home. This was the beach she walked every day.

"Yes," the cop said, looking down as the women shifted to get up. "You'll have to move."

"Since when?" Fortes asked. "This is a public beach."

"I," the officer stammered, "I, um, didn't know you lived here."

"I do," Fortes said.

The officer finally turned to leave. Fortes and her friend stayed put on that beach until dinnertime.

Months later, the Hyannis Port Civic Association, a private group of residents, tried to buy the public beach for $6,000. "Our town is changing very much," said attorney Henry Murphy, speaking in defense of the civic association proposal at the 1946 town meeting. "I can see a great change in our population as well as in our town property. To be more specific, I mean this, that we have left approximately three, I would say, substantial, old summer colonies. One is Hyannis Port, one is Wianno, and one is Cotuit. We don't have much more of that property left, and we are going to have less. It seems to me that that is an additional reason for that protection, as well as we can, of what we do have left. So I say, against the encroaching march of progress, which we cannot stop and which we want to a certain extent, but we all want to guide it, to try and keep, if we can, some of the exclusiveness and some of the charm of the Cape."

There was a public hearing where there was almost unanimous opposition to selling the land to the civic association. Murphy had argued that the civic association would incur the costs to improve the beach if they owned it—could add a playground or a tennis court—but that beach was some of the only public land where people could dock their boats in the Port. It made no sense to have it privately owned. Still, it was decided the group could lease it for a year for $100—under the stipulation "that no resident of the town shall be denied the use and enjoyment of said land so long as he complies with the same rules and regulations which apply to the members of said Association." Rose and Joe hadn't been involved with the civic association, a small neighborhood group limited to only the people living within the borders of Hyannis Port—borders established in the 1920s. If you lived within those borders—borders narrower than the borders used previously to refer to the neighborhood—you were invited to pay the dues to join the association, which also owned the pier and the West Beach Club.

Fortes, in particular, was outspoken against the beach becoming private.

"The next year the civic association came to buy the beach," Fortes recalled. "And I got up at the town meeting, two hundred people or more there, and I told them what had happened. They didn't get it. They did not get it. And I understand now that one man down there was givin' everybody a fit. Blacks comin' in."

Rose woke up early. The only movement was the gulls swooping past her window, the soft breaks of the waves below, and the outlines of the boats in the harbor pulling their moorings tight. She took out her diary as the sun came up and wrote about Cape Cod.

The vegetables grow succulent during the summer months but must be picked quickly and preserved or they will be lost. I believe this Cape Cod atmosphere influenced the Pilgrims making them appreciate God's gifts without wasting and squandering.

Over the last decade the bottom of her world had given way, but Cape Cod had brought Rose peace and stability. So it was there, not New York or Boston, where she and Joe memorialized their first son by donating an altar at St. Francis Xavier where Rose went to Mass every morning. The altar was regal, with gold navy wings placed on a sky-blue background between St. George of England and St. Joan of France. When the family went to church on Sunday mornings, they took a moment to remember their lost brother. For Rose, it became part of her daily ritual.

But Rosemary wasn't spoken of. Her sudden absence from Hyannis Port was barely remarked on. One summer she just wasn't out on the sailboat with Eunice, wasn't at the West Beach Club picnics, wasn't at the dinner table for birthdays. Then Kick was gone, too. She'd been flying with Peter Wentworth-Fitzwilliam, the 8th Earl Fitzwilliam, to Cannes—after Cannes, they'd go to Paris to see her father, Joe. Fitzwilliam, like all the boys at the Wianno Club, had fallen for Kick. Kick loved him, too. He was married but promised to leave his wife for Kick. Rose and Joe said they'd never approve. Now, the young couple were on their way to appeal to Kick's father. On May 13, 1948, their plane went down over southern France. The Kennedys were spread out across the country but when they got the news, they all made their way to Hyannis Port. A car was sent for Teddy, who was away at school. He was the first to arrive. He sat in the big, cold, empty house alone, waiting for his family to fill the silence. But now there'd only be six siblings—three of the nine gone.

Only Joe went to Kick's burial in England—everyone else mourned at the memorial Mass held at St. Francis Xavier Church, sitting in front of the altar named for their first son.

CHAPTER FOUR

It was 1951 and Rose Kennedy, in a yellow blouse and pearl earrings, gently handed her first grandchild to her mother, Josie, who sat in the cool shade of the covered porch. Bobby and his new wife, Ethel, were in Hyannis Port to show off their firstborn, Kathleen, named for Bobby's sister Kick, and just three months old in a sweet pink dress and matching bow. Pat, in a polka-dot swimsuit, stepped back from the porch to take a photo of Ethel proudly holding the new baby born on the Fourth of July. That weekend, barefoot Ethel pushed Kathleen around the grounds in a covered stroller, their bulldog never trailing far behind.

Pat swung a golf club out on a corner of the lawn, while Bobby and some friends played an aggressive game of baseball by the dunes. Jack, his crutches lying nearby, relaxed on the grass by the bushes, surrounded by young women—friends and neighbors. When there was an argument over whether Bobby was safe at third, he interrupted Jack's flirting, demanding his older brother make the final call. Bobby had grown into the most competitive of them all. Even as an adult, he'd jump right into the rosebushes lining the yard, which made up the sidelines, if it meant making a catch.

Rose and Joe were Grandma and Grandpa now. And with the death of Honey Fitz in the fall of 1950, Josie was a widow. The Big House had felt quieter that summer without his big laugh, his dirty jokes, and his too-loud renditions of "Sweet Adeline." Ethel and baby girl Kathleen were the start of a new generation of Kennedys in the Port. Bobby met Ethel through his sister Jean—the two were roommates at Manhattan-ville College, and Jean had brought Ethel back to the Big House for a Halloween weekend. "I remember arriving at the Cape and going to Jean's room and thinking how everything was so well thought out for the happiness of children and guests," Ethel said. "There were fresh flowers. There were interesting books on the bedside table." Ethel grew up in the Connecticut Skakel family, which was as loud and boisterous as the Kennedys—if not more so. She was never shy about picking up a football or grabbing the rig of a sailboat. She fit right in. The first person Bobby told that he was planning to ask Ethel to marry him was his old friend Jack Bell from over on Scudder Avenue. In 1953, Eunice married Sargent Shriver, a former *Newsweek* editor she'd met through her father. "Sarge," as he was called, was more reserved—more interested in a one-on-one conversation than entertaining a big group.

The Kennedy family was changing.

"Cape Women Invited to Be Guests of Kennedys," read the bulletin in all the local Friday-afternoon papers. "Women residents of Cape Cod will be guests of the Misses Patricia, Eunice, and Jean Kennedy at their home in Hyannis Port, Monday August 25 at 2 P.M. All women in the Cape area are invited. Congressman John F. Kennedy will address the group."

Hyannis Port was firmly Republican but there was mounting excitement about their own neighbor, their own Jack Kennedy, running for the Massachusetts Senate seat against incumbent Henry Cabot Lodge Jr. It was a big race and Jack was a long shot. The tea parties were Rose's idea. Rose and her daughters invited women in each community to come dressed in their finest, and they'd have coffee and tea served to them in elegant silver urns, with stacks of campaign materials piled high on coffee tables and couches. The women would have the opportunity to ask questions about Jack. And at the end, Rose would introduce her son, who'd say a few words about why the women should vote for him. The teas were successful—women responded well to Jack, and Rose's strategy won her son outsize media attention, too. The *New York Times* wrote about thirty-five-year-old Jack after one of the receptions: "A lean, sinewy figure with an untamed brush of brown hair overhanging his gray eyes, he has an appealingly youthful appearance. The illusion is enhanced by a suggestion of shyness . . . and by a smile which can only be described as 'boyish.'"

The excitement around Jack was growing. Rose and Joe relished the attention—they'd never used the Big House to host or socialize but now cars streamed into the Port, lining their driveway and up Marchant Avenue for teas and events for reporters and other politicians. Anything to drum up excitement for Jack. And it worked. "It was those damned tea parties," Lodge said when Jack beat him near the end of 1952.

After the buzz of the campaign, there was a shift in the Port. The neighbors had always been curious about the Kennedys; there'd always been something a little more glamorous, a little more thrilling about the comings and goings at the Big House—from Joe's Hollywood days to his ambassadorship. But now, the little boy who'd run down the streets barefoot in ratty old shorts, the boy they'd danced with at the Wianno Club or raced against on the Sound, was their state's junior senator.

Don't cut through that lawn! the neighbors whispered to their kids. *A senator lives down there. Show some respect!*

The tide broke at the end of the property on Marchant Avenue. Bubbling whitecaps of saltwater rushed in and out. As the sun slowly rose, the dark water inched up, wave by wave, and piles of spongy seaweed dotted the shrinking swath of sand. Nantucket Sound was empty and quiet.

Inside the Big House the nice china sat stacked in the white windowed cabinet in the dining room. Dark, delicately carved wooden dining room chairs were pushed under the matching glass-topped table. Fresh flowers filled a glass bowl sitting on top of a round mirror in the middle of the table. A matching bouquet sat on a tall console table in the foyer. The first floor was bathed in the early-morning light. It was a quiet morning—until the black phone in the living room vibrated with its tinny, shrill ring, which continued throughout the day.

When did Jack propose? And how?
Who's the girl?

Are they coming back to Hyannis Port?

How long will they be here?

Will they sit for an interview?

What about photos?

It was June 25, 1953, and in that day's *Barnstable Patriot* there was a two-inch story headlined: "Senator Kennedy Engaged to Girl From Newport." The article read, simply, "The marriage of the 23-year-old heiress to 'the most eligible bachelor of Capital society' will take place September 12 in Newport." Just two weeks before, thirty-six-year-old Jack had been featured in the *Saturday Evening Post*. Under the headline "The Senate's Gay Young Bachelor," Jack was pictured sailing on the Potomac and laughing with groups of young women. Journalist Paul F. Healy had written: "Many women have hopefully concluded that Kennedy needs looking after. In their opinion, he is, as a young millionaire senator, just about the most eligible bachelor in the United States—and the least justifiable one."

Jack was already engaged to twenty-three-year-old Jacqueline Bouvier by the time the article came out, but the couple had delayed the announcement, so nobody knew it yet. The engagement notice drew huge curiosity about the mysterious fiancée of the Senate's most eligible bachelor. Over the next twenty-four hours, news spread that the couple would be coming back home to Hyannis Port the following weekend to celebrate their engagement with a party at the Hyannisport Club.

As Rose and the staff readied the house, Jack sat by himself at La-Guardia Airport, waiting for Jackie. They'd made plans to meet at the New York airport to fly together to the Cape. As Jack waited and waited, waves of travelers hauled their bags to the terminal he faced. In the crowd, Jack recognized a young sports photographer named Hy Peskin, who was a fixture on the sidelines of the biggest sports events of the early 1950s, running up and down the court nearly as quickly as the players but with a heavy camera in his hands. As Peskin stepped up to the gate to check in, Jack walked up, hand extended to introduce himself.

"I'm Jack Kennedy. I'm meeting my new fiancée here—she should be here any minute—we're on our way back home for the Fourth," he said, flashing a toothy smile. "We'd love some photos, what do you think about coming back with us?"

Peskin, who knew of the young senator, hadn't photographed politicians, but he knew this was a big opportunity and agreed to do it. He found a pay phone to call his boss at *Sports Illustrated*. His boss told his counterpart at their sister publication, *Life* magazine. And within a few hours, they'd arranged for a writer to fly to the Cape to meet Peskin and the couple. Jack invited Peskin to stay at the Big House. There was always room on the second floor for an extra guest.

But as the Northeast Airlines plane began to warm up, Jackie still wasn't there. "Guess she won't make it," Jack said as he picked up his bag and walked over to an airline employee to try to make arrangements for Jackie to come on a later plane. But as he started up the ramp, a taxi pulled up with a screech. A beautiful brunette with wide-set eyes and an apologetic smile jumped out, breathless. As Jackie handed her bag to Jack, she explained she'd been stuck in traffic, and they boarded the plane just before it took off.

Not long after Jack and Jackie arrived, Peskin made his way through Hyannis, with its established Main Street, and into the tiny neighborhood of Hyannis Port. He realized there wasn't much to it. The homes he passed as he made his way to the water looked nearly identical with their cedar shingles in a rainbow of grays. Now and then there was a white clapboard house. He took a left on Marchant Avenue, turning into the driveway at the end of the road. Shaggy-headed Kennedys spilled out of the house. The back door leading from the kitchen to the vast slope of green grass overlooking Nantucket Sound swung open and shut all morning as Teddy, in his plaid swimsuit, walked in barefoot for a drink of water or a chocolate chip cookie off a tray in the kitchen. Eunice and Jean, in their halter-top suits with matching shorts, passed through into the living room, throwing their heads back in laughter. Back behind the house, Kennedys laughed and shouted over the sprinkler and the soft breaks of the Sound.

Peskin was used to directing his subjects for portraits. *Hold your hand like this; Turn your head away from me; Look up.* But that weekend, he was nearly silent as he shot more than forty rolls of film. The newly engaged couple and the rest of the Kennedys seemed to barely notice the camera pops and the reporter trailing them, notepad in hand. Jackie, however, was getting used to things. She tried to make herself comfortable in Rose and Joe's home. Quiet and observant, she seemed to be soaking in the house. Jack smiled when she came downstairs more dressed up than anyone else.

"Where do you think you're going?" he teased her. Before she could say anything—or change—Rose told him, "Oh don't be mean to her, dear. She looks lovely." Rose liked Jackie right away. She would write in her diaries that Jackie "rounded out" Jack's character. Jackie was serious and thoughtful. Like Jack, she loved to read. And like Jack, she sometimes seemed far away in her own thoughts. But while he liked books about history, she read poetry. She loved art. She eased Jack's natural intensity, encouraged him to slow down a little, to enjoy things.

Outside, more photographers and reporters gathered in the yard. There'd been so many requests for interviews and photographs of the new couple that an informal photo shoot was arranged in front of the Big House, with dozens of reporters lining up for the eleven o'clock start time. There'd never been a scene like it on Marchant Avenue. Inside, Jack led Jackie over to a corner of the TV room. Joe and Rose had hired a New York architect to update the house in 1947—enlarging the living room and extending the porch in front of the dining room. They'd also built a barbecue and built cases in the basement for the dolls Rose had collected from around the world. Joe had turned his attention to commercial real estate investing in Manhattan and, in 1945, had made the shrewd decision to buy Chicago's undervalued Merchandise Mart. Whispers that Joe had made a fortune bootlegging liquor would follow him for decades, but a thorough look at his life and career by biographers would eventually prove they were just rumors. The fact was, Joe made nearly as much money from real estate—buying and selling as well as collecting rent— as he did stocks. As the family's fortune grew, he and Rose didn't trade up for an estate in Osterville—they instead upgraded the Big House, adding on to Rose's bedroom and bathroom, installing a new shower and fixtures. They added a cedar closet in the attic. They reconstructed Rose's little cottage on the beach. And they turned Joe Jr.'s old bedroom into a TV room, which they lined with family photos.

In the TV room, Jack and Jackie examined the four large square frames on the wall: snapshots of Joe with King George VI and Queen

Elizabeth II; Joe and Princess Helena Victoria watching the trial air ma-
neuvers in 1939; Bobby and Teddy at the opening of the London Zoo;
Kick and Rosemary smiling at the camera; and the entire family lined up
on the embassy grounds. Jack told his fiancée stories about their lives in
London, their last months as a family of eleven.

With her hands clasped behind her back, Jackie leaned in to listen,
studying the ways her life would be changing. The daughter of a wealthy
stockbroker, Jackie spent her summers in the Hamptons and Newport
reading, taking ballet, or horseback riding. She wasn't rough-and-tumble
like the Kennedys, but she was a good sport as she got to know her new
family. In her crisp, sleeveless button-up blouse and pleated khaki shorts,
she tossed the football with Teddy and gamely took a swing when Jack
lightly tossed her a softball in the backyard. Cameras clicked in the background. One photographer said about Jackie, "She should be posing for
color pictures."

Jackie seemed most comfortable out on the water. Before lunch, the
siblings piled into the *Victura*. As they floated away from the long pier,
Jack climbed to the front to adjust the towering headsail. He held tight
on to the boom as Jackie sat next to him, leaning forward for the best
view of the shore of Hyannis Port, cool saltwater splashing her bare legs.
When they got back to shore, Jackie went with Eunice and Jean to find a
quiet spot on the lawn where Jackie could tell them the story of how Jack
proposed. Jack and Jackie had been introduced by their mutual friend
Charles Bartlett at a dinner Bartlett hosted in Georgetown in the spring
of 1950. After the meal, Bartlett walked Jackie out to her car, and Jack
came trailing behind, muttering shyly, "Shall we go someplace to have a
drink?" But Jackie left for Europe soon after that meeting, and Jack was
gearing up for his senatorial race. It wasn't until the winter of 1952 that
they began dating, and things progressed quickly from there.

During her courtship with Jack, Jackie had her own photography
column at the *Washington Times-Herald* where she was known as the
"Inquiring Camera Girl." That weekend in Hyannis Port, while Peskin
faded into the background, shooting candid images, Jackie waded out
shin-deep into the Sound to shoot her own photos of her handsome new
fiancé. When Peskin, the *Life* writer, and Jack walked along the shore at

the end of the shoot, Jackie asked to hold Peskin's camera and she began snapping photos of the three men, more comfortable behind the camera than in front.

For the portraits at the end of the weekend, Jack changed into a suit and Jackie went upstairs to put on a tailored A-line dress, pinning a brooch on the collar, and fastening a simple string of pearls around her neck. She made her way down the stairs at the front of the house, turning the corner into the dining room where Jack sat with the writer, that day's newspaper and a cup of tea sitting in front of him. She smoothed a patch of Jack's hair, standing on end, stiff from saltwater. Then she sat down, grabbing a section of the paper, waiting for her solo portraits with Peskin. In Peskin's portraits, Jackie looked effortless, elegant.

Life chose an informal shot for its July 20, 1953, issue, which hit newsstands just a couple of weeks later. It was the first time Jack appeared on a national magazine cover, and the couple is smiling on top of the family sailboat. The wind had hit them from behind. Jackie's thick, curly hair whipped around her cheeks and her crisp shirt collar flipped up. Jack leaned forward laughing, his white shirt cuffs rolled, his khakis soaked. And with that photograph, the world was introduced to the young, vibrant Kennedys: bare feet and windblown hair.

When Jackie got back to her quiet home, she sat down to write a note to Rose. She thanked Rose for the hospitality she'd shown her that weekend. But then she started to think about what it was going to be like to be a part of the big family she'd just gotten to know. "It seems to me that very few people have been able to create what you have—a family built on love and loyalty and gaiety," Jackie wrote. "If I can even come close to building that with Jack I will be very happy."

Their public debut taken care of, Jack and Jackie got to work planning their wedding, which would be held late that summer at St. Mary's Church in Newport, where Jackie's family had a home about two hours west of the Port. In the weeks before the wedding, Jackie flew back and forth from Newport to Hyannis Port, while the Kennedys planned a pre-celebration get-together. The Big House filled with the young Kennedys and their friends two weekends before the wedding. Teddy welcomed the group, piling people into the blue convertible and taking them for a drive down to Hyannis's Main Street to show off their hometown. When they got back to the Big House, the men tore off their shirts for a game of touch football that started on the lawn and ended on the shore behind the house. Meanwhile, the women sat on the porch watching and cheering. Jack, barefoot, rolled up his khakis to quarterback—he and the others played a version of the game called Razzle Dazzle, in which you could throw the ball from anywhere on the field. It was chaotic—more like rugby, giving an edge to the fastest players.

The Kennedys' neighbors the Harringtons wanted to host an engagement party for the couple at their house down at the edge of the golf course. In her memoir, Rose would later describe the famous scavenger hunt at that party. Among the Kennedy clan, it became the stuff of legend. It started with lists of items each team had to bring back from around the village. One of the items was "the longest object" they could find. Bobby, Pat, and their cousin Joey Gargan, now all in their twenties, were on a team together. They scanned through the list: "monster from the sea." They ran back over to the Big House into the kitchen to pull a frozen salmon from the freezer. "A menu from a famous restaurant." Easy. They drove over to Charlie's in West Hyannisport, and Joey ran in to grab one. While he was inside, Joey remembered another item from the list: "a show of courage." He eyed a police officer sitting in a booth, his gaze fixed on the hat atop his head. Without thinking much more of it, he swiped the hat, turned, and ran as fast as he could back to the car, at which point he and Bobby sped off.

Pat had split off on her own, marching around the Port determined to be the one to find "the longest object." She found something she was *sure* would win the whole darn thing: a bus. It was parked at the gas station down the street—the driver had gone inside, and when she hopped into the driver's seat, she found the keys still in the ignition. Her foot heavy on the gas, Pat turned it around, driving down the narrow streets back to the Harringtons' place. She parked it in the driveway right as Bobby and Joey were returning with the menu and police hat. Once the trio evaluated what they'd gathered, they were confident they would win.

Who could compete with a bus? When Pat, Bobby, and Joey returned to the Big House that night, the police officer whose hat they'd swiped was waiting for them—irate. Joe was down in the theater watching a movie when he heard the hubbub on the front porch. He came upstairs to see his kids trying to calm the cop. When he was all caught up on what had happened that day, his rage topped that of the hatless officer. Bobby and Joey got the brunt of the yelling.

The next morning, Joey went up to his uncle sitting in the sunroom and offered a sheepish apology. "We just got carried away," he tried to explain. "Well, Joey, don't worry about it," Joe said, the faintest smile crossing his face. "I certainly expect it's not going to happen again." Joey nodded, declaring, "I'm sure that won't happen again."

At the end of the week, the Kennedys and their friends piled into one of the family's sailboats to set off on a weekend trip up the coast of Maine. It was the last hurrah before the wedding, which was a media frenzy solidifying the Kennedys' rising status.

In the '50s, it seemed every new year brought a new Kennedy. Ethel and Bobby had their first four children back-to-back. Eunice and Sarge had their first child, a boy named Bobby, in 1954. Pat married British actor Peter Lawford that same year. Jean married Stephen Smith in 1956. Jack and Jackie spent most of their summers with her family early in their marriage but when they got away to the Port on weekends, they stayed in the narrow twin beds in Jack's childhood room downstairs in the Big House. With the kids all grown up and starting their own lives, Joe Kennedy began spending more time with his friends, like Morton Downey, the Irish American tenor who lived in the much quieter area of Hyannis Port called Squaw Island. Squaw Island wasn't farther than half a mile from the center of the Port but felt much more remote, with just a smattering of houses on the two-mile-wide peninsula. Downey bought one of the houses from the Kennedys' old neighbor, Kick's best friend Nancy Tenney, who'd moved out there after the war. After Nancy got remarried, she sold the Squaw Island house to Downey. Joe and Rose spent the summer of 1954 in the South of France, but Downey kept an eye on their busy home. He wrote to Joe, "Ethel, Eunice, the guests, and the Gargans are all in fine shape and your two houses sound like St. Isidore's Orphanage with all the kids around. I can understand easily why you're in France. I'm sure you can't hear the babies but I know the guests at Wianno aren't too happy being wakened so early by their cries." Joe wrote back to Downey in August, "I understand that Rose and I have no relatives anywhere in the world now except in my house this summer. Well, that's the way life is!" He wrote to his oldest grandson—Ethel and Bobby's second baby, named Joseph II for his grandfather—on his second birthday: "Grandpa is staying in Europe so he will live long enough to celebrate your 21st with you."

When Rose and Joe were at the Big House, with the frenzy of family enveloping their home, they each had their own method of getting away. Rose sat for hours in her new hut on the edge of the property. When she was down there everyone knew to leave her be. And she liked to visit the thrift shops around the Cape. Her favorite shop was in Sandwich, about half an hour away, where she was apt to buy the town's famous colorful glass. Joe liked reading mysteries and listening to his records. Sometimes, he took walks in the late afternoon or early evening with his pretty young secretary, Janet DesRosiers. Some evenings, he met her in her apartment in Hyannis, a little place carved into the back of a home just a few minutes from the Big House. DesRosiers, who was less than half Joe's age and with whom he carried on an affair for nearly a decade, guessed Rose must have known what was going on between them. If she did, she never let on.

Cramming all those additional Kennedys into the Big House just wasn't working. So, Bobby and his family started renting houses around Hyannis Port. One summer they were up on Scudder Avenue, the next they were on Schoolhouse Pond, a small, tucked-away pond half a mile from the Big House that was called the bottomless pond because of its muddy bottom, which made it seem like it went down forever. After having their first child, Bobby and Ethel hired Ena Bernard, a kind nanny originally from Costa Rica who quickly became like another family member. With so many young children at the same time, Bobby and Ethel had their hands full, even with Bernard's help. The summer when they rented on Schoolhouse Pond, Joseph II, their oldest son, went missing. The family looked everywhere in a panicked frenzy—for fear he'd fallen into the bottomless pond. They found him safe in another yard.

Later, it was little Bobby Jr. who caused the ruckus. Bernard's teenage daughter, Josefina, spent the summer with the Kennedys on the Cape lending a hand with the kids. While the family went over to the Big House for the day, Josefina stayed back with Bobby Jr. so the infant could finish his nap. All was quiet until there was a heavy knock at the door. Josefina went to answer it and found the milkman there with that day's delivery. Austin Bell—Jack and Bobby's old friend from down the street—was the local milkman and he always saved the chocolate milk for Bobby, because that was his favorite. Josefina thanked him, and as she closed the door to walk back to the bedroom, she heard a thud followed by a scream. She ran to the back of the house. Bobby Jr. had rolled off the bed and landed on the floor—Josefina had left him in the center of the big bed and she hadn't realized he could roll. She picked him up and rocked him, but he was inconsolable. She called over to the Big House. Bobby answered—Josefina tried to stay calm.

"Can I speak to my mom?" she asked, while Bobby Jr. continued to cry in the background.

"What's wrong?" Bobby asked. "Is everything okay?"

"It's Bobby Jr.," she answered. "Bobby Jr. fell off the bed."

"Okay," Bobby said calmly. "Well, how high was the bed?"

Josefina looked at the bed—it looked so high. "Four feet?" she said nervously.

"Four feet!" Bobby said. "You must have needed a ladder to get up onto it."

Josefina looked at it again and took a breath. The bed wasn't tall at all. Bobby Jr. was going to be fine.

"That man, I tell you what, I love him. I love him," Josefina remembered years later. "He calmed me down—he did that for everybody."

In 1952, Joe and Rose's forty-three-year-old neighbor, Kenneth Lemoine Green Jr., the one who lived in the modest clapboard house next to the Big House, had died at his other home, the one in St. Louis. Two years later, the Green house on Marchant Avenue was bought in Teddy's name. Teddy was only twenty-three and still in college, but the children all had healthy trust funds established in 1926 and 1936. Joe's goal had always been to give his sons the financial freedom to pursue public office. That meant summer homes early in their adulthood—homes most people could spend their entire lives working for and never afford. Though the house was purchased in Teddy's name, it was Bobby and his family who moved into it in 1955. While Bobby set off for a six-week-long trip to the Soviet Union with Joe's friend Supreme Court justice William O. Douglas, Ethel got her four young children all settled into the cold, empty house, signing her oldest, Kathleen, up for kindergarten at St. Francis Xavier, down the street in Hyannis.

"What a thing to leave your wife with [four] kids in Hyannis Port and nobody else was around!" Kathleen would later remember. "My poor mother with all these kids in the cold winter while her husband was gallivanting around the Earth. [It] did not make my mother happy."

On a fall weekend away from Washington in 1954 Bobby went alone up to Barnstable High School to watch the big football game between the Barnstable Townies and the Falmouth All-Stars—a fierce rivalry and one of the season's most anticipated games. Several hundred people were out there for the game, and Bobby faded into the crowd, just another townie. After graduating from the University of Virginia School of Law, Bobby had gone to work helping his older brother's Senate campaign, but once Jack won, Bobby struggled to figure out what his own future would look like. When he'd gone home to the Cape after Jack's win, Joe had pulled Bobby aside to ask him, "What are you going to do now? Are you going to sit on your tail end and do nothing for the rest of your life? You'd better go out and get a *job*." Joe made sure that happened, calling first on his friend Republican senator Joe McCarthy to bring Bobby onto his Permanent Subcommittee on Investigations, which was trying desperately to prove that Communists had penetrated the U.S. government. Bobby knew McCarthy, too—he'd been a regular visitor to Hyannis Port and had dated his sisters. After seven dramatic and explosive months, Bobby left McCarthy's committee, only to return seven months later under the committee's new chairman. Through all the back-and-forth, sports were a way for Bobby to unwind, release his aggression.

Minutes into the second half of the football game at Barnstable High, Townies coach George Parmenter subbed in a defensive player. The new player was announced as "Kennedy," but his jersey had no name, just the number 8. Earlier in the game, the number 8 jersey had been worn by Johnny McKeon, a Barnstable player who'd been thrown out for instigating a skirmish. But now, here was number 8 back on the field. It wasn't until *after* the game that everyone realized they'd been playing with Senator Kennedy's little brother Bobby.

When Bobby walked off the field, he was stopped by his dad's friend Jack Dempsey, the Massachusetts State Police lieutenant based in Hyannis who'd terrified the Kennedy kids when they were growing up. Whenever the kids were acting up, Joe threatened them with, "I'm going to get Jack Dempsey after you." When Dempsey drove by on his motorcycle, the kids dove into bushes, ran behind garages, anything to avoid catching his eye. Dempsey stepped closer to make sure it was really Bobby all dirty from the game. "What the hell are you doing here?" Dempsey asked him.

Bobby apparently just felt like playing.

He'd approached Coach Parmenter during halftime and asked if he could join the game. And the coach said yes. Bobby, who'd played junior varsity football at Harvard, ran interference, helping the Townies come from behind for the big win. Bobby wasn't a particularly skilled football player—he never did have much style or technique—but he was always the most determined one on the field. Unlike Joe Jr. and Jack, who were much bigger, Bobby had received his varsity letter at Harvard, which he earned by playing through a badly injured leg at the Yale game. He possessed a hunger. "We aren't positive that it was the play of Bob Kennedy which made the big difference," read the *Barnstable Patriot* sports pages the next week. "Possibly Falmouth simply was overawed by the presence of such a celebrity. Or, possibly they all are good Democrats and didn't want to offend anybody that close to Senator Jack."

*   *   *

One summer afternoon, Joe said to his secretary and mistress Janet DesRosiers, "Stop what you're doing." They went together to a marina in a nearby town, and he led her to the most beautiful yacht she'd ever seen. The fifty-one-footer was named *Marlin* and it had a rich mahogany double hull. The boat had been built in Quincy, Massachusetts, in 1929 and, after trading hands a couple of times, ended up being used by the U.S. Coast Guard during World War II. After being discharged after the war, the yacht was overhauled and refurbished before ending up in the yacht yard that day. Joe turned to DesRosiers to ask what she thought. "I love it!" she told him. Joe bought the *Marlin* on the spot. Joe's friend Arthur Houghton was tasked with the details of the purchase—including finding a reliable and experienced person to be the yacht's captain. Arthur asked Frank Wirtanen, a gregarious boat captain whose father had come to the Cape from Finland in 1896, if he'd be interested. Wirtanen had spent his whole life around boats. He'd been a captain in the merchant marine in World War II and drove oil tanker boats for Exxon. But this would be his first time working as a skipper for a family on a day cruiser. Wirtanen didn't know a thing about the Kennedys, but it seemed like a decent job and he said he'd take it.

Wirtanen and Joe became close, spending hours on the boat together. Rose came out every now and then, but she didn't love being out on the water like Joe and the kids. When Wirtanen and Joe were far from shore, where they couldn't see the Big House or the rest of the Port, Wirtanen would sometimes ask Joe, "When are we going to throw the clock overboard and *really* take off?" Joe's answer was always the same. "Someday, Frank, we'll do just that." Of course, Joe never would. It may have been fun to imagine another life, one with no responsibilities, no expectations, away from it all with his captain and friend. But Joe was forever tied to his children, even after they'd grown up and left home. When they were little and went out sailing, he'd putter behind them in his powerboat—when they were grown, he'd do the same in the *Marlin*.

Teddy went to Harvard, like Joe Jr., Jack, and Bobby before him. And like his brothers, he came home to the Cape every chance he got. On a summer Friday afternoon, he invited his friend John Culver to come for the Nantucket Regatta. "It's a lot of fun," Ted told his friend. "And I want you to come down and be part of my crew in the sailboat race."

"Well, Ted, I've never been on a sailboat," Culver said. "With all due respect, I haven't had a lot of experience doing that coming from Iowa."

"There's nothing to it," Teddy assured him. And they got into his car heading to the Port. They were cruising down the coast of Cape Cod Bay listening to music when a bulletin broke in. It was a storm warning—people were being advised not to go out on the water. Suddenly, the sky was black. "Well, Ted," Culver said, "I guess the sailboat trip's off!"

"Oh, there's nothing to it," Teddy said.

"Well, the fella on the radio thought there was something to it," Culver said.

Teddy shrugged it off. "There's nothing to it."

Culver trusted his friend—*he must know what he's doing*, he thought. *He lives down here*, he thought, *and I've never been on the ocean*. As they pulled onto Marchant Avenue in the afternoon, heavy storm clouds were gathered on the horizon past the Big House. "Ted," Culver said, "it looks kinda scary out there."

He waved his big paddle of a hand as if he were swatting away a fly. "Nothing to it."

When they went into the house, the cook was putting away the food from lunch. The men, who'd driven without stopping for a meal, were ravenous. She made them salmon salad sandwiches, which they wolfed down before heading to the boat. It was nearly four and they didn't have much time. Teddy rushed them out to the dock. Culver looked out to the horizon but didn't see their boat. Teddy pointed to the *Victura* bobbing beneath them. Culver, more than two hundred pounds and over six feet, looked at Teddy, who was about the same size. He'd been expecting a much bigger, steadier boat. By now, there was lightning in the distance. The *Victura* was getting knocked around by waves like a toy in a bathtub. As soon as they got in the boat, Teddy started barking orders—words Culver had never heard. *The jib! The spinnaker!* They were only out about two hundred feet when Culver leaned over the side and lost his lunch. He was distraught. He thought to himself that this was the end, that he'd die on that boat. Somehow, they made it to Nantucket at about eleven that night. Relief washed over him as he pictured a hot meal and hotel bed to lie down in. Teddy pulled out a stack of four soaking-wet seat cushions as they pulled up to a beach—those would be their pillows for the night. Culver thought about taking three, but Teddy grabbed two.

After a sleepless night, they had the race the next morning. Starving, wet, and tired, Culver watched the boat go round and round until it was mercifully over. Teddy seemed happy; Culver was happy to have survived. He looked to the horizon and there, like a mirage, was a yacht coming their way: Joe Kennedy and Wirtanen aboard the *Marlin*. Teddy explained that his dad was there to take them back home—they'd tow the *Victura* behind. It was finally over, Culver thought.

"Boys! I've got some bad news for you," Joe said through a bullhorn. "The captain says it's too rough to tow you back. You're going to have to sail back to Hyannis. But I do have something for you. I know you're probably hungry after the race."

He lowered a canteen of hot clam chowder down on a rope. Culver grabbed it, desperate, twisting off the top and chugging nearly the entirety, ribbons of chowder pouring onto his T-shirt.

"What about me?" Teddy said. "I was supposed to have some of that."

Twenty-four hours after stepping onto the *Victura*, the trip back home was calm. As the Big House came into view, the boat came to a stop. There was no wind.

"We have to get out of the boat," Teddy said. "You pull, and I'll push the sailboat." Culver couldn't believe it. Teddy jumped off and swam to the back. Culver finally made his way to the front. And, a day after taking off in the storm, they were back.

"When we were back at summer school," Culver would later tell it, "it was a whole week before I got the seaweed taste out of my mouth. And I wouldn't talk to him for two weeks."

When Jack was in town he more often than not carried his wooden crutches. His back was getting worse and worse. He never liked people to ask him how he felt. But it had gotten so bad he couldn't mask the pain from his friends and family anymore. He took quick, ginger steps to ease the pain of walking, his face twisting into a grimace. He still played football, but he'd volunteer to quarterback so he could throw for a touchdown instead of running for one. When he played tennis on his family's clay courts, he smiled and laughed as he served, but his un-natural, contorted posture gave him away. Jack had also been diagnosed with Addison's disease, a rare adrenal gland disorder that explained why he'd always had stomach issues. The faint yellow cast under Jack's sum-mer tans was another effect of his illness. For the Addison's disease, he was prescribed cortisone, which finally calmed his discomfort—but his compromised immunity still made any additional surgeries on his back a risk. Doctors came to see him in Hyannis Port and told him that despite the risks—which were significant—he should undergo surgery to fuse the discs in his spine. Joe flew back to the Cape from Europe to talk through the decision with his son.

In a room alone, the two men walked through each scenario. Jack told his father that even if his odds of survival were fifty-fifty, he'd rather die than continue with the pain he'd been living with, hobbling on crutches for the rest of his life. But Joe argued that Jack could have a full life in a wheelchair—just look at FDR, he pleaded. Joe couldn't lose another child. "Don't worry, Dad," Jack told his father. "I'll make it through."

That night Joe didn't sleep. He walked from his upstairs bedroom down to the sunroom. He sat in silence save for the sea breeze rattling the windows. He thought about the last letter that had arrived from Joe Jr. He'd written it the week before he died, but it had taken more than a week to get to the little red post office down the street.

"Dear Mother and Dad," Joe Jr. started. "I am working on something different. It is terribly interesting, and by the time you receive this letter, it will probably be released, but at this point is quite secret. . . . Don't get worried about it, as there is practically no danger."

The next day, Joe Jr. would pilot a drone plane packed with explosives that prematurely went off, leaving him dead. Joe Jr. had written with the same confident assurance Jack had shown his father hours earlier. From upstairs in her bedroom, Rose heard a raw, guttural moan, her husband's pain ripping through the house. A few weeks later, Jack flew from the Hyannis airport to New York for the surgery.

*   *   *

A reporter stood outside the Big House in November 1954. *How was Jack doing?* he wanted to know. There'd been reports that he was in dire condition, that the surgery hadn't gone well. *Could someone give a comment on the condition of the senator?*

"My son, U.S. Senator John F. Kennedy, is making good progress after his recent operation and is in no danger," Joe said. "I am issuing this report on the senator's condition on behalf of the Kennedy family because of unfounded and disturbing rumors that are being circulated, especially in Washington. These reports imply Senator Kennedy's condition is such that he will be unable to resume his seat in the Senate. Such reports are not in accordance with the facts."

And so it was written in the New Bedford *Standard-Times*. But the truth was that Jack had been read his last rites by a priest after barely surviving the spinal fusion. He wouldn't leave the hospital for another month—and when he did, it was on a stretcher. He had a second surgery in February that was successful. By the spring, Jack was on the mend. He'd recovered from the second surgery, and he finally had a reprieve from his excruciating back and stomach pain. Emotionally, he understood how close he'd come to death, and he was exuberant that he had more time.

That summer of 1955, Jack went to Osterville for dinner with a friend at the Wianno Yacht Club dining room. Like when he was a kid and had gone there for dances, Jack still liked the ritual of getting all dressed up for the evening. At the Wianno he recognized a woman he'd dated in his bachelor days and went over to talk to her. One of his longtime Port neighbors watched the interaction carefully and recounted the whole thing to writer Laurence Leamer. "Why don't we go to a motel, huh?" Jack said. "It's practically next door." The woman, who'd never slept with Jack and was there with a Hyannis Port neighbor of the Kennedys, stared at him, too stunned to speak.

"Come on, let's go," he went on. "It'll be fun."

"I'm *married*," she finally responded. "Absolutely not."

He shrugged and walked away.

Jackie knew her husband flirted with other women. She called his attractiveness his "incandescence." She joked with him about it, giving him the nickname "Magic." And it was no secret that the Kennedy men loved the attention of beautiful women—starting with Joe, who liked to joke with his sons about their love lives, whether or not they were attached. Joe had, after all, continued dating long after his wedding vows. That had been their model for marriage.

"Dear Teddy, I don't know whether you know it or not but the reports of your goings on with all these beautiful women at Cape Cod is slowly but surely driving your oldest brother insane," Joe wrote to his youngest in the fall of 1955, two years after Jack married Jackie. "There was a time when I think he thought I was a little strict with you by insisting that you have something else on your mind besides girls, but after having heard from Morton Downey that he saw you at the airport with a more beautiful girl than Grace Kelly, Jack, I am sure, has changed his whole outlook on your future."

In 1955 and 1956, Jackie had a miscarriage then a stillborn daughter. As she lay in a sterile hospital bed, devastated from the second, Jack was on a cruise in Capri. He heard about Jackie, and he still continued his trip—he didn't return to be with his wife until a friend called and insisted he return. After leaving the hospital, Jackie went to her mother's home in Newport and confided in her sister, Lee, about her marriage. She said she wasn't sure it would survive.

Thanksgiving was a Hyannis Port day for the family. There were always a few summer people who stayed through the November holiday, or families with kids who came back to celebrate together for the school break. The trees were bare, the hydrangea bushes crisp and brown, and many summer homes weren't winterized, so the Thanksgiving families layered up to gather around their dining tables for one last meal before closing up the houses until Memorial Day. For the Kennedys, Thanksgiving Thursday 1956 began like all the years before it. Thursday always started with a big breakfast of bacon, eggs, and waffles. Rose was up with the sun for the early Mass at St. Francis Xavier, but the rest of the family usually took their time, eventually piling into cars, making their way to the midmorning service. They always sat in the second row, facing the altar named for Joe Jr.

After church, they went out for a sail, even though the water was so cold a splash felt like a slap. After everyone was back on shore and cleaned up, they threw on old sweaters and skirts and heavy walking shoes before making their way over to the Big House, where dinner started promptly at one. There were no formal seating assignments—except for Rose and Joe who sat opposite each other at the heads of the long mahogany dining room table. In the middle sat four straight, polished silver candlesticks framing the centerpiece of fruit, gourds, fall leaves, and a baby pumpkin. By the time each person chose a seat, the table was set with delicate ivory Lenox china edged with gold, which Rose had purchased in London. Each setting was paired with a crystal water goblet and a crystal tumbler for milk. The Kennedys, particularly the men, drank enormous quantities of milk, and alcohol wasn't served on Thanksgiving. They jumped instead to the first course—hot clam broth on a cold day, chilled tomato juice if it was balmy.

Joe started the meal with grace: "Bless us O Lord and these Thy gifts which we are about to receive from Thy bounty through Christ our Lord. Amen." Then the bickering over the cuts of turkey began. "They all like the same thing—the white meat," said Ziptha Anderson, the family cook.

That year, 1956, there was a frisson in the air. When the plates began to clear, Jack pulled his father away from the table into the sunroom. When they came back, their arms were around each other and they had matching grins. Jack had decided to run for president, they told the family. He'd do it in 1960. He wouldn't announce it publicly for a while, but the path to the White House was charted that night on the end of that dead-end street.

After graduating from Harvard, Teddy began dating a beautiful young woman with a kind smile named Joan Bennett. They met when the Kennedys gave a talk at Manhattanville College just outside Manhattan in honor of the new Kennedy Physical Education Building on campus, which was funded by Joe. Rose had attended the school, and so had Jean, who introduced her little brother to Joan, a student at the college. Joan grew up nearby in Bronxville, but her family had long ties to the Cape. Joan's grandfather and his brothers bought a pair of clapboard houses on the Cape in 1901—decades before Rose and Joe came to town. And her father spent his summers as a boy in Hyannis Port in a pink brick house on the beach.

Teddy brought Joan home to Hyannis Port the autumn of 1957 to introduce her to his mother just before the family got to work on Jack's Senate reelection campaign. Joe was in the South of France, but Joan was racked with nerves over meeting her new boyfriend's mother. Rose quickly put her at ease, asking about Manhattanville. Teddy invited Joan back a few more times that summer. Joan was no athlete—but Teddy taught her. The neighbors noticed a pretty blond woman over on the Kennedy tennis courts. They watched as Teddy patiently explained backhands and forehands. She'd nod and mimic his motions. "She was so beautiful," remembers Tangley Lloyd, the daughter of Nancy Tenney, and Kick's goddaughter. "I mean, just so beautiful in spirit and soul."

By the end of the summer, Teddy had made up his mind that he wanted to marry Joan. He brought her to the Cape for Labor Day weekend. They went for a walk along the long, narrow beach behind the Big House, following the dunes up to Squaw Island. "What do you think about our getting married?" Teddy asked, nearly as an afterthought. "Well," Joan answered, "I guess it's not such a bad idea." Teddy sat down on the sand. "What do we do next?" he asked as Joan slid down next to him. This wasn't how she expected a proposal would go. She told him she thought he should be the one to make the plans, and he said he thought they should make arrangements to get married right away.

When Joe returned home from Europe that weekend, the couple didn't get the chance to talk to him before he went up to his room, tired and jet-lagged. The next morning, Joan walked downstairs. The house was quiet and it was a moment before she noticed Joe sitting, large and imposing, in his favorite wing-backed chair in the corner of the long living room, the big window behind him framing Nantucket Sound. She'd been so nervous to meet him the whole summer and now here he was. Joan slowly walked into the living room and sat on his ottoman.

"Do you love my son?" Joe asked. His face looked so serious behind his round glasses. She told him she did. He asked her question after question; she felt like she was sitting for an interview. Finally, Joe told Joan if she wanted to marry his son, she had his blessing.

That fall, on October 9, 1957, Jack and Jackie bought their own home in Hyannis Port for $45,948. The simple two-story house covered in gray cedar shingles on Irving Avenue was close enough to the Big House to walk barefoot. And it backed up to the house Bobby and Ethel were living in, so kids could cut through the grass to visit cousins and grandparents and go down to the beach that bordered the back of the Big House. "Grandpa wanted to keep everyone together here," Jackie said. "I fought against the idea, I thought it was too close. I wanted to be away from the compound."

Their new house had been called "Daly Cottage," after owner Jack Daly, a shoe manufacturer and colorful character who went by the name Black Jack Daly and taught Jack to swim as a kid. After young Jack survived his PT-109 boat going down in 1943, it was Black Jack Daly he'd written to say, "Dear Mr. Daly, look what you started." The Daly Cottage was more modest than the Big House, with a small living room and a cramped kitchen as well as a brick patio with a blocked ocean view.

There was a cutting garden right in the middle of all three houses, which Joaquim Rosary, a Cape Verdean local who'd grown up in Hyannis and ran the general store in town with his wife, kept looking immaculate. Everyone knew that if a home's landscaping looked particularly good, it was a house Rosary kept up. He looked after the Kennedys' hydrangeas, snapdragons and white lilies, pink lilies, honeysuckle. There were pink, white, and yellow roses. Nothing orange, though. Ethel hated orange.

As a gift, Rose and Joe helped Jack and Jackie furnish their new home. Friends of Rose and Joe's from Palm Beach put up for auction their complete collection of furniture from their home in New Hampshire after running into financial trouble. Joe and Rose purchased the complete contents of the Shea home—a 135-piece collection of seventeenth- and eighteenth-century American furniture, art, and braided rugs—and the first installment of items went directly to Jack and Jackie's home on Irving Avenue. The rest went to the Big House to replace the European antiques

Rose and Joe collected when they lived in London. To decorate both homes with the antiques, Rose hired Robert Luddington, an interior designer and antique buyer with a disposition as prim and formal as Rose's. The two were fast friends, tacking onto their business appointments lunch dates and walks around the grounds. Most of the conversations were about Rose's life but she looked after him, too. If she noticed a loose button, she'd insist on getting it fixed. They worked tirelessly on making sure both homes were picture-perfect—as American as they could be, ready for Jack's close-up. The walls in Jack and Jackie's home were painted and wallpapered to complement the elegant pine pieces, the wing chairs, dining room furniture, and end tables. There were cozy chintz couches and bright-yellow-cushioned wicker chairs.

Jack and Jackie often fell into a routine that resembled the one at the Big House—dinner at a certain time, board games in the living room. But there was a more relaxed feeling in their home. There was less touch football—Jackie finally gave it up after breaking her right ankle during one of the games. Instead, she kept a cheap little easel in a closet along with a set of inexpensive paints. She painted landscapes of the Cape, which she gave to the family as gifts. The strain of competition that set the tone at the Big House and at Bobby's wasn't there on Irving Avenue, either. Though Jack and Joe Jr. had spent most of their childhoods at each other's throats, as an adult, Jack had grown more laid-back—he was much less intense than his younger brother Bobby, who'd met his match in Ethel. When Jack and Jackie invited their friends over for cards, it never really mattered who won.

"Martha and I used to play some bridge with Jackie and Jack, but none of us was particularly interested in the game," said their friend Charles Bartlett. "He was a good competitor, he fought hard to win; but he was also a very gracious loser, he was not a bitter-ender, and it didn't undo him to lose a game of Monopoly."

Not long after they bought the place on the Cape, Jackie had a successful pregnancy with the couple's first child, a little girl they named Caroline. Jack and Jackie's marriage had survived the recent rocky years and they were looking forward. Their comfortable new Cape home would represent a fresh start.

*   *   *

In spite of their nightmare of a sailing trip, Teddy's friend from school, John Culver, came back for many more visits to the Cape. He got to know the rest of the Kennedys, and he learned that his visits would often leave him exhausted and beat up, and Teddy delighted. One summer weekend, the two rode on horseback along the fence at Joe's farm in Osterville. Teddy had put Culver on the unruliest bronco at the stables, and Culver lurched all over the place until hitting the ground as Teddy doubled over in laughter. Now, they looked over at a group of Teddy's nephews and nieces, Eunice's kids. They were on their horses and a trainer led them around the ring, holding the reins. "It's really going to be interesting how this generation turns out," Teddy said to Culver. "It's so different now than with Jack, Bobby, and me."

"Well," Culver said, "like what?"

"Well, like when we went out sailing, we had to bring in the sails and dry them in the yard or we couldn't go out again on the boat," he said. "And one time the chauffeur brought me and Joe Gargan up to the house—we were supposed to be camping, and it rained. I was about ten or eleven, and Joe was thirteen. We'd taken the sailboat down a half-mile away to camp out all night. My dad came out and said to the chauffeur, 'What are you doing with those boys? Why are those boys in the car?' And he said, 'Well, Mr. Ambassador, they called, and they were all wet, and they got rained on.' 'Well, where's their gear? Where's their boat? Put them back in the car and take them back to where you picked them up.'

"That's what we did."

It was a cold day when Joe Kennedy called his old friend Jack Dempsey, the Massachusetts State Police lieutenant, and told him to be over at the Big House the next morning. When Dempsey arrived, Joe asked him what the town had planned for kids. *Do they have anything in the works for the youngsters?* he asked. Dempsey said they didn't have anything in particular planned. "I'll tell you what. I'll give you $150,000 from the Foundation," Joe said about the foundation he'd started in his son Joe Jr.'s name after his death. "Now, you come up with something that you can build."

The attention in the family had shifted from patriarch Joe to the next generation, in particular Jack and Bobby. But in 1957, *Fortune* ran a story about Joe. The magazine estimated his fortune had grown to somewhere between $200 and $400 million, thanks to his success in stocks and commercial real estate investments. The common thread between all Joe's business ventures was that he knew a good deal and he knew how long to hold on to it before he sold. Joe Kennedy was now one of the country's richest men—easily a billionaire in today's dollars.

Dempsey set up a conference with Hyannis's religious leaders, a selectman, and other important town figures, telling them they were receiving a large monetary gift. But he kept the donor's name confidential. They talked about building an indoor pool or a gymnasium. But a teacher involved in the conversation suggested asking his students what they'd build with $150,000. More than half the class said they wanted a place to skate and play hockey. In late 1957, construction of the Lt. Joseph P. Kennedy Jr. Memorial Skating Centre, two miles from the Big House, was complete. Nearly as big as a football field, it was the only skating rink on the Cape. Joe's speech that night mirrored the note he wrote for the brochure:

Dear Neighbors of Hyannis and Barnstable: For many years my family has maintained its summer residence at Hyannisport. Here, in this lovely and friendly area, our son Joe, and his brothers and sisters lived and laughed and grew through many sunny, happy days. It was, therefore, an especial pleasure to make available through the Joseph P. Kennedy, Jr. Foundation the funds for constructing the Skating Centre which is being dedicated tonight, November 1, 1957. With sincere good wishes to all our neighbors, with thanks to all who have contributed to the planning and execution of this building and skating rink and with the hope that the Centre will be a source of community pleasure for years to come. Very sincerely, Joseph P. Kennedy.

CHAPTER FIVE

═══════════════

It was 1960—and Jack was following through on the promise he and Joe had made to the family that Thanksgiving night four years before. He began zigzagging across the country, campaigning for the Democratic nomination for president. He was only forty-two, up against frontrunners Lyndon B. Johnson, the Senate majority leader from Texas, and Adlai Stevenson, former governor of Illinois. But there was excitement around his campaign. He had a real shot.

Jack came back home as often as he could to recharge—that summer, the roses on the Cape were perfect. When he sat down for dinner with his family, he devoured lobster and corn as though he hadn't eaten in days. The crushing pressure and exhaustion that he masked when he was in public was obvious when he was with his family, like a child who cries at the end of the school day when he sees his mother. In late June, Jack, Jackie, and Caroline were back on the Cape and invited Jack's sister Jean and her kids over to dinner at their place on Irving. But Jack excused himself to go to bed early. The next morning, he and Jean went up to the club to play golf, then came home to play croquet with the kids. Their sprightly little brown dog, a Welsh terrier named Charlie, raced excitedly back and forth, yipping and chasing Jack's croquet ball. Normally, the dog's fixation would have just inspired laughs, but Jack's tension from all the campaigning was still close to the surface. Everyone froze as he screamed at the dog at the top of his lungs.

July Fourth weekend was a couple of weeks later, and the Kennedy cousins walked around the streets with their oversized Kennedy buttons and "I Like Jack" paper hats. Jackie was there with Caroline, while Jack set off for the Democratic National Convention in Los Angeles. After Jack won his spot on the ticket, he flew from California to the Cape where he was met by a hometown parade in Hyannis. Neighbors, most of whom he'd never met, cheered and waved flags as he passed. Most of the Kennedy neighbors in Hyannis Port were Republicans, but their excitement at knowing someone who was running for president trumped the fact that he was a Democrat. That didn't mean, of course, that they'd vote for him.

"Nan, I hope you're going to vote for me," Jack asked his longtime neighbor and good friend Nancy Tenney. By 1960, after her first husband had died in the war, Nancy had married Robert Coleman and they were raising their family in Connecticut. Nancy had sold the house she'd bought on Squaw Island to Morton Downey. But she still came to visit her parents at their house on Marchant Avenue in the summers, and she always got together with her friends, the Kennedy kids.

"Why would I do that?" Nancy asked Jack that night over dinner.

"Well, why wouldn't you?" he asked back.

She answered matter-of-factly, "Because I'm a Republican!"

After he won the Democratic nomination, Jack invited his running mate, Lyndon B. Johnson, and his wife, Lady Bird, to visit Hyannis Port. The plan was for the Johnsons to stay with the Kennedys at their house on Irving Avenue—an intimate getting-to-know-you for the new running mates and their wives. The extra rooms in that house, though, were quite tight. "It's a rather small house we have there, and we wanted them to be comfortable so we gave them our bedroom[s]," Jackie said. "But we didn't want them to know [they were] our bedroom[s], because we thought they might feel they were putting us to trouble."

By the time the Johnsons arrived on that drizzly Friday, the two largest rooms on the corner of the second floor were wiped clean of any sign that might give them away as the hosts' bedrooms. The closets were emptied of all Jack's suits and Jackie's dresses; every hairbrush, toothbrush, and cream removed from the bathrooms.

Jackie's sister, Lee, and her husband, Stanisław Radziwiłł, were in town that weekend as well—Jackie was always happiest and most comfortable when her sister was around. Once the Johnsons were all settled in their rooms, everyone went over to the Big House to socialize. The women sat in one part of the living room hunched over photo albums while Jackie showed off pictures she'd taken of her daughter, and the men sat in another part of the room talking business. Jackie noticed Lady Bird had three green spiral pads that she brought out one at a time to jot a note whenever she heard a name mentioned. "Does your sister live in London?" Lady Bird asked Jackie. And Lady Bird, in a tailored cherry-red suit, wrote down neatly in her notebook "Lee" and "London." Lady Bird noticed about Jackie the particular singsong way she said her name. "Lay-dee Bird." She didn't seem to notice, though, that she was staying in Jackie's bedroom disguised as a guest room for her benefit.

Over the next weeks, Irving Avenue was crowded with cars dropping off men in suits to see the new Democratic nominee. Inside, the living room drapes were pulled shut as Jack and Jackie entertained the people Jack would invite to join him at the White House. Sitting on the couch, barely noticed in the shadows, was writer Norman Mailer. He looked like he was just another Kennedy family guest. But he was there to observe them, taking notes on everything he saw. Mailer was known more for his fiction, but he'd picked Jack as the candidate to follow for *Esquire*—he'd been watching him for months. Mailer's piece was mostly about the Democratic National Convention that summer, but it was also about what he saw after, while he sat in the shadows watching Jack and Jackie entertain in that picture-perfect, classic Cape Cod cottage.

"No one had too much doubt that Kennedy would be nominated," Mailer wrote for the November 1960 issue, "but if elected he would be not only the youngest President ever to be chosen by voters, he would be the most conventionally attractive young man ever to sit in the White House, and his wife—some would claim it—might be the most beautiful First Lady in our history.

"Of necessity, the myth would emerge once more, because America's politics would now be also America's favorite movie, America's first soap opera, America's best-seller."

Jackie traveled with her husband as long as she could. But by the end of the summer, as she entered the third trimester of her pregnancy, her doctors recommended she stay put and relax. So, after most of the family had left for the season, as the Port went back to sleep for the fall, Jackie and Caroline and the dogs went back to the house on Irving Avenue.

A friend of Jackie's recommended she use the time cooped up at home to write a newspaper column—it would be a way for her to express her views and give voters a glimpse into their family life. It was a way for her to help. Jackie set up a typewriter on a small desk in her room on the second floor to work on a syndicated weekly column that was called Campaign Wife. She typed for her first column:

> For the first time since Jack and I have been married, I have not been able to be with him while he is campaigning. You can imagine how frustrating it is to be in Hyannis Port reading all that he's doing and not participating in any way. . . . The worst part was not being in Los Angeles for the nomination. To me it seemed it would surely be better to be there than sitting anxiously by the television in Hyannis Port, but my obstetrician firmly disagreed. Since then I have resigned myself and have kept up with my husband by reading several newspapers every day and by writing to Jack's many friends throughout the country.

She wrote about the hurricane that had just ripped through the Cape, tearing off a portion of their roof and downing nearly a dozen trees. And she wrote about all the questions she received about her clothes and her hairdo. She wrote that she found the attention to her style silly but that she did rather enjoy shopping. The columns were sent to editors at newspapers across the country with an option to run with it a photograph of Jackie with Jack and Caroline.

Most nights on the Cape were quiet and lonely for Jackie, except for when the phone rang late at night, echoing through the empty house. Jack would call after he was done with his events for the day, and Jackie listed off all her worries. It was hard for her to read through the papers every day and not have Jack there to reassure her about what their future might hold. But at night, when it was just the two of them on the phone, he went through her list telling her that everything would be all right, not to worry.

At the end of September, the campaign decided on another way to get Jackie involved. Since she couldn't travel to attend the debate in Chicago, she hosted a viewing party—with plenty of journalists, of course—at their house in Hyannis Port. A buffet was set up in the dining room with coffee cake, doughnuts, and cookies. A sixteen-inch TV was rented for the day and propped up on an antique desk. To accommodate the group of mostly women, the white wicker furniture from the sunroom was dragged into the living room, too. Someone complimented her pink maternity dress, asking if she bought it in Paris. Jackie replied, "A woman in Hyannis made it for me."

As Jack and his opponent, Richard Nixon, debated, it was clear how well-suited Jack was for television—calm, clear, confident. Jackie kept her eyes on the screen while the rest of the guests shifted their focus from the debate to Jackie to see her reaction. She only got up a handful of times to try and get rid of the dark streaks and waves of white bands across the TV. After the debate finished, Jack called the house from the TV studio to ask Jackie how she thought he did. She told him, "I think you were superb."

Momentum picked up for Jack. Like they had when he ran for the Senate, his sisters hosted teas to drum up support. Journalists were predicting the election might be a landslide. Jack's grandmother Josie, who'd stood quietly by her husband so many years before as he ran for mayor of Boston, watched the news from her cottage a few minutes from the beach, down the street from the Big House, as her grandson transformed that summer into a front-runner for the presidency. Josie almost never left that little cottage. From time to time, Ethel came over to sit with Josie, combing the old woman's long white hair. On one of his short trips back to the Cape, Jack went to see his grandmother. As he said goodbye, Josie said quietly to her grandson, "You're our next president."

It was Election Day in America and the Hyannis Armory was thick with smoke. Each hour that passed brought more early reports of voting tallies from out West, and journalists stationed at the large building on South Street—tucked just behind Hyannis's Main Street—pulled more cigarettes out of their packs, impatient, jittery, bored.

It was November on the Cape, perfectly crisp, not yet freezing and so clear it was hard to tell where the water ended and the sky began. The towering oaks and maples spread newly bare branches that cut across the horizon. Inside the armory, the *tik-tak* of a hundred typewriters filled the room, echoing through the high ceilings as they fired off messages about not much of anything. There was no news to report from Hyannis Port. The bulletin board on the wall where the press pool posted their dispatches said it all: "if anybody wants vast amounts of trivia about the senator's house as viewed from the chipped stone driveway, see me, bonnie angelo," read one note, typed in all lowercase. Another read, "Ethel was wearing a shocking pink wool suit when she and Bob voted at the Masonic Hall on South Street." And a rare bit of information from inside the compound: "Mrs. Shriver says Jack is smoking a cigar."

Back at Bobby's house Jack reprimanded his sister Eunice for telling the reporters he was smoking. Bobby's house was acting as campaign headquarters that week. Exactly a year earlier, Bobby's living room had served as the meeting place where Jack, his brothers, and a dozen of his closest advisors plotted out the path to Jack getting to this night—the path to the presidency. Now, the furniture from the kids' rooms upstairs had been cleared away—the children were staying next door with their grandparents in the Big House—to make a command center on the second floor. Downstairs, thirty phone lines connected directly to important voting districts had been set up in the sunroom. Two Barnstable police officers were stationed inside the house, prepared for a long night.

That morning, Jack and Jackie had taken the short thirty-five-minute flight to Hyannis after voting in Boston. When they landed, hundreds welcomed them with signs reading "WELCOME HOME MR. PRESIDENT." Jack, the exhaustion of the last year etched on his face, waved and said, "I'm glad to be back on Cape Cod." Then he added, "I plan to rest the remainder of the day. I want to see Caroline and take it easy." Then he turned to the police chief waiting there and told him, "I'd like to go directly home." As they drove off, a teenage girl belted out a song with the refrain "Welcome Home, Neighbor." Jack's cousin Ann Gargan picked them up in a sedan, driving through the police barricades with a train of cars with reporters trailing behind as they headed to Hyannis Port, which was now teeming with journalists, news trucks, cameras, and other onlookers. They didn't pass down Hyannis's Main Street for one last wave at the crowd. They went the way they always went—straight to Marchant Avenue. Four months earlier, the Hyannis Port Civic Association had held a meeting and, by unanimous vote, decided to ask the police to set up a barricade at the village limits, restricting access to only residents and their guests. The Kennedys weren't represented at the meeting, but Jack offered to do "anything short of moving out" to solve the problem of the influx of tourists coming to Hyannis Port to see him and his family.

After Jack had received the Democratic nomination for president, this sleepy corner of the Cape saw as many as three thousand cars a day passing through. The police said that sealing the entire village off from the public would be impossible. But they blocked off Irving Avenue, in front of Jack's house. As senator, Jack liked to go over and shake hands with the people who'd started coming from all across the country to meet him—sometimes frenzied, trying to grab him. "Be careful, Senator," Jack Dempsey had warned Jack, "we don't know all of these people. It's difficult for us. Somebody might try to put something in your hand."

Jackie had a towering wooden palisade fence constructed—replacing the short stockade fence that had always been there. So many people had been leaning over the stockade fence to clip their roses as a souvenir or to get a glimpse of the family inside their home, just thirteen feet from the street, that a portion of the original fence had collapsed. When Jackie made plans to have it rebuilt, she made it twice as tall to protect the lawn and give the family privacy. "Lee and Stas were staying with us and everyone could see them getting in and out of the bathtub because they had a room on the street," Jackie said about her sister and brother-in-law. "It was rather close living that summer." But when Jack came home and saw the tall fence going up, he ordered it stopped. This was his home. He didn't want to be walled off from the streets he'd grown up running down. So on Election Day, the half-finished palisade stood at the edge of the lawn, a symbol of a family deciding just how much it wanted to open itself up to the world.

Jack went over to the Big House, where his family was already gathering, for breakfast after arriving from the airport. Joe and Rose were there with Bobby and Ethel, Teddy and Joan, and his brother-in-law Peter Lawford. Everyone else would be arriving throughout the morning. Jack ate quickly, then walked back across the grass to his house to steal some quiet. He sat on his porch in the warm sun. A news airplane buzzed overhead before swooping low, within two hundred feet of his home, to snap photographs of the candidate. One of the guards stationed at the white wooden huts located all around Jack's property walked over with a magnificent display of red roses sent over from the neighbors for good luck.

Joe came across the lawn to visit with his son. After talking, Jack went inside, his home filled with the sweet smell of treats baking in the oven. The refrigerator was stacked full of containers of Jack's favorite fish chowder. He grabbed a thermos and sat out on the porch with Jackie, blankets wrapped around them.

Restless, unsure of what to do with himself, he went out to throw the football with Bobby and Teddy, then went in again to have lunch and change from his suit into a sweater, slacks, and sports jacket, then back out to walk over to Bobby's, then back to his house and up the stairs to take a nap. It was nearly four in the afternoon. There was nothing else to do but let the time slowly pass while people across the country cast their votes.

"Just about ten minutes ago, the Senator and his sisters walked over to Bob's house and remained there about ten minutes," an announcer said over a speaker in the armory. The day dragged on with almost nothing happening. Then, finally, late in the afternoon, the headquarters at Bobby's sent the armory its first bit of real news. Early returns from Campbell County in Kentucky, famous for historically voting the winner, had voted

Kennedy. Jack won fifty-six percent of the votes. The stale armory air was suddenly vibrating with excitement. The correspondents felt their lives changing—they could soon be reporting on the winner, the new president, unlike their network counterparts who were stuck with the loser.

The results rushed in now. Just after 7:00 p.m. news came from the Associated Press that they were predicting Nixon the winner. But the reporters in the armory ignored that, writing it off as typical early Republican votes. The other wire reports were all saying it was a Kennedy sweep, as had been predicted. The TVs lined up in the armory were turned up to full volume, so loud together it was hard to make out anything being said. "Who's ahead?" a reporter pushed to the back asked the person in front of him. "How many electoral votes so far?"

As the evening crept into night, the family back at Bobby's watched the newscasters explain that the computer-estimated forecast was swinging back and forth. But the early returns from the East were full of good news. Jack was carrying Connecticut and Pennsylvania. Jack walked back to Bobby's just after seven, his sisters jumping up and down with excitement when they saw him. Joe's friend Morton Downey had come over from his home on Squaw Island and belted out the ditty "Did Your Mother Come From Ireland?" in his high, lilting tenor as he passed out sandwiches. Up on the second floor, Bobby held a phone to his ear, frantically calling the campaign's representatives in each district. Phones rang, typewriters clacked, everyone talked over everyone else. Upstairs a bit of good news came in and everyone cheered, then Peter Lawford ran down the stairs waving the torn piece of news off the wires from the teletype to bring to Jack. About ten minutes later, the good news was echoed on the TVs turned on around the house. Jack looked across the living room boiling over with excitement. He was quiet.

He went over to the Big House to update his father, then he walked back to his house on Irving Avenue to have dinner with Jackie and their friend Bill Walton and to say goodnight to his daughter, Caroline. Before dinner, Jack and Walton, an old friend from Washington, settled into the sitting room, where Jack had his first drink of the day, a daiquiri. After dinner, they turned on a portable TV in the living room. The side door swung open and shut as family and friends came in and out, smiling, giggling. By ten, it looked like it would be a landslide. Over at the armory, chairs were set up on the big wooden stage, ready for Jack to give his acceptance speech. Photographers readied their lenses. Sodas at the buffet in the back of the room were replaced with glass bottles of hard liquor. Organizers were preparing for a victory party now.

But back at Bobby's place, the mood had shifted from exuberant to tense. The race was becoming tight and uneven. Jack was losing in Wisconsin, Ohio, and Tennessee. An urn of hot coffee was set up on Bobby's sunporch: preparation for a long night. Morton Downey sat quietly eating the sandwiches he'd been passing around earlier. Jack went up the stairs of his house to kiss Jackie goodnight, then Eunice, Pat, and Jean came over to see her, each taking a turn hugging her, telling her to sleep well, that they were going to stay up all night. It was midnight when Jack walked back over to Bobby's. He paced the first floor, his eyes fixed on a television. By 2:00 a.m., the Kennedy lead was down to less than a million votes. At 3:15 a.m., Vice President Nixon appeared on TV at his headquarters to chants of "We want Nixon!" Jack still had more votes, but the race hadn't been called and Nixon didn't concede. Nixon smiled as he thanked his supporters and volunteers.

Jack walked over to his future press secretary, Pierre Salinger, to say, "Tell the press I'm going to get some sleep and I won't be making any statements at this time." He walked through the kitchen out onto the connecting lawns back to his house in the black night. His sister Pat watched him fade away and whispered, "Goodnight, Mr. President." He walked up the stairs to his room and fell right asleep.

Three a.m. turned into four at the command center and Teddy and Bobby, their crisp white button-up shirts now wrinkled, their sleeves sloppily rolled, stared expressionless at a television.

The next morning as the sun rose, Bobby's house was quiet except for the sizzle of bacon coming from the kitchen. Ethel had woken up before seven to make everyone breakfast. Slowly, as the smell of the grease wafted upstairs, people made their way down. Bobby and Teddy went to Marchant Avenue to throw the football back and forth for a while.

On Irving Avenue, three-year-old Caroline and her nanny, Maud Shaw, were the first ones up. Caroline ate her cornflakes in her room so as not to wake anyone. And Shaw noticed a man in a dark suit standing outside the window. He didn't look familiar. Then it dawned on her: He's Secret Service. Jack must have won. Caroline insisted on going to wake up her father then.

"When you wake him up, I want you to give him a nice surprise," Shaw told the little girl. "Will you say, 'Good morning, Mr. President' this time?"

They went down the hall and knocked on Jack's door. They cracked open the door to find him sleeping.

"Good morning, Mr. President!" Caroline said excitedly to her father.

"Well now, is that right?" he said, looking over to Shaw in the doorway. "Am I in, Miss Shaw?"

"Of course you are, Mr. President," the nanny told him. He told her to run over to the television to read off the latest figures. She did—he was ahead. Jack asked his cousin Ann to take Caroline to ride her horse over at Grandpa's farm. "I think he wanted her out of the house, quite honestly," Gargan said, laughing when she remembered that morning.

"The dawn is breaking and the sun is shining," a rumpled reporter said into a camera. The Big House stood behind him, the sea right beyond it, placid from the protection of the old breakwall. "It's just the kind of day that is ideal for a game of touch football among the Kennedys."

After Caroline left Jack's room, Jack's aide Ted Sorensen came over to tell him the same thing—that it was all but over. Jack walked to his window and waved at the knot of press down below. He shaved. Then he went downstairs for breakfast. The race wasn't over quite yet. Jack was ahead, but it was closer than anyone had expected and Nixon hadn't yet conceded.

Bobby went over to the Big House to talk to his father, already dressed for the day in a suit and pocket square. Jean, Steve, Eunice, Rose, Ethel, Bobby, Ted, and Joan went out for some fresh air, taking a walk along the sandy, narrow causeway connecting Squaw Island to the rest of Hyannis Port. They linked arms and talked as they filled the deserted road that morning. The group made its way back to the Big House, where they sat lining the staircase talking to Joe. Jack was there, too.

When they got to Bobby's house, Salinger told them Nixon would be formally conceding soon. They all sat in front of the TV, waiting. Finally, just before 1:00 p.m., Nixon appeared on the screen. And a concession telegram arrived at 111 Irving Avenue. It was over. Jack would be president of the United States.

The house erupted. There was a mad dash to get everyone together to drive over to the armory, where most of the media was waiting—had been waiting for days now—for Jack to give his acceptance speech. Jackie was called over to Bobby's, where she took questions from the press that had been stationed there—the women reporters tasked with covering the new First Lady. "I had to see the press in Ethel's house—all those women saying, 'What kind of First Lady will you be?'" Jackie later remembered. "Those horrible women."

Photographer Jacques Lowe tried to collect everyone into one room for a group photograph. *After!* everyone told him. *We can do it after!* Finally, Lowe appealed to Joe to help him gather everyone in the sunroom. But as some came in to sit, others drifted away. And Lowe realized Jackie was nowhere to be found. When nobody was looking, Jackie had slipped outside in her overcoat to walk along the beach alone. It had been such a long few months. Her second baby was due in just a few weeks. She took in the salty air and relied on the gentle waves lapping against the shore to dull the noise she'd left behind at the Big House. Jack went down to the beach to bring her back. She went home to change into a simple red dress and black high heels. She saw Joe hanging back watching his family standing ready for the picture. Joe had tried to fade into the background during Jack's campaign, never posing for pictures with his son—he didn't want to be a distraction. He wanted it to look like Jack had done it all on his own, though, of course, Joe never stopped helping Jack. "You have to come now," Jackie said to her father-in-law as she pulled him into the room.

In the photo, the couples are all mixed and matched, with Jackie sitting on the white sofa in the front with Ted—and Ethel, Steve Smith, and Jean standing in the back corner behind the trio of Rose, Eunice, and Joe, who crowd together on a floral chair. On the right side of the frame, Pat, Sarge, Joan, and Peter stand. In the middle, there's Bobby and Jack, with his hands positioned just below his suit pockets, looking out of the frame at something. They look casual, young, and happy.

The family's motorcade—Jack in the front seat of a white Lincoln with Rose and Jackie in the back and the Shrivers and Lawfords behind them in a pink Cadillac—arrived at the armory just before two in the afternoon. Both sides of the street were lined with people ten-deep, waving American flags and cheering. Around the corner, the local principal—Johnny Linehan, the Kennedys' old sailing instructor—released all the students early so they could go to the armory to see their neighbor, the new president. Linehan warned the students, "We will all attend this speech but no one will be absent tomorrow."

The school band marched down to the armory with their instruments. The cheerleaders shouted cheers, barely audible over the roar of the crowds outside. An old school bus sat across from the building with TV cameras placed on top for a better view over the crowds. Confetti floated through the sky. Jack smiled and shook hands with the crowd lining the path to the armory. When he, Jackie, and Rose entered, the crowd's roar echoed through the cavernous building. As they walked up to the stage, the rest of the family filed in behind them. Jack spoke for just ten minutes before ending his speech by saying, "Now my wife and I prepare for a new administration—and a new baby."

He took a few questions from reporters after walking offstage. One asked him if the Summer White House would be on Cape Cod. He responded with a smile, "Well, we live on Cape Cod, don't we?"

The family walked back to the cars parked out front. When Jack's brother-in-law Peter Lawford stepped out just seconds before the new president, the crowd screamed for the debonair Hollywood star. "I was so enamored with Peter Lawford, more than anybody," said Linda Hutchenrider, who left middle school that day to wait outside the armory.

The family went back to the Big House, where Joe hosted a cocktail party. Jack sat with the dozens of reporters, going over the months that led to that day. He served himself a glass of milk punch, looking over at his mother across the living room. Joe said to a friend, "Things are never quite the same once they get to the White House."

The next day, the family went out to play a game of touch football, running across the freshly cut grass. Joe called everyone in for lunch, and when Jack and his sister Jean hung back to talk, their father called out,

"We're still waiting on you two—hurry up!" Jack turned to his sister and joked, "Doesn't he know I'm President of the United States?"

"I thought it was the funniest thing," Jean later remembered. "You may be President of the United States but you're still your father's son. It didn't matter who we were. To all of us, Dad was Number One in our house."

The grass in front of Jack's deck became the temporary stage for twice-daily press conferences for the next couple of weeks. Inside the house, Jackie kept the family's routine for the sake of Caroline. "It's practically like any other fall weekend," Jackie told reporters one rainy afternoon. But outside, Irving Avenue, which had always been a summertime street that slept in the off-season, was more alive that fall than it had ever been before. Still, the magnitude of how their lives were about to change wasn't yet sinking in. Maybe Jackie would feel different when they went back to Washington. "I feel it's very unreal—this part here," she said as the reporters jotted down her every word. "I feel terribly happy. I never thought I would."

The family left for Palm Beach. And, like every year, they all planned to be back for Thanksgiving.

CHAPTER SIX

When the president-elect left the Cape, so did the reporters, the Secret Service, and the tourists. Jack traveled between Washington and Palm Beach as he finished his transition planning, and Hyannis Port settled into its autumn doze. Jack and Jackie had planned to return to the Cape for Thanksgiving, just as they did every year. But Jackie was weeks away from giving birth to their second child, and her doctor didn't want her to fly. Jack wanted to go home to see his family for the holiday. And Joe, who was there waiting for them at the Big House, really wanted them to as well.

"I could fly by and pick up Jackie and go to Hyannis Port and we could have dinner in Hyannis Port, have Thanksgiving with the family, and come back and drop her off in Washington," Jack pleaded with future White House physician Janet Travell.

"Don't do it," she told him. "It's not worth the chance."

"But look," Jack said, "it's just an hour or so."

"Don't do it," she said.

So they stayed in Washington, and the day after Thanksgiving, John Fitzgerald Kennedy Jr. was born. A card was sent to the new baby from the Cape Cod Hospital—the mothers of the five other babies born on the same November day signed the card, which read: "We the five new citizens born November 25, 1960, at Cape Cod Hospital send the best wishes in the world to the new baby and the happy parents."

The next time Jack returned to the Cape was in the spring for his forty-fourth birthday. The neighbors didn't know he was coming, but there was an excitement inside the house as the staff prepared for Jack's first time at home as president. The phone outside the sunroom in the Big House rang just after eleven that evening.

"Mr. Kennedy's residence," answered Joe's driver, Frank Saunders.

"Tell him I'll see him in the morning," said the voice on the other line. Then the call went dead. Saunders looked at the phone. Then he realized the voice had been the president's. Jack's plane had been delayed because of the weather, so Joe had gone to bed. Even with the delay factored in, Saunders figured the president would show up before too long, so he stood out on the porch alone to smoke a cigarette and wait. Foghorns blew in the distance and the sharp early-spring wind cut through him. Saunders had started working for Joe a couple of weeks after Jack moved into the White House. He'd been working at a garage in Boston, where one of his customers worked for Joe Kennedy. The man offered Saunders a full-time job as a driver for the Kennedys—it paid $100 a week and included lodging in the Port and Palm Beach. Saunders took it and made himself at home in the dusty apartment above the Kennedy garage. Because he'd come on in the off-season, though, he hadn't yet met most of the Kennedy kids. So he didn't dare miss the chance to see Jack—the president—arriving back home.

"The warmth inside of the house was tempting, but each time I took refuge I decided quickly to move back out," Saunders later wrote, "to be standing on the porch when John F. Kennedy came home to Hyannis Port for his first time as President."

Finally, just after one in the morning, the headlights of four cars lit up Marchant Avenue, splashing the puddles on the sides of the street as they turned into the driveway in front of the porch where Saunders sat. Men spilled out of the car, none saying a word to him. Then, there was Jack. Saunders noticed how tired his young face looked. Saunders introduced himself, and Jack said hi. He took the president's suitcases into the first-floor bedroom—the one that had been Jack's as a kid. As he put down the bags, Saunders could have sworn he heard Lem Billings, Jack's old friend from school who'd joined him for the weekend, say, "Send in the broads."

"How about a glass of milk," Jack said to Saunders. "And don't mind Lem, he thinks he's still in prep school."

"Yeah?" said Billings, who was excitedly bouncing on the bed. "Well, who's asking for milk?"

Saunders handed the milk to Jack, who was absentmindedly rubbing his back. "It's good to be home, Frank," he said, then asked how his father had been doing.

While Jack was home, his neighbor on Irving Avenue, Larry Newman, a warm and friendly bespectacled author and journalist, hosted the first cocktail party in the Port for the new president. Newman had known Jack since their neighbor Morton Downey had introduced them at church. "Here he was for years just a boy running around the neighborhood, and all of a sudden he's one of the most powerful men in the world," Newman said. "That cocktail party I had was the first time a lot of people in Hyannis Port had actually met John Kennedy—or any of the Kennedys. In some ways it was kind of like there were two towns here: the one inside the fence and the other outside."

That summer, Hyannis Port's first as host to the Summer White House, was electric. The neighbors watched the presidential flag rise up the flagpole at the center of the Big House's circular driveway, the sign that Jack was arriving soon. Friday afternoons, shrill fire truck sirens cut through the quiet streets followed by the *thwap-thwap-thwap* of helicopter blades. As soon as the children in the neighborhood heard the sirens, they spilled out of their houses, squealing as they ran across lawns, jumping over fences, down Wachusett and Dale Avenues to Marchant, so they could watch Marine One land. Bobby's kids ran over from next door to line up in front of the Big House porch and Joe sat in his rocking chair proudly watching over the whole scene. As the chopper slowly lowered onto the patch of grass between the Big House and the sea, hydrangea bushes and privet bowed in its path. Thirty or so yards away was "the bullpen," as the Secret Service called the area where they instructed reporters and photographers to stand. Sometimes the agents let a couple of the local journalists they knew slip closer to the helicopter where they could get a better shot of their smiling young neighbor, the president.

Milkman Austin Bell came over with his young son to see the president. The Keavy boys were there with their families. Nancy Tenney and her children. Bobby's next-door neighbors Jack and Ginny Evans of Pittsburgh gathered friends for cocktails on the front lawn of their summer home, which they called Merview. It was one of only six houses on Marchant Avenue, and looked a lot like Bobby and Ethel's place with two stories and white clapboard. Like so many other families in the Port, the Evans family hadn't socialized much with the Kennedys before the election, but Jack Evans proudly led his group of friends from the neighborhood over the low stone wall that separated Merview from the Big House, and they each shook hands with the president until Jack was distracted by one of the kids—little John Jr. liked to sit in the helicopter to grab at the controls. As a kid, he loved anything that flew.

"Anyone for ice cream?" Jack asked as the Kennedy kids and their friends piled onto the oversized white golf cart, which the neighbors dubbed the Toonerville Trolley, and Jack drove them up to the News Shop. "Faster! Go faster!" they shouted the whole short trip up Longwood Avenue. The kids streamed into the store attached to the red post office to buy penny candy or scoops of Four Seas, an ice cream shipped over from a nearby shop by that name in Centerville. Flavors included homemade mocha chip, fresh peach, and vanilla and chocolate. Jack never carried cash, so the bill was charged to the limitless Kennedy account before they drove back to the Big House, where Joe whipped up cold daiquiris for the grown-ups.

Nancy's father, Rockwell Tenney, watched the whole scene from the top floor of his house across Marchant Avenue. After the crowds dissipated, Tenney went downstairs to examine his property, which went right up to the Big House lawn where the helicopter landed. After taking a full inventory, Tenney wrote up a bill to send the president for the damage to his outdoor furniture caused by the thick helicopter exhaust. Jack always made sure his neighbor was promptly paid.

*   *   *

More Kennedys began buying up property around the Big House. Bobby, whom Jack had named his attorney general, and Ethel were still living in the house right behind the Big House. In 1961, Ted and his wife, Joan, bought a home down the street in the quiet and most private part of Hyannis Port, the spit of land called Squaw Island, which was separated from the rest of the neighborhood by a narrow beach road. The house they bought, a ten-room, shingled cottage, was one of only a handful on the island. The year Ted and Joan bought the Squaw Island place, the property behind the Big House that had been bought in Ted's name back in 1955 was officially transferred to Bobby and Ethel. In 1963, Jean and her husband, Stephen, purchased the eight-bedroom house with the year *1787* on the chimney right at the start of Marchant Avenue for $120,000. The Big House, Jack's place, and Bobby's all backed up to one another, separated only by shrubs and some guesthouses. The family could walk back and forth between any of the properties without going onto the street or crossing the neighbors' yards. The press began referring to the grouping of the three houses as "the Kennedy Compound," and the nickname stuck. The family, which at first bristled at the moniker, eventually started calling those three homes "the Compound" as well. It was an easy shorthand.

The area around the compound was dotted with little white huts, where the summer cops were stationed to protect the Kennedys and their neighbors. Because Barnstable was a small beach town with a population that ballooned in the summer, college students, teachers, and other seasonal workers joined the police force for that part of the year only. They had a week or so of training then were given a gun. Most days, it was a boring job: asking tourists not to cut Jackie's roses, or checking for the little red stickers residents were given to put on their windshields to prove they lived there and could pass down the streets closest to Marchant Avenue. The addition of the young summer cops was an exciting development for some of the girls in the neighborhood, who occasionally brought them cakes and cookies.

Weekdays, Jack was in Washington while Jackie, Caroline, and John stayed on the Cape. Jackie spent her days on the phone with her staff back in D.C. working on White House events that were coming up in the fall, or sourcing antiques for her big restoration project at the White House. She swam or played tennis with Ethel and Eunice. She was nowhere near as competitive as her sisters-in-law were. They seemed to be out for blood while Jackie just enjoyed the exercise. Jackie's main focus that first summer, though, was preserving a sense of normalcy for her two young kids—which was, in some ways, harder in Hyannis Port than at their other homes. There was the press, whose proximity wasn't anywhere near the same at Camp David in Maryland or their country retreat, Glen Ora, in Virginia or Jackie's family home, Hammersmith Farm, in Newport or even the White House. And there were the Kennedys themselves. Jackie tried putting some distance between Caroline and John and the rest of the Kennedy cousins. There was a wildness to Bobby's brood—at their house, kids always seemed to be hanging out of windows or swinging from trees. And Eunice's kids were so fixated on all the new attention on the family.

"I just felt so strongly about those children," Jackie said. "It was hard enough protecting them in the Kennedy family, where some of the cousins—especially, Eunice's children—were so conscious of the position and would always wear Kennedy buttons and would play that record, 'My Daddy is President, What Does Your Daddy Do?'"

To put the years of Jack's presidency in perspective for their family, Jackie often talked to her kids about what life would be like when their father was no longer in the White House, no longer leaving on a helicopter every Monday morning, and they were just a regular family again.

"I'd tell them little stories about other presidents," she said, "and then there would be a president after Daddy, and then we would be living in Hyannis."

Inside the houses, a lot of things stayed the same. Dinner was after cocktails at seven. Joe still sat at the head of the table, leading the conversation. They still had movie nights in the basement of the Big House. Everyone showed up late for the 9:00 p.m. start time then argued over which movie to watch. Jack often fell asleep before the movies ended, worn out from fulfilling his duties in D.C. The compound was a safe haven—the way the houses connected meant the family could roam from house to house. And the tall fence around Jack and Jackie's property—which had stood half-built the summer before—was finished, protecting their house, which was the most exposed of the three. But as soon as they left their little corner of Hyannis Port, they were being watched. When they drove up to St. Francis Xavier Church on Sunday mornings, they passed hordes of people lining South Street waiting to catch a glimpse of the First Family. The church, which had added a west wing just a few years earlier, had never been so full inside, either. Jack and Jackie sat in the second pew on the left-hand side, with security detail in the row in front of them and the one behind. They looked ahead at the priest while everyone else looked at them. If Jackie wore a particular style of hat to church, the next week there'd be a dozen women with the exact same style.

The Secret Service called the photographers, who always seemed to be quietly waiting behind a bush, "the squirrels." Jack made a game of avoiding them. He once caught a ride to church in somebody's beat-up old station wagon and had them park it six car lengths away from the entrance. At that moment, the photographers were all training their lenses on the cars parked right in front of the church's heavy wooden doors. After Jack got a few dozen feet up the sidewalk away from the crowd, he flashed a satisfied smile for having successfully won the game, but the Secret Service cars came screeching up behind him, blowing his cover.

Joe added a private pier behind the Big House so the family could avoid the exposure of the walk down to the Hyannis Port Yacht Club pier. Now, they could set sail from right behind the house. But the local photographers who'd been covering the Kennedys since the days of Joe's ambassadorship had a leg up on the new national press in town. They knew the best time to be at the dock, when Jack went up to the golf club, and about Sampsons Island, a spot located just off the nearby town of Osterville where Jack liked to drop anchor for a quiet afternoon with Jackie or the kids. By now, the Kennedys not only had the *Marlin*, the *Victura*, and other family sailboats and motorboats, they also had a ninety-three-foot wooden presidential yacht, which Jack renamed *Honey Fitz*, in honor of his grandfather. On the easy-riding *Marlin*, the Kennedys set off after Mass for Osterville, where Jackie's good friend Bunny Mellon lived. Their yacht was surrounded by two Coast Guard boats and two navy jet boats—all four manned with military personnel as well as Secret Service agents—forming a security perimeter around the president. The press chartered their own boats, which hovered around the security boats, with long camera lenses propped on the hull like cannons. Once the small fleet made it across the Sound to Osterville, Jack, Jackie, and the kids ate lunch and sailed with the Mellons before heading back to the Port in the late afternoon.

In spite of the intrusive, constantly clicking cameras and the pops of their flashes, the relationship between the Kennedys and the press was mostly friendly. One summer afternoon a phone rang in the newsroom of the *Cape Cod Times*. It was a presidential aide shouting, "Don't do anything with those pictures until I see them!" Earlier, Jack and his friend Chuck Spalding had been lost in conversation while they were out sailing on the *Victura*, just behind the Big House, when suddenly the wooden boat jerked back with a creak. It came to a dead stop. The narrow hull was wedged between a group of rocks. Jack jumped up, adjusting the mainsail as he calmly called back to the agent in the boat behind him, "Hey, can you give us a little help? We seem to be stuck."

"Looks like you're wedged in between two big rocks, Mr. President," Jackie's Secret Service agent, Clint Hill, shouted back. "Let me see if I can rock the boat and get it moving."

Jack laughed and said he was more worried about the boat than himself and his friend. Hill managed to slide the boat out from between the boulders, and the *Victura* drifted back into open water.

The cameras hadn't missed a thing. At the request of the worried presidential aide, the photos didn't go to press the next day, but they'd been printed and shown around the newsroom. Later, at a party for the press, Jack saw the photos of his little crash.

He grinned and asked, "Why the hell didn't you use them?"

Caroline's favorite thing to do was to climb into her father's lap while he told her a never-ending story about the white shark and the purple shark. Each time she requested it, Jack started the story where he'd left off the time before. One afternoon cruising around the Sound on the *Honey Fitz*, Jack started a shark story for his daughter. Franklin Roosevelt Jr., the Under Secretary of Commerce and son of the former president, was out with them that day, his legs crossed and his shoes off. Jack glanced over at Roosevelt's feet. The shark, he told his daughter, was hungry that day. And, can you believe it, the shark's favorite thing to eat is old, dirty sweat socks! Caroline asked Jack a little nervously where the shark was as he looked into the water.

"Well," her dad said with a serious expression, "I think he is over there! And he's waiting for something to eat!"

Jack reached over and grabbed a sock straight off Roosevelt's foot and, in one swift motion, threw it over the stern.

"The only thing the shark likes more is a second sock!" Jack said, reaching over for the second sock, throwing it over the stern. Caroline shrieked with delight as she watched the socks disappear into Nantucket Sound.

Jack wanted Caroline and John out on the water with him as much as possible. He swam in the ocean with them until their little fingers wrinkled. They were so young and still needed their naps, but he pleaded with Jackie for them to come out on the boat after lunch. "They'll be cranky," Jackie told him. And they were. Eventually they fell asleep wrapped in beach towels in the boat's cabin, out of the sun, lulled to sleep by the gentle waves. "He just thought everyone would love that boat because that was his away from care," Jackie said. "It was for him what getting out on a horse was for me . . . He loved the sun and the water and no phone."

For Jackie, the best part about being out on the water was being pulled behind the boat, the gurgling of the wake drowning out everything else in the world. Jackie was a strong water-skier, but she wanted to learn to do it better. She asked Carl Wirtanen—who often helped out his dad, Frank, the captain of the Kennedy vessels—if he knew anyone who might be able to teach her some more complicated techniques. Carl called his friend, a local kid named Jim McEvoy, to ask if he wanted to ski. Jim was sixteen and doing landscaping during that summer's school break. When he said "sure," Carl told him to bring his new slalom ski to the pier.

Shortly after, Jim was at the Hyannis Port Yacht Club pier and bending down to caulk his ski when he looked up to find an imposing man with a neat crew cut and crisp suit looking down at him.

"Are you McEvoy?" boomed the man.

"How do you know that?" the teenager asked.

"I know everything," the man responded.

"What's going on here?" McEvoy asked, getting a little nervous.

"You'll be waterskiing with Mrs. Kennedy this afternoon."

"Really?" McEvoy squeaked. "I'm, uh, just here to ski with my friend, Carl." He narrowed his eyes at Carl, who was standing behind the man. It was at that moment that Jim realized the man was Secret Service. An instant later, it dawned on McEvoy, whose family was Boston Irish Catholic, that he was about to meet Jackie Kennedy. He was going to be spending his afternoon with the First Lady. *Oh my gosh*, he thought. *This is a big thing.*

For Jackie to water-ski, the Secret Service agents had to set up a protective perimeter in the water. Jet boats were used to create a boundary around where Jackie and whoever she was with would ski. Her Secret Service agent, Clint Hill, was in the boat behind her, in case he needed to quickly jump in to rescue her. The thing was, though, that Clint had received no prior water lifesaving training when he was assigned to protect the First Lady. Jackie was always looking for someone to water-ski with and when she invited Hill one afternoon, he told her: "Mrs. Kennedy, I hate to tell you, but I have never water-skied before." She looked at him wide-eyed: "Oh my goodness, I thought everyone water-skied."

That afternoon off the Hyannis Port Yacht Club pier McEvoy was struck by how polite and kind Jackie was. As they left the shore on the boat, McEvoy explained that the best way to get better on one ski was to start out on two and then drop a ski while you're out on the water, being pulled by the boat.

"The boat will circle back around and pick up that ski," he told her.

"But what if another boat hits it?" she asked him. "I can't just leave it out there. What if someone gets hurt?"

Finally, she gave it a try, her thin arms struggling to hold up her body while she balanced on one leg, her other foot dragging behind her. Each time, she fell.

"I guess I don't have it," she told the teenager as they motored back to shore.

By the time astronaut John Glenn came to visit Bobby and Ethel in the summer of 1962, Jackie *had* it. Just back from his trip orbiting Earth, Glenn and Jackie ventured out together in the water behind the *Marlin* with their skis, doing graceful figure eights and zigzagging back and forth across each other. The family cheered from the boat while hundreds of onlookers watched the show from the shore. Glenn did his best to keep up with the First Lady but toppled off his skis twice.

That day, little Caroline had her first go on skis, too, with a short turn around one of the boats with her mother. Jack burst into his biggest round of applause of the day, though, when Jackie, on a single ski and double hand grips, circled around Egg Island, ending the loop with her arms stretched out toward the stern of the *Marlin*.

There's a name Cape Codders give to newcomers—people whose families don't go back generations and who just don't quite get how things work there. They're called washashores. The Secret Service agents—men in suits who hovered around the small community—fit the definition. They were there in the church—you could always tell who was Secret Service because they never closed their eyes when they prayed; their gaze was always on the First Family. And when the Kennedys were out on the water, the agents hovered not far behind. When they steered their boats to the shallow waters, the Barnstable police shouted to them over the waves, "No, no, no, don't go over there! That's full of rocks! There are three buoys over there—don't go over there, knuckleheads!"

The agents rented a group of small cottages for the summer around the corner from the Yachtsman Motor Inn, half a mile from the compound. They shared bathrooms and bedrooms, relying on an individual twelve-dollar per diem to cover expenses. On nice summer evenings, the agents hosted cookouts on the beach that backed up to the Yachtsman, inviting the people who worked there to come out for hot dogs and burgers.

"I can remember one night, a nice-looking lady says, 'Oh, I've got something in my eye!' And the Secret Service [agent] says, 'I'm a trained medic, I'm assigned to the Secret Service,'" remembered Peter Cross, a local high school student who worked at the Yachtsman in the summer. "And he took off his sport coat and he had two guns and a knife. I said, *woah*! I almost fell over backward, I was about fourteen years old. Like holy moly, this guy's not fooling around. So, it was, for us, quite an exciting time."

The first July Fourth weekend after he became president, Jack welcomed the Secret Service agents to his hometown with cartons of his favorite clam chowder with bacon and potato chunks from Mildred's Chowder House, a little restaurant next to the airport. "I had never had clam chowder before—there wasn't a whole lot of seafood in North Dakota—but from the first taste, I realized why the president loved it," Clint Hill said. "On a cold, damp afternoon, nothing tasted better. From that point on, Mildred's chowder became a dietary staple for the Secret Service agents in Hyannis Port." Mildred's was such a regular hangout that a special red phone was installed in the restaurant, in case the agents needed to be reached while they were there.

Jackie gave specific instructions to the agents assigned to her children to help reduce the intrusion of constant surveillance. It was paramount that the agents be as unobtrusive as possible, so their friends wouldn't see them as any different. If Jackie was driving the children, the agents' car needed to be far enough behind that the kids wouldn't notice the agents if they turned around. And she didn't want to see them follow behind in boats when they were out on the Sound. If Jackie or their nanny, Maud Shaw, was with the kids, the agents were to disappear into the background—they certainly weren't to step in to help Shaw pack up the umbrellas and buckets when they went to the beach. And if they saw the kids splashing around in the water, they were to assume Jackie, Shaw, or another family member would intervene. "Drowning is my responsibility," Jackie made clear to the agents. The agents were there strictly to prevent kidnapping or other outside dangers to the kids that came from being in the public eye.

Eventually, the community adjusted to their new Secret Service neighbors. The tourists were harder to get used to. They lined the narrow streets with their cameras, stood watching the boats on the beach, crowded around the entrance to the church. Hyannis Port was a place for locals, for insiders. There were about a hundred year-round residents at that point, and five times that in the summer. There were no longer any hotels in the Port. If you wanted to stay within the boundaries of Hyannis Port proper, you had to own property or know someone. But now here were all these tourists roaming the streets. The gawkers were the hottest topic of conversation at the town watering hole: the post office. Of course, nobody ever said anything to the Kennedys. But they said it to each other—and if a reporter asked, they'd tell him, too. "They walk on the lawns," Winifred Sawyer Smith told a *New York Times* reporter as she pointed to her yard, where she was planting a border of petunias. "They steal things. They threw a beer can at dogs and hurt them. They say we're a lot of millionaires. We're far from it.

"As far as real estate is concerned, people can't sell or rent their places. Nobody wants to come into this mess. I know the people across the street wanted to rent for August, and they didn't even get a single nibble. We're not blaming anybody. It's just one of those things. This isn't a Coney Island type of thing. We like a quiet place."

As one way to deal with the congestion, new parking signs were put up in front of Sally Fowler's Shop across the street from the post office, which said you could only stay for fifteen minutes at a time. But that, too, garnered complaints from the locals. "It takes the women who go in there fifteen minutes to say hello!" George Musgrave told the *Times* reporter.

Joe's driver, Frank Saunders, heard the hubbub among the neighbors and mentioned it to his boss.

"They can kiss my arse!" Joe told Saunders defiantly.

Then Joe laughed. "You notice how Jack likes to stroll around and wave at them, say hello to them and smile at them? It's marvelous! Jack's rubbing their noses in it, Frank. It drives some of them crazy seeing that presidential flag flying here.

"Years back we lived in Cohasset and I wanted to join a club there and those narrow-minded bigoted Republican sons of bitches banned me because I was Irish Catholic and the son of a barkeep. The hell with them!"

*   *   *

In the dark basement of the Yachtsman Motor Inn down the street from the compound in Hyannis, the improv group Compass prepared to go onstage. The small group of performers were in town for the summer. And the Yachtsman was the place to be in Hyannis. Friday afternoons the press trucks arrived at the motel and for $150 each local high school kids unloaded the typewriters marked with room numbers for each journalist. On Sundays, the teenagers came back and for another $150 picked up all those typewriters and suitcases and put them back in the trucks. It was big money for a high school kid. And it was a chance to see the faces they saw on the nightly news up close and personal. If there wasn't room in any of the Kennedy houses, Jack's advisors, staffers, or guests would stay at the Yachtsman, too. It was a *scene*, with Jack's press secretary, Pierre Salinger, sliding onto the piano bench to belt out tunes for happy hour as the press corps loosened their ties and unwound at the end of the day. After Salinger's performance, the crowd made its way down to the basement for the improv set. The first hour of the show kicked off with someone in the audience throwing out a word, which dictated that the performers make up a sketch about that word. The most popular bit was by a young performer named Alan Alda. His impression of Jack Kennedy was spot-on. The audience was chock-full of reporters who that morning had fired questions at the president, and that night they fired the very same questions at Alda, who answered them as Jack. Alda spent his mornings scouring the local newspapers, keeping up with the issues of the day. Sometimes they were questions about the Cape. One of Jack's first orders of business the summer of '61 was creating the Cape Cod National Seashore. It was a bill he'd introduced back in 1959 as senator that preserved 43,000 acres of land on the wrist of Cape Cod. Those were easy questions for Alda to field. If the reporter asked a question for which he didn't have a good response, his backup answer was: "We have a Commission studying that." Sometimes Alda was joined onstage by another performer pretending to be Soviet leader Nikita Khrushchev while someone else acted the role of his translator. The guy playing Khrushchev, who didn't speak the language, babbled in fake Russian, leaving it up to the performer playing his interpreter to come up with the punch line while Alda responded as Jack.

That summer, Khrushchev was at the top of everyone's minds. On the heels of the Bay of Pigs fiasco, which threatened to derail the entire Kennedy presidency, Jack was in the middle of tense negotiations with Khrushchev over troops in Berlin. The Soviet premier wanted American troops out but Jack wouldn't budge, resolved to protect West Berlin's freedom. Jack's advisors came in and out of the house on Irving Avenue and the Big House that summer. The men walked past the barefoot neighbors making their way to the Hyannis Port pier. Instead of sails or beach umbrellas, the men carried stiff leather briefcases. Key members of the administration like McGeorge Bundy, the White House national security advisor, met with Jack in between his boat rides and games of backgammon.

At the end of one day of meetings, Jack snuck away to play a game of checkers—his favorite game—with his youngest brother, Ted. They played until just before dinnertime. Then, with Caroline tagging along, they walked over in the hazy late-day sun to the Big House. Before they got there they heard someone call from behind. It was Bundy, who'd opened the screen door of Jack's house to yell, "Mr. President, they need you on the phone. Something's come up." Jack asked his brother, "Will you walk Caroline in?" He walked back to his house while everyone else went to the Big House for dinner. Joe Kennedy sat on his deck watching the whole scene. When he was done talking to Bundy, Jack came back over for dinner with the rest of the family. Joe was the first to speak. "I know you're worried about Khrushchev," he said to his son, "but let me tell you something. Nothing is going to be more important in your life than how your daughter turns out. And don't ever forget it."

Jack wasn't defensive. He told his father he was right. Then they went back to joking around for the rest of dinner, just like any other night. Jack told his father that if he read in the news that Jack had given his nice boat model to Khrushchev, then the talks were going well. He said he wouldn't give him the model if they weren't. He joked that he wanted to keep the boat model for himself anyway, so it was a win-win. But the talks with Khrushchev were about to get more complicated.

*　　*　　*

"Bill, be sure we take the road we usually take to Mass," Jack said to his driver. "I don't want to miss my most ardent supporter."

"Absolutely, Mr. President," Bill said. He knew exactly the route. "We'll go right by him."

"Who is this great fan?" asked Red Fay, Jack's friend and advisor who was visiting for the weekend.

Jack explained that a few blocks from St. Francis Xavier Church there was a man in his eighties who came out every Sunday morning. He stood leaning on his cane right next to his mailbox, waiting for the president to drive by.

"He gives the greatest toothless smile and eager wave you've ever seen," Jack told Fay as they pulled up and Jack leaned forward, telling the driver to slow down. The old man waved. Jack smiled, a big, sincere smile. "If I had more supporters like that old pal," Jack said, "it would be a joy to read the newspapers every day."

As that first presidential summer wound down, September's fog blanketed the Cape. June on the Cape was known as the time for the honeymooners—first-timers who hadn't yet learned that the cold from winter still stuck around until then. But that sweet spot after Labor Day was for the families whose kids had moved out and were no longer married to the school schedule. Longtimers knew this was the best time to be on the Cape. Rose wasn't home yet—she'd stayed in the French Riviera a little longer than Joe because she knew hordes of press and tourists would be waiting for them when they got back. When she received the message that her dining room table was ready to be returned to the house after being repaired, she gave directions for it to stay at the shop for a few more weeks. After all, the throngs of grandchildren would just scuff it up again.

The *Caroline*, the Kennedys' private plane, was supposed to be headed for Barnstable's airport but it was redirected to New Bedford, an hour west of Hyannis Port on the mainland. Cabdriver Roger Paradise pulled up to the curb to pick up the passengers. When the plane door opened, the first one he saw walk down the steps was Frank Sinatra, in a suit and wide-brimmed hat. The singer stood in the doorway with a drink in one hand and a tennis racket in the other. Behind him followed Jack's sister Pat Lawford, Porfirio Rubirosa, the debonair playboy as handsome as Sinatra, and his wife, French actress Odile Rodin, a petite dirty blonde. Pat had a complicated relationship with her father, and she enjoyed the distance her marriage to actor Peter Lawford and their life in Los Angeles gave her. She never looked for her own home on the Cape, unlike the rest of her siblings. Having a permanent house there with the rest of her family, which sometimes felt suffocating to her, would be too close. But she and her family still came to visit in the summers. When they did, they stayed for a week or so at the Big House.

"Fifty Marchant Avenue," the group told the driver.

On the way, they asked Paradise to pull over for a pit stop at a bar called Tiny Tim's. Sinatra treated everyone at the bar to a round of drinks. Then they piled back into the cab, and continued on in the night to the dark, empty streets of Hyannis Port. When they pulled down Marchant and into the round driveway, Peter Lawford came through the door to greet his wife and their friends. Joe Kennedy stood waiting for them on the porch wearing a red smoking jacket.

Sinatra was a regular visitor those summers. He and Rubirosa were there one weekend when Joe threw a big party at the Big House. There was loud music and busloads of guests. When Joe's chauffeur, Frank Saunders, came over that night from his apartment above the garage, walking into the party, he came across his boss in a dark hallway fondling the breasts of Rubirosa's date. Saunders was carrying Joe's riding boots, which Joe wanted shined each evening, ready for his morning rides at the farm in Osterville. "My riding boots!" Joe said when he saw Saunders. "Just in time!" He and the woman laughed, Saunders later wrote, remembering each detail of that night.

On September 29, 1961, just weeks after construction began on the Berlin Wall, Khrushchev wrote to Jack from the shore of the Soviet Union's Black Sea. The letter was hand-delivered to the U.S. president and read: "As you will fully understand, I cannot at this time permit myself any relaxation. I am working, and here I work more fruitfully because my attention is not diverted to routine matters of which I have plenty, probably like you yourself do. Here I can concentrate on the main things." Khrushchev went on to write about the talks he and Jack had had in Vienna earlier in the year. He wrote about his hopes that they could find middle ground on a German peace treaty, and about how the two of them might be able to communicate confidentially through secret letters going forward so that they could come to an agreement without resorting to using nuclear weapons. "As you see, I started out by describing the delights of the Black Sea coast, but then I nevertheless turned to politics," Khrushchev wrote. "But that cannot be helped. They say that you sometimes cast politics out through the door but it climbs back through the window, particularly when the windows are open."

Jack told nearly no one about the letter, which he brought home with him to Hyannis Port. On October 16, he wrote back:

Dear Mr. Chairman: I regret that the press of events has made it impossible for me to reply earlier to your very important letter of last month. I have brought your letter here with me to Cape Cod for a weekend in which I can devote all the time necessary to give it the answer it deserves.

My family has had a home here overlooking the Atlantic for many years. My father and brothers own homes near my own, and my children always have a large group of cousins for company. So this is an ideal place for me to spend my weekends during the summer and fall, to relax, to think, to devote my time to major tasks instead of constant appointments, telephone calls and details. Thus, I know how you must feel about the spot on the Black Sea from which your letter was written, for I value my own opportunities to get a clearer and quieter perspective away from the din of Washington.

Jack went on to agree that communicating covertly through the letters would allow the two world leaders to be frank and to hopefully come to a peaceful understanding outside the view of the press and the public. The letters were the start of months of secret communications between Jack and Khrushchev that would change the course of history.

That November, it was arranged that Jack would be interviewed by a Russian journalist for a story that would appear in newspapers across the Soviet Union. It would be a valuable opportunity for the president to speak directly to the people of the Soviet Union at a time when both countries were uneasy about the ongoing negotiations pertaining to America's troop presence in Berlin. The interview would be in Hyannis Port. Khrushchev's son-in-law Aleksei Adzhubei was chosen as the journalist who'd interview Jack. Details of the interview weren't announced in advance, so few members of the press knew to expect Adzhubei when he landed at Logan Airport in Boston. He was picked up in a private limousine by the air force and driven to the Yachtsman Motor Inn, where he would be staying. Then he was taken to Jack's home, where the interview would take place: Jack in his favorite rocking chair, Adzhubei across from him in an overstuffed armchair.

That morning Larry Newman, whose house stood catty-corner to Jack's on Irving Avenue, had just finished painting a falling-apart, old picket fence, and was walking down to the Hyannis Port Yacht Club pier. As he passed Jack's fence on his way to the water just after noon, a group of Secret Service agents rushed toward him, rifles at the ready. Next, Jack walked out, then his press secretary, Pierre Salinger, followed by Adzhubei and their interpreters, all in black suits and neat ties. Jack saw his neighbor, then stopped and turned to the Russian reporter to say, "I want you to meet a typical American publisher." Adzhubei looked silently at Newman, with his filthy painting clothes and days-old stubble, then he said to the interpreter standing with him, "Ask Mr. Newman if he would like a job working for me. I could promise him enough pay for a new suit and a clean face."

Jack erupted in laughter.

Rose's dining room table was back in time for Thanksgiving. Everyone was in town except for Peter Lawford, who'd just left for Europe to film his latest project, and the three youngest Lawford kids. John, who was turning one that weekend, was sick with a cold, so he stayed back at the White House with a nanny. Newspapers across the country breathlessly covered the preparations for the president's first big family holiday.

The presidential flag was raised on the Big House lawn when Jack flew in on Wednesday. He was driven over to Hyannis Port instead of his usual helicopter ride because of the thick mist and fog that envelopes the Cape for most of the fall, making it hard to look much beyond what's right in front of you. The Secret Service cottages behind the Yachtsman were filled again. And the sightseers and police officers lined the narrow streets as many houses sat empty, shut down for the season. The families whose traditions brought them back to the Cape for Thanksgiving tossed logs in their fireplaces, which sent plumes of smoke up chimneys. From outside, the windows of their houses appeared golden through the fog.

Rose hosted the family at the Big House for cocktails Wednesday night, served with fresh local oysters and lobster tails. Everyone stayed for dinner, except for Jack and Jackie, who went down the street to their house. "Jackie probably likes to be alone for a change," Rose wrote in her diary two nights later. "She has a crowd so much."

Afterward, they went down to the basement for a movie, like they had when they were kids. But everyone was tired, and one by one they left the Big House to go to their own homes to sleep.

Thursday morning, the fog remained but Rose walked over to the golf course to play a round. It was frigid, so she wore two sweaters, a rubber rain jacket, snuggies under her slacks, and cream on her face. She liked her routine. No matter what else was going on around her. No matter what anyone else thought. She played two balls on six holes.

Thanksgiving morning was quiet. Jackie sat with Caroline, telling her the story of the first Thanksgiving. When they took their Welsh terrier, Charlie, out into the crisp fall morning he got into a fight with a neighbor dog. Reporters watching from the end of the street jotted down the scene. Both pets were okay, but the skirmish would make the front page of the *Boston Globe* the next day.

Friday morning the clouds brought rain, but still, the family played touch football on the lawn, except for Jack, who spent the day working. Defense Secretary Robert McNamara arrived with military advisor General Maxwell Taylor and others from the administration, landing their helicopters on the golf course since the Big House lawn was too soggy from the rain. That afternoon, Jack held a Defense Department budget meeting at the Big House, taking over his parents' living room, which was much bigger than his own. A dozen men with slicked hair sat hip to hip on floral couches, notebooks balanced in their laps. For lunch, Rose sent over thermoses of fish chowder to all the family houses.

Nearly every day that weekend a group of Kennedys went over to Hyannis to skate at the Lt. Joseph P. Kennedy Jr. Memorial Skating Centre. On Thanksgiving Day, Jack, Jackie, Ted, Joan, Eunice, Jean, and Pat rode over to the rink right at dusk.

"Is the rink closed?" the president asked.

"Yes," said the man closing up, "but it'll be open in just two minutes."

That weekend, Jack sat in the stands watching his nephews play ice hockey, and during open sessions, the kids skated loops over the rain-slicked ice, laughing, enjoying themselves at the rink named for the uncle they never met.

Before everyone flew back home, the family got together to celebrate Bobby's and Sarge's birthdays with lobster and ice cream. Jack, who'd been working most of the weekend, joined the celebration. He seemed happy, light. He asked his friend Fay to sing "Hooray for Hollywood." Then Ted, who never passed up an opportunity to sing, belted out "Heart of My Heart" while Eunice joined in and Joan played on the piano.

"Heart of my heart," I love that melody
"Heart of my heart" brings back a memory
When we were kids on the corner of the street
We were rough 'n ready guys
But oh, how we could harmonize

Jackie, in her pink Schiaparelli slack suit, taught everyone the latest dance craze, the Twist. She took center stage in the living room, demonstrating by swinging her hands to one side, her hips to the other, her feet staying planted on the plush rug. Music was piped through the sound system Joe had installed on the first floor a few years earlier. They each took a turn trying the move. Jack sat back in his chair with a small cigar, smiling, watching his family together, laughing and teasing like they had in that living room when they were kids.

"Jack gets a great kick out of seeing Ted dance," Rose wrote in her diary. "Ted has a great sense of rhythm but he is so big and has such a big derriere it is funny to see him throw himself around."

Finally, the group turned to the president.

"Jack," they said. "It's your turn to sing. Sing!"

"Do you know 'September Song'?" Jack asked Joan. She tapped out the chorus a couple of times. Then Jack began to sing. While the other performances that night had been raucous, laced with laughter, the room fell silent. The only sounds were Joan's notes and Jack's voice.

> *Oh, it's a long, long while from May to December*
> *But the days grow short when you reach September*

That night, after everyone walked through the night back to their beds, Rose went up to her room alone. She got out her notebook and wrote about the weekend. She was the mother of the president, and she wanted to document every historic detail. She included in her entry an aside about her husband.

> *Joe Sr. had an attack about 10 days ago and is not at all himself but quiet—complains about a lack of taste in his mouth and feels blah—he says—for first time. I have noticed he has grown old— Sargent noticed and said he was not himself. Doctor Travell was here with Jack and says cold wind and air bad for Joe but he keeps going out.*

Hyannis Port had a brief reprieve from the presidential chaos that winter and spring. The noise from the Big House resumed in June 1962. Construction vehicles clunked down the dead-end road and dug an enormous hole to the left of the Big House. Construction began on a new swimming pool in the corner of the lawn where the rock garden had been. And an elevator was built on the east side of the house—from the outside it looked like another chimney, but it allowed Joe to move from his room to the first floor and down to the theater with ease. And a wooden ramp was constructed leading out to the lawn from the first floor.

Rose and Joe were preparing to come back to Hyannis Port from Palm Beach. Just after the family had left the Cape for Florida the previous fall, Joe had been rushed to the hospital after a morning of golf. He'd suffered a debilitating stroke from a blood clot in his brain. He was partially paralyzed and his loss of speech was near total. He could barely communicate beyond the word *no*. In the months since the stroke, Joe had been working with nurses and physical therapists and had recovered to the point of being able to swim with the proper support. He'd made progress at the pool in Florida, and it was arranged for him to have a similar one built on the Cape. It was covered over with a big bubble and kept plenty warm for his comfort.

When Joe and Rose's children began arriving with their families in the summer, they each brought their kids to see their grandfather. Out on the lawn, other than the construction of the new pool and elevator, everything was the same. The breakwater still protected the waters along the shore, the waves breaking gently along the Kennedy property. Cousins still passed back and forth between the houses. They still played touch football on the Big House lawn. But inside, it was quieter. Joe's thundering voice was gone. He was confined to a wheelchair, often wearing his bathrobe, his head tilted to the side.

"We were all required to do our time with Grandpa. It scared me," Pat's oldest son, Christopher Lawford, wrote in his memoir. "I entered the living room with the awkwardness and trepidation of a kid walking into a hospital room for the first time. I was tongue-tied and terrified that whatever had stricken the great man would find its way on to me—always fearing the unexplained, involuntary physical convulsion, which would send my grandfather into painful spasms requiring a retreat back to the elevator and his upstairs bedroom and the lonely isolation of his illness."

"Nobody knew whether he was wide-awake and his brain was fully functioning or if he was basically a vegetable. They didn't know, so the assumption was that he was wide-awake," said Bobby's daughter, Kerry.

"My father would read him the newspaper every day or someone else would and they'd have the news on and then go have a discussion with him about what was going on. We, all the kids, went over every day and gave him a kiss and visited him."

Jack and Jackie didn't return to their home that summer. They decided to stay half a mile down the road on Squaw Island, across from Ted and Joan, in the house of Joe's good friend Morton Downey. The gray-shingled, two-story house was more private—and more protected—than their home. It had twelve rooms and sat on ten acres with sweeping views of the Sound. And it had a heated pool, which was good for Jack's back. The only people who came out to Squaw Island were the handful who lived there. It was separated from mainland Hyannis Port by a narrow, sandy beach road that had the Nantucket Sound to the left and a swampy marsh to the right. It was easier for agents to monitor who came and went. A communications trailer for the Secret Service was prepared on Indian Rock, the land named for the enormous boulder on the south shoreline of the isolated bluff. A neighbor's property served as the landing port for the president's helicopter.

Across from Jack and Jackie's Squaw Island home that summer, Joan sat on her terrace with Betty Hannah Hoffman, a writer for *Ladies' Home Journal*. They were surrounded by Joan's vibrant green lawn, which was edged with sweet-smelling roses and honeysuckle. Betty noted Joan's golden hair, her "geranium-pink" shorts, her flowered top, and her two babies and nephew John playing in the warm sun as the nurse looked on, speaking to the children in French. A small white phone on the terrace rang in the middle of their conversation.

"Saddle up, Joansie!" boomed the voice on the other end of the call. "We've got a two o'clock tea at Lowell, then another one at four. There's a banquet tonight in Boston and after that a coffee in Lawrence. We should be back at Squaw Island tonight. Did I tell you six are coming for lunch tomorrow? Could you get lobster?"

Joan, taking notes, answered, "Wonderful, dear! I'll be on the first plane."

Hoffman, whose assignment was to write about what it was like to marry a Kennedy, followed along as Joan packed her suitcase then drove to the airport. Thirty-year-old Ted was in the thick of his run for Senate, and when they were all on the Cape together, his older brothers—the president and the attorney general—gave him their advice on his campaign. Jack went across the street to Ted's house to help him prepare for debates. Even though his back was once again causing him pain, Jack stood on his crutches hammering away at his brother's answers until they sounded sharp, lively, and confident.

Jackie liked to tease her brother-in-law about his political ambitions. "Well, all right now, Teddy," she said. "It's clear you're going to run, and you'll probably win. Now let's figure out when your brother is going to finish with the presidency. Jack, wouldn't you like to go back to the Senate?"

Jack chimed in, "Don't be teasing Teddy about this. He's not at the point where he can take it."

Back at the Big House, Rose spent hours standing in front of the full-length mirror on her bedroom's closet door, trying on dresses, deciding what to wear for her youngest child's events. Rose had always loved the excitement of campaigns, since she was a girl supporting her father's run for mayor. It seemed like the spotlight would be on her family forever.

Ted sat on a couch at 400 Pitchers Way in Hyannis, two miles inland from the Kennedy Compound. In 1935, when Eugenia Fortes bought that little two-bedroom on the street that wound from Hyannis Port out to Hyannis, Pitchers Way was little more than a cart path. For years, she didn't have electricity. By 1962, though, her cottage had become a refuge. Since the day in 1945 that Fortes was kicked off that beach in Hyannis Port, she'd become known as a passionate defender of civil rights on the Cape, and that cottage and the small guesthouse she built behind it were always available to civil rights leaders—or anyone else in need—as they passed through. The summers of '52 and '53 lawyers Constance Motley and Robert Lee Carter took the guesthouse, bringing their paperwork to prepare for the early 1950s' trial they were working on: *Brown v. Board of Education*. Later, Thurgood Marshall stayed there when he couldn't get a room at any of the segregated inns on the Cape. "Thurgood told me,

Genny—he called me Genny," Fortes said. "'Genny, you can't cry, no matter what. You can't cry; you have to laugh.'"

Now, Ted sat on Fortes's couch surrounded by bookcase-lined walls that showed off his host's books and coin collection. Across from him was a man named David Harris, who'd just gotten off a bus on Main Street. Harris had ridden all the way from Arkansas in his best suit and tie. And when he walked down the bus steps onto the busy street, he looked around and said it "felt mighty good when I crossed that Mason-Dixon line."

Harris was the first of many Black men and women from the South who were told that jobs were waiting for them in Hyannis. They'd seen the want ads and the posters that read: "President Kennedy's brother assures you a grand reception to Massachusetts. Good jobs, housing, etc. are promised." These seekers of a better life had given up everything they knew to start over again in the North. Most had nothing more than a shopping bag with one change of clothing, and no money. The first question most had was, "Where is President Kennedy? We were told that he was going to meet us at the bus."

What they didn't know was that the Help Wanted ads had been placed by a man named George Singlemann of the White Citizens' Councils, a network of white segregationists and supremacists. There were no jobs waiting in Hyannis, or in the other towns and cities where the Citizens' Councils had sent the buses. It was a cruel stunt that had been cooked up as a reaction to the heroic Freedom Rides the year before. Civil rights activists rode buses into the segregated South—now the White Citizens' Councils were sending busloads of Black riders up north. They sent the buses to New York, Chicago, and Philadelphia. But they sent the most people to Hyannis.

"For many years, certain politicians, educators, and certain religious leaders have used the white people of the South as a whipping boy, to put it mildly, to further their own ends and their political campaigns," said Amis Guthridge, one of the White Citizens' Councils organizers. "We're going to find out if people like Ted Kennedy . . . and the Kennedys, all of them, really do have an interest in the Negro people, really do have a love for the Negro."

The Kennedys and their magazine-cover-perfect community on the sea had captured imaginations—and were now being used as a pawn in a racist charade. Lela Mae Williams was one of the people who came to Hyannis for work after seeing one of the ads. She asked the bus driver to stop before they arrived on Main Street so she could change into her finest clothes to meet the president, whose portrait, along with Bobby's, she'd had hanging on her wall in Little Rock. The pictures hung next to a portrait of Martin Luther King Jr.

The White Citizens' Councils made sure there were plenty of reporters at each stop along the way for the "Reverse Freedom Riders," as they were called in the media. They wanted to draw press attention to their stunt. By the time the first bus got to Hyannis, there was a group of nearly a hundred people waiting for them. Fortes was there—in 1961, she helped start the first Cape branch of the NAACP, and she mobilized them to make sure that when the buses arrived in Hyannis, the people were taken to a safe place where they could stay and get help finding jobs. "It was one of the most inhumane things I have seen in my years of social action work," said Margaret Moseley, a local activist who worked with Fortes.

There was a fear that having Ted, who was running for Senate, there to talk to each person as they arrived would drum up even more press attention for the White Citizens' Councils and that they'd keep sending groups up north. So, it was arranged that Harris, the first man off the bus, would meet with Ted at Fortes's home on Pitchers Way. As they sat and talked and figured out arrangements for Harris, there was a knock on the back door. Local photographer and reporter Frank Falacci stood trying to peek in. "Hi, Frank," Fortes said, keeping him busy, distracting him with conversation as Ted quietly left the house through the front door to go back to his home on Squaw Island. Thanks to Fortes, Ted's secret meeting with Harris never made it into the papers.

There was no bus stop in Hyannis then, but the buses continued to show up, letting people out in the middle of Main Street. Fortes was there reassuring them that they'd at least have a safe place to sleep and food to eat. It was the beginning of the summer season, and there were nearly no rentals available, and very few jobs. The people were taken to Cape Cod Community College, where they were given bed linens from the Red

Cross and the local jail. One of the White Citizens' Councils organizers sent a telegram to the president's Justice Department suggesting the Kennedys open their summer homes to the new arrivals. It was clear the Kennedys didn't know quite how to deal with the stunt, including what to do with the new arrivals. When Jack was asked about it at a press conference, he stumbled over his words. "Well," he started after a long pause, "I think it's, uh, a rather cheap exercise in . . ." He trailed off without finishing his thought.

That fall, as the summer season ended, the seasonal jobs on the Cape dried up. David Harris tried opening his own barbecue business on North Street. He had experience cooking and told reporters before getting on the bus that he hoped to get a good job as a chef in Hyannis Port and then "predicted he would return to Little Rock in a few years a rich man 'with a red Cadillac.'" But by October, he wasn't making enough money to keep his business afloat. And with so many people leaving with the fall, he didn't know how he'd make it through the cold months ahead. He reached out to a lawyer he knew to see if Ted Kennedy might help him financially. But he never heard back.

The Kennedys went back to D.C., and most of their neighbors went back to their second homes—which left the so-called Reverse Freedom Riders to start over again without seasonal work. When they had to leave Cape Cod Community College, some moved temporarily to Otis Air Force Base. But most returned to the South or moved to Boston, where they thought they'd have better luck finding work. Harris had to shut down his restaurant and leave the Cape. Only one family stayed in Hyannis.

Soon after Jack and Jackie returned to Washington, they began making plans for the next summer. Jack's secretary, Evelyn Lincoln, gathered photos and floor plans of properties for rent in Wianno and Oyster Harbors—two exclusive neighborhoods in Osterville. Being in Osterville—just a ten-minute drive from Jack's family—would give them the privacy they'd loved at the Downey house that summer *and* situate them closer to their friends in Osterville, like Bunny Mellon. Jackie liked Osterville, which with its fancier golf club and estates on sprawling plots of land had a different sensibility from the Port. Hyannis Port people were plenty wealthy but still liked to point out that they weren't like those snobs over in Osterville.

The house Jack really wanted, though, was the one at the dead end of Squaw Island. At the Army-Navy game that winter, Jack talked to Downey about "the house on the point," as they called it, which sat on a bluff at the island's tip. Downey told Jack he'd tried to buy it, but that the family that owned it refused to sell. Jack told his friend he was thinking of trying to rent it. But Downey said he should just use his house again. Downey and his wife, Peg, would be staying close to New York all summer—their kids were working in the city so they wanted to rent or buy a place on the North Shore of Long Island or in Connecticut so the kids could commute to work. Peg Downey wrote to Jack to make sure he knew, "Please don't feel that your using our house is in any way 'putting us out,' as we are more than happy to be in a position to contribute in a small way to your getting some rest and relaxation."

But by the time summer rolled around, the house on the point would, for the first time in decades, be available to rent for the summer. Jack would get his wish.

That fall of 1962, Jack quietly left Washington without Jackie and the kids. Usually, for his announced visits, Jack's helicopter landed right at the end of Marchant Avenue. But this time, he landed up the hill at the golf club, where he'd draw less attention. There were no crowds of kids running down the street to greet him, no lines of photographers. Jack walked along the beach in his deck shoes and leather jacket to shield the sharp autumn wind coming off the water. He'd come home to make a decision.

A U-2 flight over Cuba had detected missile installations, which the Soviets had placed there, and Jack and his team needed to quietly decide how to bring about their removal—how to prevent a nuclear war. Some of his advisors were recommending a blockade, others an air strike. Jack's decision would be the most important of his presidency.

Later that fall, Jack was back at the compound, this time with members of his cabinet. Joe's nurse, Rita Dallas, thought to herself that something serious must have been going on as the men marched through the house with serious expressions on their faces. She watched Jack, his secretary of defense, Robert McNamara, and the rest of the cabinet go outside to the flagpole to talk in private. When they went back to D.C., Jack and his team established a blockade around Cuba. It was a risky maneuver, but it worked. Khrushchev removed the missiles.

The house at the tip of Squaw Island sat on top of a bluff, overlooking Nantucket Sound from Point Gammon in the east to Wianno and Osterville in the west. The house was sprawling and covered in weathered gray shingles. The heavy front door opened into the grand first floor with dark, polished pine floors, pastel-painted plaster walls, high ceilings, and airy open rooms. There was the dining room with its heavy-beamed ceilings and the main staircase with its turned balusters. The biggest room was the main living area, which had a built-in bench seat beyond which stood the large windows looking onto the sweeping terrace. When the sun set over the Sound, the simple wooden bench seemed to change colors as it was bathed in oranges, yellows, and reds.

The house was built by local builder L. Frank Paine in 1912—just a few years after he built the Big House. For nearly forty years, the house was owned by one family—the Browns of East Orange, New Jersey. Each of the fireplaces in the ten-bedroom home was decorated with covers emblazoned with a delicate script *B* for Brown. In 1951, the house was bought by the Thun family from Pennsylvania, who took inspiration from the *B*s all around the house and named the home Brambletyde. The Thuns spent their Augusts there with their five young children and rented out the house in July. It was almost always booked—a handful of families renting it summer after summer. In 1963, though, the Thuns would be overseas for the whole summer, so, for the first time, they needed tenants for both months.

Jackie was pregnant with their third child that summer, so the privacy and calm out on the bluff was even more important. Jack, Jackie, Caroline, and John took over Brambletyde, bringing their dog Pushinka's

rambunctious new puppies, which slid across the wooden floors and pad-
ded up and down the stairs. It was Jack's idea to have the White House
dog handler, Traphes Bryant, bring all the dogs as a surprise for John and
Caroline to help ease their transition into having another sibling. The kids
spent their long summer days howling with delight as they rolled around
with the puppies in the backyard.

On Saturday nights, White House photographer Cecil Stoughton
set up a projector in the Brambletyde living room. He clicked on the
films he'd made of the family playing and relaxing in the Port the weekend before. They watched Caroline and her cousin Maria Shriver making
faces at the camera in the cabin of the *Marlin*, their wet hair sticking to
their faces, their smiles full of crooked baby teeth. They watched Jack
and little John feeding a horse out at Grandpa's farm in Osterville, the
horse more interested in the president's hair than the apple. There were
so *many* pictures and videos of the First Family by that third year of the
presidency—by then, every magazine wanted their images on the cover.
Jackie tried her best to shield the moments like these, though. The private family moments—the kids with their cousins, the dirty knees, and
the windswept hair—were just for them. The world knew about Hyannis
Port, but nobody knew their lives inside these houses. And there was
comfort in watching themselves in their happiest moments before Jack
went back to D.C. for another week of work while Jackie stayed behind
with the kids. By the time the music faded out and the film cut to black
most of the family had gone to bed. As Stoughton broke down the projector and Jack started up the main staircase, the president said over his
shoulder, "Let yourself out, Captain."

All the bedrooms at Brambletyde were upstairs. The ceilings on the
second floor were high, too, and each of the upstairs rooms was situ-
ated so it had a view of the water. Jackie made an office of the closed-in
porch off her room and spent her days there resting and painting watercolors, which she planned to make into Christmas cards to be sold to raise
money for the National Cultural Center. With the baby due at the end
of the summer, Jackie was planning ahead. She wrote up her Christmas
lists—for her family, she'd get sweaters from the Sweater Bar, the whole-
sale shop over on Route 28.

During the week, when Jack was in Washington, Jackie's end of the hall was quiet except for her quietly speaking notes into her recorder for her secretary or the song "Mack the Knife," which she played over and over that summer. At the other end of the hall, Caroline and John played happily with their nanny, Maud Shaw—their singing and giggles cutting through the stillness on Jackie's end of the hall.

"As the days went on," Jackie's personal secretary, Mary Gallagher, would later write, "I found it stranger and stranger that such a young woman could enjoy such a remote and lonely spot. Her days, for the most part, were spent in her bedroom upstairs and the adjoining closed-in porch, which served as her office. From here, as she dictated, we could feel the strong breezes and hear the lashing of the waves against the rocks. Surely, I would think to myself as I sat there, the wind and noise must be much more discernible during the stillness of the night. How could she possibly stand it?"

But Brambletyde was a haven for Jackie. She thrived on the seclusion and peace she found there. Looking out at the ocean from her bedroom, it was easy to forget the rest of the world: the reporters and sightseers over at the compound, the pressures of being First Lady, and Jack's affairs with other women, which he'd resume as soon as he left for Washington again on Monday mornings. The wind that whipped through the house and rattled the old shutters drowned out the rest of the noise.

Back at the compound, Eunice and Pat rented Jack and Jackie's house on Irving Avenue for the summer. And Bobby's wife, Ethel, was pregnant again. She was more than nine months along, but, as with the rest of her pregnancies, she didn't slow down at all. She continued to play three sets of tennis every morning. She was out on the court July Fourth weekend when she realized the baby was on his way. Ted, now a senator and sweaty in his tennis whites, joined her on Jack's Marine One helicopter, directing them up the coast to Boston. Soon, Ethel returned with her and Bobby's eighth child, little Christopher George Kennedy, who was christened at St. Francis Xavier Church in Hyannis. His godmother, Pat Lawford, wearing a white lace veil held Christopher as Cardinal Cushing gave his blessing surrounded by more than two dozen Kennedys and a cameraman in the back of the room capturing the whole thing for that night's news. Bobby hung out of the car to wave to the crowds that had gathered outside the church as he and Ethel took their new son home to Marchant Avenue.

At the start of the summer, Jack took a diplomatic trip to Europe. His presidency, after the averted Cuban Missile Crisis the fall before, was hitting a confident stride. When he returned, he was overcome with the overwhelming positive reaction to his passionate speech in Berlin. In the Brambletyde living room, the family gathered to watch the video of the trip. Jack wanted to watch it every night. By the third night, nobody but Ted would sit and watch with him.

Jack was healthier than he'd been in decades, too—his chronic back pain was fading, to the point where he could play golf again, and he could be around Caroline's horses, because of the allergy shots he'd begun taking. He was having fun with his two kids, whose personalities were showing more and more. He liked, particularly, to carve out one-on-one time with Caroline, listening to her rambling stories, asking her questions. The pregnancy seemed to bring Jack and Jackie closer—in spite of Jack's infidelity in Washington. The last weekend in July, Jack had arranged to go to the Hyannis shopping center with the kids and his friends Red and Anita Fay. When Fay got to the house to pick everyone up, he went upstairs to Jack's room and knocked. "Come in," Jack called. Fay opened the door to find Jack and Jackie in bed together, talking quietly.

"God almighty!" Fay said. "Why did you tell me to come in? I don't want to walk in here."

"Oh, that's all right," Jack told him.

That summer, even as things hit a high, Jack seemed to be preoccupied with death. There'd been death threats against him, including a bomber who'd told the authorities he'd "looked over" the Kennedy home in Hyannis Port before going to Washington. Jack started making strange comments to people around him. After a Sunday Mass, Jack turned around to face his friend Larry Newman and two White House correspondents sitting behind him, and he said, "Did you ever think if someone took a shot at me he would probably get one of you first?"

*   *   *

As the summer wound down, Jack tried to figure out how to buy Brambletyde. He loved that house, how it sat on the bluff, how you could walk into the backyard on the grass and see nothing but sea, how the end of the yard dropped twenty feet or so to the ocean below.

"Can you imagine the way they're trying to hold me up for a hundred and fifty thousand dollars for an acre and a half or two acres?" Jack said to Red Fay one afternoon.

"What do you mean, an acre and a half or two acres?" Fay said, pointing to the calm Nantucket Sound. "You own as far as the eye can see out there. That is all yours and nobody can ever take it away. When you're buying, you're paying a hundred and fifty thousand dollars for this house, you're buying yourself two hundred thousand acres right out there."

Jackie decided they should just build their own version of Brambletyde—even though they were already building a house in Virginia. Brambletyde was her favorite of everywhere they'd lived. As soon as they'd moved in, Jackie told her secretary, "Oh, I could shoot the people who own this house . . . I'd love to buy it, but I know they will never sell it!"

She asked Jack to find out who owned the empty marshlands on Squaw Island—there was talk Jack, Ted, and Morton Downey would go in together to buy the vacant land, and that was where they'd build their Brambletyde replica. Jackie had White House photographer Cecil Stoughton take photographs of the house from each angle of the exterior. And she had measurements taken of each room. In the end, the land was too expensive, and the deal fell through. Jack might have just bought Brambletyde, despite the price tag, but he was so worried about the American public knowing he'd spent that amount on another home. So, instead, he signed another lease to rent it for the summer of '64.

Liz Mumford and her mother sailed out on Nantucket Sound, behind their house. They'd been neighbors with the Kennedys for decades now— in fact, they'd been in the Port for longer than the Kennedys—but they didn't know them well. The two families said a friendly "hi" here and there, but they each minded their own business.

There was a shadow cast over Hyannis Port that week. John McKelvy, who lived at the impressive house on Irving Avenue, the one with the big columns that tourists always thought was part of the Kennedy Compound, had died at his home on Tuesday night. Everyone knew McKelvy. He'd been coming there since he was a kid in the 1920s and had bought that house in 1939. He'd been the president of the Hyannisport Club and the Hyannis Port Civic Association. There'd be services for him at his home that Thursday.

The weather was good that week—the forecast in the local paper predicted "Good Vacation Week Before Fall Storms Speak"—so Mumford and her mom were out on the water. They looked up when they heard the rip of helicopter blades. They watched it fly over their heads, past them, over to Squaw Island.

"Jackie's gone into labor," Mumford's mother said to her. "She's gone into labor, and it's way too early."

Jackie had gone along with Caroline that morning to her riding lesson in Osterville. She hadn't been there for long when she turned to her Secret Service detail and asked him to take her back to Brambletyde. She didn't feel well. They rushed her to the car, helping her into the back seat. She looked worried. The agent called the command center as they drove down the bumpy country roads back to Squaw Island. From the back seat, Jackie pleaded with him to go faster.

"I'm bringing Mrs. Kennedy back to the house," the agent said to the agent on duty at the Secret Service command center trailer outside Brambletyde. "Get Dr. Walsh to come immediately, and put a helicopter on standby. We've got an emergency."

When they got to Brambletyde, Jackie's doctor was just arriving. After a short exam, it was clear she needed to get to the hospital right away. It was five weeks before the baby was supposed to arrive. The plan was for Jackie to go back to Washington to have the baby via Cesarean at Walter Reed Army Medical Center. But because of her past difficult pregnancies, a suite had been set up at Otis Air Force Base about a half hour west of the Port, which would be easier to get to if something were to happen while she was on the Cape. The base had a handful of open cottages, so they converted one into a private suite for Jackie. Robert Luddington, who'd helped decorate all the houses on the compound and had become friendly with Rose, was brought in to make the cottage comfortable for Jackie. She liked it there, liked that it was out in the country, quiet and comfortable. The makeover, however, had become controversial. The *Washington Post* had run a story in July with photos of the suite, reporting that the air force had spent $5,000 on its renovation. Jack had flown off the handle when he saw the story.

"Did you see the *Post* this morning? See that fella's picture by the bed?" he shouted over the phone at U.S. Air Force general Godfrey T. McHugh. "And did you see that furniture they bought from Jordan Marsh? What the hell did they let the reporters in there for? Are they crazy up there? . . . That silly bastard with his picture next to the bed! I want to find out if we paid for that furniture because I want it to go back to Jordan Marsh. And that fella's incompetent who had his picture taken next to Mrs. Kennedy's bed if that's what it is. He's a silly bastard! I wouldn't have him running a cathouse! . . . You better look into it, especially when you told me they hadn't spent a cent!"

"Well, sir, this is obviously . . ." Godfrey started before Jack jumped in, shouting: "This is obviously a fuckup!"

The furniture stayed, and none of it mattered anymore on August 7. Jack was in the air somewhere between D.C. and the Cape when the baby was born in a special section of the base that had been set up for emergency surgery. Jackie delivered a four-pound, ten-and-a-half-ounce little boy by C-section. By the time Jack arrived just after one thirty that afternoon, the baby was already in an incubator. Jack asked for the base chaplain to come right away so they could baptize the baby, whom they named Patrick Bouvier Kennedy. It was clear little Patrick's breathing problems were too severe to deal with there at the base. Jackie was transferred to the suite that had been prepared for her, and Patrick was taken in an ambulance to Children's Hospital Boston. Jack went to see Jackie one more time, then helicptered home to Brambletyde to see John and Caroline before dinner. After a short visit there, he flew to Boston to be with the new baby. Jackie would need to stay at Otis while she recovered. That night, she went to sleep in the neat twin bed in the corner of the room, knowing only that Patrick had a lung condition similar to the one her first son, John, had been born with. She slept through most of the next day, too, as Jack flew back and forth from Boston to Otis to Squaw Island. He arranged for her mother to go see her at Otis after visiting with the baby, too. When Jack came to see Jackie, he tried to make her laugh. When his friend Dave Powers came with him from Squaw Island to Otis, Jack told him, "You can't let Jackie see you in that horrible suit. Pick out one of mine and put it on." Powers put on one of Jack's expensive suits, and Jack had him model it for Jackie at her little cottage on the base. She clapped and laughed, light for a moment.

Night came again. Jackie tossed and turned until four in the morning.

Just after she fell asleep, the phone in the suite next to her rang. A minute later, another phone rang down the hall. A few minutes after that, another phone rang. At 4:04 a.m., Patrick took his last breath in Boston. Jackie's doctors and Secret Service agents talked after getting the news. They decided to let Jackie sleep instead of waking her to tell her her son was gone. She didn't find out until six thirty in the morning when her doctor told her. She was devastated. She was given a sedative and slept a couple more hours until Jack arrived, puffy-faced, at Otis.

Over the next few days Jackie's friends flew in to visit her. She stayed in the cottage while Jack went to Boston for their son's funeral. When he returned, he brought John and Caroline to see their recovering mother, past the lines of reporters and photographers popping their flashes as they walked in.

After eleven days at Otis Air Force Base, Jackie left hand in hand with Jack. "Careful," he told her, as she took the two stone steps down out of the cottage.

She spent the rest of the summer at Brambletyde, and Jack came back from Washington as much as he could, sometimes making the trip midweek. Jackie spent a lot of time in her large sun-drenched room, which shared a porch with Jack's room and looked over the ocean. The weather was good that August, so the kids' nanny took them out as much as she could, leaving the house empty and quiet except for the ocean breeze that echoed off those high ceilings. When Jackie was feeling up to it, everyone sat together on lounge chairs on the downstairs stone porch, Jack making phone calls while Jackie relaxed and the kids chased all the dogs around. Jack paid special attention to his family during that time, even bringing John and Caroline up in the helicopter.

The family all got together one last time that summer for Joe's seventy-fifth birthday. They did it up big, with a plastic tablecloth emblazoned with HAPPY BIRTHDAY draped over the fine dining table, little red-and-white-striped paper party hats, and blue and yellow balloons in the shape of bunnies tied to the back of Joe's chair. He sat there in a nicely pressed baby-blue robe, with a a broad smile as his grandchildren ran around and his children sat nearby talking to him and among themselves. Jackie, with a crisp white pantsuit, sat right next to her father-in-law, gently holding his curled hand, the way she always did when they sat and talked.

As the summer wound down, the Kennedys packed up and closed down the houses for the season. Three carloads of cousins drove to the airport, unloading more than a dozen Kennedy kids, their dogs, and a couple of turtles. Eunice shepherded the chaotic crew onto the tarmac at Barnstable Municipal Airport and onto the family plane, the *Caroline*, which would take them all home before the start of the school year. Caroline and John stayed behind to go with Jackie to her parents' home in Newport, where Jack would meet them to celebrate his and Jackie's tenth anniversary.

After their anniversary, Jack made another quick trip back to the Port. In October, he was at a fundraising dinner in Boston and flew home the next day to visit with his father. They sat together watching football games. Jack went outside for walks and talked to his old friend and neighbor Larry Newman. Newman noticed that Jack seemed distracted, preoccupied by what was happening in Vietnam. "This war in Vietnam—it's never off my mind, it haunts me day and night," Jack told him. "The first thing I do when I'm re-elected, I'm going to get the Americans out of Vietnam. Exactly how I'm going to do it, right now, I don't know, but that is my number one priority—get out of Southeast Asia."

The next morning, before getting on the helicopter waiting on the lawn to take him to Otis Air Force Base, Jack turned back to look at Joe, who sat in his wheelchair on the porch. He went back and gave his father a second kiss. His friend Dave Powers watched from the helicopter. He'd never seen Jack do that before.

When Powers and Jack were both on the helicopter, the president looked out the window with tears in his eyes and said, "He's the one who made all this possible, and look at him now."

Powers later told Jackie it was almost as if Jack had a feeling it would be the last time he saw his father. The helicopter took off for Otis, where Air Force One was waiting to take Jack to Washington. A few weeks later, he'd go to Palm Beach to spend some time with Jackie before their trip to Dallas.

Tom Gunnery sat huddled in the little white hut on the edge of the Kennedy Compound. The streets were empty on that crisp, lazy November day. Most of the summer people were gone, and Jack wasn't there so there were no photographers, no sightseers. It was the time of year that year-rounders love most—golden light casting a glow across the whole Cape. That day seemed particularly quiet. There was barely a squawk or a chirp, just a stillness that settled over the Port. Gunnery, the Barnstable police officer stationed outside Jack and Jackie's place on Irving, sat watching the small TV the officers had discreetly set up in the hut to pass the time, enjoying the peace. Right around lunchtime, a newscaster broke in, taking over the fuzzy black-and-white screen. A news bulletin. About the president. Before he could find out any other details, Gunnery reached on top of the hut to pull down the antenna perched there so nobody would know about the TV set. He knew that no matter what happened to the president, the press would soon be swarming his Hyannis Port home.

Over at the Big House, the household staff was beginning to prepare for the Thanksgiving holiday the next week. The family would all be back. There was lots to be done. Rose had gone to Mass, then she and Joe had gone for a drive to enjoy the beautiful weather and the quiet. Afterward, Rose went over to the golf course to play her usual three holes. She played the fifteenth hole with her neighbor baseball player Jimmy Piersall. Then,

she and Joe had lunch together before going up to their attached bedrooms to take their naps. As she lay in her room, Rose heard a loud radio
blaring somewhere in the house. Dora, one of the family's maids, was
listening to her favorite radio program when the news bulletin broke in.
She called out to Ann Gargan, Rose's niece who took care of Joe. Ann
ran up the stairs to her bedroom and called the Secret Service agent on
duty at Jack's house, then turned on her radio for more information. Rose
walked down to Ann's room to tell her to turn down the radio. Ann told
her she didn't know anything at all but that she had heard that the president might have been shot.

"I had a mixture of reactions," Rose later wrote. "Worry about Jack, of
course, instinctively. But then a rejection of the idea that it could be something terribly serious because, after all, he had been through so much. . . .
Further, I had trained myself through the years not to become too visibly
upset at bad news, even very bad news, because I had a strong notion that
if I broke down, everybody else in the household would."

They turned on the TV to get more information. As soon as the
screen lit, the phone rang. It was Bobby. He was calling to tell them that
Jack's condition was very serious. That he wasn't expected to live. Soon
after, they learned that Jack was gone.

Outside, state police cars lined up near the compound, along with
more Barnstable police. Knots of neighbors gathered in the streets. They
stared at one another in disbelief, mostly silent or talking in hushed tones.
They all seemed to be waiting for something: more information or some
sort of comfort. An old man in a topcoat stepped away from a small
gathering and said, "Guess I'll take a walk. Glad to see you. Had to talk
to somebody . . ." A woman walked into the post office, weeping. "It's terrible," she cried. "It's a terrible thing."

Joe woke up from his nap. Ann went to tell him about Jack, but Rose
stopped her, saying they should wait until Bobby or Ted arrived. Rose
went out and walked along the beach alone. She was out there for hours
as Ann took Joe for his regular afternoon drive, not saying a word about
Jack. She took the long way, so they'd get home too late for Joe to ask
to watch TV before dinner, as he always did. They couldn't let him learn
about his son on the news. After they got home, Joe had dinner, then

Ann persuaded him to go down to the theater for a movie. The elevator in Joe's room took him straight into the basement, where tracks had been installed so he could be wheeled right to his seat in the back corner. "Today's feature film is a new Elvis Presley movie!" Joe's driver, Frank Saunders, told him as he turned on *Kid Galahad*. "How about that! Your favorite movie actor!"

Ted and Eunice arrived at Barnstable Airport just before four thirty in the afternoon and hurried into a state police car, where their old family friend Jack Dempsey sat in the driver's seat. From the small crowd gathered at the airport, someone called out, "We're sorry, Ted." His face stern, Ted didn't respond, closing the car door.

They decided to wait until the morning to tell Joe what had happened. Ted went into his father's room and ripped the television wires out of the wall, for fear he would wake up in the night and turn on the set. Rose went out again, her hair whipping around her face as she stared at the ocean, calm from the breakwater's protection. Joe's nurse, Rita Dallas, found her outside alone, shivering.

"'I walked the beach for a while,'" Dallas remembered Rose saying, "'but the sound of the ocean against the breakwaters was so rough, angry in a way.'"

The nurse told her to come inside. She'd make her a cup of hot tea.

The next morning, Ted and Eunice told their father his second son was dead. Outside his window, the flag on the lawn flew at half-mast. That day, the wind stopped and a heavy fog rolled over the Port.

On Thanksgiving morning, Rose went to Mass at St. Francis Xavier. The streets of Hyannis and Hyannis Port were quiet. Flags still flew at half-mast; black crepe still fluttered around the Barnstable Town Office Building. On Main Street, portraits of Jack hung in the front windows. Inside the Big House, the oven heated the kitchen, and cook Mathilda banged around pots and pans, preparing the meal for the family. More than once that week before, Mathilda wondered if she should give away the turkeys. But Rose indicated—in a few words, but mostly it was just understood— they would go on with their plans for the holiday. Nobody was sure if

Jackie would come but she arrived on Wednesday, flying back to the Cape with Caroline and John after visiting Jack's grave at Arlington National Cemetery. Her exhaustion showed on her face. But as soon as she arrived, she went straight to the Big House and said to the first person she saw, "I'm here to see Grandpa." Hugging against her chest the heavy American flag that had been draped over Jack's casket, she went straight to Joe's room on the second floor. She sat on a low stool next to his bed, eye to eye with him, held his hand, and said, "Grandpa, Jack's gone, and nothing will ever be the same again for us. He's gone and I want to tell you about it." She went over all of it: leaving Washington for the trip to Dallas, the shots that had been fired by Lee Harvey Oswald, and the funeral. She left the flag for Joe, telling him as she did that she was tired and was going back to her home, but that she'd be back the next day to spend Thanksgiving with him.

The next day, the dining room table was covered in a dozen pies as the family finished their meals. Everyone tried their best to act like everything was normal, like it was any other Thanksgiving. Frank Saunders came into the kitchen and asked Mathilda, "How are they doing out there?" She stopped and looked at him. "Terrible," she said. "This is not Thanksgiving. If I look at those children, I will cry." But the family went through the motions. After dinner, they all filed out of the house for their usual touch football game. That evening, Rose went for her regular walk. And up at Squaw Island, Ted had a group of friends over to drink and tell stories and laugh. The staff was dismayed at how unaffected the family seemed to be acting.

Bobby, Ethel, and their eight children, though, stayed in McLean, Virginia, that year. Bobby couldn't bear to come back to Hyannis Port without Jack there.

The day after Thanksgiving, Jackie invited *Life* magazine writer Theodore H. White to the house on Irving Avenue she'd shared with her husband. The lease at Brambletyde was up until the next year. White's limousine turned down Irving Avenue in the rain, its headlights bouncing off the fences and the naked privet hedges. Pat Lawford was with Jackie, and Jack's friends Chuck Spalding, Dave Powers, and Franklin D. Roosevelt Jr. Jackie stood to greet the writer. She wore black slacks and a beige sweater; he noticed that her eyes were "wider than pools." They went into the living room and sat on the sofa. Jackie asked him, "What shall I say?" He suggested, "How do you want him remembered?"

The rain fell heavy on the roof, the wind gently shaking the windows as she began to tell her story, holding a gold St. Christopher's medal in her hand. She told him she wanted to live where she and Jack had lived together. "I'm going to live in Georgetown. I'm going to live on the Cape. I'm going to be with the Kennedys." Then she related each detail she remembered from that day in Dallas: the sound of the gunshot, which reminded her of the backfire of a motorcycle. She spoke so clearly and calmly, twisting the ring on her finger, sitting on the couch she'd sat on with Jack so many times before.

"There's this one thing I wanted to say," she told White before he left at two in the morning. She told him she kept thinking of a line from a song Jack loved: "Don't let it be forgot, that once there was a spot, for one brief moment, that was known as Camelot."

CHAPTER SEVEN

It was cool and dreary as the town prepared for the annual Memorial Day parade in Centerville. The *Caroline* landed in Hyannis just after lunchtime on Friday with Jackie and her children, along with her sisters-in-law Pat and Jean. When they arrived at the compound, only Joe was there—Rose would arrive later from Boston. It was just six months after Jack's death and that day felt particularly heavy—they were there to honor what would have been Jack's forty-seventh birthday. Jackie had agreed to appear on a television program to mark the occasion, inviting CBS News crews to Hyannis Port to film the special. She didn't want to do this often—to become a widow whose life revolved around the legacy of her husband. She knew that for her children to have a more normal life, she would need to move past the presidency. But she wanted to cement Jack's legacy, so before she could fade into the comfort of anonymity, she would need to do a few of these. This one was about Jack's presidential library.

As Jackie walked through her house on Irving Avenue, every memory she'd made there with Jack came rushing back. His leather golf bag sat in the closet off the living room; his suits hung pressed in his closet. You could almost hear his crutches lightly rapping the speckled wood floors; the dry crinkle of the turn of newspaper pages; the creak of his rocking chair in the living room. That old house was thick with their family's memories, and full of the nothings she'd hand-picked to make it a home for them. "When I came back everything just hit me, because this was the only house where we really lived, where we had our children, where [we kept] every little pickle jar I had found in some little country lane on the Cape," Jackie said. "And nothing's changed since we were in it. All of the memories came before my eyes."

Jackie thought it would be less lonely for her, six-year-old Caroline, and three-year-old John if they stayed at the compound that summer. Jack had signed a lease to spend a second summer at Brambletyde in '64, but after he died, the family that owned the house offered to break the lease. Instead, Eunice's and Pat's families decided to use the home for the summer. Now that Jackie and the kids were back on Irving Avenue, they'd be right next door to Rose and Joe and Bobby and Ethel and their kids. Brambletyde had been so quiet. That was what Jackie had loved about it. This summer, though, she wanted the noise.

After Rose got in from the airport, she called Jackie to invite her to join her nightly walk through the neighborhood. Jackie walked over to the Big House to meet Rose, like she'd done with Jack so many times before. "It really hits, doesn't it?" she said to her mother-in-law. They walked by the small wooden huts that had been constructed along the outline of the compound that now sat empty, monuments to the years they protected the Summer White House. They wound back to their corner of the Port, Jackie back to her house and Rose to hers. As dark settled in outside the windows, Jackie went to sleep alone in that quiet house. The next morning, Rose called over to see if Jackie wanted to join her for her morning swim. Rose had been through the loss of two other children; she knew you just had to keep moving.

When Jackie went over to the Big House, the CBS crews were doing last-minute tests of their equipment, which had been damaged in a highway accident. She sat on her mother-in-law's couch. As the red camera light turned on at four thirty that afternoon and the lights shone bright on her face, Jackie kept her composure as she looked into the lens and talked about the plans for the Kennedy Library being built on the Charles River in Boston.

"Could you tell us why President Kennedy chose this particular site?" anchor Charles Collingwood asked Jackie and Bobby, who sat across from him on another sofa.

"Well, there were a number of areas that he considered," Bobby said. "One time he even thought of putting it on Cape Cod, but he wanted a place where it'd be available to students, scholars, and really easily available to the American people." Jackie had asked Bobby to be with her for the interview, and CBS agreed to it. He held her hand, steadying her nerves.

Sunday afternoon after going to church at St. Francis Xavier, Jackie and the kids packed up. More than five hundred people crowded inside the airport to see them off as they boarded the *Caroline* with Pat and Jean. Bobby was with them, too, and before he stepped onto the plane, he walked over to the fence holding back all the onlookers. He shook hands with person after person—dozens of them—before he joined his family back on the tarmac. Bobby had never paid much attention to the crowds that followed the Kennedys—that was what Jack did.

The family came back later in the season, when the Cape warmed up. The people who worked inside the Kennedy houses whispered that summer about how quickly the family seemed to move on after Jack's death. And from the outside, things looked close to normal. Over dinner at the Big House, everyone tried to laugh and tease and carry on like they always had. Jack's friends still came to visit, which made Jack feel closer. After dinner, everyone gathered around the piano like they always had, Joan playing while the family sang loudly and out of tune. But at one point, without thinking much of it, Joan started one of Jack's old favorites. As the first notes filled the house, everyone stopped singing. Tears streamed down their faces; the facade of a normal summer cracked. Everyone quickly got up and left, going back to their homes.

Rose leaned over her diary. Her mind drifted back to the summer before, when the weekends would start with Secret Service agents walking around her yard talking about the weather conditions for Jack's helicopter landing. She thought of Joe being wheeled to the porch to see his son arrive. She imagined her granddaughter running to her son's arms. She remembered the way Jack gingerly bent down, careful of his back— something she saw, because he was her son, but the rest of the world didn't notice. She thought about today, how distracted Bobby seemed, how unsure about what was next for him. Everyone in the family seemed unsure, when just last summer everything was so clear. She wrote, "I myself keep very busy all the time, as it is the only way I can keep normal and not think about the time when we were said to be the most powerful family in the world."

That June, Ted nearly died in a plane crash while he was campaigning for reelection to the Senate in Massachusetts. The weather turned while they were up in the air, and the small plane crashed when it attempted to land. Two of the people he'd been traveling with died, and Ted was left with three broken vertebrae, two broken ribs, and a collapsed lung. As Ted lay in a hospital bed in Northampton recovering, Bobby drove up from Hyannis Port.

Bobby had shifted into the family's center, like Jack had done when Joe Jr. died. When Bobby and Ted took the *Caroline* to the Cape, it was Bobby who sat in the seat Jack always took—"the President's seat," as they called it. Ted only sat there when Bobby wasn't on board. The kids all played in Bobby's backyard, which was connected to the Big House property on the right and Jack's lawn in the back. Bobby's family was growing bigger by the year, and he and Ethel were starting to think about moving to a bigger place. But for now, his little house was loud and full of life.

After months of uncertainty, Bobby's future was starting to come into sharper focus. At the end of the summer, Bobby announced he was running for a Senate seat representing New York. In November, both Bobby and Ted won. Now out of Jack's shadow, Bobby's loud voice could be heard. In the Senate, he spoke out against the war in Vietnam and was a fierce defender of civil rights, helping start a community development center in Bedford-Stuyvesant, Brooklyn—a mostly Black part of the city suffering from underinvestment—and fighting for the Voting Rights Act of 1965. "As soon as that Civil Rights thing swept over him, he was like a whole different person," said their neighbor Nancy Tenney, who'd seen him grow from a frustrated little boy to a man afire. "It was like night and day."

When the family was all back in the Port for summer weekends, the adults pulled up chaise lounges in front of Bobby's house, taking phone calls and talking to each other. Bobby walked around in his swim trunks, his skin bronze from the sun, running his hands through his hairy chest as he talked to his kids or his guests. People poured into Bobby's house each summer. The joke among the compound staff was that if you left your car door unlocked, Ethel would have someone staying in it that night. She even converted a big playhouse in the backyard into a guesthouse to account for overflow. Instead of the men in suits from Jack's administration, there were athletes like boxers José Torres and Muhammad Ali, Olympic gold medalist Rafer Johnson, or NFL player Rosey Grier, who played right along with the kids. Bobby was always the quarterback, standing in the middle of the group, huddling everyone in close to explain his plays.

"I can remember playing football with [the] Washington Redskins' Sam Huff and Rafer Johnson, being in a huddle with my father, and my father saying, 'Sam, you go long and to the left and Rafer you go long . . . and that will empty out the center. Now David, you go straight into the center and I'll throw it to you,'" Bobby's seventh child, Kerry, remembered about how her father set up her brother to be the star of the game. "He had his order of priorities straight. He was going to use all these great players but the point is the children."

But just like he was when he was a kid, Bobby was aggressive and competitive. Jack had always softened his little brother, diffusing his ferocity with a joke or a laugh when he exploded with anger after a bad play. Bobby hated to lose, and he expected the same intensity from his family. In Ethel, Bobby found his match—the two of them delighted in their intense, untamed brood. The Kennedy spouses were beginning to make their mark on the family dynamics.

From a distance, the new generation of cousins blended as they ran through the neighborhood indistinguishable to the neighbors whose lawns they ran through. Same big, toothy smiles; same thick, wavy hair; same exuberance and athleticism. There were subtle differences in the various branches, though—and there was a healthy rivalry within the family tree.

They usually split up for touch football or baseball with one side yelling, *Shrivers are better than Kennedys!* And the other echoing back, *Kennedys are better than Shrivers!* Bobby and Ethel's kids had a wildness—they always seemed to be jumping from roofs, falling out of trees and windows.

On the Shriver side, the influence of Eunice's husband, Sarge, was clear, too. Sarge, who'd been the head of the Peace Corps under Jack, was steady, gentler, more forgiving than the Kennedys. Eunice and Sarge took their time finding a house. They rented around the Port while Eunice looked at dozens of places before she finally found the perfect home in 1966 by the golf course on one of the highest points of Hyannis Port, a large house to which the Shrivers added an extra wing, making it the largest of all the Kennedy homes in the Port.

"I called the New York office to ask, 'Do I have enough money to buy this house?'" Eunice said. "And they said yes, so I assume that Daddy made grants to [us kids] and those were the grants that we used to buy the houses."

Eunice liked, too, that the house gave her family a little bit of distance from the rest of the Kennedys. It was just a ten-minute walk down the hill to Marchant Avenue, but that was enough of a walk to mean her family could have the space for a quiet afternoon when they needed one.

When Sarge was with his in-laws in Hyannis Port, he usually stood back, fading into the background, finding his own routines, while Eunice went off with her family. One afternoon, Bobby, the oldest Shriver kid, fell after running headfirst into a cousin during one of the football games on the lawn, and he began to cry. His uncle Bobby shouted the refrain he'd heard so many times from his father, Joe: "Kennedys don't cry!" Sarge walked over to his son and picked him up. "It's okay," Sarge said to his son as he helped him up. "You can cry. You're a Shriver!"

A 168-foot yacht slowly made its way up to the Big House, a growing smudge of black where the blue water met the blue sky. The people who lived along Lewis Bay were used to the sailboats and little motorboats that freckled the shoreline, and now the tour boats announcing the locations of the Kennedy homes—but nothing like this. The yacht parked about one hundred feet from shore and people walked out onto the deck, squinting at the crowds gathering below them. When the group on the shore saw the older man standing with a much younger woman, they knew it was Frank Sinatra and his girlfriend, actress Mia Farrow. Sinatra wore a short-sleeved shirt that hugged his paunchy middle, and Farrow's bright blond braids hung low, nearly meeting her bubblegum-pink pants. Sinatra and Farrow squinted at the shore and the photographers that had their big cameras trained on them. All week, the papers had been reporting that Sinatra rented a boat called the *Southern Breeze* from a Texan for $2,000 a day. He and twenty-year-old Farrow, from the TV series *Peyton Place*, brought along actresses Rosalind Russell and Claudette Colbert and their husbands for the trip. The rumors were that they were heading for Hyannis Port after their stop across the bay in Edgartown. So when the yacht turned into the bay, the photographers were ready while the neighbors reached for their binoculars, aiming them at the horizon instead of the Kennedy lawn where the helicopter used to land.

Two Barnstable police department boats circled the yacht as Sinatra took a smaller boat over to the pier, where Pat Lawford came out to greet him with a hug. He walked across the Big House lawn and disappeared inside to sit with his old friend Joe Kennedy. While Sinatra was inside, Mia walked up to the News Shop to buy a stack of the day's newspapers. After about half an hour, she met Sinatra back on the pier and they motored back to their friends waiting on the yacht. As the sun set on the horizon just beyond the *Southern Breeze*, one of the little boats traveling with the yacht motored over to the pier at the end of the Big House to pick up a woman, dressed in a simple white blouse, black pants, and a kerchief around her hair. The neighbors and photographers thought it was Jackie going over. But it was Pat, who'd been close with Sinatra for years because of their overlapping lives in California. Sarge and Eunice took their own boat over. And they all had dinner: steaks broiled on the charcoal fire on the upper deck.

That night, Rob Stewart, who'd been a summer cop protecting the compound a few years prior, had a dream he was out there on the yacht, invited to a party with the movie stars and the glamorous Kennedys. Jackie always asked Stewart to walk with her when she went to pick flowers in the garden because of the tourists who lined Irving Avenue. And once when Jackie had ordered lobsters for dinner and Jack's plane arrived too late, she gave them to Stewart to take home. When Stewart told his wife about his dream about being on the yacht, she told him: "You dream too much." The next morning, he went for a walk on the beach to see if the yacht was still there. It was gone, on to the Vineyard. He leaned over and saw an empty vodka bottle floating in and out along the shore.

As Bobby walked along the Los Angeles beach, he thought about Hyannis Port. Six of his children had been flown cross-country to give him a much-needed day of family time, a break from the busy campaign schedule that had left him exhausted that spring of '68. The enthusiasm for his presidential bid was beginning to turn up as he barnstormed through California, and now the primaries were here. But before that, he went out to the water's edge with his kids. They talked about the Atlantic versus the Pacific Oceans. Bobby said he preferred the waters of Cape Cod.

That spring, Bobby, Ethel, and sometimes their older kids zigzagged across the country as Bobby campaigned for the presidency. He was running against Vice President Hubert Humphrey and Senator Eugene McCarthy for the Democratic nomination, and there was an electricity to his campaign, which was especially clear as he passed through mostly Black or Hispanic districts. That spark of anger his neighbors had seen in him as a little boy was now directed at injustices—he was passionate and he was galvanized. He gave people hope.

Before he left for the primaries, Bobby went home to Hyannis Port to see his father.

"Dad," he told Joe, "I'm doing it just the way you would want me to—and I'm going to win." He explained to his father he was going to California in a couple of days, and that he was going to fight hard. Dinner that night was festive. But Joe's nurse, Rita Dallas, later wrote that she noticed fear and tension flashed across Rose's face when Bobby told her she'd be the mother of two presidents. After dinner, Bobby wheeled his father over to the elevator and up to his room on the corner of the second floor. He gave Joe a kiss goodbye and told him again, "I'm going to win this one for you."

After he left, construction crews descended on Bobby's house next door. Ethel had planned a surprise remodel of the house for Bobby to see when he came home. It was a quick freshen-up—new windows, fresh paint. Everyone was looking forward to the returns coming in from California, which they were sure would confirm Bobby's path to the nomination.

The morning of June 5, the nurse on duty for Joe, Bea Tripp, went to wake Rose for Mass. Ever since Jack's death, Rose had a hard time falling asleep. She paced the floors alone at night then worried she'd wake up too late to go to church. So each morning the night nurse on duty for Joe woke her. Before the nurse knocked on the door, she heard the muffled sound of a television turning on inside the room. Then the heavy door swung open, and Rose stood in the doorway.

"It's Bobby!" Rose cried. "It's Bobby!"

Then the door slammed shut again.

Her niece Ann Gargan came down the hall. She'd been called in the middle of the night and was told Bobby had been shot just after midnight at the Ambassador Hotel in Los Angeles. Ted and Jean's husband, Stephen Smith, were calling all night to give updates. Bobby was still alive but would undergo surgery to remove the bullet in his skull. Ann had been told not to tell Rose or Joe. But Rose had seen for herself when she turned on the TV that morning.

Rose called Frank Saunders and asked him to take her to Mass. She said it so quietly, he barely heard her through the phone. When he got to the Big House, Rose was ready in all white with dark glasses shielding her face. As they drove up Scudder Avenue and over to South Street to the little white church, she didn't say a word. She went in through the side door just before the services started at seven, avoiding the crowd starting to form near the front door, and made her way to the pew near the front on the left side, as she always did. She sat alone, no expression on her face. The pastor finished his sermon, addressing the congregation: "I cannot express to Mrs. Kennedy the sorrow I feel, and the sorrow I am sure you all feel, here today. We offer our sincere sympathies and prayers to her and the Kennedy family." As everyone else filed out, Rose stayed in her pew for another fifteen minutes, making the sign of the cross. When she finally left, the crowd of reporters and photographers shouted questions.

Have you talked to Bobby?

How do you feel?

When she got back home, Rose went to her room to compose herself, then she went to Joe's room, closing the door behind her. When she came back out into the hallway, she was crying. She asked Joe's nurse to go sit with him. She didn't want him to be alone. When Dallas went in, she realized the television was on, "cruelly blaring out the news," she later wrote. She turned to Joe to see tears streaming down his face.

The family's neighbor Dr. Rodger Currie offered up his house as a press center. The Curries hadn't lived there long—they'd bought the gray-shingled house down Irving Avenue from the Falveys in 1959. Now, the telephone company began installing the proper phone lines. Rose left the house again at around noon, walking through her lawn over to Bobby's, where the construction team worked on the renovation. She continued over to Jack's, lost in her thoughts, bouncing a tennis ball on Jack's driveway for a few minutes before walking back through her sons' yards to her own. Then she took the car for a drive through the streets of Hyannis Port, past the News Shop, with postcards of her family's homes spinning out front and paperback copies of *The Death of a President* on display inside. Finally, she went back home to wait for more news. For the rest of the day and night, the hum of the televisions filled the house, the staff gathering around the sets waiting for any news about Bobby's condition. He died that night, twenty-five hours after he was shot.

On Monday, after Bobby's funeral, Ted flew back home to see his father—the last living son. More than two hundred people stood under umbrellas watching the senator arrive at the Hyannis airport in the rain, with no coat or hat. He didn't say a word.

Before Bobby died, the refrain "Where is Ethel?" was the heartbeat of the RFK property—he seemed to say it without thinking, as he played football on the lawn, when he was out on the boat, as he walked around the house. That summer, after she returned to Marchant Avenue, Ethel had a jukebox installed in her garage, which played loud music day and night, drowning out the quiet.

The renovations on Bobby's house finished and the rest of the summer went on. Another summer steeped in grief. To the outside world, Ethel seemed to handle her husband's death better than could be imagined. She consoled her friends, told her family to be strong like Bobby would have wanted. But her grief could be seen in her intensity. She was halfway through her eleventh pregnancy when her husband was killed, and just as with every other pregnancy, she continued to play tennis. But now she played with a fury. After losing a doubles game with mountaineer Jim Whittaker against singer Andy Williams and writer Art Buchwald, she kneeled on the court and banged her head against it. They played a rematch in the morning, where Ethel hit the ball so hard it smashed Buchwald in the face before he could lift his racket. That day, Ethel's side won.

Bobby and Ethel's children tried to make sense of it all—this second bout of family grief feeling familiar but even more intense—and now the eyes were on *them*: How would the Kennedys go on? As people came in and out of the house, they tried to overhear the quiet grown-up conversations. There were filmmakers working on a memorial film, and writers like Arthur Schlesinger who brought over manuscripts of *Thirteen Days: A Memoir of the Cuban Missile Crisis*, which Bobby had written before he died. Newspapers were sliced up, articles clipped out about the upcoming trial of Sirhan Sirhan, the man who killed Bobby. One morning, as they stumbled downstairs for breakfast, sculptor Robert Berks sat in the sunroom shaping three clay pieces, turning them into a replica of their dead father's head.

During the long nights, Ethel locked her door, so if the children had a bad dream or couldn't sleep, they went into the room of their nanny, Ena Bernard. Bernard traveled back and forth with the family from Hickory Hill, their house in Virginia, to the Cape, where she had a small, neat room on the second floor. The children climbed into her narrow twin bed—Bernard always slept on her side to make room for the two, three, or four little Kennedys lined up against her.

Jean and her husband, Stephen, left Hyannis Port a few years after Bobby died, selling their house at the start of Marchant Avenue. Stephen had been incredibly close with Bobby. They just couldn't stand being in Hyannis Port without him there. It was so different now.

Everyone still called the house on Irving Avenue "the President's house," and they all still called the house in the middle of Marchant Avenue "Bobby's house" or "the RFK house." Of course, the Big House would always be "the Big House." But with Bobby and Jack gone and Joe unable to communicate, Hyannis Port became something of a matriarchy, with the widows left to run things, with the help of their revolving cast of governesses, sailing instructors, and "Irish bunnies," as Ted Kennedy called the young women Ethel brought over from Ireland for the summer. There were cooks who came and went and drivers. There were the regulars, locals who worked for the family, like Wilbert the landscaper, who'd been there forever, and his young apprentice, Arthur, who sometimes snuck down to the dunes to take naps. And there were the employees who were more like family—like Bernard, and Provi Paredes, Jackie's personal assistant—who went anywhere the families went. A whole little world existed in those three connected properties. The people who worked there became close. They traded stories and gossip. The hours were long, but there was such a sense of loyalty among those who worked for the Kennedys. Especially then, with everything the family had just gone through. These facilitators of Kennedy family life had a front-row seat to history. And how could anyone else understand what it was like inside the boxwood hedges of the compound?

Thursdays were when all the staff had off and the families went down to the beach club for a picnic dinner, and some of the younger women who worked for the family hitchhiked to the nightclubs, like the Mill Hill Club over in West Yarmouth, or the Melody Tent theater in Hyannis. One evening, Jackie's assistant Kathy McKeon and her friend Eileen, who worked in Jackie's kitchen, flagged down a ride on Irving Avenue. They didn't notice that the man who pulled over to pick them up was leaving from the driveway of the President's house. Once they got in, the driver turned around to ask, "Where are you girls going?" It was then they realized that his broad, friendly face was familiar. It was former secretary of defense Robert McNamara, just leaving after dinner with Jackie. But they just answered, "The Mill, please. We're going to the Mill." He drove them there, and they never said a word to Jackie.

Next door at Ethel's, when all the guests were gone, the door closed, just Ethel and the children left, the staff held their breath. Nobody ever seemed to cry outside of the youngest ones getting upset over a scraped knee. When would they collapse under the grief?

When the documentary *Robert Kennedy Remembered* aired, the family piled into the living room and huddled around the television. There was their father in his office, his sleeves rolled up, hand in a pocket, slouched in a chair, phone to his ear. Standing behind a microphone, telling his audience they should be angry at the injustices in the world, that they should do something about it. The children watched themselves, just months younger than their current selves, running in and out of frame, their father smiling his crooked smile at them. They watched dry-eyed. The tears rarely came. When you looked closely, though, you could see the cracks.

"How can Ethel handle this herself with all these kids, and pregnant with another baby?" Jackie said to McKeon one day, as she walked out to meet with David again. Twelve-year-old David had been with his father in California, alone in the hotel room watching the news coverage of his dad's assassination as it happened. David came home broken. Jackie would go over to Ethel's to sit with him quietly on the porch, holding his hand or hugging him.

Ted spent the beginning of the summer of '68 in virtual solitude. He walked for hours along the beach that connected Squaw Island to the mainland, the same beach Jack had walked along when he learned Joe Jr. was killed, where Rose had walked when she learned Jack was killed. He walked the familiar sand and sailed the familiar waters of Nantucket Sound, alone. He'd taken up painting after his plane accident four years earlier, but his art that summer was darker than it had ever been, heavy clouds on horizons, boats with taut moorings knocked past the security of the breakwall behind the Big House.

He chartered a big sailboat—a sixty-five-foot yawl with three sails. He wanted to take the family sailing—as many as could fit on the boat. They went back and forth to Nantucket a couple of times, up and down

Long Island Sound, the Vineyard, and Nantucket Sound. Jackie and the kids came, Ethel and all her kids, too. As the summer came to a close and the air turned sharp, they went all the way up to Maine. Some days Ted laughed his big, booming belly laugh, made jokes, raised hell, reveling in being surrounded by his friends and family. Other days, he woke up morose, docked the boat, and went for walks along whatever shore he swam up to. After everyone else went to sleep, Ted sat in the silence, staring up at the North Star bright in the black night as the water gently rocked the boat. "I gazed at the night sky often on those voyages," Ted wrote in his memoir, "and thought of Bobby."

It was Ted's cousin Joe Gargan who had the idea to host the women who'd been working on Bobby's campaign in Hyannis for a barbecue that summer—a way to thank the "boiler room girls," as some called them, who were hit incredibly hard by Bobby's death. They could go for a sail on the boat Ted had rented for a three-day trip to Nantucket. Twelve women flew into Hyannis, four staying at Gargan's house, half a mile up from the compound, four more at a friend's house on Squaw Island, and a few others at their family houses in Harwich. Joan Kennedy invited the group to her and Ted's house on Squaw Island. "I had told her earlier that they were all coming," Gargan said. "She invited them up to her house and had a lovely cocktail party [there] at which she was very gracious and very nice to everybody."

That night, Gargan had the group over in his backyard for steaks. The night ended with everyone jumping into the water, swimming out to the anchored boat they'd be taking for their excursion the next day. The next morning, they set sail for Nantucket. Ted wasn't at the cocktail party, or the dinner at the Gargans, and he didn't set sail with the group that morning. That summer, he also skipped one of his favorite events of the year: the Edgartown Regatta. He wasn't up for it.

Jackie walked up to the News Shop with Caroline and John in the stale late-August heat. She wore a bright yellow sundress and big black sunglasses. She was barefoot with her hair pulled into two pigtails as she bought the kids ice cream cones and gathered up a pile of magazines.

She bought *McCall's* and *Life* and on top of the stack was *Ladies' Home Journal*, with Ted and Joan's picture on the cover. The headline read "The Ted Kennedys Conquer Fear." As the tourists in the shop began to recognize Jackie, she inched closer to the magazine stand, ducking her head to avoid attention. The red-haired girl at the cash register rang her up. Then, seven-year-old John took off down the street, shirtless on his bike. That day, everyone was talking about Ted and whether he'd run for president.

"The feeling around here is that he shouldn't run," fourteen-year-old Craig Ashworth told a local reporter. Ashworth was a bait boy on a local fishing boat, and his twin brother played in a band with David Kennedy and some other kids in town. "Nobody talks about it much. I know the Kennedy kids well. They don't talk about it much either."

"This is Republican territory," said boat captain Homer Phinney. "We're all Republicans up here and have been for years. Everybody knows when Jack was elected, it was the money that did it. Everybody knows that."

Over on Squaw Island, the phone in Ted and Joan's house rang constantly as his party met in Chicago for the Democratic National Convention. After Bobby died, Ted had mostly disappeared from Washington. "He just went to the Cape and stayed there. He hadn't made any appearance in the Senate," said Milton Gwirtzman, an advisor to both Bobby and Ted. "There was a movement that he had nothing to do with to run him for President, but he just didn't want to be involved with politics at all. He later said that politics stopped being fun for him in 1968."

It was enough for Ted, at that point, to just make it through each day, trying to keep it together for his family. The whispers around town, though, were that Ted's drinking was getting worse. It was a way for him to escape, to keep moving forward, to not think about everything the family had lost in the last five years. As the summer drew to a close, Ted went back to Washington and threw himself into his work. He kept his eye on the event marked on his calendar for the middle of the next July: the Edgartown Regatta, which he'd skipped the previous summer. Ted and his brothers had been sailing in that race since Ted was a kid. It was at the Edgartown Regatta where Jack won his last race on a cold, foggy day in 1949—both Joe Gargan and Ted had been on board with him.

The whole town of Edgartown, about forty miles from the Port on Martha's Vineyard, treated the race as a holiday weekend, with celebrations and parties. Rose Kennedy always knew it was time to set the table for dinner at the end of that weekend when she saw the sails coming back home on the horizon.

The next summer came, and on Friday morning, July 18, 1969, Ted flew from Boston to Martha's Vineyard Airport to race the *Victura*, the sailboat Jack had gotten for his fifteenth birthday. The weekend of the Edgartown Regatta had finally arrived. Joan stayed home in Squaw Island, pregnant with the couple's fourth child.

The next afternoon, Ted came back to Hyannis Port. Something terrible had happened.

Rose had agreed to speak for the third year in a row at the St. Francis Xavier Church bazaar on July 19. She'd been a huge draw at the previous bazaars, with crowds gathering around her on the South Street lawn in front of the church to get her autograph or get a picture with the Kennedy matriarch. As she left the house that Saturday morning, her niece Ann called her back in. There'd been an accident involving Ted. A young woman was dead. A message was sent over to the church with Rose's regrets: she wouldn't make it to the bazaar this year.

The phone rang just after 2 p.m. at Ted's house on Squaw Island. A reporter from the *Boston Globe* asked where Ted was. Someone on the other end of the line said they didn't know. The reporter asked where Joan was. She was attempting to rest in an upstairs bedroom, the person told the reporter.

An hour later, a small, chartered plane landed at Barnstable Airport. Without waiting for directions from the control tower, the plane hurriedly taxied to the parking area. The passenger door flung open and Ted walked out, his lips in a line, his face wet with sweat. He jogged quickly to a waiting blue car. The line boy working at the airport told a reporter Ted "looked in a state of semi-shock." Ted was driven back to Hyannis Port. Black cars streamed down Irving Avenue, men in suits passing in and out of the Big House, filing into the president's old living room.

Most of Ted's siblings flew in. Jackie, who'd arrived from Greece, turned her house over to be used as a headquarters for the advisors there to help Ted. They were Jack and Bobby's men: Jack's secretary of defense, Robert McNamara, and Burke Marshall, Jack's Justice Department's civil rights division chief. When they'd last been together in Hyannis Port, they'd been advising the president or the attorney general. Now, they were huddled there trying to save the family's name and the hope of another Kennedy president.

By the time Ted landed at the airport that Saturday, it had already hit the news that a former Kennedy secretary had drowned off the island of Chappaquiddick, just to the east of Edgartown on the Vineyard. There weren't many more details out by that point. Most people didn't know yet that Ted, his cousin Joe Gargan, and Ted's friend Paul Markham, the former U.S. attorney for Massachusetts, had been at a party for the women who'd worked for Bobby, the so-called boiler room girls. Joe had rented a house on the little island, where they held a reunion for the women for a second summer in a row. Ted and one of the women, Mary Jo Kopechne, had left the party together. Ted was the one driving the car, which ran off a rickety bridge and ended up in the water below. He somehow got out of his Oldsmobile while Kopechne was left to drown. After swimming to shore Ted returned to the party, then he, Gargan, and Markham went to the scene of the accident and dove into the water, trying to get Kopechne out. They couldn't save her. They told Ted he had to report the accident as soon as possible. But he didn't report it for hours—until the next morning, when Kopechne's body was found in the car. After he finally reported the accident, Ted gave a written statement to the police on Chappaquiddick then left for Hyannis Port. But it would be days before the whole story was in the news.

In Hyannis Port, the neighbors watched out the windows as car after car drove down Marchant Avenue. Outside the Big House, more reporters were arriving by the hour. It was starting to look like '68 or '63 or even '60. The phones inside the Big House rang repeatedly.

Will the senator be making a comment?

Is anyone in the family available for a phone call?

Can you tell us anything?

Rose walked with Ted out to the flagpole in the yard, where the presidential flag had flown six summers before. Nobody could hear what she said to her youngest son. But she'd taken him outside into the heavy, humid afternoon, away from all the men coming in and out of her house. It was the one place they could talk, mother to son, without anyone listening or interjecting a political opinion.

"He was so unlike himself it was hard to believe he was my son," Rose wrote. "His usual positive attitude, which he displayed so clearly at other times of difficulty, had vanished. He was disturbed, confused, and deeply distracted, and sick with grief over the death of the young woman."

Ted went upstairs to see his father, who'd gotten worse after Jack's death and worse still after Bobby's. Ted told his father that there had been an accident. He'd stopped by a party, a woman wanted a ride to catch the ferry, he'd taken a wrong turn, they ended up in the water, and he'd gotten out. He'd tried to save her, he told his father, but he couldn't. Some things were going to be said about him, Ted said, but it was an accident.

Joe's nurse, who later wrote about the scene, watched as he nodded, patted his son's hand, and closed his eyes.

"When I talked at first to Ted after he was back in Hyannis Port he was so upset he didn't . . . the question really was where to begin," said Burke Marshall. "I advised him to have a medical examination. He truly did not know whether he might have had a medical problem. He was obviously disoriented, but he appeared coherent."

The lawyers Ted had hired in the negligence case—he was being accused of leaving the scene of an accident—had advised him not to say a word. The silence emanating from Hyannis Port, along with the image of some of the most powerful men in the country descending to form a barrier around Ted while a woman's tragic death remained unexplained, quickly turned the public mood against him. Protestors lined the streets of Hyannis Port, waving American flags and holding signs reading, "WHAT REALLY HAPPENED?" and "ANSWER OUR QUESTIONS." Thousands of letters addressed to Ted piled up in the little red post office—so many that bags had to be sent over to the bigger post office in Hyannis. It was clear Ted needed to say something. He needed to explain what happened that night; he needed to tell the public whether he'd resign his Senate seat; he needed to say something. Ted Sorensen, who'd been responsible for so many of Jack's most famous speeches, was one of the men at Jackie's house when they started drafting a statement for Ted. Something that would be the final word on what happened that night; something that would preserve the family's legacy. Milton Gwirtzman suggested adding the line, "And I know that because of this, I will never be able to seek the Presidency." Eunice, who'd arrived along with Pat, Jean, and her husband, Stephen, took that line out.

All three television networks agreed to air Ted's statement live on July 25, 1969. The sound technician arrived on the Cape to set up at Ted's house, but after driving down the narrow causeway to the island, he parked his van at the entrance. He got out, walked around to the front of the van, looked at the two pillars at the entrance to the only road onto the island, and realized he couldn't fit his equipment through. The speech would need to take place at the Big House.

Heavy TV cables snaked down Marchant Avenue, while inside Ted prepared to deliver the anticipated speech on live TV. Rose was in the sunroom with Stephen, Jean, and Pat. Joan had come over from Squaw Island. A light layer of makeup was applied to Ted's face, then he took a seat behind the desk. Books had been stacked beneath the desk and chair so that the camera was eye level for Ted, dressed in a neat suit and tie. At exactly 7:30 p.m. the feed cut in, and Ted spoke straight into the camera, gripping the white pages of his speech in his hands. Behind him, the rows of red and gold book spines and the 1790s gilt leaf and painted mirror looked familiar to people watching at home. It was where his family had stood nearly nine years earlier for their only group photograph the day Jack was elected president.

Outside, the reporters and photographers gathered around a radio that had been set up across from the tall fence surrounding Jack's house on Irving Avenue. Most had been there for days, taking notes on which powerful Kennedy ally had arrived and the comings and goings of each family member, and gossiping with one another about rumors they'd heard, but the fatigue was starting to set in. The teenagers who'd been whacking a tennis ball with their lacrosse sticks in the street stopped what they were doing, drifting closer to the radio. Kids who'd been riding their bikes through the neighborhood after dinner pulled over to listen, too. The streets were silent except for Ted's voice coming through the radio.

My fellow citizens . . .

It was the familiar voice of their neighbor who was just a couple hundred feet away, inside the house at the end of the street. In his speech, Ted walked through what happened the night of July eighteenth on Martha's Vineyard. When he talked about almost drowning on his second attempt to find Kopechne one of the reporters stopped his note-taking to chuckle to himself. A young kid shot the reporter a dirty look.

Every couple of words, Ted looked up at the camera, his brow furrowed. A few minutes in, he put down the speech, looking straight into the camera, an effort to show that he was sincere, speaking directly to the people of Massachusetts, his voters. But just behind the camera, his cousin Joe Gargan held cue cards with the next portion of the speech.

I pray that I can have the courage to make the right decision. Whatever is decided, whatever the future holds for me, I hope I shall be able to put this most recent tragedy behind me and make some further contribution to our state and mankind, whether it be in public or private life. Thank you and good night.

The camera cut to black. Outside, reporters waited, hoping Ted or someone else from the family would come out to make a comment. Nobody came out of the house. A group of shaggy-haired neighborhood kids came down the street, and one of the reporters noticed that two of them were Bobby Kennedy Jr. and his little brother David. Bobby Jr. scowled at the reporters. But David, who had a cast on his foot from a football accident days before, stopped to answer questions. He said he and some of his family had watched the speech at Ted's house on Squaw Island. Then he tried to deflect the attention to his embarrassed friend. "Interview him, he's the celebrity!" David said, before walking off to catch up with his older brother.

The reporters and photographers finally left, hurrying back to their newsrooms to file their stories on deadline. The Big House emptied out: the film crew, the reporters, the advisors. It was just the family again. Upstairs, Joe Kennedy lay in his bed. The television, which was almost always on, was turned off. He hadn't watched the speech. Ted came upstairs as soon as he was done to tell his father he'd done the best he could.

At the end of the summer, Joe's condition worsened. He barely ate. His eyes were wet with tears. On November 18, his nurse rang the bell. Everyone who was at home knew what it meant: that it was the end. Jackie ran across the lawn in her bare feet. Joan and Ted arrived and stood beside Ethel. Eunice and Sarge were there. Jean and Stephen were next to them. Joe's nurse asked for his rosary. Jackie brought it over. Rose laid it in Joe's hands. Eunice began the Our Father. One by one, each person around the bed recited a line as they looked down at Joe. Rose held her husband's hand as he took his final breath.

Ted walked the beach, as he had so many times before. Tears streamed down his face. He would rarely talk about his many moments of grief over the next decades of his life. He would almost never speak of the accident at Chappaquiddick. But in the memoir he wrote in his final years that was published after his death, he wrote about that walk on the beach: "I wondered whether I had shortened my father's life from the shock I had visited on him with my news of the tragic accident on Chappaquiddick Island. The pain of that burden was almost unbearable."

CHAPTER EIGHT

Fifteen-year-old Bobby Kennedy Jr. sat in a diner on Main Street in Hyannis as the walls around him melted. He tried to focus on the slimy plate of wormy white noodles in front of him but when he tried piercing them with his fork, they seemed to slither away. Slowly, deliberately, he chewed the heavy blob of pasta in his mouth. Was eating always so difficult? He swallowed. Then he looked up to see photos behind the counter of his father, his uncle Jack, and Jesus, each with his hands folded in prayer. A chill went down his spine.

Earlier in the night, Bobby had tried LSD for the first time, swallowing a pill given to him by a neighbor friend. He'd write about the whole experience decades later. A group of kids in town had taken the LSD in protest of local boy Charley Kirby being drafted into the Vietnam War. Bobby hung back when they draped a North Vietnamese flag across the post office intersection, but he was ready to rebel. Up until that point in his life, the teenager had never taken a drug. It was against Emperor Frederick II's rule forbidding inebriation among falconers—a credo that, as a lover of wildlife, he followed dutifully. But Bobby was starting to realize there was a lot about his parents' generation he disagreed with. Adults were probably wrong about drugs, too, he thought. Plus, one of the kids told him he'd hallucinate dinosaurs. But looking up at those images of his father, his uncle, and Jesus staring down at him, he felt like he'd made a mistake. "Until that moment everything had been a delight; my soul was happy with this strange adventure, and I was laughing along with my friends," Bobby would later write in his memoir, where he described that night. "Now things turned sour." His father, the most straight and narrow of all the Kennedys, would never have dabbled in drugs. What would he have thought of his son sitting here high? Bobby got up and left, walking the three dark, quiet miles back to his house along the streets he knew by heart. The closer he got to home, the quieter and darker it got. A living room light flashed here and there but mostly the streets were lit by the moon. *I swear*, he thought as he turned down Marchant Avenue, *I'll never do drugs again.*

Months later, Ethel and her kids were up at the Shriver house for dinner. If Ethel's cook was off, they'd go to the Shrivers' and vice versa. The doorbell rang. A group of Barnstable police officers stood at the door with news that Bobby Kennedy Jr. and the oldest Shriver boy, Bobby, were accused of possessing marijuana. The teenagers had been caught up in drug raids happening around town a few weeks earlier in early July 1970. An undercover federal agent had befriended Bobby Jr., his cousins, and some of their friends and offered the boys a ride to Cohasset to get a trained falcon Bobby had lost the week before. Bobby's arm was in a cast—he'd recently broken it after falling from a tree across from the compound trying to recapture the bird. The agent offered the ride in exchange for joints—a trade the boys were happy to make because they didn't yet have cars.

That knock on the Shrivers' door marked the start of a slow-motion nightmare for the boys. Eunice arranged for a barber to come cut her son's long hair into a crew cut. And when Sarge came home, he took the boy into his bedroom and sat him on the edge of the bed. Sarge pulled up a chair, coming face-to-face with his oldest son.

"Listen," he began, "you are a good kid. Don't listen to anybody else. I'm your father, and I am going to take care of you. Do you understand me?"

"Yes, sir," Bobby Shriver said.

The media coverage of the arrests was seismic for the small town. When the boys arrived at Barnstable County Juvenile Court, they were met by a herd of onlookers, nearly one hundred reporters, and seventeen television cameras. There were so many people by the compound that

Barnstable police were sent to control the crowds. Adding to the spectacle, the boys' uncle Ted flew from Washington to Providence, Rhode Island, before getting in a private car that would bring him to Hyannis Port. Ted told reporters, "The family informed me in Washington this morning. I'm going to the Compound to talk to the parents of the children involved. I'd rather not say any more until I find out the details of what happened."

The court agreed to dismiss the charges if the boys stayed out of trouble for six months.

Sarge took his son out of Hyannis Port to California. He issued a statement to the *New York Times*, which ran it in full. It began: "We are deeply distressed to learn that our son Bobby has been charged with possession of marijuana last month in Hyannis. He has never been involved in any such situation before, and we trust that he never will be again. If he has done anything wrong, we are sure he will make reparations in a manly and courageous manner. We love him, and for all of his sixteen years he has been a joy and a pride to us. We will help him in every way to re-establish his sense of responsibility for himself and for others, his dedication to high ideals, his personal self-confidence and dignity."

Back on Marchant Avenue, Bobby Kennedy Jr. was alone with his mother and his siblings. Ethel told her son, "You dragged the family name through the mud."

The reporters went back to their newsrooms and Hyannis Port was quiet again for a while. But that summer was just the beginning of the trouble.

The Kennedy homes were overflowing with kids and teenagers by the early '70s. While they were from the same generation, there was a wide span of ages that split the cousins into groups. It was the teenagers who more acutely understood the horrors of the previous decade. And they were angry. The rest of their peers were angry, too, and rebellious and experimental. They'd grown up in the shadow of nuclear weapons and were now thrust into a war they didn't want. They'd watched their heroes and political leaders be gunned down in the streets. *Where were you when Pres-*

ident Kennedy was shot? When Bobby was shot? When Martin Luther King Jr. was shot? The Kennedy kids, too, were learning to live without their father and their uncle and trying to figure out what their lives now meant.

When Bobby Kennedy Jr. was on the Cape, he hung out with a group of teenagers from town who called themselves the Hyannis Port Terrors. The group painted profanity on the streets, stuck potatoes in tailpipes, and broke into houses to steal booze and phones—phone thefts being their calling card.

"We wanted the cops to know it was us so we took the phones," one of the Terrors said.

They met behind someone's house or at the post office. It was a loose gang—an unofficial thing with kids coming and going from the core group. In spite of the trail they left for the cops, the kids were never caught. But the Hyannis Port Terrors had a reputation—and they terrified the younger kids. They sulked around angrily, they wore their dirty hair past their shoulders, they played Led Zeppelin and Black Sabbath on their guitars out in the garage, and their drug-dazed eyes were often glazed over.

"They were just scary," Eunice's son Tim Shriver remembered. "You know, they get all in their dark clothes and hide in bushes and go off and I think they were smoking pot before. It was like, Oh my God, these people are smoking cigarettes and going in the garage and playing heavy metal music and saying, 'If you come in here we're going to kill you.' That was more my brother Bobby, and Bobby Kennedy, Chris Lawford, a couple of other guys from around town. They'd scare the hell out of people and go set off firecrackers outside people's windows. You know, juvenile stuff. Nothing violent—but scary."

The older Robert Kennedys—that's how the kids were identified around the Port, by the names of their fathers—had a reputation unto themselves. They took the bikes they found parked at the end of the Hyannis Port pier and rode them right off the end of the dock. They shot off BB guns in the village. When Ethel was sick of her oldest kids causing trouble, she locked them out of the house. They holed up in the basement and scurried over to their neighbors' place, where the Newman kids would sneak them food. "Those kids didn't see that there was anything wrong with what they had done," their longtime neighbor Larry Newman said. "It was just a big joke to them."

Joe Kennedy II, the oldest of Bobby's sons, wasn't wrapped up in the Hyannis Port Terrors but he always seemed to seethe with anger. Joe II had wavy, dirty-blond hair, clear blue eyes, and the build of his uncle Joe Jr. He was tall and broad-shouldered—physically bigger than most of the other kids. The younger ones would go out of their way to avoid him, for fear of sparking his anger and having him chase them up a tree. The murders of two family members—played on a loop on television for years—combined with a lifetime under a microscope were bringing the oldest kids in the next generation to a boiling point. And with the tension in Hyannis Port those summers in the early '70s, sadness, confusion, and frustration were bubbling over as raw rage.

The summer after his arrest, Bobby Kennedy Jr. was in trouble again. It was close to 11:00 p.m. on a hot summer night when Bobby came out of the ice cream shop on Main Street in Hyannis carrying two cones—one for him and one for his friend Kim Kelley. Kim was sitting on the hood of Bobby's car when a local cop came over. From here, accounts of what happened next differ. The cop said the car had been obstructing traffic on busy West Main Street and that, when confronted, Bobby spat ice cream in his face. Bobby said the cop shouted profanities at Kim, that Bobby explained it was his car and Kim had permission to sit on it, and that the cop told him to drop the ice cream cones so he could be cuffed and placed under arrest for "sauntering and loitering."

His cousin Bobby Shriver bailed him out after a night in jail and he went directly to court in sandals, a blue work shirt, and patched dungarees, his long, sun-bleached hair matted. Bobby was terrified to call home to tell his mother, Ethel, that he'd spent the night in jail, and even more worried about attracting the press. It seemed as if getting a lawyer involved would just bring more attention to the whole thing. A clerk recommended he plead no contest to just be done with it without too much attention. Loitering and sauntering didn't seem like such bad crimes. He just wanted this to be over. Then the arresting officer read the charges, including that the cop was accusing Bobby of spitting on him. "That's a lie!" Bobby said. But now, even more than before, he knew the press couldn't get wind of it. He was ordered to pay $50 in court costs. He didn't have the money, and the judge gave him a week to pay. It was over, he thought, breathing a sigh of relief. But as soon as he opened the doors of the Barnstable District Court, he was met with a group of reporters shoving microphones at him, shouting questions.

Two months later, seventeen-year-old Bobby Jr. made headlines in the supermarket tabloid the *National Enquirer*. There was a report that he was going to marry Kim Kelley, the fifteen-year-old blond daughter of local bartender Frank Kelley, whom he'd been with the night of the arrest that summer. The girl's dad was quoted in the tabloid as saying, "Kim idolizes him. Bobby told me he wants to marry my daughter, but I brushed it aside."

"They're just kids," her mother, Peg Kelley, was quoted as saying. "His mother, Ethel, told him that he must live by the rules of her house or else he would have to leave home until he sees things the way the family sees them. So Bobby stays away."

But right after the *Enquirer* article came out, their friends denied it, telling the press, "It's nothing more than a high school crush."

The Kelley kids were right around the same ages of the oldest Kennedy kids. They lived down the street, through the Curries' yard and past the fence still surrounding the President's house on Irving. The Kelley girls, pretty, blond, and as adventurous as the Kennedys, were in all the same swimming classes, and went to the cookouts at the West Beach Club and dances at the Hyannisport Club. But they were year-rounders while the Robert Kennedys left each fall to go back to their home in Virginia. When the Bobby Kennedy kids began shipping off for the summers to see the world and get away from the trouble they were finding in the Port, Kim's sister Pam went along with David, the shy, fair-haired fourth child of Ethel and Bobby, when he went to work on a ranch in Colorado.

Pam and David spent the summer of '73 flirting and getting closer. When they got back to the Cape, they spent a night in the small guesthouse outside Ethel's home, the one everyone called "the Doll House." Of course, Ethel didn't know—she never would have approved. When David got up early to go with the family to church in Hyannis at St. Francis

Xavier, Pam snuck through the hedge walling off the Kennedy homes. One August day, David came home from church in a particularly good mood. He told Pam his oldest brother, Joe, had invited him to come to a party—something that rarely happened.

August 13 was one of those hot, muggy summer days on the Cape. David and Pam took the ferry from Hyannis Harbor to Nantucket Island to get to his older brother Joe's beach party. Kim Kelley would meet Pam and David there. They planned to take the three o'clock ferry back to Hyannis that afternoon. There was only room for seven passengers in the open jeep-like, four-wheel-drive Toyota. Joe got in the driver's seat, and David and Pam piled in with her sister Kim and three others. Pam was in the back with David right behind her—she held on to the roll bar and David wrapped his hands over hers. Years later, Pam would write down her memories of that day in a short book called *The Kennedy Playground*.

Everyone bumped up and down in their seats as they drove through the woods then onto the smoother asphalt roadway. Traffic was backed up with a short line of cars behind a tour bus that was driving slowly for passengers to see the Nantucket sights. Pam wrote that Joe took a short-cut through an overgrown road then back onto the main street, shifting from first gear into second. Pam, in the back, saw a station wagon full of people coming toward them. She held the roll bar tighter and David squeezed her hands as Joe sped up to get out of the way of the vehicle coming from their left. She lost her grip with the quick acceleration and suddenly she was flying, doing flips in the air until she landed with a thud on a honeysuckle bush. David was to her right, their friend Patty to her left. Pam tried to get up. But she realized she couldn't. She heard the footsteps of someone walking through the woods toward them. It was Joe, his face blanched, twisted in a look of horror. He told Pam not to move, staying with her until a medical team arrived. When she was moved onto a stretcher, a deep ache shot through her back. Still, she didn't realize how badly she was hurt.

"As I was prepared to be transported to the hospital, I recall thinking the accident and my injury might have a bright side," she wrote. "No one would bother me about what I was going to do now that I had graduated from high school."

But when she arrived at Nantucket Cottage Hospital it became clear how serious her injuries were. She'd fractured her spine. A Catholic priest had been summoned to give her last rites. Once Pam was stabilized, she was flown in a helicopter to the hospital in Hyannis, where she underwent three hours of surgery with a neurosurgeon and two assistants before being moved to an intensive care unit where she was deemed in critical condition. David and one of the other girls had been admitted to the hospital as well—David with a sprained back, the girl with a pelvic fracture. Kim and the two other girls had been treated and discharged. By the end of the week, Pam was in stable condition and moved to a private room. Rose Kennedy sent cookies, and Ted arranged for surgeons from the Lahey Clinic, where he'd been treated after his plane crash nearly a decade earlier, to come in to treat Pam. Eventually she was moved to Massachusetts General Hospital in Boston, where she spent four months undergoing rehab. David would visit once in a while, but by the time she returned to Hyannis it seemed clear to her that he wasn't willing to go down this long road of recovery with her.

One week after the accident, on Monday, August 20, Joe Kennedy II, in a suit, skinny tie, and long, wavy hair, arrived at the court back in Nantucket with his mom and his senator uncle. He was found guilty of negligent driving and ordered to pay a $100 fine. The judge told the twenty-year-old to use his "illustrious name to do a lot of good . . . rather than having to come into court like this."

"I think this court was very fair. The prosecution had a position to present and did it fairly and equitably," Ted told reporters as they left the courthouse. "Joe will have to live with the verdict."

Pam plummeted into a depression, burning the word *die* onto her stomach with the tip of a cigarette. She spent the rest of her life paralyzed from the chest down.

Every summer in the '70s, Maureen Gill and her sisters, Pat, Eileen, and Gert Murphy, sat on East Beach, the one sliver of public beach in Hyannis Port. The sisters booked the house across the street from the beach for the week, as they did every summer. Each morning, they brought along the kids, Michaela, Erin, Eileen, and Kevin, dragging their beach chairs across Iyanough Road across the sand just before ten, and set them up perfectly—not facing the water, but facing the Big House. For Maureen and her sisters, the Kennedys weren't just an important political family, they were like their own family. The sisters were Irish Catholic and grew up in New England knowing every detail about Rose and Joe, their nine kids, and all the grandkids, too.

Four times a day, a large boat full of tourists dressed in shorts, eyes squinting behind camera holes, passed by the Big House. Hyannis Harbor Tours started in 1962 when the Scudder brothers were working the gas station on Ocean and South Streets in Hyannis—Scudder's Sunoco, the family's local business—and kept getting requests for directions from customers who were looking for the Kennedy Compound. The Kennedys, they realized, were big business. The brothers decided to take a parcel of land over at the Ocean Street docks they'd received as payment for an outstanding oil bill and use it for a boat sightseeing business. When the sixty-year-old, 150-passenger boat they bought started filling up, they bought two more later in the '60s, then another in the early '70s. The boats left Hyannis and made their way toward the compound as tour guides read from a script. If the winds were blowing the right way, the guides' spiels could be heard by Hyannis Port's residents. The boat-borne lecturers pointed out anyone they guessed might be a Kennedy.

"And to your right, there's Rose Kennedy working in her garden!" a guide would excitedly announce, pointing at Nancy Tenney bent over, tending to her flowers. Sometimes the guides got it right, pointing out Jackie on water skis in the harbor. The cousins running across the lawns would sometimes look up when they heard the boats and shout "Go away!" but most of the time they ignored them. Rose found ignoring them much harder.

"One of the very annoying things in the summer here is the fact that there are four tourist boats going around each day," she wrote in her diary. "I have never been on one of these trips, but the guide seems to describe the houses in detail, how, for example, we built the swimming pool for $50,000. And for an extra 50 cents or a dollar the trip is prolonged and the group can see Teddy's home."

Maureen, Pat, Eileen, and Gert didn't go on the boat tours or the bus tours. They didn't buy souvenirs or postcards at the News Shop. They never saw themselves as tourists—they saw themselves as people who really *knew*—who *understood*—the Kennedys. They didn't need some amateurish tour guide to tell them what they already knew. It was always the same conversation. One of the sisters would start it: "Oh, they got Rose out—walking. Ethel looks drawn." Gert would say, "Oh, how old is Rose anyway?" Maureen would do the math. "Well, let's see. Jack died in '63, then Joe died in '69 making her a widow at seventy-nine, and her birthday was two weeks ago last Thursday, so she's eighty-five."

The Kennedys brought out strong feelings in a lot of people. And Hyannis Port was sacred ground. The family was one of the Cape's biggest draws up through the '70s. They built up the sand dune behind the house in part to protect the property from hurricanes—but mostly to shield the house from nosy beach walkers trying to peek into their windows. The News Shop down the street still sold postcards on a sidewalk spinning rack, under the shop's striped awning. The best-selling souvenir, which the proprietors had to reorder nearly weekly, was a porcelain plate with a picture of Jack, Jackie, John, and Caroline.

"I think the reason people like the plate is the same reason they come here at all," said Susan Hassett. "They are more or less wanting to remember the way it was, or maybe the way we thought it was, rather than the way it's all turned out."

Clifton DeMotte had worked at the Yachtsman Motor Inn in 1960, when the press and some of the campaign staff had stayed there during Jack's presidential campaign. He'd moved on to other jobs: he'd worked for the Department of Transportation, and then in navy construction in Rhode Island. Cliff had been talking. He'd been telling his colleagues he knew all sorts of stuff about the Kennedys from his time in Hyannis. He'd been saying he had dirt, particularly on Ted.

One afternoon in the summer of '71, he got a call. He was asked to meet a man named Ed Warren. They agreed to talk at a motel near the Providence Airport. Ed Warren placed a microphone on the table between them then asked DeMotte if he knew of any women-chasing from the Kennedy boys. DeMotte said he wanted to help the upcoming Republican campaign. He mentioned women who'd been involved with the Kennedy entourage. And that he knew about their drinking habits, particularly those of Jack's press secretary, Pierre Salinger.

They wrapped up the conversation. Warren put away the tape recorder and thanked DeMotte for his time. They talked one more time. But that was the end of it. DeMotte didn't know the whole story: that he'd been talking to a spy for President Richard Nixon. Ed Warren was actually E. Howard Hunt, an ex–CIA man with a fresh, new assignment on Nixon's Special Investigations Unit. The White House was looking for a source who could provide access to the Kennedy family. Someone who'd been stationed in Hyannis Port seemed like he'd be perfect to kick up some dirt on Ted in particular.

But after their conversations, Hunt decided DeMotte wasn't their guy.

"I felt that he was a nonsource," Hunt said in the 1973 hearings investigating the CIA's involvement in Watergate, "and that his previous self-advertisement as being a repository of hard information on the Kennedy camp was valueless, that he had oversold himself." They'd have to keep looking.

"I'll bet they're not having this good a good time in Miami," Ted Kennedy shouted into the wind to a reporter following him in a motorboat. It was the week of the 1972 Democratic National Convention. And as soon as Bobby died, eyes had turned to the only remaining Kennedy brother, Ted. He was, in spite of the accident in Chappaquiddick and the death of Mary Jo Kopechne, considered the odds-on favorite for the 1972 presidential race. But here he was, on his new fifty-four-foot sloop the *Patrician*, 1,500 miles away from the convention, enjoying the breeze. Instead of sporting a suit for last-minute meetings with political advisors, the forty-year-old senator was in purple pants and a yellow T-shirt signing autographs at the Hyannisport Club's caddies' camp for the next class of sixty caddies as they ate hot dogs and potato salad not far from the compound. He told anyone who was interested there was "no way" he'd agree to be the vice presidential candidate, either. It was his brother-in-law Sarge who'd step into that role.

Sarge had helped launch the Peace Corps during Jack's presidency and in 1968 he was sworn in as U.S. ambassador to France. As the summer of 1972 wound down, rumors swirled that Sarge would be Senator George McGovern's running mate. Reporters staked out the Shriver house up on the hill. When Sarge tried to sneak out on August 5, the day McGovern would be announcing his running mate, the Kennedy brother-in-law told the reporters standing behind his house that they'd get their answer that night. But they wanted to know where he was going. "I am going to visit my mother-in-law," he said. "Is that all right?" They kept asking questions. Why was he so dressed up? Was he traveling? Where would he watch the announcement? Would he return home after the announcement? He was vague with his answers, except for the last one. He said he'd be coming back home. "It's a nice home, don't you think?" All the reporters agreed that, yes, it was a nice home.

That night, McGovern announced he'd be running with Shriver. They won the Democratic nomination, but, in the general election, incumbent Richard Nixon won by a landslide. McGovern and Shriver only took the District of Columbia and Massachusetts.

Ted was a leading contender again in 1976 but, again, he sat it out. Sarge was the next one hosting fundraisers in Hyannis Port—in the summer of 1975, he told a gathering of about 170 people that he was planning to announce his presidential run that September. Eunice was there, along with Ethel, Jackie and her kids, and Rose. It was a $100-a-couple fundraiser for Sarge featuring as a centerpiece a cake iced to look like the White House. Notably, Ted skipped the event, which was hosted by candle factory owner Marvin Blank on Squaw Island just down the street from Ted's house. Ted was sailing.

When Jack had been running for president a decade before, his mother and sisters whipped up the support of women with their Kennedy Teas. Eunice borrowed the idea, hosting Shriver Teas for Sarge at the Kennedy Compound. And women came by the busload. "Nosy," one

In 1925, brothers Jack (right) and Joseph P. Kennedy Jr. stand in front of Malcolm Cottage, the house the Kennedys were renting in Hyannis Port. © JOHN F. KENNEDY LIBRARY FOUNDATION

From left to right, Rosemary, Jack, Eunice, Joe Jr., and Kick pose in the water in Hyannis Port in the 1920s. © JOHN F. KENNEDY LIBRARY FOUNDATION

In 1935, the two oldest daughters, Kick and Rosemary, stand in front of the tennis courts the Kennedys added to the backyard. © JOHN F. KENNEDY LIBRARY FOUNDATION

Joe Jr. and Jack in 1941 at the Big House with family friends, including neighbor Nancy Tenney (in floral dress). © JOHN F. KENNEDY LIBRARY FOUNDATION

Rose Kennedy with her son Bobby and daughter Jean on a couch in the Big House the summer of 1942. © JOHN F. KENNEDY LIBRARY FOUNDATION

Rose Kennedy's parents, former mayor of Boston John "Honey Fitz" and Josie Fitzgerald, often spent summers with the Kennedy family in the Big House but eventually found rental homes nearby. COURTESY OF THE BOSTON PUBLIC LIBRARY, LESLIE JONES COLLECTION

Eugenia Fortes worked for many of the Kennedy family's neighbors. It was Fortes who fought to keep the one public beach in Hyannis Port open to the public. Today, it is named for her. THE BARNSTABLE PATRIOT COLLECTION, THE WILLIAM BREWSTER NICKERSON CAPE COD HISTORY ARCHIVES, WILKENS LIBRARY, CAPE COD COMMUNITY COLLEGE

After Joe Jr. died in the war, the family donated $150,000 to create an ice-skating rink in Hyannis in his honor. Here, Joe Kennedy gives a speech at the opening of the Lt. Joseph P. Kennedy Jr. Memorial Skating Centre in 1957. THE BARNSTABLE PATRIOT COLLECTION, THE WILLIAM BREWSTER NICKERSON CAPE COD HISTORY ARCHIVES, WILKENS LIBRARY, CAPE COD COMMUNITY COLLEGE

Jack brings his fiancée, Jacqueline Bouvier, back to Hyannis Port to meet his family in the summer of 1953.
HY PESKIN/GETTY IMAGES/ALAMY STOCK PHOTO

Jack and Jackie go sailing in an image captured by photographer Hy Peskin, whom Jack met at the airport and invited to come back to the Port to photograph the weekend.
HY PESKIN/GETTY IMAGES/ALAMY STOCK PHOTO

After Jack has been announced the winner of the presidency, the family gathers for the only group photograph from that historic day. From left, Ethel Skakel Kennedy, Stephen Smith, Eunice Kennedy Shriver, Jean Kennedy Smith, Rose Kennedy, Joseph P. Kennedy, John F. Kennedy, Jacqueline Kennedy, Robert Kennedy, Edward Kennedy, Patricia Kennedy Lawford, Sargent Shriver, Joan Kennedy, and Peter Lawford.
ARCHIVIO GBB/ALAMY STOCK PHOTO

Once JFK was elected president, small white huts manned by local police officers were setup around the Kennedy Compound. THE BARNSTABLE PATRIOT COLLECTION, THE WILLIAM BREWSTER NICKERSON CAPE COD HISTORY ARCHIVES, WILKENS LIBRARY, CAPE COD COMMUNITY COLLEGE

JFK invited Soviet leader Nikita Khrushchev's son-in-law, journalist Aleksei Adzhubei, to the Big House in 1961 for an interview.

CECIL STOUGHTON. WHITE HOUSE PHOTOGRAPHS. JOHN F. KENNEDY PRESIDENTIAL LIBRARY AND MUSEUM, BOSTON

The summer of 1962, Attorney General Robert F. Kennedy poses in front of the Big House with his children Robert Jr., David, Kerry, Michael, and Courtney.

CECIL STOUGHTON. WHITE HOUSE PHOTOGRAPHS. JOHN F. KENNEDY PRESIDENTIAL LIBRARY AND MUSEUM, BOSTON

In 1962, a racist organization named the White Citizens Council lied to Black Americans in the South, saying jobs awaited them in Hyannis. Pictured here: a bus arriving in Hyannis with the so-called "Reverse Freedom Riders." THE BARNSTABLE PATRIOT COLLECTION, THE WILLIAM BREWSTER NICKERSON CAPE COD HISTORY ARCHIVES, WILKENS LIBRARY, CAPE COD COMMUNITY COLLEGE

Cousins Maria Shriver and Caroline Kennedy in the summer of 1963 aboard the family yacht, the *Honey Fitz*, named for Rose's father. CECIL STOUGHTON. WHITE HOUSE PHOTOGRAPHS. JOHN F. KENNEDY PRESIDENTIAL LIBRARY AND MUSEUM, BOSTON

John F. Kennedy Jr. drives a speedboat in the summer of 1963. CECIL STOUGHTON. WHITE HOUSE PHOTOGRAPHS. JOHN F. KENNEDY PRESIDENTIAL LIBRARY AND MUSEUM, BOSTON

John Jr. plays on the beach with family athletic director Sandy Eiler. CECIL STOUGHTON. WHITE HOUSE PHOTOGRAPHS. JOHN F. KENNEDY PRESIDENTIAL LIBRARY AND MUSEUM, BOSTON

After the death of Patrick, their third child, Jack and Jackie relax with Caroline and John Jr. on the porch of Brambletyde, the home they rented on Squaw Island. CECIL STOUGHTON. WHITE HOUSE PHOTOGRAPHS. JOHN F. KENNEDY PRESIDENTIAL LIBRARY AND MUSEUM, BOSTON

The family gathers at the Big House for Joe Kennedy's birthday in September 1963. From left, Pat Lawford, family friend Lem Billings, Ethel, Bobby, Jackie, Ted, Joan, and JFK (seated). CECIL STOUGHTON. WHITE HOUSE PHOTOGRAPHS. JOHN F. KENNEDY PRESIDENTIAL LIBRARY AND MUSEUM, BOSTON

Joe Kennedy suffered a stroke in 1961, which left him unable to walk and communicate. Each time Jack departed the Big House for the White House, Joe's nurse wheeled out the head of the family to say goodbye. This parting in 1963 occurred shortly before JFK's death. CECIL STOUGHTON. WHITE HOUSE PHOTOGRAPHS. JOHN F. KENNEDY PRESIDENTIAL LIBRARY AND MUSEUM, BOSTON

After the president's death, family friend Frank Sinatra and his girlfriend, actress Mia Farrow, sailed a yacht along the Cape with a stop in Hyannis Port to visit the Kennedys. EDWARD JENNER, COURTESY OF THE *BOSTON GLOBE* LIBRARY COLLECTION AT THE NORTHEASTERN UNIVERSITY ARCHIVES AND SPECIAL COLLECTIONS

In 1966, Jackie helped plan a simple memorial to her husband on Ocean Street in Hyannis. BARNSTABLE PATRIOT COLLECTION, THE WILLIAM BREWSTER NICKERSON CAPE COD HISTORY ARCHIVES, WILKENS LIBRARY, CAPE COD COMMUNITY COLLEGE

After Mary Jo Kopechne, who'd worked on Robert Kennedy's campaign, drowned in a car accident with Senator Edward Kennedy, people protested in front of the Hyannis Port post office. EVERETT COLLECTION INC/ALAMY STOCK PHOTO

Robert Kennedy's second oldest son, Bobby Jr. (center with his mother, Ethel, and Uncle Ted at Barnstable County Courthouse), was arrested in 1970 along with his cousin, Eunice and Sargent Shriver's oldest son, Bobby, after they were caught with marijuana.
AP PHOTO/BILL ALLEN

John F. Kennedy Jr. drew more and more attention as he got older. Here, in 1979, he makes his way down a Hyannis Port street barefoot with a boombox.
TOM WARGACKI/GETTY IMAGES

In the summer of 1983, John Jr. came home to the Cape to work on a dive ship, helping local wreckage diver Barry Clifford look for the remains of sunken pirate vessel, the *Whydah*.
BARRY CLIFFORD

In 1986, Maria Shriver married actor and bodybuilder Arnold Schwarzenegger in a celebrity-studded wedding held at the family's church, St. Francis Xavier.
ZUMA PRESS, INC./ALAMY STOCK PHOTO

Artist Andy Warhol and model Grace Jones arrived at the Shriver-Schwarzenegger party late, making a dramatic entrance. AP PHOTO

John Jr., his wife, Carolyn Bessette, and her sister Lauren went missing after flying a small plane to the Cape for a family wedding on July 16, 1999. Media immediately descended on the Kennedy Compound. REUTERS/ALAMY STOCK PHOTO

In November 2013, the Kennedys and their friends piled into a Wianno Senior sailboat for one of the last sails of the season. KENNEDY FAMILY COLLECTION

It's a Kennedy family tradition to play flag football on the Big House lawn on Thanksgiving Day. Here, the family and their neighbors play in 2015.
KENNEDY FAMILY COLLECTION

woman gave as her reason for showing up and paying the required $10. "I never got this close to the Compound before." But Sarge's campaign was short-lived—after coming in third in the Illinois primary in March, the latest hope of the Kennedys withdrew.

The Kennedy Compound officially, and quietly, had become a historic landmark in 1972. All three homes—the Big House, Bobby's place, and Jack's on Irving Avenue were part of it. When the director of the Office of Archeology wrote to Jack's best friend, Lem Billings, about the designation, explaining how important he believed the compound to be and that he hoped to move forward with giving it the National Historic Landmark status, Billings wrote back to say, "I believe the family would prefer that there be no publicity should the Compound be given this status." They got their wish—there was no fanfare when the process was completed. But that didn't stop the tourists from flowing into town to see the homes. The neighbors, two decades into Kennedy mania, began to realize their little village might never go back to what it had been. From the days of Jack's presidency until 1979, the population of Hyannis had nearly tripled, its streets lined with motels with neon signs and restaurants advertising "Leaning Tower of Pizza." Construction on the land around Main Street in Hyannis was constant, with new housing developments, restaurants, and retail. There was the draw of the Kennedys along with the growing popularity of the Cape in general as it saw an influx of retirees and people willing to make the long commute to Boston. The little neighborhood of Hyannis Port was mostly protected from the building explosion, but the fences and manicured privet hedges got higher and higher around the gray-shingled homes. And the neighbors had learned to become wary of strangers walking around, eyes darting as they looked for a familiar face. They got used to strangers on their doorsteps asking where the Kennedy Compound was, saying they just wanted to stand on the same soil Jack Kennedy stood on. While they were out running, they got used to giving wrong directions when someone they didn't recognize said they needed to know where Rose Kennedy lived because they needed to pick up their boyfriend who was working there.

And every four years, as Ted holed up in his home on Squaw Island, meeting with family and advisors to decide if this was his year to run, the neighbors held their breath, knowing the tourists, reporters, and helicopters another presidency would bring.

As the sun came up over the quiet Sound, Sandy Eiler walked up Atlantic Avenue to the Shrivers' place. Sandy was a former Canadian show diver and the first coach for the Cape Cod Swim Club in Hyannis. He'd been hired by the Kennedys as part babysitter, part athletic trainer: a one-man summer camp. Eiler was a towering presence with a big barrel chest that was always tanned a deep brown, and slicked, dark hair, and he marched around the compound wearing only his shorts and sneakers. Eiler would often say to the kids when he spotted them eyeing his large, bare stomach, "Go ahead, hit it as hard as you want to!" David and Bobby Jr. wound up and landed their biggest hit. And Sandy looked down and laughed.

Rose, who watched from her window or porch as the kids trailed behind Eiler, was driven utterly crazy by his lack of clothing. The Cape was a place where everyone dressed down: Rose wore a headscarf and comfortable, orthopedic-style shoes with slacks. The family saved their most worn-out, holey sweaters for Hyannis Port. Ted teased Joan when she got a new outfit he didn't like: "That looks great—for the Cape." But everyone was expected to be modest, covered up. Rose once sent a message to her son-in-law Sarge, "Please tell Sandy to start wearing a shirt. I am sick and tired of looking at his navel. Every year it becomes more prominent."

Eiler let himself into the Shrivers' sprawling white clapboard house on the hill and headed upstairs to the kids' room, waking them one by one. Eunice and Sarge were both fitful sleepers and would sleep late then read the newspapers, meeting everyone downstairs by breakfast time. If Eiler's first effort to wake the kids didn't work, he made a second round, tickling each one until they hopped out of bed and stumbled down the stairs. Then he cooked them whatever they wanted for breakfast as long as it was eggs. Once the Shrivers were fed and ready, Eiler went down to Ethel's and dragged *her* kids out of bed. With a child in each arm, he took them to the changing station on the beach so they could get their suits on for the day. The kids didn't get a towel unless they ran to the breakwater, touched it, and came back. Then came a morning swim. Real, precise strokes were required. If you tried to come out of the water early, Eiler stood ankle-deep in the ocean and kicked you in the solar plexus with his heel, knocking you back into the ocean.

Eiler was a constant those summers as was Ethel's governess, Ena Bernard, who started working for the family when Bobby was alive but whose role expanded after he died, relieving Ethel from some of the responsibility of caring for eleven children. With the oldest kids wreaking havoc on the Port and Ethel's emerging from a dark period of mourning with a new baby, Eiler and Bernard kept things moving for the rest of the kids. They made sure everyone got to the dock on time for their morning sailing lessons. Then there was tennis down at the Hyannisport Club. Three days a week, there was horseback riding over at Grandpa's farm in Osterville. Most days, everyone met at the dock at one, and Ethel and Eunice took all the kids out sailing with packed lunches for their two boats. Everyone knew Ethel's cooler had the good stuff—rich, decadent meals of lobster salad, fresh muffins, and cookies packed by her French-trained chef. For her boat, Eunice threw together a bag of chips and a loaf of bread and a jar of peanut butter for the kids to make their own soggy sandwiches. The two families spent hours out on the water, going over to Egg Island or just around the Sound. Ethel and Eunice were competitive. With a mischievous glance at each other, a race between the boats would start. If there was a guest, the kids would delight in trying to persuade them to go dragging behind one of the speedboats: a terrifying game in which the person holds on to a rope thrown off the back of the boat, the current pulling them below the water while they gasp for air. The only excuse for not participating was not knowing how to swim—and even then you had to make a strong case you *really* didn't know how to swim. After boating, Eiler led a game of softball over on Jackie's lawn, which was wide and flat with a permanent home plate in the middle and the grass worn to dirt in the paths between bases. If you hit the ball over the fence, that was a home run. The baseball field shared the yard space with two RVs that had no wheels and were stationed right inside the fence—housing for John's and Caroline's assigned Secret Service agents, friendly guys who always said hi to the group of kids that Eiler gathered. There was also John's airplane—after Jack died, an olive-green World War II two-seater observation plane was secretly reconditioned and shipped by truck to the compound as a gift from Grandpa Joe for all the grandchildren to play in. But John, who was five when he got the plane, loved it the most.

There were so many cousins that two teams could be assembled from just Kennedys and Shrivers—unlike when Joe Jr., Jack, and Bobby were little—but Eiler made sure they included the neighborhood kids, inviting anyone who wanted to play touch football or baseball. When Eiler dropped by the candle factory down the street from the compound to pick up his wife, Lee, who was the manager there, he asked the ten-year-old boy hanging around behind the counter if he liked baseball. Brad Blank, whose dad owned the shop, said he did. Eiler told him to be at the President's house at three that afternoon for a game.

Blank, a Hyannis year-rounder, became close with the kids right around his age—the second wave of Kennedys, a few years younger than the scary older kids. If the younger children were on a camping trip at Grandpa's lake in Osterville, the older kids showed up in the middle of the night to terrify the young ones, already jittery from a night of ghost stories by the campfire. But the younger Kennedys had their own ways of making trouble—usually by playing carefully rehearsed practical jokes.

One summer afternoon Brad Blank was the target.

"Hey, Brad, do you know what a mongoose is?" Max Kennedy, one of the youngest of the group, asked his friend.

"No," Blank responded, "I don't."

"It kills rattlesnakes and it's like the most vicious animal and we have one now," Max said excitedly. "My father was friends with this guy from India and these mongooses are indigenous to India and they're the most vicious. They're not big but their teeth and their claws are so vicious."

Suddenly, Blank realized there was a box in the room with three red Xs painted on.

"Stay away," Max warned while slowly walking closer to the box. "Don't get too close to it! It can tear a human being apart in a matter of minutes."

Blank couldn't help himself. As he kneeled to look in the box, Max clicked a remote he had hidden in his hand. A stuffed animal flew from the box, landing square on Blank, who screamed and ran outside as Max collapsed in a fit of laughter.

The next time, Blank was in on the Kennedys' scheme.

Back behind the Blank family's candle shop, there was a dumpster where the extra wax was thrown out. The group of kids decided to dive into the dumpster to fish out the extra wax. The kids told their plan to Ena Bernard, who taught them how to take the extra wax, put a base at the bottom of a pot, then insert a wick and pour the melted wax on top to make new candles. One of the kids had the big idea, though, to take their candlemaking a step further. If they went down to the shore behind the Big House, made a neat, round hole in the sand, and poured in the wax, it would make a sand candle. They were all delighted with themselves and their new innovation. They set up a stand on the street in front of the compound to sell what they dubbed "Kennedy Candles"—made with "real Kennedy Compound sand," as they advertised it. The neighbor kids had made money off the Kennedy name with their lemonade stands, why not make a buck themselves? The Kennedys and Shrivers in the bunch would delight tourists who stopped by after their bus tours to the compound. Flashing their big, toothy Kennedy grins, the kids would instantly convert a tourist to a customer. "Who's your dad?" the tourists asked each kid. Rose, impressed by her grandchildren's entrepreneurial spirit, sometimes came down to the candle stand to make cameo appearances. After packing everything up, the kids took their earnings directly to the News Shop for candy and ice cream.

The relationship with the tourists, however, wasn't strictly friendly. When the younger kids were feeling mischievous, they fashioned a contraption called a funnelator—a funnel attached to rubber tubing. A kid stood on each end of the tubing and a third held the funnel at the back, stretching it out pretty good then placing a water balloon in the widest part of the funnel. They pulled the funnelator down before letting it go, the balloon launching over the fence surrounding the President's house, landing on the crowds of tourists gathered on Irving Avenue.

As had been the case with their parents' generation, the kids, once they got a bit older, found their greatest entertainment at the evening golf club dances. There were two a week—the one in Hyannis Port and the one in Wianno. And everyone went: summer kids, locals, and the teenagers working for families as governesses. Everyone went home and got cleaned up and ready to meet at one of the kids' houses at five or six, before the dance started. "We'd go up there and would listen to music and smoke pot and drink beer and go over to the dance," said Billy Noonan, a friend of Tim Shriver's who became close with John, too. Noonan was big and loud with a resounding laugh, an affable and fiercely loyal local guy who didn't care about the legacy of the Kennedy family. He was just looking to have a good time with his friends. "It couldn't have been any more fun."

At the Hyannisport Club dance, the local band Rigor Mortis played Led Zeppelin, the Rolling Stones, and Elton John. And everyone took turns dancing with their friends. Afterward, they coupled off and went to the tower over by the first hole at the golf course. To sneak into the after-party in the tower, they had to climb a ladder up onto the roof and into a window. The best pickup line on the Cape, though, was, "Do you want to go back to the Kennedy pool?" One by one, they quietly went into the dark, steamy covered pool. At night, it was so dark under the pool's bubble cover, you couldn't see if anyone was on the other side of the pool. Any noise echoed and vibrated, risking the possibility of waking Rose Kennedy on the second floor. If she woke in the middle of the night to laughter and whispers in the pool, she rushed out to the lawn.

"Who's in here?" she yelled into the darkness one night.

"Timmy!" answered a voice.

Rose, irate, went back to her room, ready to scold her grandson Tim the next morning at Mass.

But Tim wasn't even there that night. It was the president's son, John, who collapsed in a fit of laughter with his friends as soon as his grandmother left.

While Eunice and the Shriver kids were out on the Sound racing Ethel and her kids, Eunice's husband, Sarge, wandered through the maze of pegboard-lined aisles at Bradford's Hardware on Hyannis's East Main Street. Bradford's, just off the beaten path, had been a fixture in town since 1892, long before the Kennedys came along. The original owners lived above the shop and passed the store down from generation to generation. Sarge had his own impressive career but when he was with his in-laws, he faded happily into the background. He didn't have Ted's booming personality; he hated to sail; and in his relationship with his wife, he gladly played a supporting role. And so he went to the hardware store. There was always a sprinkler that needed a part, a pen to be built for the dogs. Or, when the vacuum needed fixing, he headed over to the Sears department store where everyone knew him. Sarge learned the name of each employee, and the names of their kids. When there was dry cleaning to be picked up—everyone at the cleaner knew him by name, too.

Some days Sarge worked on his yellow motorboat, *Lucky Seven*. It always seemed to have an issue, so he'd take it over to the marina where he'd be greeted with "Hey, Sarge!" "What do you need today, Sarge?" When it was fixed, he drove it over to Baxter's, a restaurant on the Sound that had a place to dock your boat while you ate. Of course, Sarge played tennis with his kids or took them out on the boat. But he'd created his own little world just outside Hyannis Port in Hyannis. And when he was back home at the big Shriver house overlooking the water and the eighteenth hole at the golf course, he made himself busy, too. He had his routines. At the end of the day, it was Sarge who went from window to window to pull the heavy blue curtains shut. Then he went from room to room, turning on every light. He fixed himself a drink at his bar out on the simple stone patio and sat on his chaise, watching the inky waves roll onto the beach behind the compound down below.

It wasn't always easy for in-laws trying to find their place in the loud, rambunctious family. The intensity could be crushing for the kids, too, and they often had less room for escape.

"Growing up in a big, competitive, public family with countless cousins, I never allowed myself to calm down. There was relentless competition on the athletic field and in the classroom," said Sarge's son Mark. "I had a very strong sense that we kids were competing against a past that always won."

*   *   *

A woman in her midfifties walked toward the Big House porch with a nun. Her right foot dragged lightly behind her. She was tall with a beautiful round face with full cheeks and thick, dark curly hair with only a few strands of gray. She took in the house, which looked just as it had when she was last there more than thirty years before: the same green shutters, the same white shingles, the same carefully manicured lawn with its bursts of roses and annuals. The dunes along the shore had been weathered and the water lapped closer to the house. The endless Sound was pierced with the jagged stone breakwater that had been protecting the shore all those years she'd been away, just like when she grew up there on Marchant Avenue.

It was the summer of '74—five years after Joe's death—and Rosemary was home. Joe had been the one who thought it best to keep their first daughter from visiting after the lobotomy he'd arranged for her had left her severely mentally impaired. But now that he was gone, Rose finally arranged for her oldest living child to come home. Joe Jr. was gone, Kick was gone, Jack and Bobby were gone, and now with Joe gone, Rosemary returned to a house heavy with memories that she'd missed while living with the nuns at St. Coletta in Wisconsin. Rosemary sometimes wandered the grounds muttering "Kathleen," the given name of her sister Kick who was closest in age and had been dead for decades.

Rose cried to her cook, Nellie McGrail. "Nellie, I felt bad, I felt awful for Jack, Robert, Joe, but I feel worse for Rosemary, because why did God ask me to go through this?"

"Mrs. Kennedy, God used you as a tool, an implement," McGrail said to comfort Rose. They didn't talk about Joe's decision to lobotomize their daughter and to keep her away from her family for so many decades.

Rosemary became more and more incorporated into life in Hyannis Port. She stayed on the first floor of Eunice's house, a little removed from the compound. Eunice and her kids did anything they could to make her happy: trips to Four Seas ice cream shop down the road in Centerville for scoops of vanilla. A few nights a week, her nephew Anthony arranged for her to have a birthday cake, complete with lit candles and a round of "Happy Birthday."

"She wouldn't know whether it was her birthday yesterday or the day after, but she loved the cake, the candles, the singing. She loved that there was a big fuss about it," Anthony said. "She could feel that and she would smile."

Ted came over to the Shriver house from Squaw Island to see his older sister, sitting next to her for hours, telling her the same old stories over and over. "Remember when Daddy caught me with cookies in my pockets?" Ted asked. "Remember he'd take those cookies out of my pockets?" Rosemary—Rosie, he called her—beamed at her baby brother and at the memories of their shared childhood there.

Eunice took Rosemary everywhere—like she'd done more than three decades earlier. Rosemary loved being with her older sister, except when Eunice pushed her too hard, as she tended to do to everybody. But Rosemary was happy out on Ted's sailboat and sitting around the dinner table with Eunice and her kids. When Rosemary was coming, word was sent out that the pool at the Big House was closed for everyone else that week. The temperature was turned as high as it would go, since Rosemary liked it hot, and the nuns took her swimming beneath the quiet, muggy bubble that covered the pool. Rosemary had an uncanny ability to float. She could lie in the water, suspended in the clear blue pool, and just float, the top of her body skimming the water, her hair slowly suspended in a halo around her head. For twenty, thirty minutes at a time. Content.

By the 1970s Rose had been living in the house on Marchant for nearly half a century. And she had a lot of the same neighbors. There was Jack Bell—Bobby's best friend, who was now the master plumber for all of Hyannis Port. Joe had encouraged him to start his own plumbing company after he finished his training, and Rose and Joe were his first customers. Jack Bell still worked on the Big House, Bobby's house, the President's house, and most of the other houses in the neighborhood, making sure the pipes were ready when the houses were opened for the season and prepared properly after Thanksgiving. And there was Nancy Tenney, the little girl who'd run with Kick back and forth across the families' neighboring lawns, who'd moved into her father's house when he died in 1974. On Nancy's first day back home she got a call from Rose. "Nancy, you've got every light in the house on, you know," Rose said, looking across their lawns. "You need to be more frugal with your utilities."

Nancy invited Rose over from time to time. Her father, Rockwell Tenney, was one of the people who'd never approved of the Kennedys because of their Catholicism. It was no secret to Rose and Joe how their neighbors felt back then. So when Rose went over to the house across the street, now Nancy's, she put her feet up on the couch and said with a laugh, "Oh, I wish Rockwell could see me now!"

Rose's gaze fell on the old wicker chairs on the front porch. Had they always looked so worn? The white paint was starting to peel from the wicker, leaving small brown patches. The cushions were saggy and discolored from the summer heat, the autumn fog, the winter snow. She hadn't really noticed it before, but now Greek shipping magnate Aristotle Onassis sat uncomfortably in one of the tall, fan-backed wicker chairs, and they'd suddenly never looked shabbier. Rose had met Onassis a couple of times on her trips to Europe, so she knew the lifestyle his extreme wealth afforded him. And he was here, in her home on the Cape with her daughter-in-law, whom he was now dating.

Everyone working at the compound—and everyone in town—was curious about who Jackie was with. First to be the subject of the gossip mill was David Ormsby-Gore. Ormsby-Gore, who was the British ambassador to the United States when Jack was president, visited Hyannis Port several times, but it was clear to anyone who saw them together that Jackie wasn't interested in him, although the press reported that they were together.

Then there was Onassis. While Ormsby-Gore had seemed a natural match for the former First Lady, Onassis was a surprise to everyone in Hyannis Port. He was short and stout, flashy and brash, and more than twenty years Jackie's senior. "Perhaps it was this air of crude confidence and power that disturbed everyone," Joe's nurse, Rita Dallas, wrote.

Jackie and Onassis sat outside for long, leisurely lunches on her porch. He brought boxes of food with him from Greece when he came to stay on the Cape—big chunks of feta cheese floating in cloudy water, and cartons of cigarettes for Jackie and his favorite big, fat cigars. They went for walks together through the quiet streets of the Port, as if nobody else was around. They had late dinners, sitting at the Heritage House restaurant in Hyannis past midnight, long after everyone else went home. Though he stayed in the guest quarters when he came to visit, Jackie seemed happy with him, and comfortable. They were married in 1968.

"She romanced him right on the street in front of my house," Jack's old friend and neighbor Larry Newman said. "They used to have a champagne lunch here and then they would go dancing up the hill in front of my house and then would go whistling down the street to their house. And I just kept asking myself, 'How in God's name could she love that guy?'"

Rose and Nellie McGrail drove back home after an event at St. Francis Xavier Church. They took the long way, driving through the streets of Hyannis Port, up by the golf club, just talking and enjoying the morning.

"You know, Nellie, we can die right this minute and go to heaven," Rose said to her cook. At the end of the event, they'd gotten the priest's blessing. The priest had told them, "Now, if you die, you go straight to heaven."

"Yes," McGrail said to Rose, glancing over at her, so small in her seat, "that's right."

A car came driving up the narrow street toward them.

"Run into that car and let's find out," Rose said with a mischievous smile.

"No, no," McGrail said, laughing. "I'll take his word for it."

Most of the time, it was just Rose, Nellie, Rose's secretary, Barbara Gibson, and her housekeeper, Jeanette—whose name Rose mispronounced "Janet"—in the Big House, far fewer staff than when Joe had been alive. She probably would have done without a secretary except for the flood of correspondence that continued to come in for her through the Hyannis Port post office, mostly condolences for the loss of her two sons. As when Joe was alive, Rose continued to go up to the Hyannisport Club to golf; she tucked her dark hair into her swim cap to do her laps every day; and she still took her long walks around the neighborhood. She walked constantly, even in the pouring rain. She had three pairs of black walking shoes and if one got wet, she came in to change into another, leaving the soaked pair on the stove to dry.

In June 1975, three women from Vermont saw Rose on one of her walks. It was an unseasonably cold day and they recognized her despite the scarf she'd wrapped around her hair, and her winter coat, slacks, and gloves. Without hesitation, Rose invited the tourists to join her on her walk to Eunice's house up the hill. The women struggled to keep up with eighty-four-year-old Rose, who pointed out homes on their walk, including the five that belonged to members of her family. She talked about her memoir, which had been published the year before, and the fan mail she'd received, and about her grandchildren who'd come to stay with her that summer. Her grandchildren, she said, were so different from her own children. And she told these strangers how quiet her house was lately, that it was quite lonely. She told them about waiting on her porch for her grandchildren to arrive, shielded by her big sunhat and shades clipped onto her sunglasses. Just as Jack's first stop had always been to see his father, the grandchildren started each summer with a trip over to the Big House to greet their grandmother. At dinner, Rose picked up where Joe left off, leading the conversations and quizzing the grandchildren about current events.

By the 1970s, Jackie had moved on with Onassis, and Ethel was always busy with her big family and her loud house. Rose ate lunch alone, enjoying having a baked potato every day—but she just scooped out the inside, leaving the skin. She still sat down at her piano to play before each meal. McGrail knew it was time to serve her after she finished her rendition of "Sweet Adeline," the song her father always sang, the song that had let her children know it was time to come downstairs for dinner. During the fall, winter, and spring when the grandkids were at school, it was so quiet, her singing echoed through the empty house. When it was just Rose, Nellie, Barbara, and Jeanette in the house, Rose spent a lot of her time in the attic. She walked up the steep wooden stairs leading to the hot, muggy room piled with boxes, and she set aside things she wanted to save for her grandchildren and items to sell—sometimes to her own family. For $170 she sold Jackie a set of antique tin reflectors intended to go behind candles, and for $4,000 she sold Eunice an old English cream and sugar set.

Rose was also constantly making changes to her will—considering and reconsidering who to leave what to. Having survived nearly half her children and her husband spurred her to think about her family's legacy—and her own mortality. "Oh, Nellie," she said to her cook one night, "I won't want to live as long as my mother. I don't want to go through that." Josie had lived to the age of ninety-eight.

Rose rarely talked about her sons who'd died so young. The Kennedys hated to look back. But sometimes, as Rose looked at her daughters-in-law, she couldn't help but think back. "I love Jackie because she's doing such a beautiful job on the children." About Ethel, she said, "Well, I feel sorry for Ethel. I had Joe, and I had to raise my nine and she has nobody to raise eleven. And that hurts me very badly. Robert should never have gone to be president. He should have stayed to take care of his children."

At the end of the day, Rose was alone in her bedroom which she'd decorated in shades of pink and light green. Draped across the windows were white eyelet curtains that let the moonlight seep through. Rosary beads and little notes Rose had written to herself papered the room. The antique secretary desk where she liked to sit was covered with Mass cards commemorating Joe, Joe Jr., Kick, Jack, and Bobby. Also on the desk were some of her favorite snapshots—like the one of Joe Jr. in his navy uniform. The view from her room was of the empty yard, the peaceful sea.

Rose's niece Mary Lou McCarthy often called to relieve her aunt's loneliness. Mary Lou, the daughter of Joe's sister Loretta Kennedy, was just down the road at her own little cottage across from St. Francis Xavier. Mary Lou sang to Rose through the phone, offering a medley of Roman Catholic hymns, chants, and songs from Rose's childhood, the kind you didn't really hear anymore. When her eyes got heavy, Rose spoke into the receiver, "Thank you."

"You're welcome, darling," Mary Lou said. "I love you. Sleep well."

*   *   *

"Are you here by yourself?" Tom Brokaw asked Arnold Schwarzenegger. It was 1977 and they were at the Rainbow Room, where the pre-party was being held for Ethel's Robert F. Kennedy Pro-Celebrity Tennis Tournament. Schwarzenegger, a chiseled bodybuilder with an Austrian accent who'd just had the breakout role in the documentary *Pumping Iron*, was there as a guest. He told Brokaw yes, he was there alone.

"Well, I have the right girl for you," Brokaw said, enthusiastically. "You've got to meet Maria. Where's Maria? Guys, get me Maria!"

Schwarzenegger was introduced to Maria Shriver, the only daughter of Eunice, a pretty, petite brunette with thick, wavy hair, the spitting image of her grandmother Rose, who was also her godmother. When Schwarzenegger met Eunice that night, he told her, quite bluntly, "Your daughter has a great ass." After a night of dancing and flirting, Maria and her cousin Caroline invited Schwarzenegger back to Hyannis Port on their private plane. Getting invited back to the compound was, by that point, a kind of test for anyone dating a cousin. If someone could handle the hordes of cousins, the teasing, the constant competition, then they would probably fit in, so the thinking went. Schwarzenegger was game.

Two planes made their way from New York to Hyannis Port on that hot August night. The "adults," as Ethel's generation was called, took the first plane. The "kids," Kennedy and Shriver cousins in their twenties, took the second plane.

It was close to eleven by the time they landed, and Maria and Schwarzenegger went from the plane straight into the water for a late-night swim. Maria offered Schwarzenegger her brother Bobby's room, right next to hers. The next morning, Schwarzenegger woke up in the seahorse- and seashell-themed room to the sound of people running up and down the hallway and stairs. The Shrivers were getting ready for church. Schwarzenegger had no clothes but the tennis outfit he'd worn all day and on the plane the night before. The 230-pound bodybuilder was offered Bobby's much-too-small wardrobe—but the pants wouldn't pull over his thick thighs, so Schwarzenegger had to wear shorts. When they made their way over to St. Francis Xavier, all the Kennedy and Shriver cousins snickered at Maria's date. *This is hilarious! Look at his pants!*

"There was a lot here to figure out," Schwarzenegger later wrote in his memoir. "Why was there a family compound? Why have all these houses bunched all together? It was fascinating how the Kennedys circulated among themselves: 'Today we'll have cocktails at Teddy's, and then we'll have dinner at Pat's, and tomorrow we'll have breakfast over with Eunice and Sarge,' and so on."

Journalist Pete Hamill sat on the porch behind Jackie's house on Irving Avenue, his hand moving swiftly across a sketch pad as he sat quietly. The porch was almost always empty, but when Hamill was in town, he liked to sit out there and draw or paint, his curly hair thick with humidity, his expression lost in thought. Hamill had dated actress Shirley MacLaine and his love life was now of particular interest to the New York tabloids where he bounced around as a columnist. But when he was visiting Jackie on the Cape, he kept a low profile, sitting with his sketch pad or striking up conversations with one of the kids' friends. He particularly liked debating the cinematic influences of *Star Wars*. "At the heart of it, it's really a cowboys and Indians movie," he told John's friend Billy Noonan, a serious look on his face.

Jackie's social circle in Hyannis Port was similar to the one she had in New York. She liked inviting her friends or whoever she was dating after Onassis's death in 1975 to the Cape house for long summer weekends. The kids brought back their friends, too. John brought his best friend from Andover, Sasha Chermayeff, a sweet, artsy daughter of artists, for summer weekends. He showed her the hidden passageways from yard to yard—the highest shrubs, the fences with the little holes to crawl through—where they could get around the neighborhood without being detected by sightseers or photographers. "You go first and I'll duck and follow behind," he told her, delighted by the game of it all.

While kids flowed in and out of Ethel's house—"Big E," they called her—grabbing an ice cream from the cooler, a Coke from the soda machine, or a handful of candy from the candy jars, Jackie extended invitations to family members one by one. The kids looked forward to their night at Aunt Jackie's, away from the hubbub. Jackie's antique tiger maple dining room table was long and narrow. Each place setting had its own salt and pepper shakers and a big goblet of water. The chairs were tiny—except for Jackie's at the head. She had a bell next to her seat that she could step on, calling the waitstaff to retrieve something from the pantry or refresh a guest's drink.

Jackie's assistant Provi Paredes made the best daiquiris on the Cape, and she always remembered what Jackie's guests liked to eat. Paredes had been working with Jackie since the White House days, and her son had grown up with the Kennedy kids—they were like members of the family. When Jack's good friend Dave Powers came by to see Jackie, Paredes whipped up his favorite chicken dish. And after a few of her drinks, Powers slipped into his pitch-perfect Jack impression. He was terribly funny, and by that point Jackie could laugh along with him, too. Though her table was sophisticated and elegant, Jackie liked to have fun with her guests. One of her favorite questions to lighten the mood with a particularly serious dinner guest was to put them on the spot, whispering to the person sitting next to her, provoking them to ask who the stiff voted for for president. "Go ahead!" she said mischievously with a sly smile. "Just do it! Ask!"

Jackie was casual on the Cape, wearing a sundress over her bikini, or fitted white jeans with a sweater on cooler nights. She was almost always barefoot, even when walking down the street to the pier to catch a boat for an afternoon of water-skiing. In the evenings, she put on pedal pushers and white sneakers for a run along the border of the golf course up the street. At the end of her jog, she sat on the same bench every time, smoking a cigarette, striking up a conversation with whichever caddie happened to be passing through. A creature of habit.

Jackie's house, like Rose's, was locked in time. It looked exactly as it had in the 1950s—the same furniture, the same artwork on the walls. Jack's room, next to Jackie's, sat untouched. His golf caps hung in the closet. His books stood next to each other just as they had in 1963, faded after years sitting by the window. One lazy afternoon, John and Billy Noonan snuck in the room to rummage around. John opened the old seaman's chest in the corner. There on top were piles of yellowed notebooks with his father's distinctive scrawl and a bunch of official-looking documents. John slammed the top shut, and the boys walked out of the room, never discussing what they'd found.

John, Jackie, and Caroline found their rhythm those summers. Caroline rode her horse out at Grandpa's farm with her cousins Maria Shriver and Sydney Lawford. John usually avoided the football games on the lawn, preferring to tinker in the old green plane. John and his cousin Tim went diving or spearfishing. They waited for the windiest day to go out on their little flat Sunfish sailboats and surf on the waves, the dinghy flipping into the wake and righting itself again, the boys laughing as they gasped for air before flipping under the next wave.

If John saw Billy Noonan standing out on the breakwall, he made his way down the slippery rocks to meet him there. Noonan pulled in his lobster traps—and they brought what he caught to Jackie's cook, Marta, to make lobster salad the next day. For the boys, the close of the summer was marked by a bonfire at the end of Squaw Island, which everyone in the neighborhood thought was haunted.

While the kids were out, Jackie sat on the deck, sunning herself as she worked through a pile of manuscripts—Jackie started working as an editor at Viking in 1975—or she went up to the widow's walk on top of the house, where she sunbathed nude. She loved painting in the sunroom, feet bare, hair pulled back, lost in her own mind for hours. If the kids were away for the evening, she had her dinner served on a tray, painting until the sun drained from the room. Jackie's house was peaceful, quiet. It was where the other women in the family came for a moment of calm. Joan came over to play the piano, which was always out of tune because nobody else touched it. Rose came over to invite Jackie for walks. Sometimes, her friend Bunny Mellon came over from Osterville, always with a bundle of bright sunflowers in her arms to give Jackie as a gift. It was Mellon who helped Jackie plan her cutting garden behind the house, telling her what to plant and where. Jackie loved the delicate lilies of the valley, which she had placed on her breakfast tray each morning because she liked to wake up to their sweet scent.

It was Rose, though, who had the most flowers in her garden. The landscape of the Big House had been designed by Olmsted just after Joe and Rose moved in. She took good care to keep it up over the years—and she was proud of it. She called over Jackie's assistant Kathy McKeon, telling her to bring her shears to clip the most beautiful flowers to bring back to Jackie. The Secret Service, though, once caught a woman who worked for Jean sneaking around Rose's and Jackie's flowers in the night with a flashlight, clipping the best flowers to take back to Jean's house.

Another afternoon, McKeon, who happened to be looking out the window, noticed the teenage Kennedy cousins rummaging through Jackie's garden. She didn't think much of it. The next day, though, they were there again. She went out to see what they were pointing at. She bent down to examine.

Why is there a big bunch of weeds here? she thought to herself. *This flower bed is always so well taken care of.*

Then she realized what she was looking at. She ran over to find Jack Dempsey, the police chief who was by now retired but often hanging out in the Secret Service trailer. She brought him over to take a look.

"It's marijuana," Dempsey said. "How did it get here, do you know?"

"Well," McKeon replied, "I don't think the gardeners planted it."

"I have to tell Mrs. Kennedy," Dempsey said as he turned to go into the house. McKeon took a shortcut to beat him to the porch, where Jackie was sitting.

Out of breath, she blurted out, "Madam, we just found marijuana growing in the flower patch!"

Jackie stared at McKeon, stunned. "Are you kidding me?" she asked. "Oh my God, this can't get out. How are we going to fix this?"

McKeon walked with her into the kitchen, where Dempsey was waiting.

"How do we fix this?" Jackie asked him.

"Just ignore it," Dempsey told her. "We'll pull it."

"Good," Jackie said, relieved. "I don't want this to get out."

He and the Secret Service men ripped the plants up that afternoon. Caroline and John were too young to have had anything to do with it, and nobody told Rose, Ethel, or the other mothers. "I wasn't one of those tattle-tales, I wouldn't go and tell on them, no, no," McKeon said.

McKeon, a young Irish woman who'd been with the family since right after Jack's death, hurried to finish up all her duties for Jackie before the sun set, hoping to spend time with her friends who worked at the other houses on the compound, or to go out with her new boyfriend. But after Jackie put the kids to bed, when the house was dark and quiet, she always seemed to find another chore for McKeon. Could she just hang this one last picture? Could she just rearrange these things in the closet before she left? It seemed that those early-evening hours, when she would have been unwinding from the day with her husband, were the hardest for Jackie. She wanted to put off being alone.

Jackie's favorite thing in that house was an oil painting she'd done for Jack in July 1960—it hung at the end of the stairs, and it was of the Hyannis Port pier all done up with congratulation signs and fireworks for Jack after he won the nomination for president. When Jackie moved from Hyannis Port to the house she had built on Martha's Vineyard in 1979, she left that painting, along with everything else. She walked out of the house on Irving Avenue, and she didn't take a thing with her.

Two white metal chairs with patterned seat cushions were set up on the small stone patio behind Ted and Joan's home on Squaw Island. It was the last weekend of September, everything getting quieter as the Cape cooled down. Ted had traded his old, holey Cape sweaters for a black button-up shirt, black sports coat, and jeans as he sat across from broadcast journalist Roger Mudd, a good friend of Ethel's. Ted had agreed to do the interview, the first of two for a CBS News special leading up to his announcement that he'd be running against Jimmy Carter for the Democratic nomination for president in 1980. Then he'd go sailing with his youngest, twelve-year-old Patrick. The rest of the family was gone. It was just Ted and Patrick that day. He thought this would be an easy one, a quick conversation about the Kennedys, the Cape, and what the sea meant to him and the family. And it started out that way. After forty minutes, they took a break.

"Patrick, why don't you go down and get the boat and pick me up?" Ted said to his son. "I'll see these people to their van."

As Patrick walked out of sight to get the boat, Mudd asked if they could do another round of questions. Ted reluctantly agreed as his eyes darted around, looking for his son. As the cameras started rolling, Mudd asked Ted about the accident at Chappaquiddick. Ted shifted uncomfortably as Mudd said, "But you don't think because of your rapidly changing position as a national leader rather than a Senator from Massachusetts that you on your own ought to say something more to illuminate in people's minds indeed what went on that night other than saying it's all in the record?"

Ted furrowed his brow as he looked across at Mudd. His jaw tensed. He tilted his head and shifted his weight in his chair as he said, "I'll answer any question that you have right now. I'll answer any question you want to ask me. And I'll answer any question that's asked of me over the course of a campaign."

Mudd went into the details about Ted taking a right when he should have taken a left. He asked about the dirt road. He asked everything that had been asked over the last decade and that would surely be asked over and over again during a presidential run. Ted tried to answer. Then Mudd asked about Ted and Joan's marriage. The fact was, Ted and Joan had been unofficially separated for a couple of years by that point. Joan was living in an apartment in Boston, trying to deal with her alcoholism. There'd been discussions about what a presidential campaign would mean for Joan and her efforts to stay sober. As Ted tried to stay calm during the questions, it was clear that he wasn't. He'd sent out the signal that he'd be running for president weeks earlier when he told a reporter that his mother and wife were no longer against the idea of his running. But it was clear, as he sat here in his own backyard, that *he* wasn't ready yet. And that maybe he never would be.

Ted wanted the interview to be over so he could help his son with the twenty-five-foot sailboat he was trying to manage on his own. He didn't want to answer any more questions. Finally, it ended, and the camera crews packed up their equipment. As Ted and Patrick sailed away from their house on that overcast day, Ted kept saying everything was fine. But he muttered and shook his head as he looked out to sea.

The next day, Ted called Mudd and asked to set up a second interview—a chance to make up for the disastrous first. Plus, the TV special was always meant to have two portions—one on the Cape and one at Ted's office. As soon as the camera clicked on in Ted's office in Washington, Mudd asked him, "Why do you want to be president?" A simple question. But Ted, still shaky after the terrible first interview and unwilling to make the official announcement to Mudd on-air, hemmed and hawed for several minutes.

"Well, I'm . . . ," Ted started. "Were I to make the announcement to run, the reasons I would run is because I have a great belief in this country, that it is . . . there's more natural resources than any nation in the world . . ." And on and on.

He had no clear answer.

The interview ran on CBS in prime time on November 4. Ted officially announced he was running for president three days later. His advisors had persuaded him to run because polling showed he had a good chance against Carter. But the interview with Mudd had sunk any chance he had. It was over before it started. The interview made people realize that maybe Ted really didn't *know* why he wanted to be president. That maybe he was just doing what everyone expected him to. Following in the footsteps of his brothers.

Rose and Nancy Tenney went for long walks through the neighborhood. Nancy had always been the little girl next door who her daughters ran around with. Now, they were both women—women who'd been through so much loss. "After Joe died and I went back to the Cape, I then realized here was a very strong, powerful woman in every sense of the word," Nancy said. "It's been bottled up all these years being a very humble, religious wife."

On one of the walks, they were talking about all the tragedies they'd both seen. Joe Jr., Kick, Jack, Bobby, Nancy's husband, her brother. So many of the important people from their lives were gone now. "There must be one that's the worst of any of them," Nancy said. "Do you ever think of it that way? Is there even such a thing as the worst tragedy?"

For a while, Rose didn't answer. They just kept walking, the wind from the sea whipping between the houses. "Yes, there was one," Rose finally said. "It was when Joe ordered a lobotomy for Rosemary."

Nancy didn't know that her friend Rosemary had had a lobotomy—nobody knew. It would become public knowledge a decade later when an excerpt of historian Doris Kearns Goodwin's book ran in the *Washington Post*. But on that walk around the neighborhood, Nancy had just known that Rosemary was a little different than everyone else, and that one summer, she just never came back to the Cape.

"I never knew," Rose said quietly to Nancy, "Joe never told me."

"Oh, my dear," Nancy said as she hugged Rose. And they both began to cry, protected by the quiet Hyannis Port streets.

Rose had never made close friends with her neighbors. Her family had always been the center of her life—it had always been her children or grandchildren or her great-niece Kerry McCarthy, the daughter of Mary Lou, who went with her on long walks through the neighborhood now that Joe was gone. She was into her eighties by this point, though she didn't look it. Her thick hair was still a rich brown and she never left the house without it perfectly coiffed—or, otherwise, tucked under a scarf. She wore little stickers on her face called "Frownies," which were supposed to prevent wrinkles. Rose was as put-together and elegant as she'd always been. And now, she and Nancy had the comfort and familiarity that only come with living so close to someone for such a long time. After five decades, Rose was able to let down her guard. On another one of their evening walks, Eunice came down from her house up on the hill to join them.

"I love those earrings you have, Mother," Eunice said. "I wish you'd leave me those earrings."

"You have such beautiful jewelry, Mrs. Kennedy," Nancy said. "What in the name of thunder are you going to do with it all?"

"There's a little story about some of my jewelry, Eunice," Rose said to her daughter. She told her she should let her husband, Sarge, know if there was ever anything she wanted him to get her. Then she added, "Some of those things I have were from little private indiscretions."

Oh boy, Nancy thought to herself, *here we go*. She couldn't believe she'd heard Rose allude to Joe's indiscretions and she wasn't sure whether Eunice had heard it or not. Eunice had always been the most religious and pious of all the Kennedys. Nancy had always wondered if the kids knew about Gloria Swanson and the women who suddenly showed up on movie nights in the basement. She assumed the boys had noticed—but that Eunice, of all the kids, would've been the one *not* to notice. And she'd always wondered what Rose knew.

Later Nancy said to Eunice, "That was so interesting what your mother said about indiscretions."

Eunice said, "Yes, wasn't it? I wonder what she meant."

Nancy said, "I don't have any idea . . ."

Later Nancy, remembering that walk, said: "That was the only time there was a thought in my mind that she thought Mr. Kennedy was anything other than [a saint]."

CHAPTER NINE

The President's house on Irving Avenue sat empty. The Early American furniture hand-picked by Rose Kennedy for her son, then a senator and presidential hopeful, was covered by stiff, dusty slipcovers. Lights were off, kitchen cupboards empty, beds made and unslept in. Jackie's painting for Jack hung at the bottom of the staircase, as it had for two decades. A home in hibernation. Jackie had begun to spend her summers going back and forth to her new, secluded 375-acre property on Martha's Vineyard, turning it into exactly the home she wanted. It was a thirty-minute flight from the compound, nearly impossible for journalists and gawkers to get a view of, and not a neighbor in sight.

Across the lawn, at the Big House, Ted began moving his things in from his home on Squaw Island. On January 21, 1981, Ted and Joan announced they were divorcing. It was mostly amicable, but Joan dug in her heels when it came to their summer home. Ted didn't understand why she wanted it. "This is Kennedy territory," he argued. "Why don't you buy something fancier in Osterville with your Republican friends?" But Joan's family had been on the Cape for two decades longer than the Kennedys. From the upstairs window of their house on Squaw Island, she could see where her grandfather had built brick houses for himself and his two brothers. She could see where her father had gone fishing as a boy. She wasn't leaving her home. And finally, she won the battle for it. The summer after Ted moved out, things didn't change much in the Squaw Island house. Joan was there from May until September, with her three kids, Kara, Teddy Jr., and Patrick, coming and going with their friends. Joan took Patrick, a quiet boy with bright ginger hair, and his friends bluefishing off the same beach where her father fished, and they brought back their catch to fry up for dinner.

In the winters, it was mostly just Joan in the big, quiet house. She got in her car and drove the hour-and-a-half drive from Boston as the sun set early on Friday afternoon. Joan, who was by the early 1980s in Alcoholics Anonymous and in and out of sobriety, spent those cold winter days playing the piano in the empty house and looking at boxes of pictures in the attic. She walked alone on the strip of beach that led from Squaw Island down to the Big House. Joan had always loved that their house was separated from the chaos of the compound, that it was a place where she and Ted could anchor their family, and recharge away from it all. "I know I'm terribly lucky that this house is mine and that I can indulge myself by picking up and going there," Joan told a reporter writing about her new life for a women's magazine. "I'm lucky too that I am a woman who can do that—go off by, and be content with, myself."

As the summer of '82 wound down and the bright colors of the Cape faded, Ted wore a faraway expression. He was up for reelection in the Senate—two decades in office. And he was tired. But his advisors kept telling him that 1984 was his year, that it was a sure thing, that he should try just one more time for the presidency. When his kids were up with him at the Cape and they set sail on the *Mya*, the conversation inevitably turned to the race.

"Why do you want to do this?" twenty-year-old Teddy Jr. asked his father. "You tried."

Patrick was only fifteen, but he was clear, too. One fall weekend when it was just the two of them, like those weekends all those years before when it was just Ted and Bobby in that empty house, Patrick told his father he was worried. He wanted his dad around more. Again and again, Ted's children told him. But he kept asking, as if the answer might change.

The next fall, journalist and family friend Dotson Rader came to visit—he'd been on assignment covering the steelworkers' strike in West Virginia and Ted had asked him to see what working-class people thought of him running. Around the dinner table with Pat, Jean, and Ted's kids, Rader listed off the reactions: People were excited about the idea of Ted as president. Not one person, Rader said, brought up Chappaquiddick. They all thought Ted could change their lives for the better, and they said they'd vote for him. Ted nodded with relief and looked around the table. "Okay, now, who thinks I should run? Put your hand up."

Silence.

Rader put down his glass and slowly raised his hand. Everyone looked down at the table as the wind rattled the windows. Rader's hand remained the only one raised. After dinner, Rader and Ted sat on the porch, looking out over the steely water as whitecaps bubbled in. Ted went on about industrialization and manufacturing. He talked about what it meant for the military. He went on for fifteen minutes—a monologue for no one; an acceptance speech he'd never give.

The Sunday after Thanksgiving there was one last conversation. Twenty-six years earlier, Jack and Joe had emerged from the sunroom after a festive Thanksgiving meal to announce Jack would be running for president in 1960. This time, the hope for another Kennedy brother presidency that started before Ted was born with Joe Jr. was finally put to rest. On December 1, Ted held a press conference to announce he wouldn't be running. His neighbor Melissa Ludtke, whose grandmother lived up the hill in a beautiful old home and who spent hours swimming with Kara, wrote Ted a letter.

"Patrick will have his ol' Dad to pal round with, to discuss the Magna Carta with, to find that shoulder to rest his head on when exhaustion and emotions bring the fears too quickly. Kara, of course, will have her Dad to point out all the cute-looking wind surfers to, but more importantly will have her own time to gain a self-confidence which makes her more radiant every time I see her. Teddy, well he needs someone to trim the mainsail and get some weight to windward if he's going to drink champagne from that trophy on Labor Day in 1984. It seems to me you've already won a lot more than the Presidency."

*   *   *

Rose presumably shared those sentiments, having already lost two sons who'd sought the nation's highest office. Taking comfort in the fact that Ted would not be departing from the routine he'd established as a senator, she settled into quiet rhythms of her own. She'd long since recovered from a 1980 bowel surgery and, with abundant energy, still continued to read, and occasionally answer, piles of mail from readers of her 1974 memoir. And she still swam in the ocean behind her house, her swim-capped head bobbing in the waves. Every day, she went for walks through the town, keeping notes—reminders or news clips—pinned to her cardigans. And she continued to see Rosemary, who visited regularly in the summer from Wisconsin. On a hot July Sunday in 1983, with nearly no fanfare, there was a small ceremony at the Big House—no big clambake or lobster boil. For Rose's ninety-third birthday some of the nuns who'd taken care of her daughter Rosemary for nearly four decades traveled from Wisconsin to Hyannis Port. The ceremony was in honor of Rose's quiet donation of $1 million for an education program for mentally disabled adults at St. Coletta, where Rosemary lived.

On a cold Monday a few months after Rose's birthday, Jackie returned to Hyannis Port. There was a heaviness the day Jackie flew in. The next day, November 22, marked twenty years since Jack's death. Two decades since the house was bustling, preparing for a presidential Thanksgiving that wouldn't happen. When Jackie woke up that Tuesday morning, she walked over to the sleepy Big House to be with Rose. Ted had come in from Washington and that afternoon there was a small, private Mass in the living room. A short distance away, in downtown Hyannis, the Kennedys' neighbors filed into St. Francis Xavier, where a public Mass was held in Jack's honor. On the local radio and on TV, there were tributes and interviews with locals who had stories to tell about Jack. Everyone in the world remembered where they were when the president was shot. But people in Hyannis Port talked about the kid they remembered walking to the pier in tattered shorts; they told stories about him racing the *Victura*.

Ted flew back to Washington, where he was driven to Holy Trinity Church. He spoke to the audience about his favorite memories of Jack, about walking along the beach behind the Big House with its breakwater protecting it from the rest of the ocean. "He said to me when I was very young," Ted began, "on a clear day you can see all the way to Ireland."

Ted could reflect on the brothers he'd lost when he needed to, when it was expected of him on anniversaries like this. But other than that, his friends and family rarely heard him talk about his insurmountable loss. The neighbors heard stories about his drinking and guessed that was his way to numb the pain. They saw him draw all the attention in any room he walked into, but they noticed that he often had a faraway expression. They wondered what it was like for him to live his entire life in that spotlight.

When David Kennedy, Bobby and Ethel's fourth child who was now in his twenties, came back to Hyannis Port with his doctor, the compound was empty—that is, except for Rose. David had been in and out of drug rehab; he'd started and stopped at Harvard a few times; he'd been arrested. Both David and his older brother Bobby Jr. as well as their cousin Christopher Lawford had been dealing with drug addiction for a decade. Bobby Jr. had just been arrested for heroin possession. Now, David was back home at his mother's empty house trying once again to get clean under the watch of a doctor.

David had never known quite what to say to his grandmother. She was so formal, always asking him and the other kids to point out places on the maps that were plastered all over the house, always unpinning questions she'd scribbled on little scraps of paper and attached to her sweater, a pop quiz for which one could only prepare by constantly reading every newspaper, a few hefty history books, and a poetry anthology or two. David was jittery and gaunt from his years of drug use, and he had no plans to hang out with her over at the Big House. He didn't want to see anyone. But his doctor reached out to Rose's cook to see if he could go over there to eat—a way to give his days some structure and help him connect with his family.

"Mrs. Kennedy, David is over there and he is all alone and he can't go anywhere," Nellie McGrail told Rose. "Could we have him over for dinner?"

"Oh yes, Nellie," Rose said, "by all means, tell him to come tonight."

McGrail went over to Bobby's house to talk to David.

"David, your grandmother is over there alone, wouldn't you like to come?"

"Nellie, I wouldn't know what to talk about."

"Just come over. There's a picture in the dining room of your grandfather in an airplane. Speak to her about that."

That evening, David got cleaned up for dinner and walked across his lawn and over to the Big House. He stood alone in the dining room as Rose came downstairs. He looked over his grandmother's shoulder at McGrail as he said, "Grandma, I never saw this picture before."

"Oh, come on, David," Rose said, thrilled to have the chance to talk about Joe.

The next day, David's doctor sent McGrail two dozen roses with a note thanking her for breaking the ice between David and his grandmother. After that dinner, Rose and her troubled grandson were close, taking long walks together through the empty Hyannis Port streets. "She treated all of her grandchildren the same," McGrail said, "but near the end, I think she had an awful lot of sympathy and love for David."

In the mid-1980s it wasn't Rose's charity events or presidential campaigns that brought the hordes of media to Hyannis Port, but rather, Kennedy weddings. The Big House was the preferred location for the family's new generation of brides and grooms. Everyone flew into town for the wedding of Pat's daughter Sydney Lawford to James Peter McKelvy in September 1983. It was that weekend when it became clear some members of the family were drowning in drug addictions. It was one thing to hear about what relatives were going through—reading about arrests and rehabs in the news because Kennedys always made the news—and another to look them in the eye here in Hyannis Port, where echoes of a proud past were so loud.

"The night before the wedding, my dad, some of the guys, and I pulled an all-nighter in my dad's suite. As usual, booze and coke fueled the festivities—with my dad doing his best to keep up with a younger and stronger generation," Christopher Lawford later wrote about his father, Peter. And about his best friend and cousin, David Kennedy, Chris wrote: "David showed up looking a lot like the beat-up Pontiac he had driven down from the rehab he had just been kicked out of in New Hampshire . . . David's bravado was still evident but he had changed. I could see in his eyes that he was beaten, and although there was a 30-plus age difference between my dad and him, they both looked like club fighters at the end of a punishing 15 rounds—powerless to dodge the inevitable outcome . . . I had a feeling I was seeing [David] for the last time."

David died of a drug overdose the next spring.

In 1983, Rose officially gave Ted the house he'd grown up in: the Big House. Rose still lived there, but Ted was at the center of it all: the new patriarch, in many ways. True, some of the neighbors were quietly relieved that Ted's 1980 presidential run hadn't gone anywhere, having been dealt a disastrous blow by the Roger Mudd interview. They'd avoided the tumult that comes with having a Summer White House down the street. But things weren't quiet on Marchant Avenue. Ted's powerful voice, which seemed to emanate directly from his chest, echoed from the tennis court in the backyard or wafted in with the wind from his sailboat, the *Mya*, out on the Sound. "He had the loudest voice I ever heard in my life," his longtime neighbor Liz Mumford said. "You could hear it halfway across town when he started yelling."

After years of the Big House only being occupied by Rose and her small staff, suddenly the newly single senator was entertaining and hosting. The Big House was wide-awake. For Rose and Joe, Hyannis Port was a retreat—they rarely hosted or used the home for work events. That changed when Jack ran for president. And now, Ted hosted campaign events and fundraisers in the backyard. His favorite events were clambakes. His cook, Neil Connolly, pitched a big white tent on the beach and set up the folding tables with a ship's lantern as a centerpiece. Torches dotted the beach as guests arrived, making their way across the lawn and down the wooden steps at the end of the property that led from the grass to the sandy beach. Guests grabbed a mug of clam chowder then caught up as the sunset turned the sky to cotton candy.

A deep hole was dug in the sand next to the tent for the enormous seaweed-lined pans of lobsters, steamers, knockwurst, corn, and potatoes. The air was thick with the steamy, salty smell of the food and the sea. Servers came around with plastic bibs for the guests and trays of unnaturally blue Hyannis Port Martinis—Connolly's sickly sweet concoction of gin, blue Curaçao, blueberry Pucker, and a splash of cranberry juice. The night ended with thick slices of watermelon.

Down the street from the compound, Don McKeag had just moved in after his own divorce and was starting a weekly tradition: Sunday Bloody Marys. Hyannis Port is a house cocktail party kind of place, with homes close together and wide front porches, perfect for going from house to house with a drink in hand as the sun sets. And McKeag, who owned the Asa Bearse House restaurant on Main Street, was a big personality in town.

"Darling," Ted said, slapping McKeag on the back, "I heard that I had to get the ticket to Donnie McKeag's Bloody Mary party on Sunday, that it was the hottest ticket to get on the Cape."

"That's right," McKeag said. "Where is yours?"

The two men—both Irish American, both loud with big laughs, both with skin creased from the sun, and thick hair turning white at the temples—became fast friends even though McKeag was a staunch conservative. On one of their sails, Ted teased his new friend about the cheap cigars he smoked. When they got back to shore late in the afternoon, Ted told him to wait a minute and ran into the Big House and came back out with an old, beat-up wooden cigar box. Handing it over, he told McKeag, "These were my brother Jack's."

Sundays were at McKeag's; Fridays were at the Big House. They sat on the porch with steaming cups of coffee in the morning and cut through Ted's neighbor Rodger Currie's yard to get to the *Mya* to set sail for the afternoon. They were often two of the only ones left around in the off-season, too, past when Schoolhouse Pond had frozen over. One frigid February, McKeag dug his car out from the three inches of snow that had blanketed Hyannis Port. He heard someone huffing and puffing through the snow, then looked up and saw Ted's white hair and red parka. He looked distressed.

"Commander, what's going on? What happened?" McKeag asked. Ted's sailing nickname was the Commander. "Is everything all right? Come on in."

"Oh, Donnie," Ted said, as he made his way in, "I've got trouble."

"Oh, Jesus. What is it?"

"Well," Ted started, "you know, it's Valentine's Day and I gave my secretary a list of names and addresses. But she got the wrong names on the right addresses. So, Cynthia was getting a Valentine's Day card that was made out to Nancy. Nancy was getting one made out to someone else!"

"For God's sake, Teddy! You had me worried it was something serious!" McKeag said. "Well, how many were there anyway?"

"I don't know—about eleven," Ted said, hanging his head.

"Well, come on. Let's sit on the deck and have a drink."

McKeag poured two glasses of Absolut vodka with limes from the two lime trees in his yard. Settling into his seat on the deck, McKeag said, "How the hell did I ever end up with you? You're one of the most powerful men in the world—and you can't keep your mailing addresses straight."

While the President's house sat empty, frozen in the 1950s under plastic wrap, John Kennedy Jr. lived in a cramped room just down the Cape in a place called the Captain's House. It was a big white house from the 1800s that everyone said was haunted and looked an awful lot like the Big House. It was the summer of '83 and John had just graduated from Brown University. He asked family friend Barry Clifford, who owned a local scuba diving shop, if he could work for him. John had always liked diving more than sailing. And Clifford was as close as it got to a real-life pirate. The technical term for Clifford's work was *salvage diving*, but what he was doing was searching for buried treasure underwater. John was enamored with the tall, handsome, cool explorer twelve years his senior. Clifford's mission that summer was his most ambitious yet. There'd long been rumors of a wrecked ship called the *Whydah* off the coast of the Cape that had gone missing after being captured by pirates centuries ago. It was just a story, though. There'd been no evidence of the boat since it went missing in April 1717. John jumped at the opportunity to leave behind the routine and safety of Hyannis Port for the chance to find the *Whydah* with Clifford.

"Is he bringing his butler with him?" Richard "Stretch" Grey, one of Clifford's crewmen, asked when he heard John was joining. "What am I supposed to do with a Kennedy?"

John was desperate to fit in and prove himself. On his first day on the *Vast Explorer*, a sixty-five-foot lobster boat Clifford was using for the expedition, John asked what he could do to help. Grey told him he could clean the lazarette, the vile-smelling, cramped compartment in the stern of the boat that housed the rudder mechanism. For the next week, the crew barely saw John during daylight—he scrubbed until the sun went down and, after dinner, he washed the dishes. To train John for the big dive, Clifford made him swim the anchor out—the anchor needed to be pointed into the waves so that the boat wouldn't turn sideways. So Clifford attached extra chain to the anchor and told John to take it out as far as he could go behind the boat through the strong current as the motor revved. Then he had to dive down and sink the anchor into the sand facing the right direction. It was a job that needed to be done—but it was also a way for Clifford to see if John had what it took. Eventually, John proved himself.

The dive site was a square mile, thirty miles north of Hyannis Port and just off the Cape Cod National Seashore, which John's father had established two decades before. There was a small crew the day John and Clifford went to check on a spot where the magnetometer had gone off earlier. John snapped on his face mask to look into the twenty-foot hole they'd dug in the sand underwater. The ocean floor was constantly shifting—waves moving new sand to fill holes the way a beach footprint vanishes at high tide. You could dive in the same place two days in a row and it could look completely different. And that area just off the Cape was murky and full of sharks, so divers couldn't linger for long. John had barely been down there when he signaled to Clifford that he'd found something big. He wiped the sand away from the surface of the dense mass right in front of him. He pressed his microphone, then shouted into his mask: "Hey, I got something here! It looks like a pile of cannons!"

Above the surface, thunder rumbled. The current shifted the sand quickly, filling the hole with John at the bottom of it. Clifford signaled for John to come up before the hole completely caved in. John started to swim up until he felt something on his weight belt snag. He was attached to something at the bottom of the hole, while more and more sand poured on top of him. He pulled, breaking free by snapping his compass from the belt, which fell to the bottom of the hole with the cannons as John rushed up to the surface, gasping for air as he broke through. As John climbed onto the boat, the hole collapsed in on itself. John and Clifford were sure he'd been on the verge of finding something big. They'd have to try to find that spot again, though, to know for sure.

At night, Clifford took a small boat back to shore to spend time with his kids. John and the rest of the crew anchored the boat near the Beachcomber, a bar in an old station in Wellfleet, and the only place to go for a drink on the back side of the Cape's wrist. They packed clothes in a Ziploc bag and swam to shore to change. "You're All I've Got Tonight" by the Cars was always playing on the jukebox at the Beachcomber. John was the best dancer in the group, with hips that swayed right in time with the music. He smoothed his big, curly brown hair under a hat, put on sunglasses, and went the whole night without being recognized. This wasn't Hyannis Port, so nobody was expecting to find a Kennedy. John, the crew, and the women they met that night would close down the bar, then jump into the black sea, swimming their way by moonlight back to the boat. As the sun rose, they scrambled to get their dates back to shore before Clifford came back in his dinghy.

It would be decades before Clifford and his crew would again find that exact spot John explored—twenty-four years later, in fact, in 2007. When a member of the crew pulled up a shiny compass and read the inscription, he was confused. "KFJ?" he read. "JFK," Clifford corrected him. "Oh my God, that's what John lost that day." They found it attached to a mass of cannons, on top of where Clifford believes the millions in pirate treasure still lies.

Nearly 2,500 people crammed into downtown Hyannis. They snaked through Main Street and down South Street with necks stretched and eyes wide. News trucks lined sidewalks. Reporters and photographers balanced on stepladders they'd set up as close as they could to St. Francis Xavier Church on South Street. The door to Colby's Photo store, right around the corner from the church, popped open and shut as their supply of black-and-white and photo film rolls dwindled down to nothing. The darkroom in the back of the store had never been so busy.

The year was 1986 and the month was April, usually the calm before the season, a time of quiet and anticipation. But this year, Maria Shriver, the CBS news anchor and daughter of Eunice and Sarge, was marrying bodybuilder-actor Arnold Schwarzenegger. Cold and dreary Barnstable was jolted awake early. Local Chet Kelley told one of the dozens of reporters covering the wedding: "It's just like the old times." Eleanor Siscoe, who was letting the press camp out on her South Street driveway free of charge, said: "I've lived here since 1941, and I've never seen anything like this."

The last time the sleepy village had sprung to life like this, it was celebrating one of their own becoming the president. But the Shriver-Schwarzenegger wedding was pure celebrity worship. Maria was emerging as one of the most well-known of the new Kennedy generation with a journalism career that was just getting started. She wasn't marrying an Irish Catholic politician but a flashy, charismatic bodybuilder—and a Republican!—whose personality was so bright he was crossing over into mainstream fame as an action-movie hero. The social circles they brought to Hyannis for the wedding weekend were as famous as it got. People lined the streets surrounding the compound as if Marchant Avenue was a red carpet; they crowded the airport, and they piled into the lobby of Dunfey's, the local hotel that hired extra security to account for the one hundred wedding guests plus members of the press they were hosting.

"We're looking for Clint Eastwood," a teenager on a bike told a newspaper reporter as Eunice drove by unnoticed. "I am excited," said a Hyannisport Club waitress who brought her kids to the airport to look for the stars she'd be serving the next night at the reception. "I had these Lee's nails put on just for the occasion."

Diane Sawyer was there. "Dear Abby" columnist Abigail Van Buren and her husband, Morton Phillips, arrived in a white Rolls-Royce. Artist and socialite Andy Warhol showed up in his signature black turtleneck, leather jacket, black pants, round glasses, and side-parted silver wig. At his side was glamorous model, singer, and actress Grace Jones dressed in head-to-toe emerald. Their flight had touched down late at the Barnstable Airport so Jones had to change in the bathroom. She was the supermodel and dance club vocalist of the moment who'd costarred with Schwarzenegger in *Conan the Destroyer*; Warhol was a celebrity artist who was at the center of every significant social scene. Warhol had been invited without a guest—but he brought Jones anyway. She was his favorite date. They'd taken a rented yellow station wagon from the airport to St. Francis Xavier. A line of cameras popped as they smiled and waved. Photographers and onlookers screamed "Andy!" "Grace!" "There was the biggest mob I've ever seen around a church," Warhol wrote in his diaries. Inside, folding chairs lined the back of the pews, holding the overflow of guests. For the last few decades, the Kennedys were the most famous people to have entered the staid Catholic church. Neighbors memorized where the family sat; local kids stared in silence as the Kennedy, Shriver, Smith, and Lawford kids squirmed in their seats during Mass. But now, the Kennedys were the *least* famous at an event that more closely resembled a movie premiere.

Oprah Winfrey, whom Maria knew from having worked with her at a Baltimore news station and who was fresh off an Oscar nomination for *The Color Purple*, did a reading. The last time Winfrey had been a guest of Maria's for a clambake in Hyannis Port, she was so overwhelmed by the constant activity that she hid in a closet for a breather. "As an outsider, I thought, God, I'm actually here on the lawn with all the Kennedy cousins. But the games never ended," Winfrey said. "I'll never forget being in the house and someone saying, 'Where is she? Oprah, we're starting another game!' And I ran into a closet and closed the door because I'd already done three games. Enough! It was all very intense." But now, she was front and center reciting Elizabeth Barrett Browning's "How Do I Love Thee?"

After the ceremony, Schwarzenegger and Maria, grinning ear to ear, walked down the aisle to *The Sound of Music*'s "Wedding Processional," and the hundreds of guests were brought from the church to the Big House, where a big white tent was set up for the reception. The neighbors set up chairs at the end of their driveways, enjoying the show, watching each celebrity arrive. They bundled up in their comfortable Cape clothes—sweaters and sweatshirts—and curled up in blankets. It was cold and rainy, as Cape Aprils often are. It's before the hydrangeas open, before all the leaves return to the trees.

Not that you would have known it from looking at the compound, where apple trees in full bloom lined the entrance. A truckload of them had been driven in on an eighteen-wheeler two days before. What had been the Summer White House had been transformed to something more like a set—a manufactured facade. After the wedding, Maria and Schwarzenegger moved to California for a life, Maria said, far "from the madness of the whole Kennedy thing."

Three months later, as the weather turned from gray and wet to hot and hazy, cars lined up in front of the President's house again. Jackie floated from room to room as breakfast was cooked and a vacuum buzzed upstairs. Jackie's daughter, Caroline, was getting married in just a few days, and the house on Irving Avenue was alive for the first time in a decade with dozens of people rushing in and out. Jackie's friend Bunny Mellon was arranging the flowers for the front of the church where the ceremony would be held. A florist from New York hung lanterns and filled the white tents on the Big House lawn with the simple summer flowers Jackie loved. Jackie's neighbor on the Vineyard, singer Carly Simon, was there to perform at the reception. Jackie, who'd wrapped a silk scarf around her head and donned oversized sunglasses, stepped outside to talk to the Barnstable police officers about security arrangements. The officers were different from the summer cops who'd guarded the house twenty years before, but the conversations were the same. Just before 3:00 p.m. on the wedding day, the gates to the President's house opened and the crowd hushed as a Barnstable police officer came out. "How many want hot dogs and how many want hamburgers?" he asked the group of about fifty. A few minutes later, a silver limousine pulled out and the back window slowly lowered. Jackie smiled and waved as the crowd collapsed in, cheering.

Caroline, who'd barely been back to Hyannis Port after her mother moved away, was there to marry artist and design consultant Edwin Schlossberg. The night before the wedding, there'd been a moment of calm. At the Hyannisport Club bridal dinner for family and close friends, Caroline's younger brother, John, had given a toast. For as long as he could remember, it had always just been the three of them—Jackie, John, and Caroline. As much as the family had been in the public eye his whole life, their mother had guarded their little family. Now, that was starting to change. John went on to say that he wondered what the addition of Ed would do to their triumvirate. But they'd become so close that Ed had asked him to be best man. John raised a glass as he looked toward the couple and said, "I now welcome my brother-in-law-to-be to the family."

That night, inside the President's house, Caroline, Ed, Jackie, and John sat at the kitchen table laughing, telling stories, waiting for John's date to arrive. When Christina Haag, a childhood friend of John's whom he'd recently started to date seriously, arrived, Jackie's cook, Marta, put together a plate of leftovers of spinach salad and tenderloin from the rehearsal. When Haag was finished eating, Jackie told John to take her over to see the big white tents set up behind the Big House for the next day. She was so proud of how beautiful they were, above the Sound, glittering with lights.

In spite of the family's pull, St. Francis Xavier wouldn't cancel its popular Saturday Mass, so Caroline and Ed's ceremony was at Our Lady of Victory, a small, weathered church tucked away in the neighboring village of Centerville. More than two thousand spectators lined the streets around the church and flowed into the wooded hillside surrounding it. Some people climbed into trees for a better view. The crowd roared when John popped his head out of the sunroof of a limousine pulling up to the church. A few minutes later, Caroline stepped out of another limousine with her uncle Teddy. When the crowd saw the bride in her short-sleeved gown embroidered in white silk organza shamrocks and designed by her mother's friend Carolina Herrera, there was a new round of cheers. Ted patted his niece's back to calm her nerves as she smiled and waved at the crowd. Before she and Ted disappeared into the church, they turned back with a finger to their lips for an exaggerated *shhhhh* to the rowdy crowd.

Outside, they could hear the claps coming from the ceremony. But inside, they couldn't hear a thing going on outside. The pews were lined with faces less recognizable than at Maria Shriver's wedding a few months before. But Caroline's father's friends were there: Art Buchwald, Ted Sorensen, and Arthur Schlesinger. Sandy Eiler and his wife, Lee, were the first ones to arrive—for once, Eiler had covered his tan, barreled chest with a pressed dress shirt. And there was Jack Dempsey, who was still an imposing figure, big and tall with a shaved head.

No press was allowed in for the short ceremony or the reception under the tent at the Big House. Jackie's spokesperson passed out a six-page fact sheet afterward to reporters covering the event. It detailed that the food was trucked in from a high-end New York catering company. It didn't mention that the family's favorite ice cream from Four Seas was served along with a four-tiered yellow butter cake for dessert. As the melting chocolate, vanilla, and strawberry ice cream was scraped from the bottom of dishes, a fireworks display, a gift from literary editor George Plimpton, was set off with bursts of red, green, white, and blue. Under the tents, guests listened to Plimpton describe what each shell was *supposed* to look like—since fog had diluted the intended effect. "That was an imperial dragonflower, a bouquet of comet sparklers complemented by a central burst of red and gold and stunning concussion. Just spectacular."

The neighbors, who'd experienced the day from a distance, watched as the display lit up the foggy night sky with a three-minute finale of exploding white bursts.

Ted Kennedy's Senate staff knew to wrap up early on summer Fridays so he could get on the road in time to get on the water in the afternoon. He'd get into the back of his car with a stack of papers so he could work and make calls the whole long drive up to the Cape. And as much as he was out and about on the Cape and back and forth for work, his mother was a priority. She mostly stayed up in her room. Her hearing was getting worse, so Ted's voice would reverberate through the house as he said the rosary for her.

It was almost nine o'clock on a hot summer night in 1988. Ted was hosting a party for his son Patrick, who was running for a seat in the

House of Representatives for Rhode Island, and Ted's parties always started promptly at six and ended at nine, so things were winding down. Patrick's guests, who were all staying down the street at Dunfey's hotel, were deciding where to continue their evening. Ted pulled his friend Don McKeag to the side. "Can they head over to your house?" he asked. "I'll send the booze and the beers and the food."

"That's perfectly okay," McKeag said.

The group packed up and it was just Ted and McKeag downstairs. The house was quiet again.

"Before we go, Donnie, I've gotta go up and talk to my mother," Ted told his friend.

McKeag waited. And he waited. He wondered if Ted forgot he was there. So he walked carefully up the stairs then down the hallway.

"Oh, Mother," he heard Ted say. "Patrick was just so happy to have you at his party. We all were. It was such a nice night."

McKeag's eyes teared up, hearing his friend carry on the one-sided conversation with his mother. He walked quietly back down the stairs and into the kitchen and waited. The kitchen was old, displaying the same cabinets that had been there since the 1940s renovation. A visitor couldn't help but notice the linoleum floors and a scratched-up butcher block island. A few minutes later, Ted came down. "Let's get going!" he said. Neither man said a word about what McKeag had just overheard.

Along the bridle path out at the farm in Osterville where Joe Kennedy used to ride his Irish horses through the quiet, there now sat a box of a building: simple, square. It used to be a cold storage unit. Then, in the '40s, it became Joe's Twin Villa, one of the best bars on the Cape—one of the best in the state if you asked some people. It was deep in the woods—completely isolated and impossible to get to unless you knew where you were going. Inside, there was a beautiful archway, intricate woodwork along the walls, and a hardwood floor so shiny you slid right across when you were dancing. The walls were lined with wood, so on Sunday blues nights, when bands like Mr. Jelly Belly came to perform, the bass resonated so strongly through the walls that the customers felt the echo in their bones. Saturdays, the DJ played dance music. But there were rules. Up on the wall a sign read: "NO JUMPING WHILE DANCING"—on account of those slippery floors. "If one of the Kennedys slipped and fell, it was over for us," said Joe Diggs, who owned the bar. "If one of the Kennedy friends slipped and fell over—we'd never make a comeback."

Joe's Twin Villa was mostly a Cape Verdean bar—opened by Joe Gomes, who got the property from his dad, who'd immigrated from Cape Verde and built the cold storage unit to store liquor. But then Gomes was one of the first minorities in the town to get a liquor license, and he turned the building into a bar. When Gomes died in 1979, he passed it along to his grandson, Joe Diggs. The bar sat right along the Kennedy farm's bridle path—where Joe rode with Teddy when he was a boy, where the latest generation learned to love horses.

The Kennedys and their friends were regulars at Joe's Twin Villa. They waited in the long line to get in, usually upward of forty-five minutes, just like everyone else. When they got in, they piled into a booth or hopped onto the pool table, the beers flowing, cigar smoke wafting above them. Arnold Schwarzenegger loved to dance. So did John Kennedy Jr., who was beginning to draw more and more attention as he changed from a round-faced teenager to a handsome young man. One night as John stood in the back of the line snaking around the outside of the bar, someone went up to Joe Diggs, who was tending bar.

"John-John Kennedy is in the back of the line! You've gotta let him in!"

"You want to trade spots with him?" Diggs asked. "You can go ahead."

John—and the rest of the family—never got special treatment. And they were mostly left alone once they were inside. No photos, nobody asking for autographs. But it was always clear there was something special about John. "John looked in your soul and he understood it," Diggs said. "John was one of the nicest people I've ever met. I don't know anybody who said anything else but that about that man. I just don't."

Back in Hyannis Port, the crowds and the press, which had died down in the years before the back-to-back weddings for Caroline and Maria, were becoming more and more regular. In 1988, John's face was splashed on the front page of *People*. For years, thanks to his mother's fierce protection, he avoided the public eye while he was growing up. The public mostly knew him as John-John, the little boy saluting behind his father's coffin. But here he was, all grown up, there at every grocery store checkout. He was, while he was finishing up his law degree at New York University, named the magazine's "Sexiest Man Alive." His trips to Hyannis Port, which had for years been quiet, were now paparazzi frenzies. John's cousin Joe Kennedy II was elected to Congress in 1986—but celebrity now trumped politics and it was John who was the star of the show.

"There were a lot of different pressures. You walked down the pier every Saturday and Sunday and there were photographers there," said Eunice's son Mark Shriver, who was about three years younger than John. "They're looking primarily for John and Caroline. So if you were walking down the street and you saw John, you start chatting with him and you walk down the pier and you're in *People* magazine the next week. That just makes people react differently. Photographers are doing their job. You know, John's the most popular guy in America, the best-looking guy in America. And, of course, everybody thinks they're better looking than John, so you've got that dynamic going on. People were very, very competitive.

"That affects family dynamics. They take John's picture and then you're walking down and no one takes your picture. How do you think that makes you feel? If you don't feel good about it, you tell somebody to fuck off or slug somebody. And then people are running for office, which creates nervous energy, too. You've also got the stuff in the sixties, which carries into the seventies and eighties. It's not like sixty-three and sixty-eight happened and everyone forgot about it. It's just a lot of emotions and energy running around here."

For his part, John seemed mostly unaffected by the attention. In fact, some days he seemed to revel in it. In August 1988, he was at the President's house when he called his apartment in New York City to check his answering machine. His buddy Billy Noonan was flipping through the sports pages when John said, "You gotta come listen to this." It was a woman explaining in detail what she wanted to do to him sexually. "Who *is* that?" Noonan probed. John, laughing so hard he couldn't speak, shook his head. He wasn't going to tell him. "Come *on!*" Noonan pleaded.

He knew the voice sounded familiar. Finally, John told him. "Madonna," he said.

That summer, John rode around in a sporty little orange Karmann Ghia convertible, which he named Orange. He took it to the car stereo place in Hyannis to get it wired up. You could hear him coming from down the street as he blared Aerosmith and Led Zeppelin.

CHAPTER TEN

It was one of those lazy summer afternoons at the Big House in 1990. The family's new pianist, John Salerno, pushed open the back door, letting himself in, and walked through the hallway next to the kitchen into the living room. To open the lid of the baby grand piano, he had to gently push aside the framed photographs that sat on top. There was Rose and Joe Kennedy with the pope, and the kids when they were young. He popped open the top, then slid onto the bench. He'd been hired by Ted to play for Rose her favorite Irish songs and old standards—"My Wild Irish Rose," "Mother Machree," "Sweet Rosie O'Grady," and of course, "Sweet Adeline." But Rose wasn't downstairs yet, so Salerno continued warming up.

He was settling in when he heard the porch door creak open. A short man with dark skin and graying hair stood shirtless in the living room. He trailed wet footprints across the pine floors, wiping himself dry with a towel. He was coming in from the pool. He sat next to Salerno. "You sound very good," the man said with a kind smile. "I'll come back in a little while and listen to you." Then he disappeared through the front door, walking across the lawn to the RFK house. The pianist sat, confused. Several minutes later the man reappeared. He wore a crisp red shirt with a white collar. That's when it hit Salerno.

The man was Archbishop Desmond Tutu.

Tutu had been staying next door with his wife, daughter, and personal assistant at Ethel Kennedy's house, but hopped back and forth to the Big

House to swim, go sailing with Ted, and take early-morning walks on the beach. Tutu was in the U.S. for a four-week speaking tour and was at the Cape for a break, but he had to cut his trip short. Back home in South Africa, there was an escalating right-wing backlash to the efforts to dismantle apartheid. "There's a lot of tension at home," his spokesperson said. "He needs to get home more quickly than originally scheduled."

Years later, Tutu would tell an interviewer about Ted, "He took me to meet his mother, and I get so upset when the general media are negative about some of the things that have happened . . . No one has reported that he would sit by his mother and they would be singing Irish ditties together. And then he would spend time reading to his mom. I mean, it isn't something [he would reveal to the media to get better treatment, where he ever would have said] yes, I may have made mistakes but I also am a good son to my ailing mother."

Hiring a piano player had been Ted's idea. The Big House had always been filled with music since he was a kid. But after Rose had a stroke in the 1980s, she could no longer play. Rose's secretaries called the Cape Cod Conservatory and asked them to send someone over. Salerno was quiet and polite. He impressed the secretaries who were auditioning candidates, and he was hired. He played nearly every weekend Ted was home from D.C. One of Ted's assistants would call Salerno on Friday afternoons in the summer. "Ted's on his way to the Cape," they'd say. "He'll be there tonight. He's going to want you to come over tomorrow. Get ready."

Always with the short notice, Salerno would think. But he always said, "I'll be there." He ended up playing nearly every weekend at the compound, the senator joining Salerno on the bench to belt out the songs. "You've gotta give me some room!" Salerno would say, nudging his right hand past the senator to reach the keys.

Rose spent most of her time upstairs, listening to her French lesson records, taking notes in her notebooks. She used a wheelchair to get around, and she was less and less able to communicate. Still, there was a big party on the lawn for her centennial birthday. There were pink-and-white-striped tents set up on the grass, and cakes and desserts with pink and red roses made of pulled sugar. A portrait of Rose as a young girl was set up as décor. And the town passed around an enormous hand-drawn banner for everyone to sign. Rose was no longer giving interviews. After seventy years of public life, she was finally living a private one, her family speaking on her behalf.

There was a press conference before her birthday with more than fifty reporters from as far away as Spain who'd come to Hyannis Port for the occasion. Eunice rushed down the hill from her place to the Big House at around eleven that morning, running a comb through her wavy, shoulder-length hair as she walked. When she was on the Cape, Eunice was always too busy to care about what she looked like but she and her daughter, Maria, were filming a TV special on the Big House's porch. They listed off Rose's accomplishments, starting when she was a child campaigning with her father, Honey Fitz, and talked about how she quizzed her children and grandchildren at the very same dinner table that sat inside, behind them.

The family was beginning to think about what life would be like after Rose was gone. That summer, Pat had told her friend Dotson Rader that the family would remain tightly bonded after the inevitable, saying, "We're a very close family. I think the fact that there has always been a place each of us sees as home—the place on the Cape—is important." Jean told Rader she'd once asked Rose what she'd like to be remembered for, and that her mother said with a laugh, "Remember, when I'm dead not to heat the swimming pool! It's much too expensive for one person!"

A garden was planned in honor of Rose's hundredth birthday at the little triangle at the corner of Iyanough and Wachusett Avenues, just down the street from the Big House and across from the Hyannis Port Yacht Club. Paid for by the Kennedy family, forty-four rosebushes of six different varieties and two crabapple trees would be planted along a simple brick path for the Rose Fitzgerald Kennedy Centenary Garden. The bronze plaque, whose inscription had been written by a town councilman, read, "Rose Fitzgerald Kennedy at 100. A woman of valor whose effervescent spirit, compassion, and vision helped shape American history."

That summer, Rose sat on her porch with Ted. She rocked back and forth, looking out at the sea, lost in thought. "Ted," she started, "I've been with you a long time. I'm tired, and I want to go to heaven and be with my other boys."

In the years after Ted and Joan's divorce, Ted's dating and drinking were more often becoming a topic of conversation on the Cape. First there was the article in *GQ* laying bare Ted's sloppy drunken antics in and around Washington: "For his hard public drinking, his obsessive public womanizing and his frequent boorishness, he has become a late-century legend, Teddy the Terrible, the Kennedy Untrammeled. In Washington, it sometimes seems as if *everyone* knows someone who has slept with Kennedy, been invited to sleep with Kennedy, seen Kennedy drunk, been insulted by Kennedy." There was a drunken fight in 1989 outside a New York bar when someone badmouthed his brothers. Then there was the book written by a former aide alleging Ted's illegal drug use. And in 1991, Ted had been out drinking in Palm Beach with his son Patrick and nephew, Jean's son Willie Smith, when Willie was accused of raping a woman. Ted spoke at the trial at which Willie was acquitted.

In Hyannis, Ted sidled up to the bar at Dunfey's hotel down the street where he'd chat up women, or he'd meet friends for drinks at the raucous Bud's Country Lounge, or he'd accompany his nephews to Joe's Twin Villa over in Osterville—sometimes referred to by Kennedy friends as "Sloppy Joe's." There, Ted sometimes drank too much and had to be helped to his car. He was, for the most part, a good-natured drunk, his cheeks flushing crimson as he got animated telling a story after too many drinks.

Ted's weight fluctuated as well. He liked to joke, "All I got from Grandpa Fitz is fat jowls!" But the more weight he carried, the more it hurt his back, for which he wore a brace after his plane crash decades before. Some neighbors wondered what would happen to Ted, there alone with his mother in the Big House, becoming more and more unhealthy and often far away in his thoughts. While Jack and Bobby would forever be remembered as healthy and strong men—Ted moved through his fifties wearing his trauma and excess. He was now a powerful senior senator, an icon on the left who was transforming healthcare, but his hands shook, his eyes were bloodshot, and his face was red and angry with burst capillaries.

At the end of the summer of '91, anticipation of a major storm, Hurricane Bob, overwhelmed the Cape. People lined up at the grocery stores and gas stations to stock up; in Hyannis Port, patio furniture was moved to basements, boats tied up. Rose was taken to Cape Cod Hospital as a precaution because there was no generator at the Big House. So, Ted was there alone as the skies darkened and the wind whipped through the streets, snapping centuries-old oaks like matchsticks. As the waters began to roil, Larry Newman, who lived across from the compound over on Irving Avenue, looked out at the raging sea. He saw Ted taking his boat out in the storm.

"I just couldn't believe it," Newman said. "The only thing that I could think of is that the guy had a death wish. The guy wants to die."

John liked going to the Cape in the off-season after the summer crowds were gone. In the winter, when snow dusted the Cape, he cross-country skied through the golf course next to the Shrivers' house. He'd have dinner with his cousins but stay at the President's house—his house now—around the corner. Sometimes Tim Shriver and John, who were about the same age, took kayaks into the icy-cold Nantucket Sound. In the fall, he made short weekend trips when nobody else was around, calling his friend Billy Noonan.

"I'm in Boston," John said. "Let's go to the Cape for the weekend."

"I've got a girlfriend with me," Noonan told him. "Yeah, I've got one, too," John said.

Noonan picked up John and the couples made their way down an empty Route 28, catching each other up. They dropped their bags at John's house then Noonan and John went to Angelo's, the grocery store down the street, to get a bunch of food. After that, they stopped at the Hyannis Package Store, the wine and liquor shop on the small rotary that led into Hyannis Port.

"How do you know what wine to pick?" Noonan asked as they walked through the aisles.

"I look at the lowest price and then at the highest price and I pick everything right in the middle," John said, pulling out a bottle.

John and Noonan cooked for their dates, and they ate and drank wine into the evening. Then, John and Noonan squeezed up the narrow ladder behind a door in Caroline's old room which led to the attic. They opened the hatch in the corner to a rush of cool night air and crawled up to the widow's walk, the little balcony at the top of the house. A lot of the old Cape houses had them—named for the women who watched for their husbands returning home from sea. It was where Jackie used to sunbathe. But when Noonan and John were kids, it was their tree house in the sky. Now adults, the two friends sat up there, smoked weed, talked about their lives, and looked out at the endless water.

An eight-by-ten-inch Federal Express envelope with round lumps sat in the mailbox outside the Dunkin' Donuts on Main Street. A postal worker picked it up, reading the mailing address: *Kennedy Compound*. And the return address: *FBI*. Packages with an incomplete address went back to the post office, so that's where the envelope went. When the manager saw it, he called the state and local police and fire experts and told them they had a suspicious package. Everyone inside the old brick Hyannis post office was evacuated, and the surrounding streets were blocked off by police for two hours. The state fire marshal and the Hyannis Fire Department arrived, along with the FBI. For two hours, Main Street was quiet while the package meant for the Kennedy home almost three miles away was examined. Firearms experts opened the envelope to find several rolls of undeveloped thirty-five-millimeter film and a confusing note. It wasn't a bomb. There was a sigh of relief.

From time to time, these suspicious packages brought Hyannis to a standstill. And there were the tourists and crazed fans who just got too close to the compound. It was decades after the glory years of Camelot. But it still happened. By now, the intense curiosity about the Kennedys barely changed the way the family and their neighbors lived. Yes, there was the guard who patrolled the streets, paid for by the Hyannis Port Civic Association, and there were the signs. The Kennedy homes remained private residences, so there were certainly no markers announcing where they were, but the PRIVATE ROAD and BUSES TURN HERE signs were a clue you were getting close. Despite the precautions, the houses in the so-called compound remained fairly accessible—no big fences, no guard gate blocking the street.

One afternoon after getting back from a sail, Ted and Don McKeag sat in the kitchen eating soup the cook had made them for lunch. A car came down the driveway, passing right by the sign that marked the road as private. It parked and three people with cameras got out and headed for the porch.

"These people!" McKeag said. "For Christ's sake! What is it with these people? This is goddamn crazy."

"Donnie," Ted said, "if you don't like it, go out and say something to them."

"You bet your ass I'm gonna," McKeag said.

He got up and walked out into the yard.

"Is there something *wrong* with you people?" he shouted. "Can't you *read*?"

"Oh!" said a woman from the group. "We just love the Kennedys! We want to take a picture!"

"I don't care what you want! Get in your car and *leave*," McKeag said. "That's what the sign's for!"

"Oh, okay, we just wanted a couple of pictures," they said quietly as they walked back to their car in the driveway.

McKeag, irate, watched them drive back up Marchant Avenue and then turned and stomped back into the house.

"Why don't you have a guard there?" he asked Ted as he shut the door. "Why don't you have some sort of an electronic device?"

Ted's face flushed red with anger.

"Donnie," he said sternly, "I'm not going to live like a prisoner in my own house."

And they never spoke of it again.

It was January 1992 on Cape Cod. John Salerno got a call from the senator—he wanted to know what the pianist was doing on July 10. Six months away. Ted never booked anything more than a couple of days ahead of time. But that date was stuck in Salerno's mind—it was the day all those tall ships were coming into Boston, the date he'd been hired by Massachusetts governor Bill Weld to play for the occasion. "That Friday?" Salerno asked. "I don't think I can do it. I'm booked already. Governor Weld booked me."

When Salerno hung up, he began to think. *It must be something big for the senator to be calling me so far in advance. And he gives me so much work. I should do it. I should figure out a way to make it work so I can play for him.* Salerno called the Big House and gave the cook who answered a message to pass along to Ted: He'd be there. He'd play for him July 10.

A few minutes later, Salerno's phone rang.

"John. This is Bill Weld. I understand you're not coming to my party."

"Oh," Salerno stammered. "Governor Weld. Um, well, I . . ."

He heard chuckling on the other end of the line. It wasn't the governor. It was Ted's unmistakable laugh.

They talked about the plan for that summer. Ted needed a seven-piece band. But he didn't say what the occasion was. Salerno could guess, though. It must be Ted's wedding to Victoria Reggie, the lawyer he'd been dating since the year before.

Six months later, Salerno and the band arrived at the Big House, dressed in white pants, white shoes, blue blazers, pale blue shirts, and bow ties. A secretary came out to meet them, saying, "The wedding's out back on the beach. You're all overdressed!" Salerno told the band: "Okay guys, take off your jackets and ties. Roll up your pants. Take off your shoes. We're carrying all this equipment over to the beach."

The real wedding had been a week before in McLean, Virginia—a small, quiet affair with just their immediate families. This was a party—a chance to celebrate with their friends and family on the Cape.

As the sun went down and the lights from Kennedy's beachfront reflected off the still waters, Salerno played "You'll Never Know," the song Ted and Vicki always danced to. About a hundred people looked on—their closest friends, their family. Jackie was there, a scarf wrapped around her head.

Ted and Vicki had known each other for years—her parents were old family friends of the Kennedys. They'd run into each other at a dinner party at her parents' place after Vicki's divorce and from then on they were inseparable. Ted taught her to sail, and she moved into the Big House with her two young children. Vicki and Ted took Joe's old room, the room on the southeast corner that overlooks the breakwater. They could see the *Mya* docked from their window. And they watched the pair of big ospreys that nested right near the house. Ted loved those ospreys. They got their first big, black, furry Portuguese water dog and named him Splash. Splash had been lined up to be a show dog before Ted persuaded the breeder to sell the sweet, well-behaved dog. Then came Sunny, who looked a lot like Splash but was much more of a rascal. Sunny was supposed to be Vicki's dog, but both dogs gravitated toward Ted. Vicki's young children joined in the football games on the lawn with their cousins. They added new games, too—guerilla tag and red light/green light. As the growing family played below, Vicki and Ted sat on the porch watching over them.

Nearly every visitor calling the Greater Hyannis Chamber of Commerce had the same question: "How do we get to the Kennedy Compound?" The person manning the front desk could send them to Hyannis Harbor, where the boat tour picked up. They could suggest a bus tour. There was the peaceful memorial on Ocean Street, which Jackie had helped plan. But tourists wanted to learn about the president's life here, and there wasn't really anything to learn at the memorial—just a fountain to toss a coin into. The chamber staffer could give the honest, unsatisfying answer, which was that the Kennedy homes remained private property and were surrounded by more private property in a quiet, residential neighborhood. There was no house tour, no events they could attend. This wasn't like the Kennedys' Beals Street place in Brookline, which gave tours on the hour.

Wendy Northcross, who worked at the chamber of commerce within earshot of the person who answered the visitor calls, had a solution: a museum. But nothing like the big, fancy Kennedy Library and Museum in Boston. This would just be focused on JFK's life on the Cape. And the museum would be located in town—a place to send the fifty thousand tourists who called asking about the Kennedy Compound every year.

The chamber started small, with a modest exhibit in the lobby of a local hotel. From the beginning, Ted had been enthusiastic. But Jackie was resistant. How many museums, libraries, and building renamings would there be? When would it end?

It took a year to finally get the family's approval. When the conversations about the museum started in the early 1990s, Jackie had a stipulation: the exhibits needed to be in a place that was around when Jack was alive, a place where he could have spent time. In the summer of 1992, the JFK Hyannis Museum opened on Main Street, in the old town hall, a block from the armory where Jack had spoken to the nation for the first time after being elected president thirty-two years before.

On opening night, Ted walked up to a picture on the wall. He stared at the photo of himself sailing with Jack. He looked lost in the memory. "I haven't seen this in years," he said out loud.

For John, who was too young to remember most of the events on display in the museum, it was like walking through a family photo album. He came in early, before the crowds arrived, because by then he was the one they most wanted to see. He wore a baseball cap pulled low and wandered the halls, reacquainting himself with stories he'd heard about for so many years.

Rosemary, still beautiful in her seventies, was wheeled into the museum with the nuns who traveled with her everywhere she went. They took her over to the walls covered with old black-and-white photos of her childhood and color photos of her family's life after she was sent away—the years her family transformed their little town of Hyannis. The nuns rolled her up to the photos with her in them—in the water behind their home, on the lawn. She just stared and smiled.

When Jackie died in 1994, John asked his scuba diving friend, Barry Clifford, to come with him to her house on the Vineyard. He didn't want to go alone. When they arrived at her sprawling estate, the one she'd imagined from scratch, they knew something was wrong as soon as they opened the door. They went up to her room and found all her clothes drawers open. Her undergarments were strewn across the bed. A photographer had been inside and had taken pictures of her most private belongings. John was devastated. The next weekend was Memorial Day, which he usually spent at his mom's house, inviting friends. Instead, he went to Hyannis Port.

"The funeral and Arlington are going to be crazy, I won't be able to see you then," John told his friend from high school Sasha Chermayeff. "Just meet me in Hyannis. I'll see you there after it's all done."

When Chermayeff arrived on Irving Avenue, John was sitting in the kitchen, his head buried in his hands. He barely looked up when she walked into the room, so lost was he in his thoughts. Chermayeff sat with him for a while. "I wish I'd had her just a little while longer," John said. He'd wanted to have his mother as a little old lady. She'd been only sixty-four. "It's a different thing. Having both parents dead."

Chermayeff heard rustling upstairs. "What's that?" she asked him.

It was John's girlfriend, Daryl Hannah. Her dog—an old dog—had died, and she was beside herself. Hannah had whipped herself into a near panic about it and was too distracted to console John as he mourned his last living parent. John's uncle Teddy had introduced him to Hannah, a successful actress who was stunningly beautiful, tall with white-blond hair. They'd been dating for a while, and every time they were together, they attracted an unbearable crush of paparazzi. John drew enough attention on his own, but when Hannah was there it was fivefold. Things hadn't been going well in their relationship before his mother's death, and that weekend confirmed what John already knew—that it was time to end it.

John spent that weekend talking to Chermayeff about his mother and what his life would look like now. That night, he told her she could stay in his mother's room. In the past, nobody but Jackie had ever stayed in that room. John usually stayed in his dad's room, the long one on the second floor with the blue patterned wallpaper, and his friends bounced around the other small upstairs rooms. But Jackie's room, which was set off to the side in the corner, always sat open.

It was cold that May night as everyone went to their rooms to sleep. Chermayeff opened the old medicine cabinet and looked at the neat row of pill bottles with Jackie's name printed on them. She opened the drawers with Jackie's scarves, thumbed through the closet, where Jackie's casual weekend clothes still hung. Jackie had barely been in that house over the last decade. But Hyannis Port would be different with her gone.

After everyone left, John stayed in Hyannis Port for the summer. He'd always used that house more than Caroline, who spent summers with her husband in the Hamptons. And, before she died, Jackie had talked to her decorator, Robert Luddington, about John's taking over the house. Soon, the young man whom the media couldn't get enough of was using the home more and more. And when John was on the Vineyard, he invited his friends from New York or Boston to use the Hyannis Port place. He'd insist. "Just take it for the week!" he'd say. "Pick a week." The neighbors noticed there were always new people coming and going, disappearing behind the tall fence. And Provi Paredes, who'd worked for Jackie and continued to work at the President's house during the summer, greeted each guest, asking them their favorite things to eat and mixing up her signature daiquiris in the household's clunky 1950s blender.

The winter after his mom died, a limousine pulled up to John's house and parked. The few neighbors who were still around noticed. When Noonan asked John what was up with the limo in the driveway, he was vague. A friend was in town. Nothing he needed to worry about.

Then, a few weeks later, John called Noonan. His friend was living in Boston working as a stockbroker and he'd married a woman named Kathleen. John wanted them to come back to the Cape—he wanted them to meet his new girlfriend, Carolyn Bessette, a publicist for Calvin Klein who grew up in Greenwich, Connecticut. When Noonan and Kathleen walked into the house, they found John and Carolyn standing barefoot, cooking dinner in the kitchen. Carolyn was in pajama pants and one of John's old shirts. Her long, bright blond hair hung straight down her back, her toenails were painted in alternating black and white polish. She smiled when she was introduced to John's longtime best friend, and he was struck by her perfect teeth. She had big, round sapphire eyes, and long, elegant fingers that fluttered through the air as she spoke. She was strikingly beautiful.

They had dinner in the living room, kept warm by the fire roaring in the fireplace. Carolyn and John explained how they met, and Carolyn talked about her secret visits to the Cape—which Noonan had already figured out. The mystery limousine.

"I like coming to this house," Carolyn said. "I went down to Palm Beach with John, and the place was creepy. There were too many ghosts down there." Carolyn had a way of knowing whom she cared to get to know right away. And if she wanted to get to know you, her attention rained on you like a thunderstorm. "I like this house. This house has got a nice vibe to it."

John and Carolyn settled into the house as a couple. They hosted small dinner parties, the kind Jackie had always liked to have. The house was beginning to feel warm again, like a home. There was none of the chaos the RFK house was known for next door. None of the formality and pomp and circumstance of the Big House. There were dinners on the couch; daiquiris whirling in the old blender; oversized, overwashed sweaters; conversations that lingered into the night. John liked to make his guests laugh, but instead of the sly comments his mother would make to whoever was sitting next to her, he disappeared upstairs while his guests were telling stories in the living room and came downstairs dressed in an outrageous costume. It became a challenge for his guests: Who could wear the most shocking thing to dinner to create a conversation? His cousin Tim once showed up in an elaborate Barnum & Bailey's ringmaster jumpsuit.

Rose celebrated her 103rd birthday in Hyannis Port. And then her 104th. Photographers and reporters swirled around the compound whenever there were rumors that her health was in decline. Paparazzi waded out into the waters behind her home, knee-deep, lenses trained on her bedroom. Though she'd stopped giving interviews years earlier, obtaining the first privacy she'd enjoyed since she was a child, there were those who felt they—and the public—deserved to hear from her, know how she was doing, get updates on her health.

"Drive me past the Kennedy Compound," comedian Joan Rivers told her driver during one trip to Hyannis for a stand-up show. She wanted to see Rose. Who knows, maybe she'd get some material out of it. Her driver took her from busy Hyannis into the quiet Port and down Marchant Avenue. The car slowed to a stop right in front of the Big House. There was nobody around except for a tall, handsome man who sat on the porch smoking a cigarette. Rivers got out of the car and walked up the steps to the porch, her hand outstretched to the door handle.

"What are you doing here?" asked the man. Dotson Rader was there visiting his friend Pat Lawford, who was resting in a bedroom upstairs. Nobody else in the family was home.

"I want to see Rose Kennedy," Rivers said.

"Mrs. Kennedy isn't home," Rader told her.

"Okay," Rivers answered, indignant. "Then I'll just take a look around the house."

She reached back to the door, pulling it open.

"I'm sorry," Rader said. "The house is private and not open to tourists."

"Who are you?" she demanded.

"I'm a guest of the family," Rader replied. "Please leave."

They looked at each other, Rader towering over the comedian by a foot.

Finally, she turned and walked back to the car, idling in the driveway.

Rivers would still use her trip to the compound as a punch line. Except in her version, "There was Rose, rocking on the porch and not knowing she was rocking, wearing seventeen sweaters in 185-degree humidity." In Rivers's story Eunice came out to greet her, shouting, "Mother! Look who's here! It's Joan Rivers! She's such a good Democrat!" And Rose looked up at the word "Democrat." Pause for laughter here.

Just after the new year in 1995, Larry Newman was outside his house on Irving Avenue when he saw some movement by the Big House. Nurses were wheeling Rose outside for a quick breath of the fresh winter air. He gave his neighbor a wave. And they both went back inside their homes.

For the next two weeks, nobody saw Rose outside. There were rumors she'd been having trouble breathing. But then there were rumors that she'd rebounded, as she had so many times before. And did you hear, Senator Kennedy and his wife, Vicki, were supposed to go to a fundraiser in New York and never showed up? They went to Hyannis Port instead; it must mean the end is near. More and more reporters showed up outside the house. On January 22, cameras popped as more Kennedys—Maria Shriver then Jean then Pat—walked over to Marchant Avenue and into the Big House. Outside, reporters whispered, wondering if this was really the end. Inside, in her big house, once again filled with family, Rose Kennedy took her last breath right before the sun set.

The scrum of reporters standing on Scudder Avenue received word that Rose had died at five thirty that evening from complications relating to pneumonia. Ted released a statement saying that she had died peacefully and that his mother was "the most beautiful rose of all."

The next afternoon, there was a private wake at the house. Rose, elegantly dressed in pink and blue, lay in the sunroom. The winter sun poured into the first floor of the house and, as the family passed through, John Salerno sat at the piano playing the songs he'd always played for her. When Ted came downstairs, he went around the room to thank everyone for coming. When he got to his mother, he stopped. Emotion washed over his face.

"You know," he said, looking down at her, "she looks like she's going on a shopping trip to Paris."

The next day, Rose was taken up to St. Stephen's Church in Boston's North End. The O. J. Simpson trial coverage on TV was interrupted for tributes to Rose as the rest of the world mourned the loss of a great matriarch and thought back on all she'd endured. And then there was the mourning of those in Hyannis Port—a place she'd lived for most of her life but where some of her neighbors felt as though they'd never really known her at all.

"A reporter came and knocked on my door and said, tell me about Rose Kennedy," said Liz Mumford, who grew up around the corner and now lived in her family's home. She'd seen Jack become president, she'd watched the neighborhood change. "I said [Rose] didn't know who I was. I lived next door to her my whole life and she had no idea who I was."

A week later a fresh layer of snow settled on the compound and the beach behind it, filling in the tracks of the tourists and reporters and returning Hyannis Port to its winter quiet.

*   *   *

As the summer wound down in 1996, John invited Noonan and Kathleen and their brand-new baby to the house for the weekend. It would just be the five of them—no dinner parties. Provi Paredes brought out frosted Waterford goblets—engraved with the Kennedy family crest and inscribed with "John-John" and "Caroline"—from one of John's childhood trips to Ireland. As soon as Paredes left, Noonan could tell from John and Carolyn's expressions that they were about to reveal something big. Before they said a word, he knew: they were getting married. They peppered John and Carolyn with questions: When did the proposal happen? How? Where? When's the wedding?

As Carolyn and Kathleen talked about wedding details, Noonan and John went up to the widow's walk. The waves crashed on the breakwater they'd walked on so many times. John lit a cigarette, blowing smoke circles into the black night. The wedding would be small—really small—John explained. Noonan would need to keep it quiet. The details couldn't get out. John wouldn't even tell him where it was going to be.

"Do you think she's the right one?" John asked Noonan. Noonan said he thought she was. Carolyn seemed like a good fit for John, they clearly loved each other, and he thought she could handle the pressure that came with being in John's life. Outside of Hyannis Port, in the real world, there'd be overwhelming attention that nobody besides John could ever understand. He was one of the most famous, most recognizable people in the country—in the world. Yes, the paparazzi followed him to the Cape, and tourists came to gawk at him on the same streets they'd seen him run through as a child in presidential photographs. But he was protected here. Everyone here knew him—they tried to throw the paparazzi off his trail, and they didn't speak to the press. For Carolyn, it would be very different outside this bubble. But she'd be able to deal with it, John and Noonan thought.

Though John and Carolyn's wedding plans remained a secret, the press attention was a constant. Usually John stopped, smiled, and waved. Eventually he told the paparazzi assigned to him for the day, "Okay, guys, that's enough for now," and they'd back off. But one summer afternoon, he couldn't get rid of a man with a camera trailing him. He called his friend Brad Blank and said, "Meet me at my house and we'll go on the boat." When they got to the pier around the corner, John took off his shirt and handed it to Blank. He jumped in the water and swam out to the sailboat to throw the paparazzi off his trail, leaving Blank alone to launch the tender.

"What was that all about?" Blank asked when he got to the boat.

"You see that guy over there?" John said, pointing to the beach. There was a man with a telephoto lens as big as a guitar. "That guy has been following me around everywhere I've been. I think my travel agent might be tipping him off. This isn't good." And sure enough, though they were more than a mile out on the water, the photos of John, shirtless on the boat, were all over the papers the next day.

Eventually, John snapped. He'd come to Hyannis Port for Labor Day weekend in 1996, and the cameras followed. Stepping off the small sailboat onto the Hyannis Port Yacht Club dock, a crowd surrounded John. A man with a large camera walked toward him, down the pier. John grabbed a yellow bucket of water and charged.

"The pier is off limits," John said to the photographer.

"He's on his vacation, why don't you leave him alone?" a young woman said, stepping in front of the camera.

"Yeah, well, I'd love to be on vacation, too," photographer John Paparo said in his thick New York accent. Then to an older woman who walked in front of him, he said, "Hey, sweetheart, why don't you get your ass out of my way."

When he called the woman a bitch, John dumped the bucket of water over Paparo's head.

John, wearing nothing but his blue floral swim trunks, sunglasses, and backward cap, stepped off the pier onto the road in front of the club. Defiant, he walked straight ahead as Paparo kept his camera trained on him.

"Why don't you go back to where you came from?" John said, still holding the empty bucket. He moved back toward the photographer. "You're not even supposed to be on this pier!" he said, the pitch in his voice rising. As Paparo began to respond, John shouted, "Fucking mind your manners!"

"Take it easy," Paparo said, walking away.

"Yeah, I'll take it easy, and mind your manners," John said. "Don't call women bitches."

John went back to Brad Blank's car parked near the pier.

As they drove away, John cooled off.

"I better go back there," he said, pulling on a purple shirt.

He went back to the pier, where a crowd had gathered.

"You guys are like outsiders and they're just trying to be protective," John said to Paparo, motioning toward the neighbors. Paparo's shirt was still soaked through. "I apologize for pouring water on your camera. You know how much it is?"

"Well, there's a camera, there's a radio, and there's some other equipment in here," Paparo said.

"It was only half a bucket," John said. Then he cracked a smile and added, "It was a good shot!"

"It was a pretty good shot," Paparo said. "You've got pretty good aim."

John and Carolyn, who quietly wed later that month, settled into married life in the city that fall and winter. On Friday afternoons when the weather warmed, John tried to finish up at the Manhattan offices of *George*, the political magazine he founded, to get out to the Cape early. He wrapped up an edit or a last conversation in the art department offices where he liked to linger. Carolyn made her way uptown from their Tribeca loft with their black-and-white terrier, Friday, and fluffy black cat, Ruby, and they drove five or so hours on Interstate 95, the main traffic artery shooting up the eastern U.S. Pulling into the driveway of 111 Irving Avenue to that old shingled house for Memorial Day weekend marked the start of summer.

June and July were for Hyannis Port—the couple journeyed there nearly every weekend. The neighbors knew they were in town when they heard the Rolling Stones' "You Can't Always Get What You Want" coming from the old President's house. August was for the Vineyard. Jackie's place there was bigger, a little more formal with a garage turned into an apartment for guests. At the place on Irving Avenue, everyone piled into the small upstairs bedrooms. It was comfortable, with its overstuffed couch in the living room, perfect for sitting around and watching TV in bare feet. John and Carolyn almost always brought friends for the weekends, filling the house with people they knew from New York. They weren't the type to demand private time or a romantic getaway. They liked to be around their friends. Paredes was always there waiting for their arrival—she and her son spent their summers in the Port. To John and his friends, it was Paredes, whom he'd known since he was a child, who made that house a home. Spending time with her was half of what John looked forward to about Hyannis Port. Paredes was the one who kept things moving, too. Like at 5:00 p.m., you knew she'd put a tray of cheese and crackers out on the deck and pour the tart lime daiquiris. Friday and Ruby rolled around in the grass while friends caught up. Sometimes a family member or one of John's old childhood friends from Hyannis Port stopped by. After cocktails in the yard, the group would head inside for one of Paredes's home-cooked meals.

Sometimes John and Carolyn snuck away for breakfast in town. After the weekend morning rush, they'd slide behind a table at Gourmet Brunch, a modest diner with low ceilings and comfortable booths in a building set back from Main Street in Hyannis. It's one of those places with an endless menu, but where people mostly order eggs or waffles. John and Carolyn liked to go late in the morning, ten thirty or so, and the owner, Joe Cotellessa, sat them at table six, the one facing the window, instead of looking into the restaurant where they might be recognized. And if someone did happen to catch their eye, the person was on their way out, not waiting for a table, and therefore less likely to bother them. John and Carolyn brought a stack of newspapers, drinking cup after cup of coffee as they waited for their omelets.

The couple began to plan their future: where they would live, if they'd have kids.

Michael Kennedy sat at Joe's Twin Villa, the only source of noise that night in the quiet corner of Osterville farmlands. The bar was alive with people dancing on the slick wooden dance floor, or shouting their drink orders across the bar. Michael was the spitting image of his father, Bobby—his distinguishing features being a big smile full of long teeth and eyes that crinkled at the corners. There was no blending in for him—when you saw him, you knew he was a Kennedy. And in 1997, he was the Kennedy everyone was talking about. He'd been accused of the statutory rape of his underage babysitter. (The investigation was called off when the babysitter refused to cooperate.)

As the bartender poured drinks, he kept his eye on Michael. All through the night, as patrons had more and more to drink, they went up to Michael to make a comment about the accusations. Michael sat there silently.

Just a few months later, thirty-nine-year-old Michael died on a trip to Aspen. Michael was the one who inherited his father's relentless competitiveness on the football field, who often dove into the bed of rose-bushes lining the Big House yard, emerging covered in thorns. He died in an accident playing catch with a football as he made his way down a ski slope on New Year's Eve. He was the second of Ethel's sons to die.

Michael's body was flown from Colorado to Hyannis Port in the borrowed jet of actor and family friend Kevin Costner. Inside the RFK house, as it was still called, Michael's siblings piled into the cold bedrooms upstairs where they'd played as children. That house got so frigid in the winter that their sister Kathleen once kicked a hole in the wall to build a fireplace to keep warm. "It wasn't until . . . I found myself in an upstairs bedroom in Hyannis Port with my brothers Max, Douglas, Chris, and Bobby and our sister Rory, that I realized he was truly gone," Ethel and Bobby's oldest son, Joe II, later wrote.

At the Barnstable Airport photographers camped out, trying to get a picture of Kennedys coming to mourn. To avoid them, Carolyn arranged to be picked up on the tarmac. Still, a car chased her all the way to Hyannis Port, where she hopped out and slipped through a dead privet hedge and behind the tall fence, barely avoiding being photographed.

Outside, TV trucks lined the narrow neighborhood streets, parked half on the road, half on the neighbors' lawns. Reporters lined up against barricades shouting questions at anyone who walked by. Finally, Joe II, now a congressman, came out to the street corner where the reporters stood. He walked up to a microphone as boom mics hovered over his head. His family stood behind him, among them his sister Kerry and her husband, Secretary of Housing and Urban Development Andrew Cuomo. Also there as part of the family's united front: Kathleen and Bobby Jr., whose face was wet with tears.

"There have been so many ways that Michael touched our lives, that Michael touched others who in turn have touched ours," Joe told the crowd, which furiously took down notes as he spoke. "All of us wanted to say thank you to the people who have helped us get through this period."

Kathleen, the oldest child and now the lieutenant governor of Maryland, added, "This has been a very, very tough and difficult time, a time of terrible sadness since this awful tragedy."

Family and friends washed in and out of the house the day of the wake. Maria Shriver and Arnold Schwarzenegger came to town that night with actress Glenn Close. Victoria, Michael's estranged wife, was there, along with her father, sportscaster Frank Gifford. John walked over from his house, his dog at his side. A tent was set up near the Kennedy houses with a buffet for the hundreds of people. Most of the food sat uneaten.

Down the street from Hyannis Port, behind a row of pine trees, the funeral was held at Our Lady of Victory in Centerville, the Kennedy family's new church. (They'd left St. Francis Xavier because of its conservatism.) A thin rope tied between bare trees and orange-and-white barricades opposite the entrance held back the throngs of press. Inside, holiday cards lay on the organ to the side of the pulpit, and the nativity scene from Christmas services more than a week earlier covered the first few pews. Just after ten in the morning, Mass opened with a letter of sympathy from President Bill Clinton.

Joe spoke: "Michael had amazing physical gifts as an athlete. And like all gifted athletes, he was fearless—on the slopes, on water skis, wherever he could test himself at the edge. This was one of the glories of his life and it should not be diminished by his loss. He was not made for comfort or ease."

Bobby Jr. invoked his brother's "personal issues," which he said were "not about malice or greed. They were about humanity and passion. . . .

His transgressions were the kind that Christ taught us are the first and easiest to forgive."

Afterward, the family was told there was only room for one person in the hearse taking Michael's body to the cemetery in Brookline. But all the brothers went, Bobby and Joe squeezing into the front seat with the driver. Max, Douglas, and Chris crowded into the back with Michael's coffin for the hour-and-a-half drive.

Six months later, on July Fourth weekend, everyone was back in Hyannis Port. Ted had put the word out that there'd be a family reunion—and attendance was mandatory. By now he had grandchildren and great-nieces and -nephews who'd never met one another. There was a tent set up behind his house and he brought photographer Ken Regan up to orchestrate a big family photo with all 106 members of the family. There was face painting for the little kids and tours of the Big House. Pat, Eunice, and Jean gave the tours, walking the kids from room to room, including the living room overlooking Nantucket Sound where they'd sung songs with their mother, the formal dining room where Joe Jr. and Jack had fought over the last piece of chocolate pie, and the bright sunroom where their father had told them their brother Joe Jr. had died. They pointed out the pictures that lined the walls—of dignitaries, celebrities, politicians, and their own family dressed up for important events when they were the most powerful family in the world.

Ted rented a boat large enough to fit everyone and sailed to a stretch of land about half a mile out for a picnic. Rosemary, who was down from St. Coletta, stayed on shore. Everyone else had to be on time—the land where the picnic was to be held came and went with the tide, so they had only four or five hours before the water swallowed up the land again. They made it out there, set out food, but that day, the tide wasn't cooperating. The water crept up, closer and closer to the family and the picnic. They quickly packed everything up and gathered back onto the boat. With everyone together, they sailed around the Sound. They were out about three miles when suddenly John jumped off the boat. Everyone gasped. They watched his head bob up and down as speedboats raced around him. When they got back to the beach, John wasn't there yet. Carolyn's eyes darted across the water, looking for his dark hair to surface again. A few minutes later he came up for air, swimming to shore with a proud smile, and the family burst into cheers and claps. The Kennedy cousins grew up being told they came from Wexford, the Irish port town. They were told they had saltwater in their blood and that they should never be scared of the sea. Controlled recklessness was a family tradition.

"Don't you ever do that again," Carolyn told her husband sharply.

Everyone went to clean up before the family photo—John and Carolyn walked back to their place, the Shrivers up the hill, the Robert Kennedys to Ethel's. The photographer and his assistants ran house to house shouting, "Come on! You've got to come now!" Everyone lined up in their freshly pressed sundresses and collared shirts, salty hair combed into place. The kids lined up in a row in front, except the youngest, who were held by their parents.

"Are we ready?" Ted boomed from the back.

"John and Carolyn aren't here," the photographer answered.

"Well, you know where they are!" Ted responded, the crowd erupting in laughs.

Ted sent one of the kids up to John's house, and he brought them back down to the water where everyone was waiting, frozen in their posed positions. With their arms linked, John in khakis and a white shirt and Carolyn in jeans and a black sweater, both flushed with embarrassment, they ducked down at the front of the group with the children. Everyone cheered when they arrived, Eunice clapped, and Ted spun his finger in the air indicating to the photographer to quickly snap the photos.

The family broke off into smaller groups for portraits—the men gathered together, then individual family units. Carolyn wandered around the Big House lawn barefoot, leaning forward into handstands, as comfortable as could be. She and John came back together every few minutes to tease each other and kiss. That weekend, John and Carolyn were the picture of a healthy, young couple. They seemed happy, carefree.

*   *   *

A few months later, in the fall, John's friend Sasha Chermayeff, her husband, and their two children came to visit for the weekend. The toddlers ran through the house and yard, shrieking with delight. As Carolyn and John lay in the grass with them, the kids crawled on top of John and tried to balance their little feet on his bare chest. When they went sailing, Chermayeff's daughter, Olivia, got scared as the mast whipped back and forth and, with panic in her eyes, reached not for her dad who stretched out his arms to hold her, but for John. John threw down the ropes he was holding and took the little girl. She calmed down and fell right to sleep in his lap, her head resting on her big orange life jacket. A look of pride washed over John's face as he held the sleeping toddler.

That night Chermayeff took the kids upstairs to give them their baths and get them ready for bed. She kneeled over the tub, washing off the sweat and saltwater, barely noticing John had stopped to lean against the doorframe and watch her. "You guys are the best parents," he finally said. He came into the bathroom, sitting on the toilet lid. Chermayeff was an artist and her husband, Philip Howie, was a sculptor. They'd bought a little old house in the country, in the Catskills, New York, and were going back to the city a couple of days a week. But they were thinking of moving upstate full-time. John's life could be so overwhelming—the paparazzi, his work, the pressures on him—and when he was with Chermayeff and her family he was calm, at peace. He called them his second family. He loved how central the kids were in Chermayeff's life. They were different from the New York City families he'd grown up around—and the ones that he saw his friends and his sister starting now. Their weekends weren't booked up with classes and activities.

Carolyn was great with Chermayeff's kids, too. They told her long, nonsensical stories the way little kids do, and she focused her big blue eyes on them, listening as if what they were telling her was the most interesting thing she'd ever heard. She nodded along, asked them the right questions. And they adored her. But Carolyn wasn't ready for kids. She couldn't imagine pushing a stroller with a little Kennedy while being chased by the paparazzi. John thought she could handle the attention, like he had his whole life. And so did she. But the cracks were beginning to show.

"I definitely want kids," John told Chermayeff that night after the kids were bathed and put to bed. "Look at Bobby," he said about his cousin Bobby Jr., whom he was growing closer to, "he's got five!"

In the summer of 1999, John and Carolyn spent a lot of their time on the Vineyard when they weren't traveling for work. They were expected to go to more meetings with advertisers to help drum up fresh interest in *George*, which was floundering. The pressure weighed heavily on them. And the constant presence of paparazzi and media attention made Carolyn increasingly anxious.

If that weren't enough, John's cousin Anthony Radziwill—the son of Jackie's sister, Lee, and John's closest cousin and best man at his wedding—was at the Vineyard for the summer, in his tenth year of battling cancer, and not expected to live much longer. Anthony had come to the island with his wife, Carole, for what he called a vacation, but the seriousness of his condition was on everyone's minds. John had already started writing Anthony's eulogy, and Carolyn was pouring all her energy into taking care of Anthony and Carole, one of her closest friends.

With all that, John and Carolyn's relationship couldn't help but be affected. They didn't talk about it, though—they just kept moving forward. "There was a deep sadness that was entering in," said Chermayeff. "And I think Anthony's sickness was the symbol: the place where everybody could kind of let go of all the weight. You could go and visit a hospital and then cry together and relieve a whole lot. But [John and Carolyn] weren't really addressing their own personal problems. That's why I think their relationship was starting to tank, because they just weren't really giving it the time . . . needed to really unpack what was wrong with it, what they needed to change."

There was also growing tension between John and Caroline. John, Carolyn, Caroline, and her husband, Ed, were deciding what to do with the house on Irving Avenue—among other things. The house had remained mostly unchanged since their father's death more than thirty years earlier—his room as it had always been, behind a closed door. Jackie had barely changed things, and when she died, neither had John and

Caroline. So the house remained a time capsule of the most celebrated period of the Kennedys' lives. The history was important to John. But it was becoming clear that the house was also full of incredibly valuable things—items that should be properly preserved and archived. The papers and pictures tucked away in old trunks and closets weren't just family heirlooms, they were American history. In 1996, John and Caroline had auctioned off some of the things from the house—a rocking chair, some of Jackie's jewelry. But there was so much more.

John had considered taking a step away from Hyannis Port, maybe even selling the house. His accountant told him to keep it—it made more financial sense to just use it on the weekends, even taking into account the cost of flying back and forth. And John had always wanted his kids to have access to the house one day. But the previous Thanksgiving weekend in Hyannis Port, John had said to Noonan: "I'm thinking about selling the house. I want you to buy it. It would do my heart good for somebody to use that house. Especially a young family."

"You want to keep this house, you want to bring your children here," Noonan told him. "It was your father's only home. Plus, Carolyn loves it here."

"She does and she doesn't," John said. "We really don't get any privacy."

Noonan had a young family and didn't want to take on the expense of buying the property. John offered to give him the loan to buy it. "I don't want Ethel Kennedy as a neighbor," Noonan told him. "Sorry."

He suggested John sell it to someone in his family so he could visit when he wanted.

"They'll turn it into an event hall," John said.

John and Carolyn decided to keep the house—and to update it so it would be a place where they'd be comfortable spending more time. The crisp burn mark from a hot frying pan was still there on the Formica countertop from when John was a kid, covered for decades by a cutting board. The drafty old windows let in the chill when they came for weekends in the fall. John didn't want to replace them with aluminum or change their size—he wanted them to be wood, and to look like they'd always looked. For months they made careful decisions about how to make the house more livable. As John and Carolyn's relationship deteriorated, the house came to represent what their lives *could* be.

That summer, the weight of everything was nearly unbearable for Carolyn. She'd stopped working out, stopped seeing her therapist, stopped talking about going back to school. She seemed aimless—except for her laser focus on making that house perfect for her and John. "Do you think Mummy would like the wallpaper?" she called to ask Noonan, referring to Jackie. She'd picked a shamrock pattern for Jackie's old upstairs bedroom. She was trying to figure out the hardwood floors—which Jackie had decorated with Cape Cod speckling decades before. It's a particular way of painting, where the brush is dipped in paint then flicked over the floor like a priest performing a baptism—a classic Cape cottage style. Carolyn wanted the floors sanded and updated but was having trouble getting the stain just right. The more she worked on the house, the more it became a symbol of a normal future, of peace.

That summer, there was another big family wedding, for John's cousin Rory—Ethel and Bobby's youngest child—at the Big House. While John and Carolyn were in town for the wedding, they planned to check in on the renovations happening at their house. They were set to meet on Saturday with Robert Luddington. Jackie had always told Luddington the house would one day belong to John—and now the designer was gathering fabric samples and taking measurements to get everything ready for the interior update. As they worked on the house, John told Noonan he was ready to really settle down, start a family. He wanted a little boy named Flynn. But Carolyn still couldn't imagine bringing into their tumultuous lives a baby whose existence would make the media glare in Manhattan even worse.

When Noonan suggested they make 111 Irving their main residence, Carolyn said, "I can't live there year round." He told her, "Try to fix it up and if everything happens the way it's supposed to and you live in Hyannis Port, it's not a bad place to live." "Alright," she said, "I'll think about it."

Noonan and his wife, Kathleen, had planned to meet John and Carolyn and some of their other friends for dinner in Nantucket on Friday,

July 16—the day before Rory's wedding—to celebrate the Noonans' fifth wedding anniversary. Then they'd all go back together to Hyannis Port. John called a couple of times that evening and each time gave a new reason why they were running late: he'd been wrapped up at work; plans had changed; they needed to wait for Carolyn's sister, Lauren; they were stopping by the Vineyard. Finally, they all just agreed to meet back at John's house after they landed to share a bottle of champagne.

So Noonan and Kathleen left with their Hyannis Port friends Brian and Miriam O'Neill on their boat to Nantucket. They went out and enjoyed their dinner, but when they got back to the boat, the captain told them a thick mist had settled over the Cape. They wouldn't be able to get back that night to Hyannis Port safely. They'd need to stay put. Noonan and O'Neill figured they'd see John in the morning and have their champagne toast later. They sat in the back of the boat, staring up at the sky. As they laughed and caught up, O'Neill noticed that there were no stars above them. The mist swallowed the lights, and the night was pitch-black.

Just past midnight, the overnight maintenance worker at the Hyannis airport went to look at the far end of the airport where John usually parked his plane. It wasn't there. He looked through the logbook, which confirmed John never landed that night. As it neared two in the morning, the phone rang at the Big House. It rang and rang, echoing through the rooms.

Slowly, the family began to wake up, realizing that John and Carolyn never made it to the Vineyard or Hyannis. When the Noonans and the O'Neills woke up the next morning on the boat, the captain told them he'd just gotten off the phone with the mainland. John, Carolyn, and Lauren were missing.

Phones across Hyannis rang. John Salerno had spent the prior two weeks going over to Ethel's house, figuring out the music for Rory's wedding that was supposed to be that day. There were thirty-five musicians booked—Rory had wanted a bagpipe band, a string quartet for before the wedding, and a musician for the ceremony. The groom's pickup band would play the reception. One by one, each musician was told: there'll be no wedding today. In the tailor shop down the street in Hyannis, the little flower girl dress and the suit for the ring bearer would hang suspended in plastic wrap for days.

By daybreak, news vans lined the narrow Hyannis Port streets and white satellites dotted the sky surrounding the compound, broadcasting a constant stream of "no news" updates, filling the hours though there was nothing new to report. "At the top of the two's we'll just do Q and A," an NBC News producer said into her cell phone. "We'll use that as a scene setter."

For the local journalists, it was a repeat of Michael Kennedy's death a year and a half earlier. On July 22 the front page of the local paper read, "This moment, when the world's media descends on the Kennedy Compound, is a ritual deeply embedded in modern American life. . . . The Greek chorus is among us again." The reporters knew by now to wait at the corner of Irving and Scudder for someone from the family or a spokesperson to come out to give a quote. But there were so many of their peers here this time. The international press jostled for any place they could park and stand along the residential streets, waiting by their vans, calling their producers, and doing live shots every few hours. But the pattern of the day continued: there was no news, no updates.

Thick cables snaked across the streets. A wall of tripods balancing cameras bordered Marchant Avenue, which was blocked off. Barnstable police had already planned for coverage down by the Big House for Rory's wedding, but when the press started to arrive to cover John and Carolyn's disappearance, they sent backup. There were fifteen police officers covering the area at one point. The phone company was so overloaded that it added a hundred extra phone lines to deal with the crush. Rental cars and cabs were booked up, so reporters hired stretch limousines to drive them around Hyannis Port. It was like nothing the neighbors had ever seen.

As the heat rose, reaching ninety degrees with suffocating humidity, and the search for John, Carolyn, and Lauren stretched on, neighborhood kids passed out Popsicles and sold water bottles for three dollars. "Never mind the water, I'll give you five dollars for a bathroom," a *USA Today* reporter told one of the children. When the water ran out, camera crews dipped plastic cups to scoop the melted ice from the coolers that had held the water bottles. The heat and the crowds and the waiting became unbearable.

Plastic bottles and stubbed cigarette butts gathered where the concrete met manicured grass. The trucks growled, their diesel fumes souring the air, wafting into the open windows of the houses without air-conditioning. Some of the neighbors tried to ignore it and go about their day. "I'll be better when it's over," one woman told a reporter as she tended to her wilting annuals.

Sam Barber, a local artist and friend of the Kennedy family, sat in his yard down the street from the Big House. He set up his easel and moved his left hand gracefully across the canvas, creating a tranquil sailboat race. Sam knew John, who waved when he ran by his house on the beach in the mornings, and he'd known Jackie, who'd bought his paintings. He edited out the disarray surrounding him, painting a serene scene, as if it were any other day on the Cape.

In Hyannis, Rob Stewart, the summer cop who'd grown close with Jackie and had seen John toddle around the yard, was working at the funeral home. On his way to work, he'd heard on the radio that John, Carolyn, and her sister were missing. His boss told him, "Don't say a word but you've gotta get three gurneys, three hearses, three vans, three of everything ready." In a news van parked out front, a photojournalist with a camera around his neck stared at the funeral home, looking for signs of movement—a signal that they were getting things ready for the worst. But it would be days before there was any news.

Along the beach behind the Big House, Bobby Jr. and his younger brother Max and their wives stood on the sand gazing out at the water, on the same shore where John's father had walked and grieved after his older brother, Joe Jr., had fallen out of the sky. Cameras popped at the chance to capture for the next day's paper a shot of the family looking distraught. But where else could they go? This was their home, where their family was. And so, as the world watched, they moved through one of the worst days of their lives, once again staring at the unthinkable. Caroline stayed away from all of it, at home on Long Island with her husband and three children.

Inside John's house, time stopped. When Noonan and Kathleen got back there on Saturday morning, Billy noticed the flag in front of the Big House still flew at full staff. A good sign, he noted. They walked past the gate of John's house, with their son's initials carved into the cement, in through the back door into the kitchen, expecting to find John sitting at the table reading the paper, laughing at what a big deal they were making over nothing. He wasn't there. Paredes looked up as they walked into the house. "Where's John? Is he with you, Billy Noonan?" Noonan told her he wasn't.

He probably knew then that John wasn't coming back, but he lied to himself a little longer, for as long as he could. Noonan picked up the phone to call his friend and John's cousin, Tim. This was all just a big misunderstanding, they told themselves. They knew John would come home. It was John! He was always causing their hearts to stop with his impulsive changes of plan. They laughed about it. "You know that John's out on the wing of the plane and Carolyn's yelling at him to do something," Noonan said, looking around the living room, which was newly transformed into Carolyn's vision for her and John's future: fresh wallpaper, crisp new upholstery, newly stained floors.

But as the hours stretched on and the wall of media began closing in on the house, something inside changed. They couldn't keep pretending he was coming back. Noonan called Anthony Radziwiłł over on the Vineyard. "You need to come up here," Noonan told him. "No," Anthony said. "I need to stay here. I can't come up there. I can't see you."

Cousins and friends passed both ways through the gate on Irving Avenue. The media parked their trucks along Irving but walked around to Marchant, closer to the Big House, not realizing that anyone inside John's house would come and go through the front entrance, right where they'd parked their trucks.

The phone inside the house kept ringing: Journalists hoping for a quote from anyone who would answer. John's friends used their clunky cell phones to call the outside world for updates while the landline inside kept ringing and the TV in the living room blared cable news, which was being broadcast from a few feet away. Debris from the plane had been recovered from the waters—Lauren's suitcase, Carolyn's prescription bottle—the news anchors told them through the television. Everyone inside the house was trapped in a nightmare, bombarded with messages from the outside. Next door, a Mass was held under the tent that had been set up for Rory's wedding. Billy remembered Tim telling him that Caroline had called and said not to let anyone else in the house.

Pinky, a friend John knew through his cousin Tim, paced the yard. He was so nicknamed because his cheeks flushed when he got angry. And he was angry that weekend, walking back and forth under the apple tree inside the property's fence listening to the reporters on the other side. Noonan and Pinky threw apples over the fence, shouting, "Shut up! You're liars!"

Finally, that afternoon Tim and Noonan had the hard conversation. John wasn't coming home.

That night, after the sun set, Noonan went up to the widow's walk, staring out at the sea, wondering where his friend was, willing him to come back home. The night blurred into a new morning, which blurred into another night.

On Monday, Noonan and Pinky went with another friend to Otis Air Force Base, where John's father had landed on Air Force One all those years before. "We're gonna find this fucker," they said to each other with empty bravado. When they got there, the commander told them it was no longer a search-and-rescue mission. It was a recovery mission.

It was over.

Noonan and Pinky went out to dinner that night with their friend Brad Blank, John's cousin Mark Shriver and his wife, Jeannie, and Paredes. They picked a cheap Italian restaurant in town, one with candle wax dripping down a Chianti bottle as a centerpiece. They told stories about John and about Hyannis Port. They laughed. It was their own private wake. After the bill was paid, Noonan went back into the night, back to John's quiet house, up to John's bedroom. The President's bedroom. He lay down, thinking to himself this was the last time he'd be in this house. He could see into his future, and he knew it would always be too painful to be here in Hyannis Port. Like Carolyn had said the first time they met, Hyannis Port had never felt heavy with ghosts, the way the Kennedy house in Palm Beach had. It always felt full of life. But without John, there was nothing left for him here. He fell asleep, the weight of the last few days finally taking over. The next morning, as the sun reflected off the ocean, Noonan opened his eyes and noticed John's comb. He thought of the old Yeats poem:

As 'twere all life's epitome.
What made us dream that he could comb grey hair?

On July 21 at 10:30 a.m., the bodies of John, Carolyn, and Lauren were found seven and a half miles off the shore of Martha's Vineyard. Ted and his two sons were taken by Coast Guard helicopter to the navy ship where they were briefed on the recovery effort. The bodies were brought up that afternoon, and later examination of the plane by the National Transportation Safety Board determined the cause of the crash was "failure to maintain control of the airplane during a descent over water at night, which was a result of spatial disorientation."

John, like his father, like his uncle Bobby, his uncle Joe, his aunt Kick, and his cousins Michael and David, would live forever in Hyannis Port frozen in time. People would keep coming to their homes because they saw the pictures of them running through the grass spotted with clover. The neighbors would always have their stories about when they knew the Kennedy who died too young. The mail, much of it addressed simply to "The Kennedy Family, Hyannisport," started arriving at the post office on Tuesday, and by Wednesday the small building was flooded with thousands of cards and letters for the family.

Later that week, Ted gave his eulogy for John, invoking that same Yeats poem about the gray hair. And telling his own stories of how he'd remember his nephew and Carolyn—and how he wanted the world to remember them.

"How often our family will think of the two of them, cuddling affectionately on a boat, surrounded by family—aunts, uncles, Caroline and Ed and their children, Rose, Tatiana, and Jack, Kennedy cousins, Radziwiłł cousins, Shriver cousins, Smith cousins, Lawford cousins—as we sailed Nantucket Sound," Ted said in his eulogy. "Then we would come home, and before dinner, on the lawn where his father had played, John would lead a spirited game of touch football. And his beautiful young wife, the new pride of the Kennedys, would cheer for John's team and delight her nieces and nephews with her somersaults."

The ashes of John, Carolyn, and Lauren, along with three American flags and three wreaths with red, yellow, and white flowers, were taken onto a navy destroyer on July 22. Ted, Caroline, Tim Shriver, and Willie Smith were some of the seventeen family members who went along. A brass quartet played as the ship steered into the choppy waters between the Vineyard and Hyannis Port. The family cried as the ashes were taken to the rear of the ship and then laid to rest at sea.

A friend of Ted's says it was John's death that finally broke him. He, like his mother, Rose, was one of the lucky ones to grow old in Hyannis Port. But that meant living through each one of the tragedies.

CHAPTER ELEVEN

A small crowd gathered at the little beach at the end of Wachusett Avenue, down the street from the Big House. There were reporters and photographers there for a naming ceremony—East Beach would no longer be East Beach. The Barnstable County Sheriff's Office had donated a boulder with a twenty-by-thirty-inch plaque proclaiming the new name and the beach's history. East Beach was not being renamed for any of the Kennedys—the name most of the world associated with this little neighborhood. It was being renamed for Eugenia Fortes, the Cape Verdean woman who'd been kicked off that beach six decades before and had been fighting ever since to keep it public—one of the only slivers of public land in the private and exceedingly expensive neighborhood.

The plaque read:

THE TOWN OF BARNSTABLE DEDICATES THIS PUBLIC BEACH TO EUGENIA FORTES, WHOSE TIRELESS EFFORTS ON BEHALF OF ALL RESIDENTS HAVE EARNED HER THE REPUTATION AS THE "TOWN WATCHDOG." HER ABILITY AND COURAGE TO SPEAK WHERE OTHERS DARED NOT, PRESERVED RIGHTS OF ACCESS FOR ALL. EUGENIA'S DECADES OF VIGILANCE IN THE TOWN OF BARNSTABLE PUBLIC MATTERS WILL FOREVER TEACH US THE VALUE OF GOOD CITIZENSHIP AND THE MEANING OF HUMAN RIGHTS.

Fortes's fight to keep the beach public didn't end in the 1940s. After the Hyannis Port Civic Association was allowed to lease the land, they tried to buy it again in 1961. Fortes went to the annual town meeting, where she stood up to say: "Mr. Moderator, I would like to ask the civic association are they going to segregate the beach as they have done in the last fifteen years since they have taken it over?"

The president of the civic association, George Shannon, responded: "We have never at any time wanted, enforced, or asked for segregation of that beach." But Fortes won the battle in 1961—the beach remained public.

Fortes, her hair now white and cropped short, went to the beach renaming in a floral collared shirt and slip-on shoes. Fortes had always been in the background—nobody knew how she helped Ted Kennedy navigate the Reverse Freedom Rides in 1962, or that she was such a regular at the town meetings advocating for justice that she had her own rocking chair there. Now, she stood proudly next to the boulder as reporters asked her questions and photographers snapped her portrait.

"I feel very honored to know that a beach is to be named after me," Fortes said. "I hope it will be a public beach until the ozone layer decides to kick us out."

Fortes died two years later. The Eugenia Fortes Beach remains a public beach.

After John and Carolyn died in 1999, John's cousin Anthony Shriver rented the house on Irving Avenue for a few summers while John's estate and his sister, Caroline, decided what should happen to it next. The house had been in John's and Caroline's names since their mother died in 1994. Anthony thought about buying it; he thought maybe if he was patient, he'd get his chance. But in June 2004 Ted bought his brother's house for $3 million—almost double the assessed value of $1.7 million. As the house's landlord, Ted said he'd rent the property to family, primarily Anthony. But eventually, Ted's oldest son, Teddy Jr., moved in with his wife, Kiki, and their children. Teddy Jr. and Kiki did their own renovation, replacing the windows and the old gray shingles, taking out the clunky steam radiators, ripping out the old kitchen and the wallpaper with the delicate baby-pink flower pattern Jackie had picked out and that Carolyn had loved. Some things were repurposed—the sink in Jack's bathroom was saved, moved to the bathroom in the guest bedroom.

That wasn't the only change. Joan sold her Squaw Island home that she'd fought for in the divorce from Ted. Max Kennedy, Bobby and Ethel's ninth child, sold his waterfront house for almost $6 million in 2006. The same year, a local newspaper printed a headline: THE KENNEDYS ARE LEAVING HYANNIS PORT. It seemed like a long chapter for Hyannis Port was coming to a close. But Joan continued to rent the home she'd sold— a deal she'd struck with the buyer, according to her neighbors. Max, his wife, and their children kept coming for summers, too, finding a different place to rent each time, but always close enough to sail from the Hyannis Port Yacht Club nearly every day. When their daughter, Noah Isabella Rose, was just two days old, Max and Vicki brought her out on a sailboat and let Nantucket Sound rock her gently to sleep.

Eunice and Sarge still lived in the house up the hill. Ethel was still in her home. Jean and Pat still came to visit, years after Jean sold her house on Marchant Avenue. When Pat's oldest son, Christopher, wrote his memoir about his years of drug addiction, talking about the pressures of growing up in his famous family and his days in the Hyannis Port Terrors, Pat and Eunice proudly went around Hyannis to each store that sold the book and moved Christopher's front and center.

Ted and his wife, Vicki, drove up to the Big House on a Friday night in spring 2008. It was clear and peaceful in Hyannis Port—before the Memorial Day and end-of-school crowds arrived. They went to bed in their room upstairs, the one that had been Ted's father's room, with the view of the Sound. The next day, Ted's nephew Anthony was hosting a charity bike ride for his nonprofit organization for people with developmental disabilities. The ride would start at the Kennedy Library in Dorchester and end in Hyannis Port with a concert and a clambake. Before their day got started Saturday morning, Ted and Vicki got up, had their coffee in the sunroom, read the papers. Just after eight, Ted walked through the living room, past his mother's piano that sat in the corner, where it always had. He suddenly felt unsteady and disoriented. He told himself fresh air would help—sitting and looking out at the sea always did. But his vision blurred, and he sat down to steady himself. Then everything went black.

Barely a minute had passed when their assistant, Judy Campbell, found Ted collapsed on the floor and called out to Vicki, who was still waiting for Ted to come back to the sunroom. Vicki ran into the living room. "Call 911 right now!" she told Campbell. As Campbell made the call, Vicki sat with her husband, kissing him, telling him everything would be okay. Five minutes later, the paramedics arrived, rushing into the house. While they got Ted ready for the ambulance, Vicki called as many members of their family as she could. She knew as soon as Ted left the house, as soon as an ambulance left Marchant Avenue with red sirens blaring, it would be all over the news. She wanted the family to hear it from her first. After arriving at Cape Cod Hospital just three miles away, Ted was taken in a medevac helicopter to Massachusetts General Hospital in Boston. Shortly after he arrived, he was told he had a brain tumor.

Four days later, Ted came home in a black SUV—earlier than expected. It was another clear day on the Cape and there was a crowd of cameras and reporters lined up along Irving Avenue, ready for him when he arrived. "How are you doing, Senator?" shouted one journalist over the *click, click, click, click* of the cameras as the front passenger-side window rolled down, revealing Ted in a suit. He put his hand out the window to wave. "Well," he said, giving a thumbs-up, "glad to be back home." "Good luck, Senator!" "Good luck, Senator!" the crowd shouted as the car turned down Marchant Avenue. "That was emotional," said one photographer as the car parked in front of the Big House. Ted and Vicki got out, walking across the front yard as Sunny and Splash ran excitedly, tails wagging as Ted bent down to pet their heads. After going inside to change into their sailing gear—matching windbreakers, Ted's with his name embroidered on the chest—Ted and Vicki walked down to the pier to board their fifty-foot wooden sloop, the *Mya*, with the dogs. The local reporters gathered there wanted to know if he'd be racing in the annual Memorial Day race, the Figawi. Ted loved the Figawi. He and Vicki laughed as she said, "Stop talking about the Figawi! Is this a conspiracy? I want to know!" Ted later wrote in his memoir about that two-hour trip out on the Sound:

> Sailing, for me, has always been a metaphor for life. But on Wednesday, May 22, the day I left Massachusetts General, as Vicki, the dogs, and I stepped aboard *Mya*, docked and waiting for us at the pier in Hyannis Port, our sail was more than a metaphor: it was an *affirmation* of life. *Mya* cut smartly through the sparkling waters of Nantucket Sound under a brisk wind—the same waters on which Jack had taught me to sail more than sixty-five years earlier. Everything seemed back to normal, except for the crowd of cameramen and reporters who awaited us onshore.

A few weeks later, after sailing nearly every day, Ted started chemotherapy.

Six months after his diagnosis, Ted had his annual day-after-Thanksgiving party at the Big House with Vicki as his cohost. He looked happy and at ease, safely surrounded by his friends and family. His favorite ritual at these parties played out when all the guests moved into the living room to gather around Rose's piano. On this day Ted slid behind the piano and sang "Some Enchanted Evening." There was sadness in the room as guests considered whether this might be his last party at that house. It was only him, Eunice, and Jean left from the original nine. Rosemary had died in 2005, Pat in 2006.

But that night, Ted didn't seem worried. He looked at peace.

The next summer, Eunice and Sarge went to Hyannis Port at the end of July, as they always did. When their kids were young, they piled dogs and suitcases into their cars and towed a horse trailer behind them for the long drive from Maryland. Now, Sarge was in the advanced stages of Alzheimer's. But still, they did the things they loved in Hyannis Port. They looked out over the sea from their stone porch; they went sailing.

Sarge and Eunice were only home for a couple of weeks when Eunice was rushed to Cape Cod Hospital. Her kids and grandchildren came home right away. They went back and forth from the hospital to the Shriver house. They swam in Nantucket Sound, like Eunice loved to do. They walked along the empty beach. They said their goodbyes to their mother, their grandmother. And they waited.

Eunice died at Cape Cod Hospital early in the morning on August 11, 2009. Her kids arranged for a Mass at her home, and her youngest son, Anthony, insisted there was a place for her in the living room, in front of the big picture windows, her favorite place in the house.

The home was filled with family. Ted, who was very ill by that point, was there. Two weeks after saying goodbye to his sister, on a cloudy, gray night, Ted died at home, in the Big House.

Rob Stewart, who'd worked as a summer cop outside the President's house half a century earlier, was working at the local funeral home the day Ted died. His boss sent Stewart down to the Big House to collect a few things for the funeral because he knew the compound best. Stewart's hair was now white, the crinkles around his eyes etched in. When the police officers blocking off the street saw him coming, they waved him through the barricades. Stewart noticed that though there'd previously been a switchboard in the Big House, there was now in its place a small, neat office with two computer screens where Ted had worked at the end of his life. It was a little thing, but Stewart's picture of that house had been cemented on Election Day 1960—and now it wasn't the same.

"Just shows how things change," said Stewart.

Ethel wanted the grandkids to see a real, live turkey for Thanksgiving in 2010. Ethel and Jean were the last of their generation. Ethel was once again left as the head of a family she thought she'd always have support in leading. After Ted and Eunice died, Jean mostly stopped going to the Cape. It was too painful, too heavy with their absence.

But that Thanksgiving, Ethel was determined to make it special. So she asked her son Bobby Jr. to go get a turkey—a live one. He went over to Brewster and picked out a big black-and-white bird, wrangled it into the back of his car, and drove it home. As soon as he opened the door, the turkey escaped, running wild through the neighborhood for three days. It was chaos. But Ethel's plan worked. The grandchildren shrieked with delight as they chased the bird around the compound.

A new normal was setting in. The next summer, Ted's youngest son, Patrick, and his wife, Amy, had their wedding at the Big House, which had sat empty since Ted's death two years earlier. Patrick and Amy were making plans to take over the garage at the back of the property, where Ted and Bobby had spent those cold fall nights alone, talking about life. Patrick and Amy would be starting their family, bringing new life to the old garage. Patrick was newly sober when he married Amy—like some of his cousins, he'd lived through serious drug addiction. In 2015, he published his memoir about the pressures and expectations of being a Kennedy, about his parents' alcohol abuse, his mental illness, and about how dangerous family secrets can be. For so many years, the family ethos was "Kennedys don't cry." There were things you just didn't talk about—the affairs, the drug use, the pain of all the loss. That was starting to change. Amy and Patrick's wedding would be the last public event at the Big House. Marchant Avenue was finally quieting down.

It was the summer of 2012 and a crowd was gathered outside Bobby Kennedy Jr.'s house on Irving Avenue, around the corner from his mother's house on Marchant. There were photographers with raised cameras popping their flash over the tall hedge. Hordes of other people bunched up around the driveway, hoping to get a glimpse. Inside the hedge border, pop star Taylor Swift played volleyball with Bobby Jr.'s eighteen-year-old son, Conor, and his siblings and friends. With candy-apple-red lips and matching nails, a boatneck sweater with red, white, and blue stripes, and short blue shorts, Swift served the ball unfazed as the crowd looked on. Aiden, Conor's little brother, took the garden hose and pulled it over to where the crowd was gathered on the street just on the other side of the hedge. He turned it on, shooting a stream of water onto the fans and photographers standing on Irving Avenue. Swift dropped the ball, running over to the eleven-year-old.

"Don't you dare do that," a family friend remembers her saying. "These are my fans. This is how I make a living, and these people are the reason I'm here."

Then Swift walked barefoot to pose with the fans, walking along the paved street talking to them, as if she were reuniting with friends, catching them up on her day. Swift had been in Hyannis Port earlier in the summer for the annual July Fourth parade. The Kennedys always picked a theme and decorated Ethel's golf cart to join the parade, which snakes through Hyannis Port streets, tossing candy to kids from decorated floats and cars. At the end, everyone met up at the West Beach Club, where free Popsicles were distributed, then the Kennedys and their friends broke off to head up the hill to the Shriver house. Swift went along and spent most of the afternoon hanging out with Patrick Schwarzenegger—the eighteen-year-old aspiring-actor son of Maria Shriver and Arnold Schwarzenegger. Everyone assumed Swift and Patrick were dating until a few weeks later when she was with Conor, playing volleyball at his dad's house. Swift and Conor were suddenly inseparable, sailing together, going for walks, being driven up to Four Seas for cookie dough ice cream. Swift's fans followed along everywhere she went. And the paparazzi were never far behind.

That summer, Nancy Tenney was looking for someone to buy her family's home at the tip of Marchant Avenue. The Tenneys and the Kennedys had both been there since the 1920s, their family houses passed down through the generations. That rambling old house was a part of who she was. But she was in her nineties. "It's time," Nancy told her family. The house sat for sale for two years with a few price drops. But it was pulled off the market when Swift, who was fresh into her relationship with Conor, bought the thirteen-room house for $4.9 million. All that separated the singer-songwriter's new home from the Big House lawn was a simple, low white picket fence.

"She is just spectacular," Ethel—Conor's grandmother—said about Swift after the purchase went through. "She's just sensational inside and out. She's very kind. You know what she really is? She's game. She had never sailed before; she sailed. She had never gone dragging before; she dragged. She played anything that everyone else was doing. And she was good at it, and no fuss. And I'm happy that we'll be neighbors. I'm thrilled."

Swift came and went from Hyannis Port. The construction teams got to work updating the house Rockwell Tenney had built nearly a hundred years before. The singer was never there. She and Conor broke up. And three months after buying 27 Marchant Avenue, she sold it for nearly $6 million.

"My mother adored Taylor and referred to her as 'the songbird,' " Tangley Lloyd, Nancy's daughter, said. "[Swift's] family renovated my grandfather's 1920 house and resold it at a much larger price. Security was a huge problem for the family and Hyannis Port was just not the place. Watch Hill [Rhode Island], where Taylor moved next, was a much better venue for her to fend off the ever-present paparazzi."

As Ethel Kennedy entered her nineties, she spent more and more time in Hyannis Port. Her house was often full of her children, her friends, and her grandchildren. Sunday mornings, she hosted breakfast—and there was a new family tradition of the kids climbing her two-story roof. The most outgoing of Ethel's grandchildren was her daughter Courtney's only child: a girl with dirty-blond hair named Saoirse. Courtney's husband was Paul Hill, a man from Ireland who'd made headlines as one of the Guildford Four, who were wrongly accused of the IRA bombings in 1974. From when she was a little girl with her father's Irish accent, Saoirse spent a lot of her time on the Cape with her mother and grandmother; she loved the water and spending time with all her cousins and aunts and uncles. She was close with her Gramma Ethel—the two liked sitting together in Ethel's cozy living room on her overstuffed sofas to watch Patriots games. Over time Ethel had switched from the Washington Redskins to the Patriots—and Saoirse loved quarterback Tom Brady.

Saoirse was a big personality, beautiful with round eyes, full cheeks, and a warm smile. People in town took note when they met her. When Saoirse dropped off half a dozen pieces to get tailored in town, the seamstress noticed the name on the receipt and asked Saoirse if she was a Kennedy. "Yes, I am," she replied. "Ethel's my grandmother." The seamstress excitedly told her, "You are my first fourth generation! I've had so many of the third generation. But you are my first fourth generation! I wish I had a bell I could ring." Saoirse laughed. While some of her cousins would politely smile when they heard things like this from neighbors, feigning interest, Saoirse sat in the shop, listening to the seamstress share her memories of her mom, her grandmother, and her great-grandmother Rose.

When Courtney went to her painting lessons with Sam Barber, she'd set down her brush and step away each time Saoirse called. When Saoirse joined her mother for a lesson one morning at his crowded warehouse studio, Barber told her, "You're beautiful. You should model in New York City." She blushed. But Saoirse was never in the public eye. She was just another girl, another one of the Kennedy cousins in Hyannis Port. Unless you knew her well, you might not have known she'd battled depression since middle school.

On the last night of July 2019, she'd just finished a twenty-five-page paper for Boston College. She'd spent a week in her uncle Bobby Jr.'s garage working on it, and she was so proud to be done. That night she would celebrate. She had dinner with Ethel, watched the Democratic presidential primary debate, then went to a karaoke bar and drag show with a friend. She came home at 2:00 a.m., singing and dancing with her friend in the guest cottage at the back of Ethel's property. The next day, she would fly to Los Angeles. The trip was all planned. She and her friend went to bed in her uncle Douglas's bedroom upstairs at Ethel's. But Saoirse never woke up.

On Thursday afternoon, Barnstable police sped down Marchant Avenue to respond to a 911 call. Saoirse was rushed to Cape Cod Hospital where she was pronounced dead. Weeks later, an autopsy report listed the cause of death as "acute methadone and ethanol toxicity in combination with other prescription medications." Saoirse died of an accidental overdose.

At her funeral at Our Lady of Victory in Centerville, her uncle Tim Shriver spoke. He talked about a dinner a couple of months before, which Saoirse insisted be outside to take advantage of the beautiful, crisp spring night. Tim asked his cousin what she wanted to learn in her twenty-second year—she'd just had a birthday in May. She answered right away: "I want to learn to love myself."

Tim told the crowd that that night had run through his head again and again in the days since her death. He'd thought about what it was like to grow up in Hyannis Port, the pressure to succeed, to be great, to do great things. And he thought about the days since Saoirse died. He'd felt a shift.

"That question is echoing in my soul now," he said. "This village of Hyannis Port that we know for its celebrities and scions, for daredevils and night owls, for parties and pathbreakers—has changed. Everywhere, there is a gentleness here now. A love. A deep and breathtakingly beautiful vulnerability. Eyes are meeting. Voices are softening. Laughter is gentler. We are not afraid to cry anymore.

"We prize bravery here but all of a sudden, bravery has become facing our pain, the most brave thing any of us can do. We prize beauty here but all of a sudden, beauty has become welcoming the light within each of us. We prize success here but all of a sudden, success has become loving ourselves and one another without judgment."

That afternoon, Tim's youngest brother, Anthony, took the family out sailing. Dozens of cousins piled into boats, gliding through the water for hours. Later that week, they went out to the red-and-white buoy marked with the *HH* for Hyannis Harbor, which Saoirse liked to jump from. It was a summer ritual the newest generation had created: climb to the top of the bobbing structure. It's unsteady and covered in sharp barnacles but when you get to the top you're rewarded with the most beautiful view. Saoirse loved the Cape like her mother, Courtney; she was outgoing like her great-uncle Joe Jr.; she liked to test limits like her grandfather Bobby. She loved climbing to the top of that buoy. That day, two days after burying Saoirse, one by one, her family plunged into the cold Nantucket Sound.

As the family mourned together, there was the familiar background click and hum of cameras and news trucks. It wasn't until she died that the public knew who Saoirse was. She was a young Kennedy. And she died at the compound. So it made national news.

Kerry Kennedy, one of Saoirse's aunts, deeply felt the loss of her niece's passing, but tried to keep in perspective the press's sometimes oppressive attention: "When Saoirse died, there was a press pool at the top of the driveway, a press pool by the pier and in some ways you just really don't want that invasion of privacy at that moment, and you also don't want to have to be thinking about what am I wearing down the pier today? Should I be wearing this bathing suit because it's a little bit more modest in case there's a photographer there? That's an invasion of private space you don't want to be dealing with when you're in the midst of mourning. So there's that piece of it, but much more important to me: I think that the press is there because people really love what my father stood for and what Jack stood for, and what Teddy stood for, and what Eunice stood for."

Eunice and Sarge's third son, Mark, bought a home just behind the old post office, which is no longer painted red. Mark's house is covered in classic gray shingles and tucked behind hedges: a prairie-style Cape with a beautifully manicured lawn. He sat on the porch as his kids played in the backyard with their cousins. He was in his fifties and possessed the Kennedy's thick, dark hair, big, toothy smile, and political background— he served in the Maryland House of Delegates before losing in his run for Congress in 2002. As Mark watched his kids run in and out of the yard, he said, "I'm done with the past, really. It's about what's happening today, what's going to happen tomorrow."

There was a shift after Joe Kennedy died in 1969. But there was an even bigger change in the family when Ted died in 2009. He'd been the center of the family for so long—the face of an earlier era, the one who'd carried the torch for his brothers. The man who lived in the Big House. Since Ted died, the Big House has sat empty—the property of an organization named for him. Rose Kennedy wanted that home to be a place where the public could learn about her family, she was so proud of it—but mostly it's used to host exclusive events for the various Kennedy cousins' organizations. There are no family dinners taking place there, no viewings happening in the still-working theater in the basement. There are no grandchildren running across the yard. The tennis court sits unused as vines snake up the fence around it. The house is dark and quiet. Suspended in time. Marchant Avenue feels different with that hole at its center. But Hyannis Port is in most ways the same. Same little yacht club, same pier, same breakwater. If you see a family riding bikes down the street or piled into a golf cart and you look closely for those signature Kennedy traits—it's likely you'll see them. Some summers there are a dozen Kennedy houses in the Port—some are rentals, many are homes the family has bought over the last decade or so. In 2017, Tim Shriver bought a six-bedroom house with a saltwater pool. There's Bobby Kennedy Jr. on Irving Avenue in the house with the trampoline in the yard and the unruly hedges, which the neighbors like to complain about. Kerry Kennedy has a simple clapboard house tucked away on one of the residential streets away from the water—she has a lush garden and a handful of chickens. Her brother Christopher lives in Brambletyde—the house his uncle Jack fell in love with in 1963— on Squaw Island. Anthony Shriver has the house his parents Eunice and Sarge lived in up on the hill. Teddy Jr. still lives in the President's house. Patrick Kennedy and his wife, Amy, completed their meticulous renovation of the garage on the Big House property, turning it into a comfortable two-thousand-square-foot home. Some of the Kennedys, like Ethel's son Max, rent for the summers. Others stay with relatives— Maria Shriver visits her brother Anthony's home most summers, and Kathleen Kennedy Townsend stays with her mom, Ethel.

Old-timers like to say that the constant renovations are ruining the look of the Port—and it's true that the houses are getting bigger, edging closer to the corners of their property. But the truth is, that's *always* happened here. Joe Kennedy doubled the size of the old Malcolm Cottage back in the 1920s. Families have grown over the decades—and the descendants who can afford it buy up houses close to their old family homes, giving their clan a bit more space, like the Kennedys did in the 1950s when they created their so-called compound.

Now, sixty years after the Kennedy presidency, there's no longer a Kennedy in Congress let alone the White House. The family still plays a significant role in Democratic politics—in 2022, Caroline Kennedy and Ted's widow, Vicki, both held ambassadorships. But these days, Kennedys lose runs for elected office more often than they win. In the summer of 2020, Joe Kennedy III—the ginger-haired grandson of Bobby and Ethel—ran in the primary for a Senate seat. Navy "KENNEDY FOR SENATE" signs dotted lawns throughout Hyannis Port that summer—mostly at the homes of his relatives. His cousins and aunts and uncles phone banked for him in their backyards. That fall, he lost.

Today, there are hundreds of Kennedy cousins who haven't run for office that you've never heard of. But still, there's Hyannis Port. It's what's left of Camelot. The museum down the street from the house still celebrates the family's legacy, and people come from around the world to visit. The gift shops still sell shirts with Jack's face. And when Bobby Kennedy Jr., never far from the spotlight thanks to his famous name, advertised a chance to visit the "Kennedy Compound" in March 2020 in exchange for a ten-dollar donation to Children's Health Defense, his anti-vaccination organization, people paid. If he was any other lawyer espousing dangerous theories, nobody would listen. But he's leveraged his name and his family's legacy—and so they do.

"The Kennedy Compound is the iconic cluster of homes on the Nantucket Sound in the Atlantic Ocean where my family has lived for one hundred years," Bobby Jr. said in a video about the contest. "President Kennedy grew up there as did my father, Robert Kennedy, my uncle Senator Kennedy and now over one hundred and five Kennedy children, great-grandchildren and great-great-grandchildren . . . many of whom you'll meet on your visit to the compound!"

Bobby Jr.'s sister Kerry hosts a similar auction—hers is for the RFK Human Rights foundation, which advocates for racial justice. "You and a friend will enjoy a personal tour of the Kennedy Compound and have lunch with Kerry Kennedy in Hyannis Port!" read the auction details. The opportunity to do just that was bid up into the thousands. There's also the RFK foundation golf tournament, which brings celebrities like Bill Murray and Martin Sheen to town to play on the Hyannisport Club's eighteen holes, the same course Jack played on, and where Rose liked to go to avoid the hubbub of her son's presidency—where Jackie took her walks, sitting to have a cigarette with the caddies.

"I think a lot of people use this place now for business, to be honest with you," said Anthony Shriver, who for years has hosted a bike ride fundraiser out of Hyannis Port for his nonprofit, Best Buddies International. "For lack of a better word, it's commercializing the experience here for people—give them the Hyannis Port experience—but now it's kind of a free-for-all. Now there's always someone hovering or walking around.

"When I was a kid, there were tons of tourists here and lots of buses were here all the time. They'd dump out people everywhere. But, you know, we had little businesses we made money off like selling the candles. The vibe and the energy was really different then. It was more like they were there, and then we'd retreat to our house.

"So the idea of bringing those kinds of people into our houses and entertaining . . . we never thought we'd do that. As my mother would say: if we're using it for a good cause and helping people with it, that's the right use of it all."

For Rose and Joe, the Big House was a family home—a retreat away from the public eye. But as the kids got older, as the public became more interested, and particularly after Joe died, it was Rose who opened the doors. When the paparazzi took pictures of the family, she told her grandchildren, "The editor told him to get your picture. And it would be mean to get him in trouble with his boss when he's just trying to do his job." Once, in her eighties, when she met a tourist on one of her walks through the neighborhood, she was asked for directions to the Kennedy Compound. The tourist didn't realize they were talking to the family matriarch. Rose led them back through the narrow streets over to Marchant Avenue and let them in the front door. Rose said she worked at the house, so she was able to come and go as she pleased. She walked them around, watching their expression carefully, so proud to see the reaction to the family and home she'd created.

Back in 2009, Jean sat at the dinner table at the Big House with Ted and Vicki. Jean began to sing:

There'll be bluebirds over
The white cliffs of Dover

She sang slowly. Nearly speaking the words. Next, Ted sang an old favorite. And Vicki sang a show tune. They all knew this was likely their last summer together. Ted had been diagnosed with a brain tumor. He knew he didn't have much time. And he wanted to spend it at home—in the

Big House surrounded by the people who'd known him his whole life. He and Nancy Tenney across the street would catch up together for hours, taking turns sitting on each other's porches, sharing memories about Joe Jr. and Kick and Jack and Bobby. Jean and Ted liked to tease each other through dinners that last summer. Since back when they were kids, the youngest in the bunch, they loved to imitate British accents, like the ones they heard as children when they lived in England, when their father was ambassador to the Court of St. James's, when it was all just beginning.

"Oh, Teddy, what are you doing over there, sitting in your chair?" Jean asked, slowing her vowels.

"Oh, I'm just looking at you, you ugly thing," Ted said, matching her accent. They'd go back and forth until one made the other break into laughter.

Jean, who'd been the ambassador to Ireland in the '90s, had sold her house on Marchant Avenue years before, so she rented a house for a few weeks that summer to be with Ted. When the lease was up, she stayed at the Big House. She didn't want to leave her little brother. And she made him so happy.

Jean and Ted sat together on the porch, where their mother had sat watching them, their thick, wavy hair now white with age. And they looked out at the ocean, listening to the waves roll in, watching the rocky waters on the other side of the breakwall, following the ospreys as they darted across the water back to their nests.

"You know the sea, it's talking," Ted always said. "It's talking to us."

AUTHOR'S NOTE

The community of Hyannis Port is a fiercely private one. They've dealt with journalists, writers, photographers, and tourists for decades now. When you mention the name Kennedy, they won't let their facial expressions reveal their feelings about the family—many Port families decided generations ago, "We don't talk about the neighbors." But in the nearly three years I spent working on this book, I was able to earn the trust of more than 120 sources, many of whom have never spoken publicly, as well as a dozen members of the Kennedy family, who shared personal stories about their lives in Hyannis Port. To me, this isn't a story about a former president. It's a story about a small community and an incredibly famous and influential family and their impact on each other. It's a story about home, and the people we are when no one but the neighbors is looking.

I signed my book contract in February 2020. Weeks later, the world shut down. The illustrious John F. Kennedy Library in Boston was closed to in-person research for the duration of my project. But thanks to its extensive digital collection as well as its patient, kind, and creative archivists, especially Abigail Malangone, I was able to get access to the oral histories, letters, documents, and photographs I needed to bring the Summer White House years to life. I also worked closely with so many wonderful local Cape organizations. Tales of Cape Cod, a nonprofit dedicated to preserving Cape history, was a godsend. President Gene Guill invited my family into his home, facilitated introductions, shared interviews, and was a beacon of support for this project. The Zion Union Heritage Museum, the Marstons Mills Historical Society, the Hyannis Public Library, the Wianno Senior Class Association, the Whydah Pirate Museum, the Historical Society of Old Yarmouth, and the Cape Cod Cape Verdean Museum & Cultural Center were all invaluable—these organizations opened their doors, invited me to Zoom meetings, dug into their archives, introduced me to members, and provided inestimable background and context, which helped me understand the rich history of the town of Barnstable. The John F. Kennedy Hyannis Museum is such a special place on Main Street Hyannis, and founders Wendy Northcross and Rebecca Pierce-Merrick, as well as board members Dick Neitz and Lynne Poyant, and director of Programs and Operations Jennifer Pappalardo were especially helpful, sharing their stories and allowing me access to their current and previous exhibits and interview projects (including wonderful unpublished interviews with Senator Edward M. Kennedy and those who knew and worked for the family who have since passed). The Sturgis Library in Barnstable has given researchers a great gift by digitizing all their local newspaper archives. I wondered many times during the quarantines and travel restrictions of 2020 and 2021 how I could have written this book without them. Rebekah Ambrose-Dalton, archivist and reference librarian for the William Brewster Nickerson Cape Cod History Archive and the Wilkens Library at Cape Cod Community College, led me through these wonderful resources, including undigitized press coverage, the *Barnstable Patriot* archives, and local books that are no longer in print. And James M. Shea, the former curator for the Edward M. Kennedy Institute for the United States Senate, who spent more than two years archiving the Big House, was an incredible resource.

Off-Cape, I relied on the archives of the Brooke Russell Astor Reading Room for Rare Books and Manuscripts at the New York Public Library, the Leo Damore papers in the Special Collections and Archives at Kent State University, The HistoryMakers Oral History Digital Archives, University of Virginia Miller Center's Edward M. Kennedy Oral History Project, the *Boston Globe* digital archives, the New Bedford *Standard-Times* archives, the New York Public Library's Women's Magazine

Archives, and countless other local newspapers' digital archives. Seeing the Port through the eyes of the nation gave me an important perspective.

I also relied on the reporting of all the writers and journalists who came before me—many of whom also talked me through their reporting and research, sharing insights and sometimes even unpublished transcripts and documents. Kennedy biographers Steven M. Gillon, David Nasaw, Larry Tye, James W. Graham, and Laurence Leamer were all generous with their time and resources and wrote extensive books that covered different portions of the Kennedys' lives on the Cape. *Kathleen Kennedy: Her Life and Times* by Lynne McTaggart and *The Lost Prince: Young Joe, The Forgotten Kennedy: The Story of the Oldest Brother* by Hank Searls were enormously helpful in informing me about the siblings who died so young, as was *The Fitzgeralds and the Kennedys: An American Saga* by Doris Kearns Goodwin. I'm also grateful for the insights of the memoirs of those who lived and worked on the compound, including Edward M. Kennedy, Rose Kennedy, Rita Dallas, Maud Shaw, and Frank Saunders. *Old Hyannis Port* by Larry Newman and Paul Fairbanks Herrick, and local journalist Leo Damore's two books about the Kennedys on the Cape, helped me understand the world of the 1920s–1960s in Hyannis Port thanks to their research and interviews with Port neighbors who have since passed. Local journalist Matt Pitta shared his radio coverage of the Kennedy family over the years. Gabrielle Emanuel of Boston's NPR station GBH produced a must-listen-to investigation into the Reverse Freedom Riders. I wish I'd had the chance to talk to so many of the local reporters and photographers who spent their careers camped out at the end of Marchant Avenue but who have since died—I almost feel like I know them through their bylines: particularly Lou LaPrade, Gordon Caldwell, and Frank Falacci.

In 2020, journalist and Kennedy friend Dotson Rader invited me to his Manhattan apartment to share his memories of Hyannis Port. At the end of our conversation, he mentioned that he'd been working with Senator Kennedy before his death on an oral history project about the compound. It took nearly a year to get all the approvals necessary, but I was lucky enough to be the first researcher to use this invaluable trove, which included an intimate tour of the Big House during which Senator Kennedy took Rader from room to room sharing his memories, and, also, rare interviews with neighbor Nancy Tenney and family nurse Luella Hennessy. This material was foundational to my project.

I can't thank enough the wonderful people of Barnstable who invited me into their homes and their lives for nearly three years. I conducted interviews on the bench in front of the News Shop, on sprawling porches overlooking Nantucket Sound, in the shadow of the Kennedy Memorial on Ocean Street, in weathered rocking chairs, over homemade cookies and lemonade and boxes of yellowed photographs and letters. I was introduced to neighbors who were walking by while I did interviews, and neighbors who reached out to me because they heard from another neighbor what I was working on. There are too many to list them all here, and their names make up many of the citations at the back of the book because they are the ones who made this work what it is by sharing their memories. But to name just a few: I met Peter and Michelle Cross on my first trip to Hyannis in 2019 and they spent their afternoon driving me around and sharing stories about Peter's father, who was a selectman when President Kennedy was in office. John Kennedy Jr.'s closest friends helped me understand his life in Hyannis Port—Billy Noonan and I sat in creaky Adirondack chairs for hours one hot summer afternoon in 2020, and he shared his memories until long after the sun went down, his big voice echoing through the night. Billy tells a hell of a story and his detailed and poignant memoir, *Forever Young: My Friendship with John F. Kennedy Jr.*, also helped me retrace his and John's steps on the Cape. Mark Grenier taught me the rich architectural history of Hyannis Port complete with a long and winding driving tour down the Port's hidden paper roads. The Frazees shared their extensive family research about Brambletyde—the family has avoided the media for decades, but they decided it was finally time to share the story of their special home. Also hugely helpful were the families of Eugenia Fortes, Frank Wirtanen, Sam Keavy, Nancy Tenney, Jack Bell, and Sandy Eiler, who helped me understand these important Hyannis Port figures. Those who worked at the compound like Edgar Gunnery, David Crawford, Robert Stewart, Josefina Harvin, Kathy McKeon, Joan Ellis, and John Salerno as well as neighbors and close friends of the family like former senator Paul Kirk,

Brad Blank, Don McKeag, Tom Holmes, Brian O'Neill, Melissa Ludtke, Phillip Scudder, Joe Diggs, Jim Shay, Liz Mumford, Sam Barber, John Kelley, Paul Stewart, Jim Manley, and Barry Clifford provided invaluable insight. I'm so grateful for their trust and their time.

And, of course, I owe a heartfelt thank-you to the members of the Kennedy family who took me sailing, gave me tours of their homes, introduced me to neighbors, shared their photo albums, and sat for hours opening up about their lives on the Cape: Kerry Kennedy, Kathleen Kennedy Townsend, Timothy Shriver, Mark Shriver, Christopher Kennedy, Anthony Shriver, Matthew Maxwell Taylor Kennedy, Victoria Strauss Kennedy, Kerry McCarthy, Robert F. Kennedy Jr., Cheryl Hines, Patrick Kennedy, and Amy Kennedy. Many of you told me you're not a family that likes to reminisce—I appreciate your doing it with me anyway.

My wonderful literary agent, Susan Canavan, has been my partner in this whole process and I couldn't be more grateful. My fantastic fact-checker, Hilary McClellan, helped me sleep at night by double- and triple-checking every minute detail of this nearly hundred-year tale. It's been a dream getting to work with Scribner, which has been so supportive of this story from the beginning—including my esteemed editor, Rick Horgan, his assistant, Olivia Bernhard, and senior vice president and publisher, Nan Graham.

I've had some amazing editors and mentors in my years writing for newspapers and magazines and I often thought of their advice as I wrote this book: Kate Lewis, Brooke Seigel, Madison Vain, Kelly Stout, Ryan D'Agostino, Michael Shain, Robert Rorke, Linda Stasi, Don Kaplan, Michael Starr, Margi Conklin, and Carla Spartos, to name a few. And especially *Esquire* editor in chief Michael Sebastian, my editor, mentor, and friend whose years of encouragement gave me the confidence to tackle this book.

Writing a book during a pandemic truly takes a village. Thank you to Muriel Watt and Rick Brown for your support and for filling in with childcare during the two worst years of the pandemic, in which I also happened to be writing a book with a young child. And thanks to my parents and brother, George, Maurice, and Michael Storey, for your encouragement and for supporting my writing all these years.

Thank you to my friends and family for being a sounding board for so many of the stories in the book and for all your words of encouragement. And to my dear friend Gregory E. Miller, one of the first people I told about this project: we were supposed to celebrate our first books together; I miss you every day.

Thank you to Finn for being so patient and so curious. I love you, and I hope one day you look back at these summers we spent on the Cape and remember them as fondly as so many of the people in this book do. Watching you play in the sand at Eugenia Fortes Beach, slurp oysters, and eat drippy ice cream cones at Four Seas helped me understand why the people of Hyannis Port love it so much.

Most of all, thank you to Heath Brown, who encouraged me to write this book, who read early drafts, who kept our son miraculously busy and happy when I was too wrapped up in interviews, research, and writing, who was my own personal presidency expert, who helped me put stories in context and asked the right questions, who kept me fed and sane. Thank you, and I love you.

NOTES

PROLOGUE

1 **Ted Kennedy walks:** Dotson Rader interview with Edward M. Kennedy, August 28, 2003, Miscellaneous Accessions collection, JFK Library. (Hereafter JFKL.)

1 **The kids had always squabbled:** Luella Hennessey Oral History Interview, November 26, 1964, John F. Kennedy Oral History Collection, JFKL.

2 **"You look out over that water":** Dotson Rader interview with Edward M. Kennedy, August 28, 2003, Miscellaneous Accessions collection, JFKL.

2 **Ted's father, Joe, calling him:** Edward M. Kennedy, *True Compass: A Memoir* (New York: Twelve, 2009), 19.

2 **his brothers in the attic playing toy soldiers:** Dotson Rader interview with Edward M. Kennedy, August 28, 2003, Miscellaneous Accessions collection, JFKL.

3 **sister-in-law Jackie taught everyone in the family how to dance the Twist:** Amanda Smith, ed., *Hostage to Fortune: The Letters of Joseph P. Kennedy* (New York: Viking, 2001), 699.

3 **1790s gilt leaf and painted mirror:** "The Kennedy House in Hyannis Port: An American Political Family at Home," James M. Shea research files, prepared 2015.

3 **Joe's stroke:** David Nasaw, *The Patriarch: The Remarkable Life and Turbulent Times of Joseph P. Kennedy* (New York: Penguin, 2012), 775.

4 **gunned down in Dallas:** Kennedy, *True Compass*, 209.

4 **where he learned his third son had been shot in California:** Rita Dallas, *The Kennedy Case* (New York: Putnam, 1973), 299.

4 **where his youngest son told him:** Kennedy, *True Compass*, 292.

4 **He watches a family of ospreys:** Caroline Raclin Oral History, November 11, 2009, Edward M. Kennedy Oral History Project, University of Virginia Miller Center.

4 **"This is where my mother lived for the last thirty, thirty-five years":** Dotson Rader interview with Edward M. Kennedy, August 28, 2003, Miscellaneous Accessions collection, JFKL.

4 **Ted has been thinking a lot lately about the past:** Cal Fussman, "What I've Learned: Ted Kennedy," *Esquire*, January 1, 2003.

CHAPTER ONE

5 **on about three acres:** Town of Barnstable Assessing Division, https://gis .townofbarnstable.us/Html5Viewer/Index.html?viewer=propertymaps&run= FindParcel&propertyID=286023&mapparback=286023%27%20target=.

5 **craggy breakwater:** Town of Barnstable, *The Seven Villages of Barnstable* (Town of Barnstable, 1976), 141.

5 **L. Frank Paine:** Paul Fairbanks Herrick and Larry Newman, *Old Hyannis Port, Massachusetts: An Anecdotal, Photographic Panorama* (Reynolds-DeWalt: New Bedford, MA, 1968), 35.

5 **picked up and moved:** Leo Damore, *The Cape Cod Years of John Fitzgerald Kennedy* (Hoboken, NJ: Prentice-Hall, 1967), 10.

6 **until 1928:** "Real Estate Transfers," *Hyannis Patriot*, Thursday, November 15, 1928, 13.

6 **doubled its size:** Charles Leveroni, "Private Talky in Cape Home," *Hyannis Patriot*, June 13, 1929.

6 **Rolls-Royce:** Damore, *The Cape Cod Years*, 19.

7 **Old Orchard:** Doris Kearns Goodwin, *The Fitzgeralds and the Kennedys: An American Saga* (New York: St. Martin's Press, 1991), 124.

7 **Honey Fitz on the trains:** Dotson Rader interview with Edward M. Kennedy, August 28, 2003, Miscellaneous Accessions collection, JFKL.

7 **Nantasket Beach:** Nasaw, *The Patriarch*, 48.

8 **Cohasset:** Nasaw, 81.

8 **"It was petty and cruel":** Goodwin, *The Fitzgeralds and the Kennedys*, 326.

9 **Rose's birthday:** Rose Fitzgerald Kennedy, *Times to Remember* (Garden City, NY: Doubleday, 1974), 98.

9 **breakwater:** Herrick and Newman, *Old Hyannis Port*, 11

9 **the Taggarts' place:** Elizabeth Mumford, interview with author, May 15, 2020.

9 **FBO:** Nasaw, *The Patriarch*, 99.

10 **"I know it's terrible to tell you":** Nasaw, 93.

10 **"Pesky skeeters!":** "Mosquito Meeting," *Yarmouth Register*, August 8, 1925.

10 **capsized:** "Three Children Capsized," *Hyannis Patriot*, August 13, 1925.

10 **1926:** Nasaw, *The Patriarch*, 98.

10 **"least successful ventures in child rearing":** Kennedy, *Times to Remember*, 175.

11 **He looked in Oyster Harbors:** Dotson Rader interview with Edward M. Kennedy, August 28, 2003, Miscellaneous Accessions collection, JFKL.

11 **neighbor James Woodward:** Damore, *The Cape Cod Years*, 20.

11 **Joe had his eye on the biggest house:** Dotson Rader interview with Edward M. Kennedy, August 28, 2003, Miscellaneous Accessions collection, JFKL.

11 **In November 1928:** "Real Estate Transfers," *Hyannis Patriot*, November 15, 1928.

11 **create an addition:** Charles Leveroni, "Private Talky in Cape Home," *Hyannis Patriot*, June 13, 1929.

12 **weekly allowance:** Kennedy, *Times to Remember*, 119.

12 **Background about hotels:** Herrick and Newman, *Old Hyannis Port*, 37–38.

13 **golf course . . . renovation:** William L. Healy, MD, *Hyannisport* (FCI Digital: West Carrollton, OH, 2020), 70.

13 **Wednesday picnic:** Janice Cliggott, interview with author, July 17, 2020.

13 **Megathlin's drugstore, and the Idle Hour Theatre:** Jennifer Longley, *Hyannis and Hyannis Port* (Charleston, SC: Arcadia Publishing, 2002), 57.

13 **Colonial Candle of Cape Cod:** Longley, *Hyannis and Hyannis Port*, 27.

13 **but Rose always went alone:** Dotson Rader interview with Nancy Tenney, December 2, 2000, Miscellaneous Accessions collection, JFKL.

14 **Keavy boys:** Allison Falkenberry, interview with author, August 18, 2020.

14 **Bell boys:** Deborah Blakely, interview with author, January 31, 2022.

14 **Tish Mumford:** Elizabeth Mumford, interview with author, May 15, 2020.

14 **Rockwell Tenney's credo:** Tangley Lloyd, interview with author, December 20, 2020.

14 **they connected a long string:** Dotson Rader interview with Nancy Tenney, December 2, 2000, Miscellaneous Accessions collection, JFKL.

15 **Rudy Vallee's or Fred Waring's voice:** Hank Searls, *The Lost Prince: Young Joe, the Forgotten Kennedy* (New York: Ballantine Books, 1977), 49.

15 **BoBeWiJo:** Searls, *The Lost Prince*, 49.

16 **Joe Jr. fell in love:** Searls, 51.

17 **"leave an unprotected shin unkicked":** Damore, *The Cape Cod Years*, 26.

17 **"I knew what he was doing. And he knew that I knew":** Kennedy, *Times to Remember*, 104.

17 **twenty-eight stitches:** Joan Meyers and Goddard Lieberson, eds., *John Fitzgerald Kennedy: As We Remember Him* (New York: Atheneum, 1965), 7.

17 **Jack mistakenly took:** This scene is a compilation of the three versions of the story appearing in Searls, *The Lost Prince*, 52; Kennedy, *True Compass*, 17; and Kennedy, *Times to Remember*, 125.

19 **Boston police commissioner:** Dotson Rader interview with Nancy Tenney, December 2, 2000, Miscellaneous Accessions collection, JFKL.

19 **"No matter what anyone else had done":** Goodwin, *The Fitzgeralds and the Kennedys*, 326.

19 **"It's solitary confinement not splendor I need":** "The Campaign: Pride of the Clan," *Time*, July 11, 1960.

20 **Blackburn said:** Laurence Leamer, *The Kennedy Women: The Saga of an American Family* (New York: Ballantine, 1994), 182.

20 **Communion:** "Hyannis," *Hyannis Patriot*, August 8, 1929, 4.

20 **Sikorsky amphibious plane:** Damore, *The Cape Cod Years*, 21.

21 **in January 1928:** Nasaw, *The Patriarch*, 115.

21 **Honey Fitz, had had public affairs:** "John Fitzgerald: Mayor of a Bigger, Better, Busier Boston," National Park Service, https://www.nps.gov/articles/000 /john-fitzgerald-mayor-of-a-bigger-better-busier-boston.htm.

21 **"I was told if I wanted to be in the club":** Dotson Rader interview with Nancy Tenney, December 2, 2000, Miscellaneous Accessions collection, JFKL.

22 **Duesenberg:** Dotson Rader interview with Nancy Tenney, December 2, 2000, Miscellaneous Accessions collection, JFKL.

22 **September 1929:** "Ex-Mayor and Mrs. Fitzgerald Observe 40th Wedding Anniversary at Summer Home," *Hyannis Patriot*, September 19, 1929.

CHAPTER TWO

25 **the Toll House Inn:** Edward M. Kennedy, *The Fruitful Bough: A Tribute to Joseph P. Kennedy* (Privately Printed, 1965), 177.

25 **the renowned Olmsteds:** "Job #9199, Joseph P. Kennedy, Hyannisport, MA," Olmsted Archives, Frederick Law Olmsted NHS, NPS.

26 **long-planned renovation of the Hyannisport Club:** Healey, *Hyannisport*, 75.

26 **donations from other members, like Joe:** Nasaw, *The Patriarch*, 178.

26 **Odd Fellows Parade:** "Odd Fellows Parade," *Hyannis Patriot*, June 5, 1930.

26 **"a golden interval":** Goodwin, *The Fitzgeralds and the Kennedys*, 424.

26 **far end of the porch:** Dotson Rader interview with Edward M. Kennedy, August 28, 2003, Miscellaneous Accessions collection, JFKL.

26 **"Murder":** Kennedy, *True Compass*, 31.

27 **"We would sit in our house":** Ralph G. Martin, *A Hero for Our Time: An Intimate Story of the Kennedy Years* (Greenwich, CT: Fawcett Crest, 1984), 21.

27 **kids' fingernails:** Dotson Rader interview with Luella Hennessey, May 19, 2000, Miscellaneous Accessions collection, JFKL.

27 **"Coming in second was just no good":** Goodwin, *The Fitzgeralds and the Kennedys*, 326.

28 **"my spies in New York":** Dotson Rader interview with Edward M. Kennedy, August 28, 2003, Miscellaneous Accessions collection, JFKL.

28 **tucked a bag of beer:** Deborah Blakely, interview with author, January 31, 2022.

28 *Dumbo* and *Snow White*: Kennedy, *True Compass*, 31.

28 **"My friend Sancy":** Dotson Rader interview with Nancy Tenney, December 2, 2000, Miscellaneous Accessions collection, JFKL. Story about women visiting also told by neighbor Harry Fowler in Laurence Leamer, *The Kennedy Women*, 230. Story of Joe pinching women is also in Lynne McTaggart, *Kathleen Kennedy: Her Life and Times* (Garden City, NY: Doubleday, 1983), 19.

28 **"Teddy, I think it's time for you to go to bed":** Kennedy, *True Compass*, 35.

29 **But in 1932:** Stan Grayson, *The Wianno Senior Story: A Century on Nantucket Sound* (Thomaston, ME: Tilbury House Publishers, 2013), 57.

29 **a boat labeled number 94:** Grayson, *The Wianno Senior Story*, 57.

29 **where they'd nailed pins and hooks:** Dotson Rader interview with Edward M. Kennedy, August 28, 2003, Miscellaneous Accessions collection, JFKL.

30 **Jimmie MacLean:** Grayson, *The Wianno Senior Story*, 57.

30 **"If there was a tough race":** Dotson Rader interview with Nancy Tenney, December 2, 2000, Miscellaneous Accessions collection, JFKL.

30 **"All the kids in the neighborhood":** Sam Keavy interview with Patrick Ramage, "Cape Codders Remember the Kennedys," *Tales of Cape Cod*, DVD, 2020.

30 **"a little slow":** Kennedy, *Times to Remember*, 164–65.

31 **stuck with a would-be suitor:** Searls, *The Lost Prince*, 85.

31 **A tradition at the dances was for the girls to throw a shoe:** Dotson Rader interview with Nancy Tenney, December 2, 2000, Miscellaneous Accessions collection, JFKL.

31 **Rose and the family's governess, Alice Cahill:** Lynne McTaggart, *Kathleen Kennedy: Her Life and Times*, 11.

31 **"Make sure to take Rosemary with you!":** Kennedy, *Times to Remember*, 164–65.

32 **Eunice still invited her to come crew:** Eileen McNamara, *Eunice: The Kennedy Who Changed the World* (New York: Simon & Schuster, 2018), 23.

32 **Thomas Bilodeau:** Thomas Bilodeau Oral History Interview, May 12, 1964, John F. Kennedy Oral History Collection, JFKL.

33 **friend from school Dave Hackett:** David L. Hackett Oral History Interview, July 22, 1970, John F. Kennedy Oral History Collection, JFKL.

33 **"Rules for Visiting the Kennedys":** William Peters, "You Can't Run Away from Being the President's Brother," *Redbook*, June 1962, 72.

33 **"I suppose if you're not used to it":** Gail Cameron, *Rose: A Biography of Rose Fitzgerald Kennedy* (New York: Putnam, 1971), 105.

33 **Ralph "Rip" Horton Jr.:** Joan Blair and Clay Blair, *The Search for JFK* (New York: Putnam, 1969), 26.

34 **three-week trip to Russia:** Goodwin, *The Fitzgeralds and the Kennedys*, 474.

34 **"I don't want to hear any more of it":** Dotson Rader interview with Edward M. Kennedy, August 28, 2003, Miscellaneous Accessions collection, JFKL.

34 **"Hitler is building a spirit":** Smith, *Hostage to Fortune*, 131.

35 **"That's Daddy," Pat told Nancy:** Dotson Rader interview with Nancy Tenney, December 2, 2000, Miscellaneous Accessions collection, JFKL.

35 **Bobby was eleven, just a hair over five feet:** Smith, *Hostage to Fortune*, 306.

35 **"Bobby was a brat!":** Dotson Rader interview with Nancy Tenney, December 2, 2000, Miscellaneous Accessions collection, JFKL.

36 **Eighteen-year-old Rosemary was away at camp that summer:** Nasaw, *The Patriarch*, 263.

36 **appendicitis:** Luella Hennessey, "Bringing Up the Kennedys," *Good Housekeeping*, August 1961, 53.

36 **"Do you smoke?":** Hennessey, "Bringing Up the Kennedys."

37 **"Teddy!" Honey Fitz shouted:** Dotson Rader interview with Edward M. Kennedy, August 28, 2003, Miscellaneous Accessions collection, JFKL.

37 **Joe Jr. got his own boat:** Goodwin, *The Fitzgeralds and the Kennedys*, 460.

38 **"Teddy was darling":** Dotson Rader interview with Nancy Tenney, December 2, 2000, Miscellaneous Accessions collection, JFKL.

38 **"Hit it, squirt!":** Eileen Keavy Smith, interview with author, September 1, 2020.

38 **Rose's sister Agnes:** Ann Gargan Oral History, October 21, 2005, Edward M. Kennedy Oral History Project, University of Virginia Miller Center.

38 **maid of honor:** Nasaw, *The Patriarch*, 41.

38 **The *Victura* was repaired:** "Early Files," *Barnstable Patriot*, July 18, 1996.

38 **Teddy's first race:** John F. Kennedy, "Kennedy, Joseph P., Jr.: As We Remember Joe" (1945), JFKL.

39 **The lead editorial in the local paper:** "Our New Ambassador," *Hyannis Patriot*, December 16, 1937.

39 **"I am now a member of at least":** Goodwin, *The Fitzgeralds and the Kennedys*, 524.

40 **they were met with new neighbors:** Longley, *Hyannis and Hyannis Port*, 114.

40 **the McMillan Cup:** "Harvard in Front in Yachting Series," *New York Times*, June 24, 1938.

41 **the sand black with a blanket of birds:** "Terns Claim Ambassador's Beach," *Hyannis Patriot*, July 6, 1939.

41 **had hired Norton Sherman:** Dotson Rader interview with Edward M. Kennedy, August 28, 2003, Miscellaneous Accessions collection, JFKL.

CHAPTER THREE

43 **they watched their friend George Mead:** Charles Spalding Oral History Interview, March 14, 1968, JFKL.

44 **The former mayor and his wife, Josie, had rented a house on Lighthouse Lane:** Kennedy, *Times to Remember*, 358.

44 **"She is much happier when she sees the children just casually":** Smith, *Hostage to Fortune*, 394.

45 **1888 baton from conductor:** "The Kennedy Family Home in Hyannis Port," James M. Shea research files, prepared 2015.

45 **"You can come riding if you're downstairs in five minutes!":** Kennedy, *True Compass*, 17.

45 **nicknamed his favorite horse Mount Sinai:** Cameron, *Rose: A Biography*, 108.

45 **The family had a farm in Osterville:** Kerry Kennedy, interview with author, July 15, 2021.

45 **If it was low tide:** Dotson Rader interview with Edward M. Kennedy, August 28, 2003, Miscellaneous Accessions collection, JFKL.

45 **Joe mounted his horse:** Kennedy, *True Compass*, 19.

46 **"The summer of 1941 was":** Kennedy, 17.

46 **Joe Jr. took the *Victura* for one last race on July 10:** Damore, *The Cape Cod Years*, 61.

46 **sell their home in Bronxville, New York:** Rose Kennedy letter, December 5, 1941, John F. Kennedy Personal Papers, JFKL.

47 **Rosemary suddenly stopped coming home to the Cape:** Dotson Rader interview with Nancy Tenney, December 2, 2000, Miscellaneous Accessions collection, JFKL.

47 **draped with thick, dark curtains:** Kennedy, *True Compass*, 47.

47 **Cape Cod experienced its first air raid:** "Cape Cod on Alert," *Yarmouth Register*, December 12, 1941.

47 **Cape Cod Secretarial School:** "Secretarial School Students Prepare to Aid in War Effort," *Barnstable Patriot*, July 9, 1942.

47 **Jean went to the Red Cross:** Kennedy, *Times to Remember*, 284.

47 **Pat, then eighteen, wrote to her older brother Jack:** Pat to Jack, July 10, 1942, John F. Kennedy Personal Papers, JFKL.

48 **the kids' first friend died in the war:** "Lt. George Mead Jr. Killed in Solomon Islands Battle," *The Dayton Herald*, September 23, 1942.

48 **Kick, in particular, was devastated:** McTaggart, *Kathleen Kennedy*, 120.

48 **Joe converted the farm in Osterville:** Nasaw, *The Patriarch*, 554.

48 **September 1943:** Kennedy, *True Compass*, 83.

49 **she received a phone call just after eight:** Nasaw, *The Patriarch*, 557.

49 **the kids . . . found out:** Kennedy, *True Compass*, 75.

49 ***Boston Evening Globe:*** Leif Erickson, "Kennedy's Son Hero of PT-Boat Saga," *Boston Evening Globe*, August 19, 1943.

50 **"To Ambassador Joe Kennedy":** Searls, *The Lost Prince*, 182.

50 **Nancy opened the letter from Kick:** Tangley Lloyd, interview with author, December 30, 2020.

51 **Jack received a letter from Joe Jr.:** Kennedy, Joseph P., Jr.: Letters and telegrams, 1940–1944, John F. Kennedy Personal Papers, JFKL.

51 **Pat, Jean, and Eunice were next door with Nancy:** Dotson Rader interview with Nancy Tenney, December 2, 2000, Miscellaneous Accessions collection, JFKL.

51 **Family finding out about Joe Jr.'s death:** This scene is a compilation of the points of view in Kennedy, *Times to Remember*, 323, and Kennedy, *True Compass*, 85; "Ex-Envoy Kennedy, Crushed by Son's Death, Remains in Seclusion," *Boston Globe*, August 15, 1944.

52 **She called Joe's good friend:** Pete MacLellan interview with Larry Tye, Larry Tye private notes.

53 **Wilbert, the caretaker:** Frank Saunders, *Torn Lace Curtain* (New York: Henry Holt & Company, 1982), 13.

53 **Jack invited his navy friends:** Blair and Blair, *The Search for JFK*, 356.

54 **Billy Cavendish died:** Goodwin, *The Fitzgeralds and the Kennedys*, 695.

55 **his father's chauffeur, David Deignan:** Dotson Rader interview with Edward M. Kennedy, August 28, 2003, Miscellaneous Accessions collection, JFKL.

55 **Next door, the McKelvys were trapped, too:** Longley, *Hyannis and Hyannis Port*, 122–24, and "Family Rescued at Hyannis Port," *Barnstable Patriot*, September 21, 1944.

56 **The Hyannisport Club . . . had the roof ripped straight off:** Herrick and Newman, *Old Hyannis Port*, 34.

56 **The old, scratched-up floors:** "Hyannis Port 1941–1942," Joseph P. Kennedy Personal Papers, JFKL, and Dotson Rader interview with Edward M. Kennedy, August 28, 2003, Miscellaneous Accessions collection, JFKL.

56 **it had once been illegal:** Dot, "The King's Pines," Webster Historical Society, June 26, 2016, https://websterhistoricalsociety.org/?p=309.

57 **the first Catholic president:** Damore, *The Cape Cod Years*, 75.

57 **Jack's navy buddy Jim Reed:** Blair and Blair, *The Search for JFK*, 357.

57 **He followed the victory with a two-week vacation back:** "Kennedy Awarded Degree at Colby; Son Wins Big Vote," *Barnstable Patriot*, June 20, 1946.

57 **bringing his sister Eunice and the family cook, Margaret Ambrose:** Blair and Blair, *The Search for JFK*, 518.

58 **Jack and Eunice brought Mary Pitcairn:** Blair and Blair, 544.

59 **Fortes's nephew remembered about his aunt:** Robert Cutts, interview with author, November 29, 2021.

59 **Fortes had sailed with her mother to the States in 1920:** Eugenia Fortes interview, July 20, 1978, *Tales of Cape Cod*, DVD, 2020.

60 **"They're not happy":** "Eugenia Fortes Talks About Her Reputation for Honesty," The HistoryMakers Oral History Digital Archives, August 21, 2004.

60 **One summer day in 1945:** "Black History on Cape Cod," Cape Cod Chamber of Commerce, and "Eugenia Fortes Sustains Legacy, Could Make History," *Boston Herald*, September 17, 2008.

60 **"Our town is changing very much," said attorney Henry Murphy:** Barnstable Town Meeting 1946, Verbatim Minutes, 187–88.

61 **Rose and Joe hadn't been involved with the civic association:** Civic association member, interview with author.

61 **"The next year the civic association came to buy the beach," Fortes recalled:** "Eugenia Fortes Describes Refusing to Vacate a Segregated Beach in Hyannis, Massachusetts in 1946," The HistoryMakers Oral History Digital Archives, August 21, 2004.

62 **"The vegetables grow succulent":** Rose Kennedy diary entry, Hyannisport, October 15, Rose Kennedy Papers, JFKL.

62 **donating an altar at St. Francis Xavier:** Searls, *The Lost Prince*, 268.

62 **She'd been flying with Peter Wentworth-Fitzwilliam, the 8th Earl Fitzwilliam:** Barbara Leaming, "Inside the Scandalous Life of JFK's Sister, Kick Kennedy," *Harper's Bazaar*, April 25, 2016.

62 **A car was sent for Teddy:** Edward M. Kennedy Oral History, November 29, 2006, Edward M. Kennedy Oral History Project, University of Virginia Miller Center.

62 **memorial Mass held at St. Francis Xavier Church:** "Memorial Mass Tues. For Kathleen Kennedy," *Barnstable Patriot*, May 20, 1948.

CHAPTER FOUR

63 **Rose Kennedy, in a yellow blouse and pearl earrings:** Harrison Engle, director, *The Lost Kennedy Home Videos*, DVD. Produced by Stanley Moger. A&E Television, 2011.

63 **he'd jump right into the rosebushes:** John Culver Oral History, June 2007, Edward M. Kennedy Oral History Project, University of Virginia Miller Center.

63 **Honey Fitz's death:** "John Fitzgerald: Mayor of a Bigger, Better, Busier Boston," National Parks Service.

64 **"I remember arriving at the Cape and going to Jean's room":** Kennedy, *Times to Remember*, 112.

64 **The first person Bobby told:** Deborah Blakely, interview with author, January 31, 2022.

64 **In 1953, Eunice married Sargent Shriver:** "Miss Eunice Kennedy Becomes Bride of Robert Shriver, Jr.," *The Palm Beach Post*, May 24, 1953, 17.

64 **"Cape Women Invited to Be Guests of Kennedys":** "Cape Women Invited to Be Guests of Kennedys," *Yarmouth Register*, August 22, 1952, 7, and "Cong. J. F. Kennedy to Be Guest Speaker," *Barnstable Patriot*, August 21, 1952.

64 **The *New York Times* wrote about thirty-five-year-old Jack:** Cabell Phillips, "Kennedy Campaign: Case History of a Senate Race," *New York Times*, October 26, 1952.

65 **"It was those damned tea parties":** "The Campaign: Pride of the Clan," *Time*, July 11, 1960.

65 ***Don't cut through that lawn!:*** Ellen Cliggott, interview with author, July 17, 2020.

65 **It was a quiet morning:** "Senator Kennedy, Fiancée Spend 'Quiet' Weekend," *Barnstable Patriot*, June 25, 1953.

66 **thirty-six-year-old Jack had been featured in the *Saturday Evening Post*:** Paul F. Healy, "The Senate's Gay Young Bachelor," *Saturday Evening Post*, June 13, 1953.

66 **Jack sat by himself at LaGuardia Airport:** "Kennedy, Bride-to-Be Enjoy Cape Weekend," *Boston Globe*, June 27, 1953.

66 **sports photographer named Hy Peskin:** Preston Reynolds and Adriana Reynolds, interviews with author, October 28, 2019.

68 **"Oh don't be mean to her, dear":** Kennedy, *Times to Remember*, 375.

68 **an informal photo shoot:** "Senator and Fiancée Spend Weekend on Cape," *Boston Globe*, June 29, 1953.

68 **Joe and Rose had hired a New York architect:** "Hyannis Port Decorating Correspondence, 1927–1960," Joseph P. Kennedy Personal Papers, JFKL.

68 **Joe made nearly as much money from real estate:** Nasaw, *The Patriarch*, 586.

69 **With her hands clasped behind her back, Jackie leaned in to listen:** Hy Peskin photographs, Getty Images, June 1953.

69 **One photographer said about Jackie, "She should be posing for color pictures":** "Senator and Fiancée Spend Weekend on Cape," *Boston Globe*, June 29, 1953.

69 **Jack and Jackie had been introduced:** Charles Bartlett Oral History Interview, January 6, 1965, JFKL.

70 **When Jackie got back to her quiet home:** Smith, *Hostage to Fortune*, 662.

71 **Teddy welcomed the group:** Engle, *The Lost Kennedy Home Movies*.

71 **The Kennedys' neighbors, the Harringtons:** Kennedy, *Times to Remember*, 377.

72 **"I'm sure that won't happen again":** Kennedy, *Times to Remember*, 378.

72 **Eunice and Sarge had their first child:** Bobby Shriver biographical information, One.org, https://www.one.org/us/person/bobby-shriver/.

72 **Pat married:** "Lawford to Wed Patricia Kennedy," *New York Times*, February 13, 1954.

72 **Jean married:** "Miss Jean Ann Kennedy Married; Wed in Lady Chapel of St. Patrick's to Edward Smith," *New York Times*, May 20, 1956.

72 **Downey bought one of the houses:** Tangley Lloyd, interview with author, December 30, 2020.

73 **"Ethel, Eunice, the guests, and the Gargans are all in fine shape":** Morton Downey to Joseph P. Kennedy (undated), Joseph P. Kennedy Personal Papers, JFKL.

73 **"I understand that Rose and I have no relatives anywhere in the world":** Joseph P. Kennedy to Morton Downey, August 23, 1954, Joseph P. Kennedy Personal Papers, JFKL.

73 **He wrote to his oldest grandson:** Nasaw, *The Patriarch*, 678.

73 **Her favorite shop was in Sandwich:** "Undated notes: Antique shopping on Cape Cod," Rose Fitzgerald Kennedy Personal Papers, JFKL.

73 **pretty young secretary, Janet DesRosiers:** Janet DesRosiers Fontaine, *A Good Life: A Memoir*. Self-published, November 18, 2015.

73 **One summer they were up on Scudder Avenue:** Kathleen Kennedy Townsend, interview with author, July 5, 2021.

74 **Bernard's teenage daughter, Josefina:** Josefina Harvin, interview with author, January 11, 2022.

74 **Austin Bell . . . was the local milkman:** Brooks Smith, interview with author, July 20, 2020.

74 **Kenneth Lemoine Green Jr.:** "Kenneth Lemoine Green Jr. Dies; Funeral Wednesday," *St. Louis Post-Dispatch*, April 28, 1952, and property records obtained from Town of Barnstable Assessing Division, requested July 12, 2021.

75 **the children all had healthy trust funds:** Michael C. Jensen, "Managing the Kennedy Millions," *New York Times*, June 12, 1977.

75 **Though the house was purchased in Teddy's name:** Kathleen Kennedy Townsend, interview with author, and property records obtained from Town of Barnstable Assessing Division, July 12, 2021.

75 **Bobby went alone up to Barnstable High School:** Lou Howes, "Kennedy Scion Debuts with Townies," *Barnstable Patriot*, October 28, 1954.

75 **"You'd better go out and get a *job*":** Arthur M. Schlesinger, *Robert Kennedy and His Times* (Boston: Houghton Mifflin, 1978), 99.

75 **Bobby left McCarthy's committee:** Larry Tye, *Bobby Kennedy: The Making of a Liberal Icon* (New York: Random House, 2016), 37.

76 **Joe threatened them with, "I'm going to get Jack Dempsey after you"** and

"What the hell are you doing here?" Dempsey asked him: John F. Dempsey Oral History Interview, June 10, 1964, JFKL.

76 **varsity letter at Harvard:** Jack Newfield, *RFK: A Memoir* (New York: Plume, 1969), 43.

77 **"Stop what you're doing":** DesRosiers Fontaine, *A Good Life.*

77 **The boat had been built in Quincy, Massachusetts:** "1930 Commuter Yacht Marlin," Christies, https://www.christies.com/en/lot/lot-919473.

77 **Frank Wirtanen, a gregarious boat captain:** Edward M. Kennedy, "Slightly Salty," *Cape Cod Standard-Times,* 1967, and Ed Wirtanen, interview with author, May 11, 2021.

77 **Wirtanen would sometimes ask Joe:** Ed Wirtanen, interview with author, May 11, 2021.

77 **On a summer Friday afternoon, he invited his friend John Culver:** John C. Culver Oral History Interview, May 12, 2003, JFKL and John C. Culver Eulogy for Edward M. Kennedy.

79 **volunteer to quarterback:** Jacqueline Kennedy Onassis and Arthur Schlesinger Jr., *Jacqueline Kennedy: Historic Conversations on Life with John F. Kennedy* (New York: Hyperion, 2011), 15.

80 **Addison's:** Kirk LeMoyne Billings Oral History #6, July 22, 1964, JFKL.

80 **"Don't worry, Dad":** Goodwin, *The Fitzgeralds and the Kennedys,* 774.

80 **"Dear Mother and Dad," Joe Jr. started:** Smith, *Hostage to Fortune,* 598.

81 **"My son, U.S. Senator John F. Kennedy is making good progress":** Damore, *The Cape Cod Years,* 144.

81 **spinal fusion:** Carl Sferrazza Anthony, *As We Remember Her: Jacqueline Kennedy Onassis in the Words of Her Family and Friends* (New York: HarperCollins, 1997), 95.

81 **Jack went to Osterville for dinner with a friend:** Leamer, *The Kennedy Women,* 442.

82 **"incandescence":** Sferrazza Anthony, *As We Remember Her,* 88.

82 **Joe wrote to his youngest in the fall of 1955:** Smith, *Hostage to Fortune,* 670.

82 **Jackie had back-to-back miscarriages:** Sferrazza Anthony, *As We Remember Her,* 95.

82 **Jackie went to her mother's home in Newport:** Thurston Clarke, *JFK's Last Hundred Days: The Transformation of a Man and the Emergence of a Great President* (New York: Penguin, 2013), 11.

82 **Thanksgiving Thursday 1956:** Jacqueline Kennedy as told to Joan Younger, "Our Thanksgiving: What It Means to Us," *Ladies' Home Journal,* November 1960.

83 **Jack pulled his father away from the table:** Goodwin, *The Fitzgeralds and the Kennedys,* 787, and Kennedy, *True Compass,* 116.

84 **a pair of clapboard houses on the Cape in 1901:** Sally Jacobs, "Prime Time with Joan Kennedy," *Boston Globe Magazine*, July 9, 2000.

84 **in a pink brick house on the beach:** Betty Hannah Hoffman, "What It's Like to Marry a Kennedy," *Ladies' Home Journal*, October 1962.

84 **The neighbors noticed a pretty blond woman:** Tangley Lloyd, interview with author, December 30, 2020.

84 **Joan proposal story:** Leamer, *The Kennedy Women*, 472.

85 **on October 9, 1957:** National Register of Historic Places Inventory Nomination Form, United States Department of the Interior National Park Service.

85 **"Grandpa wanted to keep everyone together":** Sferrazza Anthony, *As We Remember Her*, 89.

85 **"Daly Cottage":** Herrick and Newman, *Old Hyannis Port*, 54.

85 **Joaquim Rosary:** Kerry Kennedy, interview with author, July 15, 2021, and Tom Holmes, interview with author, January 28, 2022.

85 **Shea collection and Luddington background:** Robert Luddington interview with Patrick Ramage, "Cape Codders Remember the Kennedys," *Tales of Cape Cod*, DVD, 2020.

86 **Jackie breaking right ankle:** "Mrs. Kennedy Breaks Ankle Playing Football," *Boston Globe*, November 18, 1955.

86 **"Martha and I used to play some bridge":** Meyers and Lieberson, *John Fitzgerald Kennedy: As We Remember Him*, 67.

87 **"interesting how this generation turns out":** John Culver Oral History, June 2007, Edward M. Kennedy Oral History Project, University of Virginia Miller Center.

87 **"I'll give you $150,000 from the Foundation":** John F. Dempsey Oral History Interview, June 10, 1964, JFKL.

88 **But in 1957, Fortune:** Tye, *Bobby Kennedy: The Making of a Liberal Icon*, 8.

88 **Dempsey set up a conference:** John F. Dempsey Oral History Interview, June 10, 1964, JFKL.

88 **Joe's speech that night mirrored:** "The Joseph P. Kennedy Jr. Memorial Skating Centre" brochure, William Brewster Nickerson Cape Cod History Archives, Wilkens Library, Cape Cod Community College; and Damore, *The Cape Cod Years*, 156.

CHAPTER FIVE

89 **that summer, the roses on the Cape were perfect:** Kennedy, *Times to Remember*, 400.

89 **Jack, Jackie, and Caroline were back on the Cape:** "Hyannis, 24–25 June 1960," Rose Kennedy Personal Papers, JFKL.

90 **"I Like Jack" paper hats:** Maud Shaw, *White House Nanny: My Years with Caroline and John Kennedy Jr.* (New York: New American Library, 1966), 64.

90 **"Nan, I hope you're going to vote for me":** Tangley Lloyd, interview with author, December 30, 2020.

90 **"It's a rather small house we have there":** Jacqueline Kennedy Onassis Oral History, interview 1, January 11, 1974, by Joe B. Frantz, LBJ Library Oral Histories, LBJ Presidential Library.

91 **Jackie was always happiest and most comfortable when her sister:** Pierre Salinger, *With Kennedy* (Garden City, New York: Doubleday, 1966), 100.

91 **"Does your sister live in London?":** Jacqueline Kennedy, *Jacqueline Kennedy: Historic Conversations*, 84.

91 **Lady Bird noticed about Jackie:** Lady Bird Johnson Oral History Interview XLIII, November 23, 1996, LBJ Presidential Library.

91 **writer Norman Mailer:** Arthur M. Schlesinger Jr., *A Thousand Days: John F. Kennedy in the White House* (New York: Houghton Mifflin, 2002), 62. Originally published by Random House, 1988.

91 **"No one had too much doubt that Kennedy would be nominated":** Norman Mailer, "Superman Comes to the Supermarket," *Esquire*, November 1960.

92 **A friend of Jackie's recommended:** Sferrazza Anthony, *As We Remember Her*, 118.

92 **She typed for her first column:** Publicity Division, September 1960: 10–16 (page 114 + 115), Papers of John F. Kennedy, JFKL.

93 **Most nights on the Cape were quiet and lonely:** Jacqueline Kennedy, *Jacqueline Kennedy: Historic Conversations*, 57.

93 **"A woman in Hyannis made it for me":** Mary Cremmen, "Listening Party," *Boston Globe*, September 27, 1960.

93 **"I think you were superb":** Mary Cremmen, "Jacqueline to Jack: You Were Superb," *Boston Globe*, September 27, 1960.

93 **Jack's grandmother Josie:** Associated Press, "Grandmother Tells Kennedy 'You're Our Next President,'" *The Idaho Statesman*, August 8, 1960.

93 **Ethel came over to sit with Josie:** Robert F. Kennedy Jr., interview with author, October 23, 2020.

94 **the Hyannis Armory was thick with smoke:** Theodore White, *The Making of the President 1960* (New York: Harper Perennial, 2009), 11. Originally published by Atheneum, 1961.

94 **"if anybody wants vast amounts of trivia about the senator's house":** *Dennis-Yarmouth Register*, Friday, November 11, 1960.

94 **Jack reprimanded his sister Eunice:** White, *The Making of the President 1960*, 18.

94 **Exactly a year earlier:** White, *The Making of the President 1960*, 49.

94 **Two Barnstable police officers:** Martin Hoxie, interview with author, July 24, 2020.

95 **"I'm glad to be back on Cape Cod":** "Kennedy and His Wife Vote Here as Partisan Hundreds Cheer," *Boston Globe*, November 8, 1960.

95 **"I want to see Caroline and take it easy":** Relman Morin, Associated Press, "Kennedy Looks Confident Over Vote Outcome," *Lawrence Daily Journal-World*, November 8, 1960.

95 **Ann Gargan picked them up in a sedan:** "Kennedy and His Wife Vote Here as Partisan Hundreds Cheer," *Boston Globe*, November 8, 1960.

95 **They didn't pass down Hyannis's Main Street:** Frank Falacci, *Cape Cod News*, December 17, 1964.

95 **the Hyannis Port Civic Association had held a meeting:** United Press International, "Kennedy Offers Olive Branch to Cape Neighbors," *Salt Lake Tribune*, August 1, 1960.

95 **"Be careful, Senator":** John F. Dempsey Oral History Interview, June 10, 1964, JFKL.

95 **Jackie had a towering wooden palisade fence constructed:** White, *The Making of the President 1960*, 6.

95 **"Lee and Stas were staying with us":** Jacqueline Kennedy, *Jacqueline Kennedy: Historic Conversations*, 82.

96 **Jack went over to the Big House for breakfast:** White, *The Making of the President 1960*, 7.

96 **Jack's favorite fish chowder:** Jacqueline Kennedy, *Jacqueline Kennedy: Historic Conversations*, 57.

96 **he went out to throw the football with Bobby and Teddy:** Frank Falacci, "Kennedy Refuses to Claim Victory Despite Rising Lead," *Boston Globe*, November 9, 1960.

96 **"Just about 10 minutes ago, the Senator and his sisters walked over to Bob's house":** George McKinnon, "Hyannis Armory Scene of Waiting," *Boston Globe*, November 9, 1960.

97 **"Who's ahead?" a reporter pushed:** Mary Cremmen, "'Longest Hours of Life,' Jacqueline Says of Wait," *Boston Globe*, November 9, 1960.

97 **Joe's friend Morton Downey had come over:** Kenneth P. O'Donnell and David F. Powers with Joe McCarthy, *"Johnny, We Hardly Knew Ye": Memories of John Fitzgerald Kennedy* (Boston: Little, Brown, 1972), 256.

97 **dinner with Jackie and their friend Bill Walton:** O'Donnell and Powers, *"Johnny, We Hardly Knew Ye,"* 256.

97 **to say goodnight to his daughter, Caroline:** White, *The Making of the President 1960*, 16.

98 **Sodas at the buffet in the back of the room:** White, 14.

98 **Jack went up the stairs of his house to kiss Jackie goodnight:** Jacqueline Kennedy, *Jacqueline Kennedy: Historic Conversations*, 97.

98 **At 3:15 a.m. Vice President Nixon appeared on TV:** "CBS News Election Night 1960: 11:35 P.M. E.T.–6:19 A.M. E.T.," https://www.youtube.com /watch?v=hcm494i-tiw.

98 **Jack walked over to his future press secretary, Pierre Salinger, to say:** Martin Hoxie, interview with author, July 24, 2020.

98 **Three a.m. turned into four at the command center:** Jacques Lowe, *JFK Remembered: An Intimate Portrait by His Personal Photographer* (New York: Gramercy Books, 1993), 92.

98 **On Irving Avenue, three-year-old Caroline and her nanny, Maud Shaw:** Maud Shaw, "My Life with Caroline and John-John," *Ladies' Home Journal*, December 1965.

99 **"I think he wanted her out of the house, quite honestly":** Ann Gargan Oral History, August 11, 2005, Edward M. Kennedy Oral History Project, University of Virginia Miller Center.

99 **"The dawn is breaking and the sun is shining":** Richard J. Levine, "From Gold to Football," *Cornell Daily Sun*, November 10, 1960.

100 **a concession telegram arrived at 111 Irving Avenue:** "Nixon Waits Until 12:47 to Concede," *Boston Globe*, November 9, 1960.

100 **"What kind of First Lady will you be?'":** Jacqueline Kennedy, *Jacqueline Kennedy: Historic Conversations*, 97.

100 **Photographer Jacques Lowe tried to collect:** Lowe, *JFK Remembered*, 101.

100 **Jackie had slipped outside in her overcoat:** Mary Cremmen, "Jackie Walks Alone, Then Faces Spotlight," *Boston Globe*, November 10, 1960.

100 **"You have to come now":** Jacqueline Kennedy, *Jacqueline Kennedy: Historic Conversations*, 97.

101 **white Lincoln:** President-elect John F. Kennedy: November 9, 1960, Hyannis Armory, https://www.youtube.com/watch?v=8DvBSM99eKQ.

101 **pink Cadillac:** Lawrence J. Arata Oral History Interview, 1964, JFKL.

101 **the local principal . . . released:** Linda Hutchenrider, interview with author, July 22, 2021.

101 **Johnny Linehan, the Kennedys' old sailing instructor:** Rob Stewart interview with Patrick Ramage, "Cape Codders Remember," *Tales of Cape Cod*, DVD, 2020.

101 **"Well, we live on Cape Cod, don't we?":** George McKinnon, "Kennedy Calls for Supreme Effort," *Boston Globe*, November 9, 1960.

101 **served himself a glass of milk punch:** Falacci, *Cape Cod News*, December 17, 1964.

101 **"Things are never quite the same once they get to the White House":** Benjamin A. Smith II, Oral History Interview, December 29, 1964, JFKL.

102 **"We're still waiting on you two—hurry up!":** Kate Storey, "Jean Kennedy Smith's Private Family Stories," *Town & Country*, June 18, 2020.

102 **temporary stage for twice-daily press conferences:** Falacci, *Cape Cod News*, December 17, 1964.

102 **"It's practically like any other fall weekend":** Associated Press, "Jacqueline Says It's All Very Unreal," *Titusville Herald*, November 11, 1960.

102 **The family left for Palm Beach:** Merriman Smith, United Press International, "Kennedy Takes Off for Florida," *Redlands Daily Facts*, November 11, 1960.

CHAPTER SIX

103 **"I could fly by and pick up Jackie":** Janet G. Travell Oral History, January 1, 1966, JFKL.

103 **A card was sent to the new baby:** "Best Wishes Mailed to New Baby," *Barnstable Patriot*, December 1, 1960.

104 **"Mr. Kennedy's residence":** Saunders, *Torn Lace Curtain*, 37.

105 **hosted the first cocktail party in the Port for the new president:** Peggy Eastman, "Summer of '61 Belonged to JFK," *Cape Cod Times*, 1991.

105 **The neighbors watched the presidential flag:** Clint Hill and Lisa McCubbin Hill, *Mrs. Kennedy and Me* (New York: Gallery Books, 2012), 87.

105 **"the bullpen":** Lou LaPrade and Gordon Caldwell, "Out of Terror and Shock, Thoughts of Happier Days," *Cape Cod Standard-Times*, November 22, 1973.

106 **Milkman Austin Bell came over:** Gregory Bell, interview with author, February 8, 2022.

106 **The Keavy boys were there with their families:** Allison Falkenberry, interview with author, August 18, 2020.

106 **Nancy Tenney and her children:** Tangley Lloyd, interview with author, December 30, 2020.

106 **Bobby's next-door neighbors:** On background interview with author.

106 **Nancy's father, Rockwell Tenney, watched the whole scene:** Martin, *Hero for Our Time*, 372.

107 **The house they bought, a ten-room, shingled:** Property records obtained from Town of Barnstable Assessing Division, August 5, 2021.

107 **eight-bedroom house with the year 1787:** Herrick and Newman, *Old Hyannis Port*, 16.

107 **at the start of Marchant Avenue for $120,000:** "Kennedy Kin Buy Home," *New York Times*, September 15, 1963.

107 **The press began referring to:** Mary Cremmen, "'Longest Hours of Life,' Jacqueline Says of Wait," *Boston Globe*, November 9, 1960.

107 **They had a week or so of training:** Martin Hoxie, interview with author, July 24, 2020.

107 **brought them cakes:** Elizabeth Mumford, interview with author, May 15, 2020.

107 **Jackie spent her days on the phone with her staff:** Mary Barelli Gallagher, *My Life with Jacqueline Kennedy* (Philadelphia: David McKay Co., 1969), 276.

108 **"I just felt so strongly about those children":** Jacqueline Kennedy, *Jacqueline Kennedy: Historic Conversations*, 341.

109 **added a west wing:** Longley, *Hyannis and Hyannis Port*, 51.

109 **a dozen women with the exact same style:** Tom Holmes interview with Patrick Ramage, "Cape Codders Remember the Kennedys," *Tales of Cape Cod*, DVD, 2020.

109 **"the squirrels":** Peggy Eastman, "Summer of '61 Belonged to JFK," *Cape Cod Times*, 1991.

109 **beat-up old station wagon:** Brooks Smith, interview with author, July 20, 2020.

109 **Joe added a private pier:** "Kennedys Get Permit," *New York Times*, May 11, 1961.

109 **Sampsons Island:** Don Walsh, "Focusing on JFK Days," *Cape Cod Times*, November 20, 1983.

109 **friend Bunny Mellon lived:** Meryl Gordon, "How Bunny Mellon Re-invented the White House Rose Garden," *Vanity Fair*, September 22, 2017.

110 **Their yacht was surrounded:** Hill and McCubbin Hill, *Mrs. Kennedy and Me*, 94.

110 **a phone rang in the newsroom of the *Cape Cod Times*:** Lou LaPrade and Gordon Caldwell, "Out of Terror and Shock, Thoughts of Happier Days," *Cape Cod Standard-Times*, November 22, 1973.

110 **Clint Hill, shouted back:** Hill and McCubbin Hill, *Mrs. Kennedy and Me*, 158.

111 **Franklin Roosevelt Jr., . . . was out with them that day:** Meyers and Lieberson, *John Fitzgerald Kennedy: As We Remember Him*, 207.

111 **"I think he is over there!":** Janet Lee Bouvier Auchincloss Oral History Interview, September 5, 1964, JFKL.

111 **"They'll be cranky," Jackie told him:** Jacqueline Kennedy, *Jacqueline Kennedy: Historic Conversations*, 337.

112 **She asked Carl Wirtanen:** Jim McEvoy, interview with author, July 14, 2020.

113 **biggest round of applause of the day:** Frank Falacci, "Caroline Water Skis, Too," *Boston Globe*, July 23, 1962.

113 **closed their eyes when they prayed:** Patrick Butler interview in *At the Center of the World: Hyannis Port and the Presidency of John F. Kennedy*, JFK Hyannis Museum Video, 2008.

113 **"don't go over there, knuckleheads!":** Peter Cross interview, "Barnstable Remembers: JFK: A Beloved Neighbor," Hyannis Public Library, May 2017.

113 **twelve-dollar per diem:** Hill and McCubbin Hill, *Mrs. Kennedy and Me*, 89.

113 **"'Oh, I've got something in my eye!'":** Peter Cross interview, "Barnstable Remembers: JFK: A Beloved Neighbor," Hyannis Public Library, May 2017.

114 **"I had never had clam chowder before":** Hill and McCubbin Hill, *Mrs. Kennedy and Me*, 89.

114 **Jackie gave specific instructions to the agents:** Hill and McCubbin Hill, *Mrs. Kennedy and Me*, 331.

114 **"Drowning is my responsibility":** Memorandum by Lynn S. Meredith, Special Agent, Children's Detail, February 16, 1961, Secret Service responsive records obtained by author Steven M. Gillon through *Gillon v. Department of Homeland Security Civil Action* and shared with author.

115 **"They walk on the lawns":** "Sightseers Upset President's Town," *New York Times*, May 30, 1961.

115 **"They can kiss my arse!":** Saunders, *Torn Lace Curtain*, 73.

116 **for $150 each local high school kids:** Peter Cross interview, "Barnstable Remembers: JFK: A Beloved Neighbor," Hyannis Public Library, May 2017.

116 **Pierre Salinger, sliding:** J. David Crawford, interview with author, July 30, 2020.

116 **Alan Alda:** Alan Alda, interview with author, December 16, 2020.

117 **Jack snuck away to play a game of checkers:** Kennedy, *True Compass*, 203.

118 **"Bill, be sure we take":** Paul B. Fay Jr., *The Pleasure of His Company* (New York: Harper & Row, 1966), 224.

118 **Rose wasn't home yet—she'd stayed in the French Riviera a little longer:** Kennedy, *Times to Remember*, 40.

118 **redirected to New Bedford:** Dick White, "Cabby's Passenger Top of the Heap," *New Bedford Standard-Times*, May 17, 1998.

119 **"My riding boots!":** Saunders, *Torn Lace Curtain*, 79.

119 **On September 29, 1961:** *Foreign Relations of the United States, 1961–1963, Volume VI, Kennedy-Khrushchev Exchanges*. Office of the Historian, U.S., Government.

121 **Adzhubei when he landed:** "K Son-in-Law Here to See Kennedy," *Boston Globe*, November 25, 1961, and "Transcript of Interview with the President by Aleksei Adzhubei, Editor of Izvestia," November 25, 1961, The American Presidency Project, UC Santa Barbara.

121 **That morning Larry Newman:** Larry Newman, "Across the Street from History," *Cape Cod Times*, November 20, 1983.

121 **all in black suits and neat ties:** "Interview with Aleksei Adzhubei, Editor of Izvestiya, in Hyannis Port, 10:10AM," November 25, 1961, JFKL.

121 **sick with a cold:** Frank Falacci, "Caroline's Dog Steals the Show at Kennedy Thanksgiving," *Boston Globe*, November 24, 1961.

122 **Welsh terrier, Charlie:** Falacci, "Caroline's Dog Steals the Show."

123 **Defense Department budget meeting at the Big House:** "President John F. Kennedy at a Defense Department Budget Meeting in Hyannis Port, Massachusetts," JFKL.

123 **"Is the rink closed?":** Frank Falacci, "Rugged! That's Our Kennedys," *Boston Globe*, November 25, 1961.

123 **"Hooray for Hollywood":** Fay Jr., *The Pleasure of His Company*, 241.

123 **Schiaparelli slack suit:** "Thanksgiving 61," November 1961, Rose Kennedy Personal Papers, JFKL.

124 **"Do you know 'September Song'?":** Fay Jr., *The Pleasure of His Company*, 241.

125 **Construction began on a new swimming pool:** "Preparations Under Way for Arrival of Kennedys," *Cape Cod Standard-Times*, June 13, 1962.

125 **debilitating stroke:** Nasaw, *The Patriarch*, 776.

125 **"We were all required to do our time with Grandpa":** Christopher Kennedy Lawford, *Symptoms of Withdrawal: A Memoir of Snapshots and Redemption* (New York: William Morrow, 2005), 81.

126 **"Nobody knew whether he was wide-awake":** Kerry Kennedy, interview with author, March 23, 2020.

126 **it had a heated pool:** Betty Hannah Hoffman, "What It's Like to Marry a Kennedy," *Ladies' Home Journal*, October 1962.

127 **Jack stood on his crutches:** Fay Jr., *The Pleasure of His Company*, 226.

127 **"It's clear you're going to run":** Edward M. Kennedy Oral History, March 23, 2005, Edward M. Kennedy Oral History Project, University of Virginia Miller Center.

128 **The summers of '52 and '53:** *Tales of Cape Cod* Interview with Eugenia Fortes, July 20, 1978, William Brewster Nickerson Cape Cod History Archives, Wilkens Library, Cape Cod Community College, https://archive.org/details/FortesEugeniaAllTracks.

128 **"Thurgood told me, Genny":** Sean M. Walsh, "Two Hyannis Women, Two Amazing Lives," *Register*, February 9, 1995.

128 **"crossed that Mason-Dixon line":** Gabrielle Emanuel, "The Cruel Story Behind the 'Reverse Freedom Rides,'" NPR, February 29, 2020.

128 **"President Kennedy's brother assures you":** "Cape Grumbles More About Cost of Kennedy's Stay Than Influx of Negroes," *Boston Globe*, June 10, 1962.

128 **"Where is President Kennedy?":** Emanuel, "The Cruel Story Behind the 'Reverse Freedom Rides.'"

128 **they sent the most people to Hyannis:** Clive Webb, "'A Cheap Trafficking in Human Misery': The Reverse Freedom Rides of 1962," *Journal of American Studies*, 38.

129 **Lela Mae Williams:** Emanuel, "The Cruel Story Behind the 'Reverse Freedom Rides.'"

129 **"most inhumane things":** TCC TV 35, Tales of Cape Cod Collection, Wil-

liam Brewster Nickerson Cape Cod History Archives, Wilkens Library, Cape Cod Community College.

129 **it was arranged that Harris:** TCC TV 35, Tales of Cape Cod Collection.

130 **"a rather cheap exercise in":** "White Citizens' Action Criticized by Kennedy," *New York Times*, May 10, 1962, and Emanuel, "The Cruel Story Behind the 'Reverse Freedom Rides,'" NPR.

130 **"predicted he would return to Little Rock":** "Little Rock Ships Negro to Hyannis Port by Bus," *Boston Globe*, May 11, 1962, 12.

130 **Harris had to shut down his restaurant:** "Freedom Rider Harris Sees Outlook Dim at His Barbecue Pit," *Barnstable Patriot*, October 4, 1962.

130 **Jack's secretary, Evelyn Lincoln, gathered photos:** Evelyn Lincoln Correspondence, 1962, John F. Kennedy Personal Papers, JFKL.

131 **"the house on the point":** Peg Downey letter, 1962, John F. Kennedy Personal Papers, JFKL.

131 **for the first time in decades:** Bob and Alex Frazee, interview with author, January 27, 2021.

131 **he landed up the hill at the golf club:** Martin, *A Hero for Our Time*, 463.

132 **Joe's nurse, Rita Dallas, thought to herself:** Dallas, *The Kennedy Case*, 40.

132 **top of a bluff:** Bob and Alex Frazee, interview with author, January 27, 2021.

133 **Pushinka's rambunctious new puppies:** Traphes L. Bryant Oral History Interview, May 13, 1964, JFKL.

133 **Cecil Stoughton set up a projector:** Cecil W. Stoughton Oral History Interview, September 18 and 19, 2002, JFKL.

133 **Video descriptions:** "Hyannis: Squaw Island, July 21–22, 1962," and "Hyannis Port and Squaw Island, August 1963," JFKL.

133 **All the bedrooms at Brambletyde were upstairs:** Bob and Alex Frazee, interview with author, January 27, 2021.

134 **painting watercolors:** Martin, *A Hero for Our Time*, 524.

134 **speaking notes into her recorder:** Martin, 207.

134 **"As the days went on . . . I found it stranger and stranger":** Barelli Gallagher, *My Life with Jacqueline Kennedy*, 276.

134 **Jack's affairs with other women:** Barbara Leaming's *Mrs. Kennedy: The Missing History of the Kennedy Years* (New York: Free Press, 2002) relies on White House visitor logs to establish a timeline of when Jack's mistresses came to see him.

135 **realized the baby was on his way:** Christopher Kennedy, interview with author, July 31, 2020.

135 **christened at St. Francis Xavier:** Michael Fitzmaurice, "President Kennedy at Nephew's Christening 1963," Reuters.

135 **speech in Berlin:** LeMoyne Billings Oral History #11, January 9, 1966, JFKL.

135 **Jack wanted to watch it every night:** "At the Center of the World: Hyan-

nis Port and the Presidency of John F. Kennedy," John F. Kennedy Hyannis Museum.

135 **the allergy shots he'd begun taking:** Clarke, *JFK's Last Hundred Last Days*, 29.

135 **"Come in," Jack called:** Paul B. Fay Jr., Oral History Interview, November 1970, JFKL.

135 **a bomber who'd told the authorities:** UPI, "Bomber Says Money Behind Murder Plot," *Waco News Tribune*, December 17, 1960.

136 **"Did you ever think if someone took a shot at me":** Larry Newman, "Across the Street from History," *Cape Cod Times*, November 20, 1983.

136 **"a hundred and fifty thousand dollars for an acre and a half or two acres?":** Paul B. Fay Jr. Oral History, November 11, 1970, JFKL.

136 **"Oh, I could shoot":** Barelli Gallagher, *My Life with Jacqueline Kennedy*, 275.

136 **marshlands on Squaw Island:** Gallagher, *My Life with Mrs. Kennedy*, 292.

136 **he signed another lease:** Bob and Alex Frazee, interview with author, January 27, 2021.

137 **Liz Mumford and her mother:** Elizabeth Mumford, interview with author, May 15, 2020.

137 **John McKelvy:** "Services Held Today at Hyannis Port for John E. McKelvy," *Barnstable Patriot*, August 8, 1963.

137 **"I'm bringing Mrs. Kennedy back to the house":** Hill and McCubbin Hill, *Mrs. Kennedy and Me*, 239.

138 **Robert Luddington, who'd helped decorate:** Luddington interview with Patrick Ramage, "Cape Codders Remember the Kennedys," *Tales of Cape Cod*, DVD, 2020.

138 **She liked it there:** Janet G. Travell Oral History Interview, January 20, 1966, JFKL.

138 **"Did you see the *Post* this morning?":** Telephone Recordings: Dictation Belt 23D.1. Furniture at Otis Air Force Base, July 25, 1963, JFKL.

138 **"That silly bastard":** Telephone Recordings: Dictation Belt 23D.2. Furniture at Otis Air Force Base, July 25, 1963, JFKL.

138 **Jackie delivered a four-pound:** "Mrs. Kennedy Given Blood," *Boston Globe*, August 7, 1963, 1.

139 **he flew to Boston:** Gerald Hazard, interview with author, July 27, 2020.

139 **He arranged for her mother to go see her:** Gerald Hazard, interview with author, July 27, 2020.

139 **"that horrible suit":** O'Donnell and Powers, *"Johnny We Hardly Knew Ye,"* 437.

139 **phone in the suite:** Hill and McCubbin Hill, *Mrs. Kennedy and Me*, 239.

139 **Jackie left hand in hand:** Shaw, *White House Nanny*, 157.

139 **"Careful":** "Hyannis Port, August 1963: 7–14," JFKL (4:38).

140 **the kids' nanny took them out:** Shaw, *White House Nanny*, 157.

140 **Joe's seventy-fifth birthday:** "Weekend at Hyannis Port: Birthday Party at Hyannis Port for Joseph P. Kennedy, Sr.," September 7, 1963, JFKL.

140 **cousins drove to the airport:** "Kennedy Youngsters Bid Cape Farewell," *Boston Globe*, September 9, 1963.

140 **Jack went outside for walks:** Martin, *A Hero for Our Time*, 499.

141 **"He's the one who made all this possible":** O'Donnell and Powers, *"Johnny We Hardly Knew Ye,"* 42.

141 **Tom Gunnery sat huddled:** Edgar "Tom" Gunnery, interview with author, November 8, 2019.

141 **There was barely a squawk:** "Cape Codders Recall the Day Their President Was Killed," *Cape Cod Times*.

141 **Rose had gone to Mass:** "Hyannis Port Wept Quietly for a Friend," *Cape Cod Standard-Times*, November 23, 1963.

142 **She called out to Ann Gargan:** Gail Cameron, "The Kennedy Nobody Knows," *Ladies' Home Journal*, June 1966.

142 **"I had a mixture of reactions":** Kennedy, *Times to Remember*, 478.

142 **Knots of neighbors:** "Hyannis Port Wept Quietly for a Friend," *Cape Cod Standard-Times*.

143 **"Today's feature film is a new Elvis Presley movie!":** Saunders, *Torn Lace Curtain*, 215.

143 **where their old family friend Jack Dempsey:** "'Jack is Dead' . . . Father Is Told by Senator," *Cape Cod Standard-Times*, November 23, 1963.

143 **ripped the television wires:** Kennedy, *True Compass*, 209.

143 **Joe's nurse, Rita Dallas, found her outside alone:** Dallas, *The Kennedy Case*, 11.

143 **black crepe:** "President Kennedy's Summer 'Home Town' Returned to a Measure of Normalcy," *Barnstable Patriot*, November 28, 1963.

143 **portraits of Jack hung in the front windows:** Saunders, *Torn Lace Curtain*, 226.

144 **"I'm here to see Grandpa":** Dallas, *The Kennedy Case*, 240.

144 **"How are they doing out there?":** Saunders, *Torn Lace Curtain*, 226.

144 **Bobby couldn't bear to come back to Hyannis Port:** Associated Press, "Bob Kennedy Remains at His Estate," *Uniontown Morning Herald*, November 29, 1963.

145 **"wider than pools":** Item III-A: Copy of White's 19 December 1963 Transcript of Interview Notes, Theodore H. White Personal Papers, JFKL.

CHAPTER SEVEN

147 **Memorial Day parade in Centerville:** Frank Falacci, "JFK . . . He Would Have Been 47 Today—Family Gathers," *Boston Globe*, May 29, 1964.

147 **His leather golf bag:** Kathy McKeon, *Jackie's Girl: My Life with the Kennedy Family* (New York: Gallery Books, 2017), 122.

147 **"When I came back everything just hit me":** Kennedy, *Times to Remember*, 548.

148 **break the lease:** Bob and Alex Frazee, interview with author, January 27, 2021.

148 **"It really hits, doesn't it?":** Kennedy, *Times to Remember*, 548.

148 **CBS crews:** Falacci, "JFK . . . He Would Have Been 47 Today—Family Gathers," *Boston Globe*, May 29, 1964.

148 **"Could you tell us why President Kennedy chose this particular site?":** CBS News Special transcript, May 29, 1964, as broadcast over the CBS Television Network.

149 **He held her hand:** "The Kennedy Case," 254.

149 **More than five hundred people:** Frank Falacci, "Crowds See Kennedys Off at Cape," *Boston Globe*, June 1, 1964.

149 **The people who worked inside the Kennedy houses:** Saunders, *Torn Lace Curtain*, 226.

149 **Joan playing while the family sang:** "Summer, Hyannis, 1963–1964," Rose Kennedy Personal Papers, JFKL.

150 **three broken vertebrae, two broken ribs:** Ned Potter, "Edward M. Kennedy Escaped Death in 1964," ABC News, August 6, 2009.

150 **Collapsed lung and hospital location:** Kennedy, *True Compass*, 219.

150 **"the President's seat" as they called it:** Peter Collier and David Horowitz, *The Kennedys: An American Drama* (New York: Summit Books, 1984), 327.

150 **"he was like a whole different person":** Dotson Rader interview with Nancy Tenney, December 2, 2000, Miscellaneous Accessions collection, JFKL.

151 **Bobby walked around in his swim trunks:** Lawford, *Symptoms of Withdrawal*, 82.

151 **left your car door unlocked:** Josefina Harvin, interview with author, January 11, 2022.

151 **"I can remember playing football":** Kerry Kennedy, interview with author, March 23, 2020.

151 *Shrivers are better than Kennedys!:* Saunders, *Torn Lace Curtain*, 58.

152 **added an extra wing:** Anthony Shriver, interview with author, July 14, 2021.

152 **"'Do I have enough money to buy this house?'":** Dotson Rader interview with Eunice Shriver, August 28, 2003, Miscellaneous Accessions collection, JFKL.

152 **One afternoon, Bobby, the oldest Shriver kid, fell:** Mark Shriver, *A Good Man: Rediscovering My Father, Sargent Shriver* (New York: St. Martin's Griffin, 2013), 46.

152 **A 168-foot yacht:** Associated Press, "Frank Sinatra and Mia Farrow Back at Island," *The Bradford Era*, August 9, 1965.

153 **Southern Breeze:** Gerard F. Weidmann, "Sinatra Hires Police Guards," *Boston Globe*, August 9, 1965.

153 **Mia walked up to the News Shop:** Edward Jenner, "Jacqueline, Other Kennedys Sup on Sinatra Yacht," *Boston Globe*, August 8, 1965.

153 **But it was Pat:** Associated Press, "It Was Pat Lawford, Not Jacqueline—Roz," *Boston Globe*, August 13, 1965.

153 **That night, Rob Stewart:** Rob Stewart, interview with author, July 16, 2020, and "Cape Codders Remember the Kennedys," *Tales of Cape Cod*, DVD, 2020.

154 **As Bobby walked along the Los Angeles beach:** Theodore White, "The Wearing Last Weeks and a Precious Last Day," *Life*, June 14, 1968.

154 **"I'm doing it just the way you would want me to":** Saunders, *Torn Lace Curtain*, 296.

155 **Ever since Jack's death:** Rita Dallas with Maxine Cheshire, "My 8 Years as the Kennedys' Private Nurse," *Ladies' Home Journal*, March 1971.

155 **Rose called Frank Saunders:** Saunders, *Torn Lace Curtain*, 303.

155 **"I cannot express to Mrs. Kennedy the sorrow I feel":** Alan B. Sheehan, "Rose Kennedy Flies Alone to N.Y. City," *Boston Globe*, June 6, 1968.

155 **When she finally left:** Saunders, *Torn Lace Curtain*, 303.

156 **When she came back out into the hallway:** Dallas, *The Kennedy Case*, 301.

156 **Dr. Rodger Currie:** Frances L. Broadhurst, "Hyannis Port Quiet, Gloomy, Sad," *Middletown Times Herald Record*, June 6, 1968.

156 **they'd bought the gray shingled-house:** Property records obtained from Town of Barnstable Assessing Division.

156 **Now, the telephone company began installing the proper phone lines:** Sheehan, "Rose Kennedy Flies Alone to N.Y. City," *Boston Globe*, June 6, 1968.

156 **She continued over to Jack's:** Sheehan, "Rose Kennedy Flies Alone."

156 **paperback copies of *The Death of a President* on display inside:** Sheehan, "Rose Kennedy Flies Alone."

156 **More than two hundred people stood under umbrellas:** "Kennedys Gathering at Hyannis Port Compound," *Boston Globe*, June 10, 1968.

156 **"Where is Ethel?":** "The Kennedy of Hickory Hill," *Time*, April 25, 1969.

157 **The renovations on Bobby's house:** "Kennedys Gathering at Hyannis Port Compound," *Boston Globe*, June 10, 1968.

157 **After losing a doubles game with mountaineer Jim Whittaker:** "The Kennedy of Hickory Hill," *Time*, April 25, 1969.

157 **There were filmmakers:** Carolyn Wood, *Class Notes: A Young Teacher's Lessons from Classroom to Kennedy Compound* (New York: White Pine Press, 2021), 84.

157 **During the long nights:** Josefina Harvin, interview with author, January 11, 2022.

157 **Jean and her husband, Stephen, left Hyannis Port:** "Kennedy Compound House Sold," *Greenfield Recorder* (AP report), August 28, 1973.

158 **"Irish bunnies":** McKeon, *Jackie's Girl*, 139.

158 **Arthur, who sometimes snuck down to the dunes to take naps:** Kathy McKeon, interview with author, December 17, 2021.

158 **younger women who worked for the family:** Kathy McKeon, interview with author, December 17, 2021.

159 **When the documentary:** Wood, *Class Notes*, 107.

159 **"How can Ethel handle this":** McKeon, *Jackie's Girl*, 196.

159 **summer of '68 in virtual solitude:** Mieke Tunney, "My Friend Joan Kennedy," *Ladies' Home Journal*, 1974.

159 **his art that summer was darker:** Burton Hersh, *Edward Kennedy: An Intimate Biography* (Berkeley, CA: Counterpoint, 2010), 295.

159 **He chartered a big sailboat—a sixty-five-foot yawl:** Kilvery Dun Gifford Oral History, July 13, 2005, Edward M. Kennedy Oral History Project, University of Virginia Miller Center.

160 **"I gazed at the night sky often on those voyages":** Kennedy, *True Compass*, 294.

160 **It was Ted's cousin Joe Gargan:** Joe Gargan Interview, Leo Damore papers, Kent State University Special Collections and Archives, February 15, 1983.

160 **"I had told her earlier that they were all coming":** Joe Gargan Interview, Leo Damore papers.

160 **Ted wasn't at the cocktail party:** Joe Gargan Interview, Leo Damore papers, Kent State University Special Collections and Archives, February 9, 1983.

160 **Jackie walked up to the News Shop:** Betty Flynn, "Far from the Tumult," August 28, 1968, *Boston Evening Globe*, 1.

161 **"He just went to the Cape and stayed there":** Milton Gwirtzman Oral History, August 5, 2009, Edward M. Kennedy Oral History Project, University of Virginia Miller Center.

161 **The whispers around town:** Hersh, *Edward Kennedy: An Intimate Biography*, 295.

161 **It was a way for him to escape:** Kennedy, *True Compass*, 422.

161 **It was at the Edgartown Regatta:** Grayson, *The Wianno Senior Story: A Century on Nantucket Sound*, 105.

162 **time to set the table for dinner:** Kennedy, *Times to Remember*, 532.

162 **on Friday morning, July 18, 1969:** Stephen Kurkjian, Richard Powers, and Robert L. Turner, "One Fateful Week: A Chronology," *Boston Globe*, July 27, 1969.

162 **St. Francis Xavier Church bazaar:** Frank Falacci, "Meant for Fun, Hyannis Port Once Again a Haven for Sadness," *Boston Globe*, July 20, 1969.

162 **The phone rang just after 2 p.m.:** Falacci, "Meant for Fun, Hyannis Port Once Again a Haven for Sadness."

162 **Ted walked out:** Falacci, "Meant for Fun, Hyannis Port Once Again a Haven for Sadness."

163 **Jackie, who'd arrived from Greece:** Dallas, *The Kennedy Case*, 330.

163 **The neighbors watched out the windows:** Tangley Lloyd, interview with author, December 30, 2020.

164 **Rose walked with Ted out to the flagpole in the yard:** Dallas, *The Kennedy Case*, 330.

164 **"He was so unlike himself":** Kennedy, *Times to Remember*, 532.

164 **Ted went upstairs to see his father:** Dallas, *The Kennedy Case*, 330.

164 **"When I talked at first to Ted":** Hersh, *Edward Kennedy*, 373.

165 **Milton Gwirtzman suggested:** Milton Gwirtzman Oral History, May 2009, Edward M. Kennedy Oral History Project, University of Virginia Miller Center.

165 **The sound technician arrived:** Leo Damore, *Senatorial Privilege: The Chappaquiddick Cover-up* (Washington, D.C.: Regnery, 1988), 201.

165 **whacking a tennis ball:** William S. Workman, "They Kept Long Vigil Outside of Kennedy Home," *Boston Globe*, July 26, 1969.

166 **cue cards:** Damore, *Senatorial Privilege: The Chappaquiddick Cover-up*, 205.

166 **shaggy-haired neighborhood kids:** Workman, "They Kept Long Vigil Outside of Kennedy Home," *Boston Globe*, July 26, 1969.

167 **On November 18, his nurse rang the bell:** Dallas, *The Kennedy Case*, 343.

167 **"I wondered whether I had":** Kennedy, *True Compass*, 292.

CHAPTER EIGHT

169 **Fifteen-year-old Bobby Kennedy Jr.:** Robert F. Kennedy Jr., *American Values: Lessons I Learned from My Family* (New York: HarperCollins, 2018), 382.

170 **drug raids:** Alan H. Sheehan and Andrew F. Blake, "A Kennedy, a Shriver Face Drug Charges," *Boston Globe*, August 6, 1970.

170 **ride in exchange for joints:** John Kelley, interview with author, August 15, 2021.

170 **"Listen," he began:** Shriver, *A Good Man*, 100.

171 **"The family informed me in Washington":** Bill Kovach, "Robert Kennedy Jr. And Cousin, Shriver Son, in Marijuana Case," *New York Times*, August 6, 1970.

171 **He issued a statement to the *New York Times*, which ran it in full:** Kovach, "Robert Kennedy Jr. And Cousin, Shriver Son, in Marijuana Case," *New York Times*.

171 **"You dragged the family name through the mud":** Kennedy Jr., *American Values*, 384.

172 **"We wanted the cops to know"**: On background interview with author.

172 **"They were just scary"**: Tim Shriver, interview with author, May 20, 2020.

172 **"Those kids didn't see"**: Leamer, *The Kennedy Women*, 660.

173 **for fear of sparking his anger**: Brad Blank, interview with author, July 20, 2020.

173 **It was close to 11 p.m.**: Associated Press, "Robert F. Kennedy Jr. Fined $50 On 'Sauntering, Loitering' Charge," *Danville Register*, August 24, 1974.

173 **shouted profanities**: Kennedy Jr., *American Values*, 384.

174 **"Kim idolizes him"**: UPI, "Young Kennedy Reported Planning to Get Married," *Naugatuck Daily News*, October 8, 1971.

174 **"high school crush"**: UPI, "15-Year-Old for RFK Jr.," *Kingsport News*, October 7, 1971.

174 **ranch in Colorado**: Pamela Kelley Burkley, *The Kennedy Playground* (Hyannis, MA: Sandpiper Books, 1990), 4.

175 **"I recall thinking the accident"**: Kelley Burkley, *The Kennedy Playground*, 11.

176 **fractured her spine**: "Pamela Kelley Listed as Stable," *Barnstable Patriot*, August 16, 1973.

176 **three hours of surgery**: "RFK's Son Overturns Car; Two Girls Seriously Hurt," *Madison Capital Times*, August 14, 1973.

176 **David with a sprained back**: "Centerville Girl Badly Hurt in Nantucket Jeep Accident," *Register*, August 16, 1973.

176 **Rose Kennedy sent cookies**: Kelley Burkley, *The Kennedy Playground*, 11.

176 **where he'd been treated after his plane crash**: Associated Press, "Edward Kennedy Won't Need Operation on His Back," *New York Times*, August 14, 1964.

176 **"illustrious name to do a lot of good"**: Associated Press, "$100 Fine Levied in Accident," *Findlay Republican Courier*, August 21, 1973.

176 **Pam plummeted into a depression**: Kelley Burkley, *The Kennedy Playground*, 12.

176 **She spent the rest of her life paralyzed**: Pamela K. Burkley Obituary, *Cape Cod Times*, December 3, 2020.

176 **Maureen Gill and her sisters**: Michaela Murphy, interview with author, September 17, 2021.

177 **a large boat full of tourists**: "Tourist Boats at Hyannis Port, Fall 1968," Rose Kennedy Personal Papers, JFKL.

177 **Hyannis Harbor Tours**: Philip Scudder, interview with author, July 28, 2020, and Hy-line Cruises, "History," https://hylinecruises.com/history/.

177 **"And to your right"**: Tangley Lloyd, interview with author, December 30, 2020.

177 **"Go away!"**: Wood, *Class Notes*, 95.

178 **Maureen, Pat, Eileen, and Gert didn't go on the boat tours:** Michaela Murphy, interview with author, September 17, 2021.

178 **"Oh, they got Rose out—walking":** Michaela Murphy, "Eye Spy," *The Moth*. Recorded: April 16, 2004. Location: New York City. Aired: January 9, 2018. The Moth is a nonprofit storytelling group.

178 **sand dune behind the house:** Dotson Rader interview with Edward M. Kennedy, August 28, 2003, Miscellaneous Accessions collection, JFKL.

178 **"I think the reason people like the plate":** Carol McCabe, "At the Kennedy Compound, They Look and Remember," *Providence Journal*, August 17, 1975.

178 **Clifton DeMotte:** "Hearings Before and Special Reports Made by Committee on Armed Services of the House of Representatives on Subjects Affecting the Naval and Military Establishments," U.S., Government Printing Office, 1975.

179 **"I'll bet they're not having this good a time in Miami":** Michael Widmer, UPI, "Ted Kennedy Has a Ball Far Away from Miami," *Naugatuck Daily News*, July 12, 1972.

180 **Reporters staked out the Shriver house:** Paul Langner, "Shriver Leaves Hyannis but Fails to Duck Press," *Boston Globe*, August 6, 1977, 14.

180 **fundraiser for Sarge:** Shelly Cohen, Associated Press, "More Than 170 Turn Out for Shriver Party," *Greenfield Recorder*, August 18, 1975.

181 **"I never got this close to the Compound before":** Associated Press, "Shriver Teas the Latest Thing at Hyannis Port," *Aiken Standard*, February 3, 1976.

181 **after coming in third:** Seth S. King, *New York Times*, March 17, 1976.

181 **historic landmark in 1972:** National Register of Historic Places Inventory Nomination Form, United States Department of the Interior National Park Service, September 8, 1972.

181 **the population of Hyannis had nearly tripled:** Fred Bayles, Associated Press, "Hyannis Outgrows Kennedys," *Kannapolis Daily Independent*, November 28, 1979.

181 **"Leaning Tower of Pizza":** "Back to New Middle School for Barnstable," *Register*, June 15, 1972.

181 **While they were out running:** Elizabeth Mumford, interview with author, May 15, 2020.

182 **Sandy was a former Canadian show diver:** Karl Eiler, interview with author, October 22, 2021, and Cape Cod Swim Club, "History," https://www.teamunify.com/team/neccsc/page/home/historyswim-stars.

182 **"Go ahead, hit it as hard as you want to!":** Lawford, *Symptoms of Withdrawal*, 95.

182 **"That looks great—for the Cape":** Betty Hannah Hoffman, "What It's Like to Marry a Kennedy," *Ladies' Home Journal*, October 1962, 97.

182 **"Please tell Sandy to start wearing a shirt"**: Barbara Gibson, *Life with Rose Kennedy* (New York: Grand Central Publishing, 1986), 44.

182 **If Eiler's first effort to wake the kids:** Jim Shay, interview with author, July 27, 2020.

183 **Eiler stood ankle-deep in the ocean:** Christopher Kennedy, interview with author, July 31, 2020.

183 **With a mischievous glance:** Jim Shay, interview with author, July 27, 2020.

183 **dragging behind one of the speedboats:** Jim Shay, interview with author, July 27, 2020.

184 **There was also John's airplane:** Associated Press, "WW2 Observation Plane to be Toy for John-John Kennedy, 5," *Racine Journal-Times Sunday Bulletin*, May 29, 1966.

184 **When Eiler dropped by the candle factory:** Brad Blank, interview with author, July 20, 2020.

186 **"listen to music":** William Noonan, interview with author, July 25, 2020.

186 **Bradford's Hardware:** Anthony Shriver, interview with author, July 14, 2021.

187 **a fixture in town since 1892:** Bronwen Howells Walsh, "Bradford's Hardware in Hyannis Sold to New Owners but Legacy Continues," *Barnstable Patriot*, October 30, 2019.

187 **when the vacuum needed fixing:** Brad Blank, interview with author, July 14, 2021.

187 **Sarge who went from window to window:** Anthony Shriver, interview with author, July 14, 2021.

187 **"Growing up in a big, competitive":** Shriver, *A Good Man*, Chapter 5.

188 **Her right foot dragged lightly behind her:** Gibson, *Life with Rose Kennedy*, 63.

188 **"Nellie, I felt bad":** Nellie McGrail Oral History Interview, September 12, 1991, John F. Kennedy Oral History Collection, JFKL.

188 **She stayed on the first floor:** Anthony Shriver, interview with author, July 14, 2021.

189 **"Remember when Daddy caught me with cookies in my pockets?":** Tim Shriver, interview with author, May 20, 2020.

189 **When Rosemary was coming:** Kathy McKeon, interview with author, December 17, 2021.

189 **uncanny ability to float:** Tim Shriver, interview with author, May 20, 2020.

189 **There was Jack Bell—Bobby's best friend:** Deborah Blakely, interview with author, January 21, 2022.

190 **"Nancy, you've got every light in the house on":** Tangley Lloyd, interview with author, December 30, 2020.

190 **Rose's gaze fell on the old wicker chairs:** Kennedy, *Times to Remember*, 522.

190 **"crude confidence":** Dallas, *The Kennedy Case*, 318.

191 **Heritage House:** Robert Ward, "Cape Cod Commuters," *Boston Globe*, October 18, 1968.

191 **Though he stayed in the guest quarters:** McKeon, *Jackie's Girl*, 200.

191 **"She romanced him":** Leamer, *The Kennedy Women*, 642.

191 **"You know, Nellie, we can die right this minute":** Nellie McGrail Oral History Interview, September 12, 1991, JFKL.

191 **whose name Rose mispronounced "Janet":** Gibson, *Life with Rose Kennedy*, 24.

192 **black walking shoes:** Nellie McGrail Oral History Interview, JFKL.

192 **three women from Vermont:** "Residents Take Walk with Rose Kennedy," *Burlington Daily Times-News*, July 27, 1975, 24.

192 **shielded by her big sunhat:** McKeon, *Jackie's Girl*, 119.

192 **having a baked potato every day:** Nellie McGrail Oral History Interview, JFKL.

193 **she sold Jackie a set of antique tin reflectors:** Gibson, *Life with Rose Kennedy*, 56, 84.

193 **"I won't want to live as long as my mother":** Nellie McGrail Oral History Interview, JFKL.

193 **"I love Jackie because":** Nellie McGrail Oral History Interview, JFKL.

193 **Rose's niece Mary Lou McCarthy often called:** Kerry McCarthy, interview with author, November 30, 2020.

194 **"Are you here by yourself?":** Arnold Schwarzenegger with Peter Petre, *Total Recall: My Unbelievably True Life Story* (New York: Simon & Schuster, 2013), 222.

195 **Journalist Pete Hamill:** William Noonan, interview with author, July 25, 2020.

195 **best friend from Andover:** Sasha Chermayeff, interview with author, November 12, 2021.

195 **Jackie extended invitations:** Christopher Kennedy, interview with author, July 31, 2020.

196 **salt and pepper shakers:** William Sylvester Noonan with Robert Huber, *Forever Young: My Friendship with John F. Kennedy Jr.* (New York: Viking, 2006), 32.

196 **She had a bell:** Kathy McKeon, interview with author, December 17, 2021.

196 **Powers slipped into his pitch-perfect Jack impression:** William Noonan, interview with author, July 25, 2020.

196 **pedal pushers and white sneakers:** Paul Stewart, interview with author, July 1, 2020.

196 **John and Billy Noonan snuck into the room:** Noonan with Huber, *Forever Young*, 138.

197 **diving or spearfishing:** Tim Shriver, interview with author, May 20, 2020.

197 **lobster traps:** William Noonan, interview with author, July 25, 2020.

197 **Joan came over to play the piano:** McKeon, *Jackie's Girl*, 135.

197 **delicate lilies of the valley:** McKeon, *Jackie's Girl*, 134.

198 **McKeon, who happened to be looking out the window:** Kathy McKeon, interview with author, December 17, 2021.

199 **an oil painting she'd done for Jack:** William Noonan, interview with author, July 25, 2020.

199 **"Patrick, why don't you go down and get the boat and pick me up?":** Kennedy, *True Compass*, 368.

200 **"But you don't think because of your rapidly":** "CBS Reports: Teddy," CBS News, directed by Andrew Lack, written by Roger Mudd, November 4, 1979.

201 **"a very strong, powerful woman":** Dotson Rader interview with Nancy Tenney, December 2, 2000, Miscellaneous Accessions collection, JFKL.

202 **It would become public knowledge a decade later:** Doris Kearns Goodwin, "The First Tragedy," *Washington Post*, March 23, 1987.

CHAPTER NINE

205 **Jackie had begun to spend her summers:** William Noonan, interview with author, July 25, 2020.

205 **Ted and Joan announced they were divorcing:** Kennedy, *True Compass*, 394.

205 **"your Republican friends?":** Adam Clymer, *Edward M. Kennedy: A Biography* (New York: William Morrow, 1999), 354.

206 **Joan was there from May until September:** Jean Libman Block, "Joan Kennedy: My Life on My Own," *Good Housekeeping*, 1983.

206 **"I know I'm terribly lucky":** Block, "Joan Kennedy: My Life on My Own."

206 **"Why do you want to do this?":** Edward Kennedy Jr., Kara Kennedy, Patrick Kennedy Oral History, July 8, 2008, Edward M. Kennedy Oral History Project, University of Virginia Miller Center.

207 **journalist and family friend Dotson Rader:** Dotson Rader, interview with author, April 8, 2021.

207 **"Patrick will have his ol' Dad to pal round with":** Clymer, *Edward M. Kennedy: A Biography*, 8, and quoted with permission by Melissa Ludtke.

208 **a 1980 bowel surgery:** Gloria Negri, "Rose Kennedy Is 'Convalescing Very Nicely,'" *Boston Globe*, September 26, 1980.

208 **pinned to her cardigans:** Kerry Kennedy, interview with author, March 23, 2020.

208 **For Rose's ninety-third birthday:** Susan Lampert Smith, "Kennedys Give $1 Million to St. Coletta," *Wisconsin State Journal*, July 23, 1983.

208 **Jackie returned to Hyannis Port:** Thomas Oliphant, "United in Grief," *Boston Globe*, November 23, 1983.

208 **the kid they remembered:** "Mourners Go to Mass at Hyannis Church," *Cape Cod Times*, November 20, 1983.

209 **"He said to me when I was very young":** Associated Press, "20th Anniversary of JFK Death—a Tribute by Sen. Kennedy," *Boston Globe*, November 23, 1983, 2.

209 **When David Kennedy:** Nellie McGrail Oral History Interview, September 12, 1991, JFKL.

209 **Bobby Jr. had just been arrested:** Associated Press, "Robert F. Kennedy Jr. Admits He Is Guilty in Possessing Heroin," *New York Times*, February 18, 1984.

209 **"Mrs. Kennedy, David is over there and he is all alone":** Nellie McGrail Oral History Interview, JFKL.

210 **"The night before the wedding":** Lawford, *Symptoms of Withdrawal*, 278.

211 **Rose officially gave Ted the house:** Town of Barnstable Assessing Division property records, https://www.townofbarnstable.us/Departments/Assessing/Property_Values/Property-Display.asp?ap=0&searchparcel=286023&searchtype=address&mappar=&ownname=&streetno=&searching=yes&streetname=marchant&Start=&Offset=.

211 **"He had the loudest voice I ever heard in my life":** Elizabeth Mumford, interview with author, May 15, 2020.

211 **His cook, Neil Connolly:** Neil Connolly with Elizabeth Benedict, *In the Kennedy Kitchen: Recipes and Recollections of a Great American Family* (New York: DK Publishing, Inc., 2007), 88.

212 **Hyannis Port Martinis:** Neil Connolly with Elizabeth Benedict, *In the Kennedy Kitchen*, 242.

212 **Don McKeag had just moved in:** Don McKeag, interview with author, July 7, 2020.

213 **John Kennedy Jr. lived in a cramped room:** Barry Clifford, interview with author, July 7, 2020.

213 **John was enamored:** William Noonan, interview with author, July 25, 2020.

214 **"Is he bringing his butler with him?":** Barry Clifford with Paul Perry, *Expedition Whydah: The Story of the World's First Excavation of a Pirate Treasure Ship and the Man Who Found Her* (New York: William Morrow Paperbacks, 2000), 124.

214 **magnetometer had gone off:** Barry Clifford, interview with author, July 7, 2020.

215 **anchored the boat near the Beachcomber:** Barry Clifford, interview with author, July 7, 2020.

215 **Nearly 2,500 people crammed into downtown Hyannis:** Susan W. Lyon, "Thousands Line Street for Shriver Wedding," *Cape Cod News*, April 30, 1986.

216 **Colby's Photo store:** Fred Bodensiek, "Just Like Old Times," *Barnstable Patriot*, May 1, 1986.

216 **"It's just like the old times":** Bodensiek, "Just Like Old Times," *Barnstable Patriot*.

216 **"I've lived here since 1941":** Deirdre Donahue and Susan Reed, "A Hyannis Hitching," *People*, May 12, 1986.

216 **"We're looking for Clint Eastwood":** Karyn Bober Kuhn, "We're Looking for Clint," *Register*, May 1, 1984.

217 **"There was the biggest mob":** Andy Warhol, *The Andy Warhol Diaries*, ed. Pat Hackett (New York: Twelve, 2014), 739.

217 **"God, I'm actually here on the lawn":** "Oprah Talks to Maria Shriver," *O, The Oprah Magazine*, June 2008.

217 **Elizabeth Barrett Browning's "How Do I Love Thee?":** Susan W. Lyon, "Thousands Line Street for Shriver Wedding."

217 *The Sound of Music's* **"Wedding Processional":** Jay Mulvaney, *Kennedy Weddings: A Family Album* (New York: St. Martin's Press, 1999), 104.

218 **apple trees in full bloom:** Bodensiek, "Just Like Old Times," *Barnstable Patriot*.

218 **"madness of the whole Kennedy thing":** McNamara, *Eunice: The Kennedy Who Changed the World*, 288.

218 **Jackie floated from room to room:** William Noonan, interview with author, July 25, 2020.

218 **Bunny Mellon was arranging:** Mulvaney, *Kennedy Weddings*, 115.

218 **A florist from New York hung lanterns:** Christina Haag, *Come to the Edge: A Love Story* (New York: Random House, 2012), 144.

218 **"How many want hot dogs":** Bonnie Winston, "At the Compound, Onlookers Started the Reception Early," *Boston Globe*, July 20, 1986.

219 **"I now welcome my brother-in-law-to-be":** Noonan with Huber, *Forever Young*, 95.

219 **spinach salad and tenderloin from the rehearsal:** Teresa M. Hanafin, "Wedding Party Starts at the Beach," *Boston Globe*, July 19, 1986.

219 **Jackie told John to take her:** Haag, *Come to the Edge*, 144.

219 **More than two thousand spectators lined:** Fox Butterfield, "Caroline Kennedy Wed in Cape Cod Church," *New York Times*, July 20, 1986, 1.

219 **white silk organza shamrocks:** Mulvaney, *Kennedy Weddings*, 112.

220 **Sandy Eiler and his wife, Lee:** Melissa Dribben, "Caroline Kennedy Takes a Husband," *New Jersey Record*, July 20, 1986.

220 **And there was Jack Dempsey:** Noonan with Huber, *Forever Young*, 93.

220 **six-page fact sheet:** Butterfield, "Caroline Kennedy Wed in Cape Cod Church," *New York Times*.

220 **Plimpton describe:** Robert Littell, *The Men We Became: My Friendship with John F. Kennedy Jr.* (New York: St. Martin's Griffin, 2004), 121.

220 **He'd get into the back of his car:** Jim Manley, interview with author, October 26, 2021.

221 **"Can they head over to your house?":** Don McKeag, interview with author, July 8, 2020.

221 **Joe's Twin Villa, one of the best bars on the Cape:** Joe Diggs, interview with author, July 27, 2020.

222 **on the front page of *People*:** "JFK Jr: The Sexiest Man Alive 1988," *People*, September 12, 1988.

223 **John's cousin Joe Kennedy II was elected:** "Kennedy, Joseph Patrick II," United States House of Representatives: History, Art & Archives, https://history.house.gov/People/Detail/16214.

223 **"There were a lot of different pressures":** Mark Shriver, interview with author, July 15, 2020.

223 **"You gotta come listen to this":** Noonan with Huber, *Forever Young*, 95.

CHAPTER TEN

225 **pianist, John Salerno, pushed open the back door:** John Salerno, interview with author, July 2, 2020.

225 **Tutu had been staying next door with his wife:** Dan Ring, "Tutu, Kennedy Meet at Hyannis Compound," *Cape Cod Times*, June 2, 1990.

226 **"He took me to meet his mother":** Archbishop Desmond Tutu Oral History, May 13, 2006, Edward M. Kennedy Oral History Project, University of Virginia Miller Center.

226 **Cape Cod Conservatory:** John Salerno, interview with author, July 2, 2020.

226 **her centennial birthday:** Vanessa Parks, "The Greatest Mother of Them All," *Cape Cod Times*, July 16, 1990.

226 **hand-drawn banner:** David Still II photo, "Banner Year," *Barnstable Patriot*, July 19, 1990.

227 **more than fifty reporters from as far away as Spain:** Yumiko Watanabe, "Foreign Journalists Swarm to Cover U.S. 'Royal Family,'" *Cape Cod Times*, July 16, 1990.

227 **filming a TV special:** "Rose Kennedy Turns 100 Years Old in 1990," https://www.youtube.com/watch?v=HfrTpA0u-nM.

227 **"We're a very close family":** Dotson Rader, "She Wanted to Inspire and She Did," *Parade*, July 22, 1990.

227 **forty-four rosebushes:** Christopher Noxon, "A Rose for the Rose of the Kennedys, Hyannis Dedicated Garden," *Register*, July 25, 1991, 5.

227 **"I've been with you a long time":** Nellie McGrail Oral History Interview, September 12, 1991, JFKL.

228 **First there was the article in *GQ*:** Michael Kelly, "Ted Kennedy on the Rocks," *GQ*, February 1, 1990.

228 **drunken fight:** UPI, "Kennedy Involved in Bar Incident," January 20, 1989.

228 **former aide alleging Ted's illegal drug use:** Richard E. Burke with William and Marilyn Hoffer, *The Senator: My Ten Years with Ted Kennedy* (New York: St. Martin's Press, 1992).

228 **Ted sidled up to the bar:** Tom Holmes, interview with author, July 17, 2020.

228 **he'd accompany his nephews to Joe's Twin Villa:** Joe Diggs, interview with author, July 27, 2020.

228 **"All I got from Grandpa Fitz is fat jowls!":** Ann Gargan Oral History, 2005, Edward M. Kennedy Oral History Project, University of Virginia Miller Center.

228 **his hands shook:** Kelly, "Ted Kennedy on the Rocks," *GQ*, February 1, 1990.

229 **People lined up at the grocery stores and gas stations:** John Black, "The Preparations," *Register*, August 22, 1991, 3.

229 **Rose was taken to Cape Cod Hospital:** Herbert Mathewson interview with Patrick Ramage, "Cape Codders Remember the Kennedys," *Tales of Cape Cod*, DVD, 2020.

229 **"I just couldn't believe it":** Laurence Leamer, *Sons of Camelot: The Fate of an American Dynasty* (New York: William Morrow, 2004), 346.

229 **he cross-country skied:** Noonan with Huber, *Forever Young*, 143.

229 **"I'm in Boston":** William Noonan, interview with author, July 25, 2020.

230 **It was where Jackie used to sunbathe:** McKeon, *Jackie's Girl*, 130.

230 **An eight-by-ten-inch Federal Express:** "Bomb Scare Clears Main Street, Hyannis," *Register*, June 20, 1991, 2.

231 **"For Christ's sake! What is it with these people? This is goddamn crazy":** Don McKeag, interview with author, July 8, 2020.

231 **John Salerno got a call from the senator:** John Salerno, interview with author, July 2, 2020.

232 **Salerno played "You'll Never Know":** John Salerno, interview with author, July 2, 2020, and wedding program.

232 **Ted and Vicki had known each other for years:** Victoria R. Kennedy Oral History, April 8, 2010, Edward M. Kennedy Oral History Project, University of Virginia Miller Center.

233 **Sunny was supposed to be Vicki's dog:** Caroline Raclin Oral History, November 11, 2009, Edward M. Kennedy Oral History Project, University of Virginia Miller Center.

233 **Nearly every visitor calling the Greater Hyannis Chamber of Commerce:** Wendy Northcross, interview with author, November 15, 2019.

234 **"I haven't seen this in years":** John Leaning and Paul Gauvin, "Kennedys, Cape Are Part of Each Other," *Cape Cod Times*, January 2, 1998.

234 **He came in early, before the crowds arrived:** Wendy Northcross, interview with author, November 15, 2019.

234 **Rosemary, still beautiful in her seventies, was wheeled into the museum:** Lynne Poyant, interview with author, July 12, 2021.

234 **all her clothes drawers open:** Casey Sherman, "20 Years After John F. Kennedy Jr.'s Death, Barry Clifford Remembers," *Boston Herald*, July 7, 2019.

235 **"The funeral and Arlington are going to be crazy":** Sasha Chermayeff, interview with author, November 12, 2021.

236 **before she died, Jackie had talked to her decorator:** Robert Luddington interview with Patrick Ramage, "Cape Codders Remember the Kennedys," *Tales of Cape Cod*, DVD, 2020.

236 **he invited his friends from New York or Boston:** Rose Marie Terenzio, interview with author, May 22, 2020.

236 **a limousine pulled up:** William Noonan, interview with author, July 25, 2020.

237 **"I like coming to this house":** William Noonan, interview with author, July 25, 2020.

237 **Paparazzi waded out into the waters:** Dotson Rader, interview with author, April 8, 2021.

237 **"Drive me past the Kennedy Compound":** "Five Minutes with Joan Rivers," *Barnstable Patriot*, July 23, 1998, 20.

238 **"What are you doing here?":** Dotson Rader, interview with author, April 8, 2021.

238 **Except in her version, "There was Rose":** "Five Minutes with Joan Rivers," *Barnstable Patriot*, July 23, 1998.

238 **Just after the new year in 1995:** Sean M. Walsh, "Rose Fitzgerald Remembered for Her Strength, Love of Family," *Register*, January 26, 1995.

238 **a fundraiser in New York:** Sean Polay, "Familiar Scene Ends on Note of Sorrow," *Cape Cod Times*, January 23, 1995.

239 **Rose had died at five thirty that evening:** "Rose Kennedy Death Announcement," 7News Boston WHDH, https://www.youtube.com/watch?v=H-Z eFJeyB8Q.

239 **John Salerno sat at the piano:** John Salerno, interview with author, July 2, 2020.

239 **"a shopping trip to Paris":** Don McKeag, interview with author, July 8, 2020.

239 **"A reporter came and knocked":** Elizabeth Mumford, interview with author, May 15, 2020.

239 **A week later a fresh layer of snow:** Alisha Tuba photo, "Peaceful Aftermath," *Barnstable Patriot*, February 2, 1995.

240 **frosted Waterford goblets:** Noonan with Huber, *Forever Young*, 152.

240 **"Do you think she's the right one?":** Noonan with Huber, *Forever Young*, 156.

241 **"Meet me at my house and we'll go on the boat":** Brad Blank, interview with author, July 20, 2020.

241 **A man with a large camera:** *Inside Edition*, September 1996, https://www
.youtube.com/watch?v=RZvXAbPKUKQ.

241 **When he called the woman a bitch:** Noonan with Huber, *Forever Young*, 21.

242 **John tried to finish up at the Manhattan offices:** Rose Marie Terenzio, interview with author, May 22, 2020.

242 **the art department offices where he liked to linger:** Kate Storey, "The Inside
Story of John F. Kennedy Jr.'s *George* Magazine," *Esquire*, April 22, 2019.

242 **black-and-white terrier, Friday, and fluffy black cat, Ruby:** Rose Marie
Terenzio, interview with author, May 22, 2020.

242 **Rolling Stones' "You Can't Always Get What You Want":** McKeon, *Jackie's
Girl*, 291.

242 **August was for the Vineyard:** Rose Marie Terenzio, interview with author,
May 22, 2020.

243 **To John and his friends, it was Paredes:** Rose Marie Terenzio, interview with
author, May 22, 2020.

243 **they'd slide behind a table at Gourmet Brunch:** John Cotellessa, interview
with author, July 16, 2020.

243 **Michael Kennedy sat at Joe's Twin Villa:** Joe Diggs, interview with author,
July 27, 2020.

244 **He'd been accused of the statutory rape:** Sara Rimer, "A Kennedy Faces the
Fallout from a Scandal," *New York Times*, July 10, 1997.

244 **He died in an accident:** Michael Janofsky, "Favorite Game for Kennedys
Took Deadly Turn on Slopes," *New York Times*, January 2, 1998.

244 **borrowed jet of actor and family friend Kevin Costner:** Names & Faces,
Washington Post, 1998.

244 **Kathleen once kicked:** Kathleen Kennedy Townsend, interview with author,
July 5, 2021.

244 **"I found myself in an upstairs bedroom":** Joseph P. Kennedy II, "We Happy
Few," *Esquire*, June 1, 1998.

244 **arranged to be picked up on the tarmac:** Noonan with Huber, *Forever Young*,
197.

245 **"There have been so many ways that Michael touched our lives":** Mike Karath,
"Hilltop Church Offers Family Privacy," *Cape Cod Times*, January 1998.

245 **because of its conservatism:** Tim Shriver, interview with author, May 20,
2020.

245 **"personal issues":** Laurence Leamer, *Sons of Camelot*, 494.

246 **the family was told there was only room for one person in the hearse:** Joseph
P. Kennedy II, "We Happy Few," *Esquire*, June 1, 1998.

246 **attendance was mandatory:** Melody Miller Oral History, July 15, 2008, Edward M. Kennedy Oral History Project, University of Virginia Miller Center.

247 **Wexford, the Irish port town:** Kennedy Jr., *American Values*, 294.

247 **"Don't you ever do that again"**: Ken Regan Oral History, Edward M. Kennedy Oral History Project, University of Virginia Miller Center.

248 **in the fall, John's friend Sasha Chermayeff**: Sasha Chermayeff, interview with author, November 12, 2021.

249 **John had already started writing Anthony's eulogy**: Carole Radziwiłł, *What Remains: A Memoir of Fate, Friendship, and Love* (New York: Scribner, 2005), 234.

249 **"There was a deep sadness"**: Sasha Chermayeff, interview with author, November 12, 2021.

249 **Jackie had barely changed things**: William Noonan, interview with author, July 25, 2020.

250 **In 1996, John and Caroline had auctioned off some of the things from the house**: Lisa Anderson, "Homey Pieces of Camelot," *Chicago Tribune*, February 9, 2005.

250 **"I want you to buy it"**: William Noonan, interview with author, July 25, 2020.

250 **"They'll turn it into an event hall"**: William Noonan, interview with author, July 25, 2020.

250 **crisp burn mark**: McKeon, *Jackie's Girl*, 291.

250 **drafty old windows**: Kathy McKeon, interview with author, December 17, 2021.

251 **She'd stopped working out**: Radziwiłł, *What Remains*, 222.

251 **"Do you think Mummy would like the wallpaper?"**: William Noonan, interview with author, July 25, 2020.

251 **They were set to meet on Saturday**: Robert Luddington interview with Patrick Ramage, "Cape Codders Remember the Kennedys," *Tales of Cape Cod*, DVD, 2020.

251 **little boy named Flynn**: William Noonan, interview with author, July 25, 2020.

251 **When Noonan suggested**: William Noonan, interview with author, July 25, 2020.

251 **dinner in Nantucket on Friday, July 16**: Noonan with Huber, *Forever Young*, 5.

252 **O'Neill noticed that there were no stars**: Brian O'Neill, interview with author, July 28, 2020.

252 **the overnight maintenance worker**: Radziwiłł, *What Remains*, 236.

252 **the captain told them he'd just gotten off the phone**: Brian O'Neill, interview with author, July 28, 2020.

252 **John Salerno had spent the prior two weeks**: John Salerno, interview with author, July 2, 2020.

252 **In the tailor shop**: Janet Cook, interview with author, July 9, 2020.

253 **"At the top of the two's"**: John Watters, "Once Again, Hyannis Copes with Tragedy—and the Media Blitz," *Register*, July 22, 1999, 1.

253 **"when the world's media descends":** Watters, "Once Again, Hyannis Copes with Tragedy—and the Media Blitz."

253 **There were fifteen police officers:** Tim Demarce, "The Nation Stood Vigil," *Cape Cod Times*, July 22, 1999.

253 **reporters hired stretch limousines:** David Still II, "Responding to Another Kennedy Tragedy," *Barnstable Patriot*, July 22, 1999.

253 **"Never mind the water, I'll give you $5 for a bathroom":** Watters, "Once Again, Hyannis Copes with Tragedy—and the Media Blitz."

253 **camera crews dipped plastic cups to scoop the melted ice:** Local reporter, interview on background with author.

254 **"It'll be better when it's over":** Still II, "Responding to Another Kennedy Tragedy."

254 **Sam Barber . . . set up his easel:** Watters, "Once Again, Hyannis Copes with Tragedy—and the Media Blitz."

254 **Jackie, who'd bought his paintings:** Sam Barber, interview with author, July 18, 2020.

254 **Rob Stewart:** Rob Stewart interview with Patrick Ramage, "Cape Codders Remember the Kennedys," *Tales of Cape Cod*, DVD, 2020.

254 **Caroline stayed away:** Tina Cassidy, "Privately, a Very Private Survivor Grieves," *Boston Globe*, July 19, 1999.

254 **They walked past the gate of John's house:** Noonan with Huber, *Forever Young*, 215.

255 **"Where's John?":** William Noonan, interview with author, July 25, 2020.

255 **"You know that John's out on the wing":** William Noonan, interview with author, July 25, 2020.

255 **"You need to come up here":** William Noonan, interview with author, July 25, 2020.

255 **Debris from the plane had been recovered:** CNN, "Searchers Scale Back Hunt for Kennedy Plane as Night Falls," July 17, 1999.

255 **a Mass was held under the tent:** Noonan with Huber, *Forever Young*, 216.

256 **"Shut up! You're liars!":** William Noonan, interview with author, July 25, 2020.

256 **"We're gonna find this fucker":** William Noonan, interview with author, July 25, 2020.

257 **the bodies of John, Carolyn, and Lauren:** Lynne Duke, "Bodies of Kennedy, Bessettes Brought to Shore," July 22, 1999.

257 **cause of the crash:** Don Phillips, "NTSB Says Disorientation Likely Caused JFK Jr. Crash," July 7, 2000.

257 **"The Kennedy Family, Hyannisport":** Still II, "Responding to Another Kennedy Tragedy."

257 **Ted gave his eulogy for John:** Richard Pyle, "Sen. Kennedy Delivers JFK Jr. Eulogy," Associated Press, July 24, 1999.

258 **The ashes of John, Carolyn, and Lauren:** CNN, "Remains of JFK Jr., Wife and Sister-in-law Buried at Sea," July 22, 1999.

258 **finally broke him:** Lester Hyman Oral History, October 6, 2008, Edward M. Kennedy Oral History Project, University of Virginia Miller Center.

CHAPTER ELEVEN

259 **The Barnstable County Sheriff's Office:** "New Beach Honors a Civil Rights Leader," *Register*, August 26, 2004, 1.

260 **"Mr. Moderator, I would like to ask":** "The Naming of Fortes Beach," *Barnstable Patriot*, December 19, 2003, 6.

260 **"I hope it will be a public beach":** Joe Burns, "Changing Times," *Register*, August 26, 2004, 1.

260 **John's cousin Anthony Shriver rented:** Anthony Shriver, interview with author, July 14, 2020.

260 **June 2004 Ted bought his brother's house for $3 million:** Town of Barnstable Assessing Division property records, https://townofbarnstable.us/Departments/Assessing/Property_Values/Property-Display.asp?ap=0&searchparcel=287065&searchtype=address&mappar=&ownname=&streetno=111&searching=yes&streetname=Irving%20Avenue&Start=&Offset=.

261 **steam radiators:** Mark Grenier, interview with author, November 10, 2020.

261 **ripping out the old kitchen and the wallpaper:** John F. Kennedy Hyannis Museum, "The JFK Centennial Auction" brochure, August 2017.

261 **Some things were repurposed:** Mark Grenier, interview with author, November 10, 2020.

261 **The Kennedys are leaving Hyannis Port:** Jack Coleman, "The Kennedys Are Leaving Hyannisport," *Providence Journal*, October 22, 2006.

261 **When their daughter, Noah Isabella Rose:** Matthew Maxwell Taylor Kennedy and Victoria Strauss Kennedy, interview with author, October 24, 2020.

261 **Pat and Eunice proudly went around Hyannis:** R. Scott Reedy, "Growing Up Kennedy," *Register*, December 22, 2005, 17.

261 **a charity bike ride:** Tania deLuzuriaga, "At Charity Ride, a Missing Luminary at the Finish Line," *Boston Globe*, May 18, 2008.

262 **He suddenly felt unsteady and disoriented:** Kennedy, "Prologue," *True Compass*.

262 **Four days later, Ted came home:** "Kennedy Home in Hyannisport," *Patriot Ledger* video footage, May 22, 2008, https://www.youtube.com/watch?v=hdize2DAIxk.

263 **Ted had his annual day-after-Thanksgiving party:** Mike Barnicle, "Barnicle on Kennedy: Of Memory and the Sea," *Time*, August 27, 2009.

263 **Sarge was in the advanced stages of Alzheimer's:** Schwarzenegger, *Total Recall*, 579.

263 **Eunice was rushed to Cape Cod Hospital:** Shriver, *A Good Man*, 199.

264 **"Just shows how things change":** Rob Stewart interview with Patrick Ramage, "Cape Codders Remember the Kennedys," *Tales of Cape Cod*, DVD, 2020.

264 **Jean mostly stopped going to the Cape:** Paul Schwartzman, "What the Political Spotlight Reveals About William Kennedy Smith," *Washington Post*, December 10, 2014.

264 **asked her son Bobby Jr. to go get a turkey:** Eric Williams, "Curious Cape Cod: A Wild Turkey Tale, Starring the Kennedys," *Cape Cod Times*, November 24, 2020.

265 **Amy and Patrick's wedding would be the last public event:** Patrick J. Kennedy, *A Common Struggle: A Personal Journey Through the Past and Future of Mental Illness and Addiction* (New York: Blue Rider Press, 2016), 347.

265 **Aiden, Conor's little brother, took the garden hose:** Brad Blank, interview with author, July 20, 2020.

266 **afternoon hanging out with Patrick Schwarzenegger:** Brad Blank, interview with author, July 30, 2020.

266 **being driven up to Four Seas:** Doug Warren, interview with author, July 8, 2020.

266 **cookie dough ice cream:** Stephanie Steinberg, "Hyannis Port Welcomes Taylor Swift, Sort Of," *Boston Globe*, August 22, 2012.

266 **"It's time," Nancy told her family:** Tangley Lloyd, interview with author, December 30, 2020.

266 **thirteen-room house:** Property records show house was purchased with LLC; *Vanity Fair*, "Taylor Swift Fights Back About Her Love Life, the Hyannis Port House—and Has Words for Tina Fey and Amy Poehler," March 5, 2013; and Lloyd confirmed to author in interview that Swift was the buyer.

266 **"She is just spectacular":** "Taylor Swift New Hyannisport Neighbor Says Ethel Kennedy," CapeCast, October 12, 2012, https://www.youtube.com/watch?v=ZcwE0-S9Azw.

267 **"My mother adored Taylor":** Tangley Lloyd, email to author, February 1, 2022.

267 **there was a new family tradition:** Christopher Kennedy, interview with author, July 30, 2020.

267 **Washington Redskins to the Patriots:** Brad Blank, interview with author, July 30, 2020.

267 **Saoirse dropped off half a dozen pieces to get tailored in town:** Janet Cook, interview with author, July 9, 2020.

268 **Courtney went to her painting lessons with Sam Barber:** Sam Barber, interview with author, July 18, 2020.

268 **battled depression since middle school:** Saoirse Kennedy-Hill, "Mental Illness at Deerfield," *Deerfield Scroll*, February 3, 2016.

268 **On the last night of July 2019:** Bobby Kennedy Jr., "My Eulogy to Saoirse," eulogy as published on Medium.com, August 7, 2019.

268 **respond to a 911 call:** Boston 25 News Staff, "Granddaughter of Robert and Ethel Kennedy Dies at Kennedy Compound," Boston 25 News, August 2, 2019.

268 **Tim asked his cousin:** Tim Shriver, "Saoirse Roisin Kennedy Hill: My Eulogy to Saoirse." Eulogy quoted with his permission.

269 **It was a summer ritual:** Brad Blank, interview with author, July 20, 2020.

269 **"When Saoirse died, there was a press pool at the top of the driveway":** Kerry Kennedy, interview with author, March 23, 2020.

270 **losing in his run for Congress in 2002:** Jo Becker, "In Upset, Van Hollen Beats Shriver," *Washington Post*, September 11, 2002.

270 **"I'm done with the past, really":** Mark Shriver, interview with author, July 15, 2020.

271 **Tim Shriver bought a six-bedroom house:** David L. Harris, "A Kennedy Buys a $3.3 Million, Six-Bedroom Home on Cape Cod," *Boston Business Journal*, August 21, 2017.

271 **two-thousand-square-foot home:** Kathryn Romeyn, "A Kennedy Family's Hyannis Port Compound Carriage House Turned Cottage," *Architectural Digest*, August 15, 2018.

272 **Bobby Jr. said in a video:** "Go Sailing with Robert F. Kennedy Jr. at the Kennedy Compound in Hyannis Port, MA," March 2020.

272 **"You and a friend will enjoy a personal tour":** "Tour the Kennedy Compound, Have Lunch with Kerry Kennedy & Sail with Ted Kennedy, Jr in Hyannis Port, MA," CharityBuzz.com.

272 **"use this place now for business":** Anthony Shriver, interview with author, July 16, 2021.

273 **"The editor told him to get your picture":** Kennedy Jr., *American Values*, 45.

273 **Rose led them back through the narrow streets:** Brad Blank, interview with author, July 20, 2020.

273 **Jean sat at the dinner table:** Interview with Caroline Raclin, November 11, 2009, Edward M. Kennedy Oral History Project, University of Virginia Miller Center.

274 **"You know the sea, it's talking":** James Sterling Young Oral History, 2016, Edward M. Kennedy Oral History Project, University of Virginia Miller Center.

INDEX